LIBERTY & EQUALITY IN CARIBBEAN COLOMBIA

1770-1835

D1073806

Aline Helg

LIBERTY & EQUALITY

in Caribbean Colombia

1770–1835

The University of North Carolina Press

Chapel Hill & London

© 2004
The University of North Carolina Press
All rights reserved

Designed by Eric M. Brooks
Set in Monticello by
Tseng Information Systems, Inc.

The paper in this book meets the guidelines
for permanence and durability of the Committee
on Production Guidelines for Book Longevity
of the Council on Library Resources.

Library of Congress
Cataloging-in-Publication Data
Helg, Aline, 1953–
Liberty and equality in Caribbean Colombia,
1770–1835 / Aline Helg.
    p. cm.
Includes bibliographical references and index.
ISBN 0-8078-2876-9 (cloth: alk. paper)
ISBN 0-8078-5540-5 (pbk.: alk. paper)
1. Blacks—Colombia—Atlantic Coast Region—
History. 2. Colombia—History—18th century.
3. Colombia—History—19th century. 4. Blacks—
Race identity—Colombia—Atlantic Coast
Region. 5. Social classes—Colombia—Atlantic
Coast Region—History. 6. Discrimination—
Colombia—Atlantic Coast Region. 7. Colombia—
Race relations. I. Title.
F2281.A79H45   2004
305.896′08611—dc22   2004001708

cloth   08 07 06 05 04   5 4 3 2 1
paper   08 07 06 05 04   5 4 3 2 1

Parts of this book have been
reprinted in revised form from
"Simón Bolívar and the Fear
of *Pardocracia*: José Padilla in
Post-Independence Cartagena,"
*Journal of Latin American
Studies* 35, no. 3 (August 2003):
447–71; "A Fragmented
Majority: Free 'of All Colors,'
Indians, and Slaves in Caribbean
Colombia during the Haitian
Revolution," in *The Impact of
the Haitian Revolution in the
Atlantic World*, edited by David
Geggus, 157–75 (Columbia:
University of South Carolina
Press, 2001); and "The Limits
of Equality: Free People of Color
and Slaves during the First
Independence of Cartagena,
Colombia, 1810–1815," *Slavery
and Abolition* 20 (August 1999):
1–30.

TO MALIKA

Now the night was rising from the land itself and began to engulf everything, the dead and the living, under the marvelous and ever-present sky. No, he would never know his father, who would continue to sleep over there, his face forever lost in the ashes. There was a mystery about that man, a mystery he had wanted to penetrate. But after all there was only the mystery of poverty that creates beings without names and without a past, that sends them into the vast throng of the nameless dead who made the world while they themselves were destroyed forever.

ALBERT CAMUS, The First Man

CONTENTS

ILLUSTRATIONS

MAPS, FIGURE, & TABLE

Maps

Figure

Table

ACKNOWLEDGMENTS

There are many people whose time, interest, and support made this book possible. Foremost among them are David Bushnell, who read the entire manuscript twice with the eyes of the Colombianist and the Latin Americanist, and Karen Carroll, who meticulously edited it not only during my residence at the National Humanities Center but after my return to Austin as well. I am immensely grateful to Eduardo Posada-Carbó, Matt Childs, and Mauricio Tenorio Trillo for their careful reading of the manuscript and insightful comments. Special thanks also go to Kathryn Burns, Eduardo Restrepo, Michael Hanchard, Norman Whitten, Denise Spellberg, K. Russell Lohse, and Jeanne Helg-Emery for their stimulating reading of specific chapters. I thank the graduate students of my seminar "Postslavery Afro-Latin-America," in particular Rachel Pooley and Mauricio Pajón, for their comments on the comparative conclusion. I am grateful to Susan Long for her hand drawing of the maps and chart, and to Joseph Sánchez for the reference for the fourth illustration (uniform of the mulatto and black militiamen). At the University of North Carolina Press, I thank Elaine Maisner for her continuing faith in my manuscript and Stevie Champion for her careful copyediting.

A preliminary interpretation was published in the journal *Slavery and Abolition*, for which I thank Anthony McFarlane for his constructive comments. Parts of some chapters were first presented at conferences and later published in edited volumes. I thank Adolfo Meisel Roca and Haroldo Calvo Stevenson for inviting me to the Third and Fourth Symposia on the History of Cartagena de Indias in the Nineteenth and Eighteenth Centuries, respectively. I am grateful to David Geggus for inviting me to the conference on "The Impact of the Haitian Revolution in the Atlantic World" at the College of Charleston, South Carolina, and to Gonzalo Sánchez and María Emma Wills for inviting me to the symposium "Museo, memoria y nación" in Bogotá. I thank Nils Jacobsen for his invitation to the conference on "Political Cultures in the Andes, 1750–1950" at the University of Illinois at Urbana-Champaign and for his engaging comments on my paper.

My deep gratitude goes to Franklin W. Knight for his stimulating friendship and his trust in this project. Many friends and colleagues have helped me with their intellectual support and warm encouragement: Thomas and Carolyn Palaima, Peter Jelavich, Charlie Hale, Virginia Hagerty, Margo Gutiérrez, Milton Jamail, Jonathan Brown, Edmund Gordon, Robert Abzug, James Sidbury at the University of Texas at Austin, and Francisco A. Scarano at the University of Wisconsin in Madison. My research in Bogotá would not have been possible without the expert help of Guiomar Aya Dueñas. There I learned a lot from my conversations with Fabio Zambrano, Guiomar Dueñas Vargas, Fernán González, Orlando Fals Borda, the late Dora Rothlisberger, and Manuel Zapata Olivella. In Cartagena, my thanks go to Gloria Bonilla, Alvaro Casas, Edgar Gutiérrez, Father Efraín Aldana at the Centro Afro-Caribe, and Alfonso Múnera, and in Barranquilla, to Aquiles Escalante and Dolcey Romero.

For their assistance I would like to thank the personnel at the Benson Latin American Collection of the University of Texas at Austin, the Archivo Histórico Nacional de Colombia and the Biblioteca Nacional de Colombia in Bogotá, the Archivo Histórico de Cartagena, the Archivo Eclesiástico de Santa Marta, the Archivo General de Indias in Seville, the Archive of the Ministère des Affaires Etrangères in Paris, and the Public Record Office in London. Additional thanks go to Father José Marino Pineda, who opened the archives of Cartagena's archbishopric and parishes to me and let me work in his office while he attended his parishioners.

I am indebted to the institutions that financed research for this project: the Swiss National Fund for Scientific Research, the American Philosophical Society, and the Center for African and African American Studies and the Institute of Latin American Studies (Mellon Fellowship) at the University of Texas at Austin. Part of the writing was achieved thanks to a residential fellowship at the National Humanities Center in North Carolina, derived from a grant from the National Endowment for the Humanities, and a Faculty Research Assignment from the University of Texas at Austin.

Finally, the making of this book, like most others, was a complex journey. I am grateful to my mother, Jeanne Helg-Emery, for being such a generous grandmother in times of intense research and writing. This book is dedicated to my daughter, Malika. Thanks to her companionship from start to finish across two continents, this journey was also an adventure full of joys and discoveries.

LIBERTY & EQUALITY IN CARIBBEAN COLOMBIA
1770-1835

INTRODUCTION

In 1991 Colombia adopted a new democratic and pluralistic constitution that recognizes the ethnic and cultural diversity of the country, protects minorities, and acknowledges the existence of Indians in the nation by assigning two senatorial seats to the indigenous communities.[1] Finally putting an end to the 1886 constitution, which for more than a century provided Colombians with a highly centralized political system that denied diversity, the new constitution admits de facto that the forces of regionalism have won over centralism and that the process of whitening Colombia's population through *mestizaje* (racial mixing) and Catholic education have not been fully achieved. The creation by the 1991 constitution of two senatorial seats for indigenous communities acknowledges the long-standing organization of Indians who have held to their land, traditions, and languages since the Spanish conquest. However, the new constitution does not challenge the image of Colombia as a patriarchal mestizo (of mixed European and indigenous ancestry) nation. Nor does it break the silence that Colombian elites have kept since the early nineteenth century over the substantial contribution of people of African descent to the formation of the nation, except in Transitory Article 55. This article, adopted reluctantly by the Constitutional Assembly to respond to the grassroots mobilization of the nonrepresented black associations, announced that within two years the government would legalize the traditional communal landholdings of "black communities" located on the Pacific Coast.[2]

In the summer of 1993, after much activist lobbying, Colombian blacks eventually gained some legal recognition, in Law 70 of Negritudes [*sic*]. This law focuses on the "black communities" along the rivers of the Pacific Basin; it acknowledges their ancestral communal land ownership and protects their cultural identity.[3] However, by stressing "Afrocolombian ascendancy," cultural homogeneity, and distinctiveness, as well as location in a specific rural riverine region, the law de facto excludes blacks in other areas as well as *zambos* (of mixed African and indigenous ancestry) and mulattoes from "blackness." Interestingly, Colombians of mixed African ancestry in other parts of the country did not protest these omissions. Nor did they seize the opportunity provided by the Law of Negritudes, which guaranteed land as well as cultural and political rights, to question its racial, ethnic, and regional determinism and to demand similar rights for themselves. Only a few mulatto intellectuals from the Caribbean Coast attempted, with little success, to capitalize on the movement leading to the law in order to raise the racial consciousness of people of partial African descent.[4]

Whereas the 1991 constitution enabled Indians, who make up only 2 percent of Colombia's population, to permanently secure two senatorial seats out of one hundred and obtain community ownership of 22 percent of the national territory, Law 70 resulted in few changes for most Colombians of mixed and "full" African ancestry.[5] In addition to the riverine dwellers of the Pacific Basin, who gained an avenue to communal land ownership, in Caribbean Colombia the descendants of Palenque de San Basilio, a former maroon community near Cartagena, have secured the exclusivity of the region's *negritud*. But at the same time the vast majority of blacks in Caribbean Colombia have been excluded from *palenquero* "ethnic" blackness and from the benefits of Law 70, and they continue to face racial discrimination without legal protection.[6] Arguably, the Law of Negritudes' principal achievement has been to bring some Colombian blacks out of the "invisibility" (to use the word of the late anthropologist Nina de Friedemann) to which they had been confined since independence and, by doing so, to initiate a national debate on issues of race.[7]

INVISIBILITY OF AFRO-CARIBBEAN COLOMBIANS

Colombian blacks' invisibility sharply contradicts the fact that today Colombia has the third largest population of African origin in the Western Hemisphere after Brazil and the United States. Although mestizos comprise the most numerous racial group among the country's 44 million inhabitants, almost one Colombian out of three is of full or mixed African descent.[8] The Caribbean Coast is the region of Colombia that is most densely populated by people of mixed African descent; it also includes black enclaves consisting of former *palenques* (maroon communities formed during the colonial period). The sparsely inhabited Pacific lowlands are Colombia's "blackest" region, where about 90 percent of the population is of full or mixed African origin. Black communities and people of mixed African descent are also numerous in the south, particularly in the upper Cauca Valley and along the Patía River, and along the central Magdalena River.

Undoubtedly, the two-century-old tradition of presenting Colombia as a mestizo nation has greatly contributed to black Colombians' invisibility. The Andean dominant discourse of mestizaje, which ultimately aims at the whitening of the population and the disappearance of "full" blacks and Indians, has severely restricted the ways in which Afro-Colombians can express their distinctiveness without excluding themselves from the nation. It has incited them to minimize their racial identity and the role of racial exclusion in national formation. Moreover, the long-lasting insistence on Colombia being a mestizo—Euro-Indian—nation has historically played down its African component. Thus, unlike many Afro-Cubans, Afro-Brazilians, and African Americans, few Colombians of partial African descent have identified with African ancestry and blackness. In fact, only Colombians of full African descent in the Chocó, the Pacific Coast, and some black enclaves, such as Palenque de San Basilio and the Patía Valley near Popayán, have tended to assert blackness. But even in the Pacific region, ethnic or racial identity remains weak and fragmented. There, unlike the Indian communities that claimed their ethnic distinctiveness to collectively justify special rights, historically Afro-Colombians have sought to discreetly "blend in" rather than affirm their difference. Thus, the newly formed black associations have lacked a tradition of joint struggle and a common vision to create viable national or regional movements following the Law 70 of Negritudes.[9]

The absence of a collective black- or African-derived identity is particularly noticeable in Colombia's Caribbean region. There, people of mixed African descent comprise the majority of the population and had a long history of close interaction with the Afro-Caribbean world until the early twentieth century, when road, and later air, transportation improved connections with the Andean interior. This neglect of an Afro-Caribbean identity has been manifest in the terms traditionally used to define the region's population—the *costeños*—and the region itself—la Costa or the Atlantic Coast—as well as in studies of its particularism. In *Costeñismos colombianos* (1942), *cartagenero* priest Pedro María Revollo rooted the idiosyncrasy of the region's language in its alleged first inhabitants, the Andalusians, without even mentioning the Amerindians and the Africans.[10] Nor did the nineteenth-century geographical and historical essays and collections of documents written by costeños acknowledge that most of the region's population was of African descent.[11] Without doubt, these works offer irreplaceable data for the study of the region and its inhabitants and constitute the first postindependence costeño attempt to counterbalance Andean-centered histories and to present the nation and its history from the unique perspective of the Caribbean region.[12] When we take into account that, symptomatically, New Granada's most important national scientific expedition during this period, the Comisión Corográfica (1850–59) led by geographer Agustín Codazzi, did not cover the Caribbean region, these works are irreplaceable. Yet their authors focused on the white elite and included the lower-class population of color only as anonymous participants in the background. Simultaneously, however, Andean Colombians have tended to racialize the image of their Caribbean fellow citizens, whom they commonly have described as mulattoes. Until the 1970s, Andean writers and authors of textbooks often ascribed to costeños the contradictory psychosocial traits imputed to mulattoes by pseudoscientific racism: lazy but at the same time active, brave but irresponsible, fun-loving, promiscuous, and noisy.[13] According to anthropologist Peter Wade, these stereotypes fed Andean Colombians' perceptions of costeños in the mid-twentieth century and still exist today.[14] Starting in the late 1970s, historians from the region have forcefully reclaimed its Caribbeanness, renaming it *Caribe colombiano*. However, with the exception of Alfonso Múnera, they have been less willing to highlight the importance of the African component in its racial makeup and, consequently, to discuss the role of race and racism in the historical development of the region.[15]

The invisibility of Afro-Caribbean Colombians is also noticeable in the pantheon of the region's heroes and political leaders, who were almost exclusively white males. The most notorious of them was Rafael Núñez (1825–94), who from a regionalist Liberal became the national president who implemented Colombia's centralist and clerical constitution of 1886.[16] Among the few nonwhite public figures, the most well known and the one Colombians generally mention to illustrate absence of racism in the nation, is the light *pardo* (mulatto) Juan José Nieto (1804–66), a merchant, self-taught writer, and politician of modest origins who remained faithful to the Liberal ideals of liberty and federalism until his death. Nieto progressively assimilated into the Liberal elite and earned the rank of general by participating in the civil war of the "Supremes" (1839–42). Under the national presidency of General José Hilario López, Nieto became governor of the province of Cartagena (1851–54). With the Conservatives back in power, in 1859 Nieto launched a coup that caused a civil war within Caribbean Colombia and pitted Cartagena Province against the New Granadan nation. In 1861, at the zenith of his career, Nieto was elected president of the sovereign state of Bolívar, a position from which he was evicted in 1864, after the coastal provinces reintegrated the nation. Nieto owed his success to his intellectual

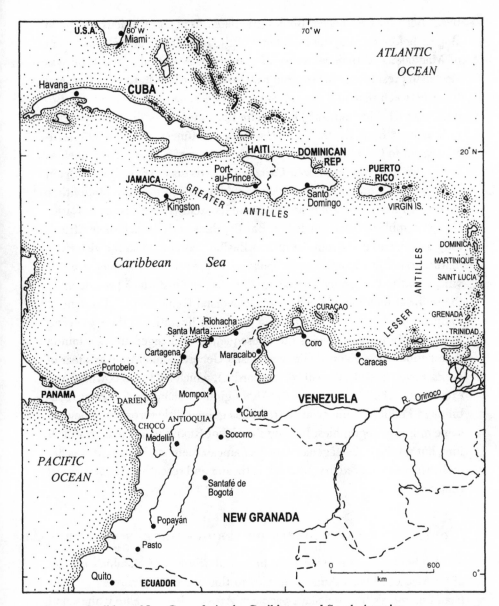

MAP I. Caribbean New Granada in the Caribbean and South America

and military talents, his assimilation into the Liberal elite through his marriage to the daughter of a patriot patrician of Cartagena, and his systematic avoidance of the issue of race.[17]

The other politician often cited to show absence of racism was Luis A. Robles (1849-99), symptomatically known in Colombia as "*el negro* Robles." Born near Riohacha, Robles graduated from a prestigious college in Bogotá before gaining the confidence of the inhabitants of the department of Magdalena as their secretary of education. A radical Liberal, he was elected to preside over the sovereign state of Magdalena in 1877 and, several times between 1876 and 1894, to represent his state in the Congress in Bogotá, where he distinguished himself for his oratorical skills and unyielding radicalism.[18] Recently, thanks to the work of Múnera, some mulatto leaders crucial to Caribbean New Granada's process of independence, such as Pedro Romero, who organized Cartagena's artisans of color against Spain in 1810 (see Chapter 4), have begun to achieve the historical visibility they deserve. Since the Law of Negritudes and its exclusive application in Caribbean Colombia to Palenque de San Basilio, Benkos Bioho, a former African king and the mythical founder of San Basilio, has embodied the victorious maroon rebel in Colombian textbooks as well as in statues erected in his village and in Cartagena.[19] In contrast, today few historians provide more than a brief mention of the more controversial General José (Prudencio) Padilla, a pardo who played a leading role in the liberation of the region and Venezuela in the early 1820s but subsequently challenged the continuing domination of the colonial elite and raised General Simón Bolívar's fear of *pardocracia* (literally, the rule of the pardos), which led to his downfall and execution in 1828 (see Chapter 6). Although the Colombian Congress rehabilitated Padilla's memory in 1831, he has gained little recognition beyond some military biographies. In 1887 the city of Riohacha erected a statue of him, but no site in Cartagena bears his name or memory. His house was demolished and replaced first by a movie theater and recently by a commercial center.[20]

ORIGINS OF THE NEGLECT OF AFRO-CARIBBEAN COLOMBIA

This book seeks to uncover the historical origins of Colombia's neglect of its Afro-Caribbean dimension. Key to this neglect is the role of Caribbean Colombia's free and slave people of African descent, elite whites, and Indians during the crucial period of nation formation in which the country reportedly transformed from a colonial hierarchical caste society into a raceless independent nation founded on mestizaje and whitening. I attempt to answer three related questions: Why did Caribbean Colombian lower classes of color not collectively challenge the small white elite during this process? Why did race not become an organizational category in the region? Why did the Caribbean Coast integrate into Andean Colombia without asserting its Afro-Caribbeanness? By answering these questions, I hope to help explain Colombia's long-lasting self-representation as a mestizo nation, with the exception of the indigenous and black communities defined by the 1991 constitution and Law 70.

In the 1770s one-fifth of the population of Colombia (then known as New Granada) lived in the Caribbean region stretching along the seacoast and into the interior.[21] The inhabitants were predominantly free blacks, mulattoes, and zambos.[22] Slavery was nevertheless an important feature in the region. The coast's principal city, Cartagena de Indias, had been the main port of entry for African slaves imported by Spanish South America, and the majority of workers employed by the region's sugar plantations and cattle ranches were slaves. Thus Caribbean New Granada was demographically an important part of the African diaspora in the Americas. Indians resettled in indigenous villages made up 18 percent of the population, and several Indian nations continued to defy Spain's sovereignty on the vast uncontrolled periphery. Whites represented only 11 percent of coastal inhabitants, and the region's small white elite had good grounds to fear for its survival if people of African descent rebelled autonomously or in alliance with Indians.

Indeed, on various occasions from the late colonial period to the 1820s, conditions seemed conducive to a social revolution in Caribbean New Granada. The region was the scene of much violence, notably the Spanish expeditions of forced resettlement in the 1770s and early 1780s, the devastating wars for independence during the second decade of the nineteenth century, and a civil war in 1831. The position of the white elite was further weakened, and control by the state and the Catholic Church was often nonexistent. Yet free people of African ancestry did not seize such opportunities or take advantage of their demographic superiority to gain power over whites and impose their rule in any part of the region. Nor did they attempt to unite across class, color, and residential lines or to organize autonomously or in union with slaves and Indians to achieve equality and liberty on their own terms.

Free people of African descent gained legal equality as a result of a process in which their actual demographic importance accounted for much, and in which they shared historical agency with the colonial state and the white creole elite. A first step toward racial equality was the royal extension of military privileges to militiamen of African descent in the 1770s. A second step, in 1811, was the decision by Cartagena's white creole elite to admit free African men and their full or mixed male descendants to the body of citizens—in opposition to the decision of the Spanish Cortes (Parliament) to grant suffrage only to male Spaniards, Indians, and mestizos. A third step, in the 1820s, was the suppression in Colombia's constitution and laws of any reference to race in the rights and duties of the free male population. Nevertheless, these three steps were secured by free people of color, who effectively asserted their equality by participating in the region's socioeconomic and political development and its military defense. In some cities they staged massive demonstrations to force town councils to declare independence in 1810–11. Also, free men of African descent were overrepresented in the armies that fought against Spain until the early 1820s, and as a result some of them gained high-ranking military positions. Yet most proindependence demonstrations by free people of color were not self-directed initiatives but part of a movement organized by radical patricians. Furthermore, enlistment in the proindependence armies was often violently imposed on men. In addition, in Caribbean New Granada (unlike in southern New Granada) slaves did not collectively rebel to speed up emancipation, nor did the free people of color demand abolition. In fact, slavery was abolished only in 1852, when it had almost disintegrated as the combined result of the virtual end of the slave trade in the 1790s, the turmoil of the wars for independence, natural death, the 1821 free womb law, and British pressure, as well as slaves' self-purchase and the offer of freedom made to male slaves who joined the Spanish and "patriot" armies.

This book shows that, throughout the period, the people of African descent of Caribbean New Granada chose various forms of revolt, resistance, and adaptation, none of which were racially based or encompassed the entire region. People employed a wide combination of individual, local, and/or transient strategies such as flight, legal action, patronage networks, ritual kinship, manipulation of elite divisions, negotiated support for political leaders, and shows of force. Race did not become an organizational category also because the small white elite, which never became an export planter class, was too weak and divided to articulate a racial ideology as a means of oppression. Instead, to maintain their power, elite whites granted equality to free men of color at the onset of independence and continuously relied on patronage networks including lower-class people of color. Weakness, division, and avoidance of racist ideologies by the elite of society mirrored the same salient features at the bottom: localism, internal rivalries, and silence on the issue of race. The strategies employed by Caribbean New Granadan people of color resulted in individual social mobility and specific spheres of popular autonomy, notably culture, but simultaneously militated against building an autonomous sociopolitical consensus to collectively improve the conditions of people of African descent and lower-class people in general. In other words, if creative forms of survival, accommodation, acquiescence, and resistance were used extensively in the region and could be individually effective, their impact on economic structures and the socioracial hierarchy was limited. Indians were more successful at jointly struggling, but their victories were local or in the borderlands. The regional elite could not unite and overcome its provincialism to preside over the formation of a strong Caribbean entity. Lower- and upper-class failure at region building enabled the highlands' elite to construct the Colombian nation as Andean, white, and mestizo and to minimize its Afro-Caribbeanness.

Several factors help to explain these developments. Caribbean New Granada's territory was deeply fragmented, lacked an integrated network of communication, and was surrounded by a vast uncontrolled frontier. As a result, people tended to identify more with individual cities, towns, and villages than with the Caribbean region or New Granada as a whole. In addition, the traditional competition between Cartagena and Santa Marta for the monopoly of foreign trade and the domination of the region caused other towns and villages not to unite against dependency on the Andean center but to oppose or align themselves with Cartagena or Santa Marta according to circumstance, which led to civil war during the struggle for independence and in 1831. Moreover, people's identification with local communities, still conceived as hierarchical, corporative entities headed by elite whites, precluded local and regional organization along class and/or racial lines.

Throughout the period, state and church supervision hardly extended beyond a handful of important cities and left most villages, slave haciendas, and the hinterland with little or no official control. Against this background, the small white elite lived off cattle ranching, agriculture for the regional markets, and legal and contraband trade. Although some members of the white elite possessed degrees in law or theology, few qualified as intellectuals or had a regional vision. The elite failed to become an export planter class and was weakened by clashing economic interests and intraregional rivalries. It also was divided along political lines, first between advocates of full Spanish colonialism, autonomy, and independence, and, in the 1820s, between supporters of the 1821 constitution and those championing Bolívar's semimonarchical constitution.

People of African descent too were divided. With occupations ranging from property owner to artisan, day laborer, and slave, they could not mobilize collectively on the basis of class and race. Colonial racial categories did not overlap with status, as blacks, mulattoes, and zambos could be slave or free. By 1800 few individuals were African-born, making the appeal to Africa as the common origin tenuous, even among "full" blacks. Moreover, free people of African descent regardless of color tended to view themselves as superior to slaves (and Indians) and to dissociate their cause from that of more disfranchised members of society. In the cities, the existence of a socioracial hierarchy among the free people of color—assigning "full" blacks to the lower strata and allowing for some wealthy light mulattoes to enter in the white category—prevented their joint action. In contrast, in several rural areas free blacks, mulattoes, and zambos had intermarried to such an extent and were in such an overwhelming majority that color distinctions were more fluid. Yet, because the rural population was geographically fragmented and isolated and because the power was located in the distant cities, the urban socioracial hierarchy handicapped mobilization in the entire region.

The demographic predominance of women among both the slave population and the urban free population of African descent, as well as women's socioeconomic importance in the whole region, also explain people of color's preference for improvisation and adaptive strategies of resistance. In addition to non-Western cultural traditions, female preponderance in cities and the migratory quality of many men's employment (notably ranching and transportation) resulted in a high incidence of female-headed households. Society and the economy thus depended on women as reproducers (mothers) and as producers (workers).[23] Because of the simultaneous demands of childbearing, childrearing, and work, women of color tended to focus their struggle on survival and local and specific concerns rather than on access to institutional power. This affected overall mobilization, making massive revolt not the preferred form of protest. In fact, Caribbean Colombian women resourcefully utilized the law and existing spaces of freedom to make gains. Through the wars, epidemics, and sieges that characterized many of the years after 1810, they were influential in the strategies of flight and adaptive survival used by local communities, which minimized the loss of lives. Where women largely outnumbered men, as in the slave and free populations of African descent in the principal cities, some women had children with white men, contributing to the fuzziness of the region's racial categories.

The indigenous population was even more scattered and fragmented than the free people of color. Huge distances and deep cultural differences separated the autonomous indigenous nations on the periphery, yet they continued unsubdued as colonial and republican authorities lacked the means to carry out any policy toward them. Those Indians who settled in colonial villages were less successful in maintaining distinct ways of life. Several communities were forcibly resettled or broken up during the Spanish campaigns of resettlement. As a result, most became small enclaves in the vicinity of towns and villages inhabited by non-Indians. But some indigenous communities saw the wars for independence as opportunities to redefine their relations with exploitative authorities and settlers. In the area of Santa Marta, they massively fought for the defense of Spain, whereas some villages along the Magdalena River struggled for independence. Although, with the advent of the republic, Indians became legally equal, in fact they were second-class citizens. When in 1833 the state began to dismantle their communal lands, their localized protests could not overturn the process, except on the frontier.

HISTORIOGRAPHY

Colombia's arduous process of nation making has received the scholarly attention of several historians. Anthony McFarlane has analyzed in depth Colombia's transition from colony to early postindependence fragmentation. Five decades ago, at the beginning of a productive career as a Colombianist, David Bushnell wrote a pioneering study of the experiment of Gran Colombia (composed of Venezuela, New Granada, and Ecuador) following independence in 1821; he later published, among other works, a broad interpretation of the making of modern Colombia, aptly subtitled *A Nation in Spite of Itself.*[24] Hans-Joaquim König and Margarita Garrido have skillfully examined nation formation during the early nineteenth century through constitutions, political discourses, and local claims. Frank Safford and Jaime Jaramillo Uribe have shed light on the contradictions between society and elite ideology. More recently, Victor Uribe-Urán has examined the role of lawyers in the process of nation formation, whereas Rebecca Earle has shown that Spain's mismanaged reconquest from 1815 to 1821 was a key factor in the achievement of independence.[25] However, these historians have tended to focus on Andean, rather than Caribbean, Colombia.

In fact, Caribbean Colombia, with its population of African descent, was little known outside of the country until the publication of the Nobel Prize novel *Cien años de soledad* (One Hundred Years of Solitude) by Gabriel García Márquez in 1967.[26] In Colombia, historical interest in the region paralleled the rise of peasant movements in the 1970s to regain control of their lands taken over by latifundia owners. Two studies by Colombian sociologist Orlando Fals Borda on population and modes of agrarian production in Cartagena Province since the early colonial period, designed to provide a historical framework to the ongoing struggle, fostered several works on the socioeconomic effects of the development of haciendas in eighteenth-century Caribbean Colombia.[27] Yet it was Fals's publication of the four-volume *Historia doble de la Costa* (Double History of the Coast) in 1979-86 that brought the social history of Caribbean Colombia to the forefront. A militant work aimed at promoting popular mobilization, *Historia doble* focuses on the rivers' rural communities rather than the urban popular classes and slaves in general. It minimizes the role of race and tensions within the popular classes to stress the democracy of their "amphibious" culture in contrast to the presumably more violent culture of central Colombia.[28]

Whatever its limits, Fals's work is thought-provoking and has generated new interest in the region among younger Colombian scholars. Although not directly addressing the issue of race, in the late 1980s they began to stress the Caribbean characteristics of the region, which they renamed *Caribe colombiano*, in contrast with the neutral terms of *la Costa* or "the Atlantic Coast." Among these historians, Gustavo Bell (governor of the department of Atlántico in the early 1990s) has examined Spain's failure to reestablish control of the Caribbean provinces during the reconquest as well as the impact of intercity rivalry on Caribbean Colombian regionalism after independence. Adelaida Sourdis de De la Vega has produced some pioneering work on Cartagena during the first phase of the independence movement. Writing on the same subject, but from a more innovative perspective, Múnera has stressed the conflict between the creole elites in Cartagena and Bogotá and the role played by mulatto artisans in Cartagena's independence in 1811. Adolfo Meisel Roca and María Aguilera Díaz have thoroughly examined the demography of Cartagena in 1777. Dolcey Romero has published a well-documented study of slavery in Santa Marta until its abolition in 1852.[29] Eduardo Posada-Carbó has examined in depth Caribbean Colombia's socioeconomic and political development between 1870 and 1950.[30] Together, the works of these historians have informed my book in decisive ways, and I consider some of their specific arguments in the chapters that follow.

Until recently, the history of Colombians of African descent has been of limited scholarly interest. Most anthropologists had focused on Indian communities until the pioneering works on Palenque de San Basilio by Aquiles Escalante (inspired by Melville J. Herskovits) and on Chocó by Rogerio Velásquez.[31] Since the 1980s Jaime Arocha, Nina S. de Friedemann, Michael Taussig, and Peter Wade have written thought-provoking studies on blacks in the Pacific region and, to a lesser extent, in southern Cauca and the Caribbean Coast.[32] For their part, historians have often neglected the Afro-Colombian experience except in relation to colonial slavery. More generally, however, works on Colombians of African descent have focused on the Chocó, the Pacific Coast, and rural communities of the southern Cauca Valley.[33] Little research has been done on the population of mixed African descent of the Caribbean Coast, except on recent developments. In a now classic but slightly deterministic study of Colombia's family and cultural structures, Virginia Gutiérrez resolutely placed the Caribbean region within the country's "Negroid cultural complex," together with the Pacific region.[34] Focusing on Cartagena in 1970, social scientists Mauricio Solaún and Sidney Kronus argued that the city's fluid and "gentle" race relations have prevented the rise of strong racism and organized racial violence. Two decades later Joel Streicker concluded that racial discrimination and prejudice permeate Cartagena's society, although they are encoded in a discourse on class and gender. More recently, Elizabeth Cunin has shown how in Cartagena, with Law 70, the appropriation of negritud by palenqueros has left other blacks unable to claim blackness and to protest racism.[35]

PURPOSE AND SUMMARY

This book examines the historical development of Caribbean Colombia within the comparative perspective of the Americas. It places itself within the growing scholarship on elite and popular classes as well as regionalism in the making of Latin American independence, which has resulted in challenging works on Mexico, Peru, Brazil, and Cuba but has seldom focused on Colombia—a major, yet little studied, country.[36] After 1810 Caribbean Colombia, barely connected to the rest of the country, could well have become a strong united region—perhaps even a separate nation—with its own distinct economy, racial makeup, and culture. Yet it did not. Building on Wade's analysis of the regionalization of race in Colombia, I show that, in a national racial system in which mestizaje is understood as progressive whitening through the mixture of whites and Indians, elite and lower-class silence on the region's Afro-Caribbean component allowed for its depreciation as a "mulatto" space by the Andean interior and encouraged racism against the poor of apparently full African ancestry within the coastal society.

This study complements the historiography of African-derived societies, which generally has focused on slave societies (with a small but powerful planter elite and a predominantly slave population of African descent), such as most Caribbean islands and the U.S. South. There, while free people of African origin remained internally divided and seldom associated their struggle for equality with slaves' struggle for abolition, race became an organizational category after independence. By examining a society in which the majority consisted of free people of color (i.e., a society with slaves) and African ancestry has not been an identity for political organization, I expose the diversity prevalent in a multiracial society where slavery was only one of several labor systems and I show the increased difficulty this diversity represented for popular mobilization. I also provide landmarks for the processes of independence and abolition in Venezuela, a Caribbean-Andean nation with a substantial population of mixed African descent that, like Colombia, has received little scholarly attention. Moreover, my examination of the complex configuration of historical circumstances that generate a weak race consciousness in Caribbean Colombia provides an enlightening complement to the extensive scholarship on Brazil, which has highlighted the role of the "mulatto escape hatch," clientelism, and patronage, as well as the open frontier in preventing racially based mobilization while simultaneously fostering antiblack racism.[37]

This book expands the scholarship on frontier societies and Indian resistance to colonialism by studying a case in which the frontier remained unconquered; the problem has been one of "opening a frontier" that offered few opportunities for wealth except contraband and was inhabited by outcasts and unsubdued indigenous nations.[38] Unlike in Argentina or the United States, in Caribbean Colombia there was no pressure from a growing white population eager to settle on the frontier, nor did the state have the means to conquer and "civilize" the frontier, as in Brazil. As a result, up to the present the Caribbean frontier has been dominated by indigenous and marginal groups; simultaneously, its marginality and isolation explain its continuing centrality for illegal activities.

Finally, this study participates in the ongoing debate on slave resistance initiated by Eugene Genovese, who accords a central role to the French and Haitian Revolutions in the outburst of slave rebellions after 1790.[39] In Caribbean Colombia the ideals of 1789 or 1804 found a more receptive audience among free people of color than among slaves. No major revolt along Haitian lines erupted despite continuing white fears to the contrary, because no alliance formed between the slave minority and the free people of color and because flight to the uncontrolled frontier, self-purchase, and enrollment in the Spanish and patriot armies provided individual opportunities for self-liberation. Indeed, as indicated by Michael Craton and David Geggus, the factors leading to slave revolt were complex and often simultaneously forward and backward looking. Moreover, the conditions that made the Haitian Revolution possible were unique, and, not surprisingly, although it was followed by a wave of genuine and rumored conspiracies and revolts throughout the Greater Caribbean, nowhere did massive rebellions take place until the very distinct Bussa's Rebellion in Barbados in 1816, the Demerara Revolt in 1823, and the Jamaican Baptist War in 1831–32.[40]

The contribution of this book to the nascent field of gender studies during the transition from slavery to free labor and from colonialism to independence in Latin America is more limited than I had hoped, because most documents I located featured men only. Still, my findings agree with studies stressing continuity in conditions for females and their public roles from colonialism to independence and follow recent analyses of women's fundamental economic role and active practice of citizenship. I demonstrate not only the extraordinary demographic and economic importance of women in Caribbean Colombia's major cities, but also their influence in the broader society in shaping culture and strategies of mobilization, resistance, and adaptation that pursued survival rather than individual rights and access to institutional power.[41]

The first three chapters of the book analyze the dynamics of power, race, and class in Caribbean New Granada, starting from the unconquered frontier and moving progressively to the region's main cities. Chapter 1 examines the indigenous and runaway communities established on the vast border of Caribbean Colombia and Spanish failure to conquer them militarily, politically, and spiritually during the eighteenth century. Chapter 2 analyzes the countryside, highlighting the extreme fragmentation of the region's territory and social fabric. It documents the eighteenth-century expansion of landlord fiefdoms and slave haciendas in contrast with the state's and the church's limited authority, and it considers lower-class strategies to resist loss of land and cultural imposition. Viewing the city as the center of state, church, and white elite power, Chapter 3 compares the culture and the economic and socioracial structure of Cartagena, Mompox, Santa Marta, Riohacha, and Valledupar to explain the continuing rivalry between these cities. It also examines the different means employed by free people of color and slaves, particularly women, to challenge elite rule and to individually, and sometimes collectively, pursue liberty and equality.

Chapter 4 focuses on Caribbean New Granada's First Independence (1810–21). It compares the competing processes of independence in Cartagena and Mompox, and contrasts them with Santa Marta's continuing allegiance to Spain. It examines how elite divisions and intraregional wars prevented the formation of a common regional project. Simultaneously, it discusses class, racial, and gender divisions and the forces of localism and patronage to explain why free people of color and slaves did not take advantage of the general breakdown of order to impose their rule and to end slavery in any part of the region. It shows how the brutal Spanish reconquest in 1815 and the pursuit of the war until independence in 1821 further weakened the Caribbean elite at the regional and national levels and led to increasing defection, flight to the frontier, and individual strategies of survival among the population of African descent.

The last two chapters look at the achievements and limits of the early republic (1821–35) from the perspective of Caribbean New Granada as a whole and the issues of race and class. Chapter 5 analyzes the impact of the 1821 constitution and early republican reforms of Gran Colombia on the Caribbean region in the broader context of elite fear of a revolution along Haitian lines. It examines the different meanings free men of color gave to their new legal equality and how they struggled to recover from the devastation of the war rather than to gain power. Weak church and state presence, and a *hacendado* class only slowly reemerging from the war also explain the lack of open sociracial conflict in the region. Chapter 6 analyzes the challenges of pardo General José Padilla to the sociracial hierarchy of Cartagena in 1824 and 1828 and his subsequent downfall ending with his execution in 1828, highlighting the role played by race and by Bolívar's fear of pardocracia in the process. The chapter then turns to an examination of the growing challenge Riohacha, Santa Marta, Mompox, and several towns along the lower Magdalena River posed to Cartagena as capital of the newly created Magdalena department, culminating in a successful revolution in 1831. Launched under the banner of Liberalism, the revolution used the martyrdom of Padilla to rally supporters but carefully avoided the issues of racial equality and slaves' freedom. Although it ended the centralization in Cartagena stipulated by the 1821 constitution, it also reinforced the Caribbean region's alignment on Andean New Granada's bipartisan politics initiated by the rival projects of Bolívar and General Francisco de Paula Santander.

The conclusion considers the Caribbean New Granadan case vis-à-vis other multiracial societies in the Americas with an important population of African descent during the Age of Revolution. It assesses why it did not become a strong region within independent New Granada. It reexamines the reasons that led to free people of African descent achieving legal equality at the outset of the republic in contrast with slaves gaining freedom only three decades later. Finally, the conclusion highlights how territorial fragmentation, localism, patronage, the existence of a vast frontier, and smuggling prevented lower-class mobilization against a seemingly vulnerable white elite.

1

FRONTIERS

In 1789 the archbishop-viceroy of New Granada, Antonio Caballero y Góngora, remarked that "disorder" was the fundamental problem of his jurisdiction, centered in Santafé de Bogotá. The most fertile valleys were underpopulated and in desperate need of a labor force, whereas the infertile deserts, vast forests, and steep mountains provided refuge for numerous unsubdued Indians as well as "criminal and fugitive men who fled society to live without law or religion." The "disorder of the viceroyalty," he believed, originated in the conquest, when the Spaniards did not attempt to colonize and populate the land but to exploit its resources using indigenous labor. As a result, the inhabitants concentrated in areas already populated by Indians, to which slaves were added, leaving huge regions almost unoccupied.[1] No other region of New Granada was more characteristic of this pattern than the three Caribbean provinces of Cartagena, Santa Marta, and Riohacha, where Spain failed to control the frontiers and backlands inhabited by "savage" Indians and runaway free people of color.

INDIAN NATIONS

The Caribbean region of New Granada had no secure boundaries. The approximately one thousand miles of seashore extending from the Gulf of Urabá to the Guajira Peninsula were easily accessible to foreign corsairs, smugglers, pirates, and invaders. In the 1690s the Scottish attempt to establish a colony in the Darién and the successful seizure of Cartagena by a French fleet under the command of Admiral Jean Bernard Louis Desjean Pointis had fully exposed the vulnerability of the coast to sea attacks. Since then, Spain sought to increase control by adding new fortifications and by forming in 1775 a *matrícula de mar* (navy register) to expand the coast guard.[2] Despite these efforts, Dutch, British, and French smugglers and corsairs still called in, even near Cartagena.[3] Understandably, during the

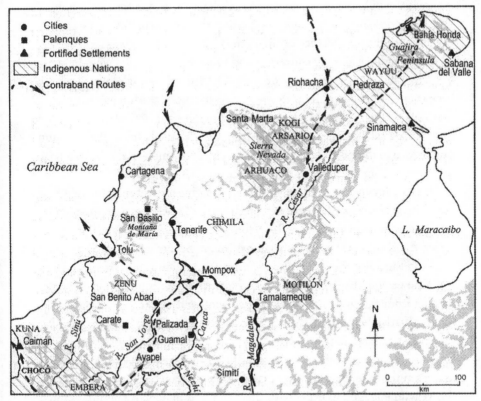

MAP 2. Indigenous nations, fortified settlements, palenques, and contraband routes in Caribbean New Granada, ca. 1770

Haitian Revolution, news that rebellious French slaves and free men of color were deported to Caribbean shores or escaped by sea alarmed New Granada's authorities.[4] With the threat of a slave revolt from the sea, the Caribbean region seemed all the more uncontrollable.

Likewise, the borderlands remained unguarded. The Guajira Peninsula, in the east, was the unconquered territory of some 30,000 Wayúu (or Guajiro) Indians, who periodically attacked settlements in Riohacha Province. In the west, the territory was almost entirely controlled by sovereign Indians: the Emberá in the south of the Sinú and San Jorge Valleys, and an estimated 10,000 Kuna (or Cuna) in the region of the Atrato River and in the Darién. The mountains of the Sierra Nevada, between Riohacha and Santa Marta, belonged to three indigenous groups: the Arhuaco, the Kogi, and the Arsario. Until the mid-eighteenth century, the Andean Cordillera between Riohacha and Ocaña comprised several areas held by the Motilón, whereas the hilly region east of the Magdalena River was the stronghold of about 10,000 Chimila Indians.[5] According to a concerned New Granadan official, indigenous defiance of Spain meant that these regions gave refuge to "other Indians already converted and to licentious people, who, in order to escape the punishment they deserve for their crimes, take refuge in the barbarians and induce them to greater restlessness."[6] Moreover, it meant that these regions tended to favor Spain's enemies and actively participated in contraband. This was particularly the case with the Kuna in the west and the Wayúu in the east, both of whom had intense commercial relations with the British from Jamaica and the Dutch from Curaçao.

In 1761, for instance, Spanish military engineers Antonio Arévalo and Antonio de Narváez y la Torre explored the Gulf of Urabá, accompanied by a translator and ten black men. They found ample evidence of an alliance between the Kuna and the British against Spain. Several communities traded cacao and tortoise shells for clothes, arms, and ammunition from the British. One cacique had reportedly received the title of captain and a golden scepter from the governor of Jamaica. Another traveled in a pirogue flying the British flag. When the engineers offered the Kuna caciques Spanish royal titles to land and the salaries of captains of Indians, most of them refused these inducements on the grounds that the British had told them that Spain's aim was to take over their lands.[7] Similarly, on the coast of Riohacha, the Wayúu engaged in trade with the British from Jamaica and the Dutch from Curaçao. They bartered lumber, dyewood, salt, cattle, and mules for arms and ammunition.[8] Such exchanges showed not only the importance of the commercial ties of Indians with Spain's rivals but also their will to militarily defend their lands.

ROCHELAS AND PALENQUES

Weakened by unconquered Indians on the periphery, the vast territory of Caribbean New Granada situated within the frontier was far from operating as an integrated unit. Unlike central New Granada, which is divided by three high-peak cordilleras, the coastal region is mostly fertile tropical lowland, except for the Sierra Nevada and the arid Guajira Peninsula. A complex network of rivers runs from the center of the viceroyalty to the Atlantic Ocean, the most important of them being the Magdalena River, which meets the Cauca River near Mompox and flows into the Caribbean Sea near Barranquilla. Two other waterways are the San Jorge River, which runs through the southern region between Ayapel and San Benito Abad before flowing into the Cauca River, and the Sinú River, on the west of the Cauca, which flows into the Caribbean Sea north of Lorica. The Atrato River linked the gold-producing Chocó to the Gulf of Urabá. However, neither the Magdalena nor any of the other rivers were easily navigable; moreover, the Atrato flowed through the territory of the Kuna, who continuously attacked boats and travelers. Although well connected to the Caribbean Sea, neither Cartagena nor Santa Marta, the two largest port cities on the coast, had direct access to the Magdalena River, the viceroyalty's main waterway. Besides the rivers, a few trails connected colonial towns and villages, but periodic floods and rain rendered them precarious. Most tracks to the coast cut through the territories of unsubdued and occasionally unfriendly Indian nations.[9] Not surprisingly, with such an embryonic communications system, the backlands situated beyond Caribbean New Granada's cities, villages, and haciendas fully escaped the supervision of colonial institutions.

Thus, in addition to the Indians in the unconquered nations, until the 1770s an estimated sixty thousand people lived out of the reach of the colonial state and the Catholic Church, scattered in small illegal settlements called *rochelas*, established in the forests, hills, and swamps along the rivers, and in isolated huts housing nuclear families.[10] As these men, women, and children did not leave their own testimonies, their conditions can only be roughly sketched on the basis of reports written by their adversaries during the Bourbon era. According to one of them, Spanish lieutenant colonel Antonio de la Torre y Miranda, who in the mid-1770s led expeditions against such communities in the hinterland west of Cartagena:

[The *arrochelados*] are the descendants of the military and naval deserters, of the numerous stowaways who without license or job passed to these dominions, of the black male and female slaves who ran away or escaped from the justice of their masters, and of others who, having committed some homicides or other crimes sought shelter from their excesses by dispersing in order to free themselves, some from punishment, others from servitude, having among them many Indian men and women who, mixed with mestizo, black, and mulatto women, propagated an infinity of racial mixes (*castas*) difficult to verify.[11]

Ten years later, another of their conquerors, Franciscan friar and veteran army officer Joseph Palacios de la Vega, also stressed that the arrochelados along the San Jorge, Cauca, and Nechí Rivers south of San Benito Abad formed a predominantly male, mixed population of Indians, zambos, blacks, and mulattoes among whom the boundaries of race and original status were difficult to establish. Nevertheless, some rochelas were more racially homogeneous, notably those formed by Indians who had fled the *pueblos de indios* (segregated indigenous villages) to which they had been forcibly assigned in order to return to their own ways of life in adjacent forests. Other rochelas, founded by African runaway slaves and their descendants, were predominantly black.[12]

Life on the margins of the colony allowed arrochelados to form sexual unions and families that displayed little observance of the Catholic norms, especially monogamy and the interdiction of consanguineous unions. To his great dismay, Antonio de la Torre reported that in the mangrove swamps near Cartagena men and women spent the night together fishing in small boats: "From such a disorderly and brutal mixture of the two sexes, which in some cases extended to daughters, sisters and sisters-in-law, some family kinships were formed that were so intertwined that it would be difficult for the most consummate Theologian to sort them out."[13] For his part, Palacios de la Vega lamented that, in the rochelas he destroyed, it was common for mothers to have children from several fathers and for men to live with several concubines concurrently.[14] The Bourbon conquerors often were appalled to find arrochelados drinking alcohol and dancing to the rhythm of drums, their bodies barely covered below the waist, in complete sexual proximity. According to La Torre, these dissolute mores, together with the unusually high fertility levels of the region's women, explained why families of arrochelados were so large. It was not exceptional, he claimed, for a father having two or three unmarried daughters to end up with twelve or fourteen illegitimate grandchildren—a household of more than thirty persons.[15] But limited concern for the Catholic norms did not mean that most rochelas were egalitarian and peaceful communities, despite the fact that they did not own slaves. According to Palacios de la Vega, some were characterized by internal violence and abuse, especially against women and children. Most women, he asserted, had been kidnapped and forced into multiple concubinage by male arrochelados, who exploited their children's labor and kept them unbaptized.[16] Nevertheless, several colonial reports claimed that arrochelados lived a life of idleness and earthly pleasures because nature generously provided all the fruits, starchy food, game, and fish they needed. Seemingly, their only struggle was against the voracious insects, and their only industry was to make illegal liquor or pan gold for contraband. Bishop Diego de Peredo of Cartagena alleged that in the plains of Tolú the laziness of arrochelados led them to steal a lot from each other, whereas La Torre claimed that women "had never performed any [work]."[17]

No doubt, these reports magnified the immorality and brutality existing in rochelas to justify conquest, even when Palacios de la Vega's description of domestic abuse and men's kidnapping of women and girls is not at odds with the picture of male violence against women and children observed in other frontier societies.[18] Moreover, the extensive destruction of arrochelados' homes and crops by La Torre and Palacios de la Vega contradicts their own statements of idleness. Closer to the reality of the arrochelados, though gender biased, was their portrait by French traveler Gaspard Mollien. In 1823 he described the scattered nuclear families established along the Magdalena River as busy settlers growing corn, root vegetables, and fruits in a hostile environment characterized by isolation: "The life of the inhabitant of the Magdalena is not idle. Alone, he takes care of everything, he does not expect any help from society; he must be at the same time an architect, a hunter, a fisherman, a skillful worker. . . . He never rests." However, by Mollien's own admission, "Man cannot live alone," and subsistence farming was impossible without the contribution of a wife and children. Together, they grew food crops, planted and harvested corn, fished, and produced lard. Whereas men hunted, women and children tended the poultry, ground the corn, and prepared the meals. In addition, they continuously faced disease, natural disasters, and dangerous reptiles and insects. In such conditions, few newborns survived, few adults reached old age, and most families comprised only a father, a mother, and two or three children. Mollien concluded, not without some racial and climatic determinism: "One does not live long with the evils from which these people suffer, and which are common to all mixed races in the tropics."[19] Similarly, the arrochelados' failure to observe Catholic baptism, marriage, burial, and communion, often lamented by colonial officials, resulted largely from the lack of priests serving outside cities and the most important villages. Some ministers charged expensive fees to perform the sacraments that many arrochelados simply could not afford. Thus, arrochelados generally did not get married in church, often neglected to have their children baptized, and sometimes buried their dead in the woods.[20]

In addition to rochelas, several palenques had existed since the early seventeenth century, when heterogeneous groups of Kongo, Angola, Arará,

Family of Indian fishermen on the Magdalena River. (Alcide Dessalines d' Orbigny, *Voyage pittoresque dans les deux Amériques* [Paris: L. Tenré, 1836])

Mina, and Karabalí runaway slaves formed them around Cartagena, in the lower Cauca River, and in the vicinity of Valledupar and Riohacha.[21] Although by the 1690s many palenques had been destroyed by military expeditions, some became officially recognized as peaceful hamlets of free blacks. For example, the 1780 census returns for the village of Santa Catalina, between Cartagena and Barranquilla, included two haciendas and one palenque comprising three households and thirteen dwellers.[22] More well known is Palenque de San Basilio, near Cartagena, to which the bishop of Cartagena granted the status of an autonomous black community in the 1710s, after all attempts at conquest had failed.[23] In exchange for a general pardon and freedom, the palenqueros agreed not to shelter new runaway slaves and not to accept any white residents except a Catholic priest.[24] In 1772 Cartagena's Bishop Diego de Peredo noted that they "keep to themselves without mixing with other peoples," speaking "a particular language" (derived from the Bantu family). They governed themselves autonomously in all political, military, and administrative matters and were accountable solely to the province's governor in Cartagena. The only outside authority in the community was the priest, who administered to 396 parishioners as well as 90 slaves from adjacent haciendas.[25] The fact that slaves could be kept on haciendas in the direct vicinity of San Basilio suggests that, until 1772, the palenqueros complied with the agreement reached earlier in the century.

In the 1770s several other palenques survived, but without the status of an autonomous black community. The mangrove swamps of Matuna and the thickly covered Mountain of María near Cartagena still provided refuge for small groups of runaway slaves who lived off fishing and raising small crops. According to Antonio de la Torre, they also harassed nearby haciendas, and their mores were contrary to the Catholic canon.[26] South of Mompox, the palenques formed by runaway slaves from the gold mines of northern Antioquia in the seventeenth century continued to exist, protected by their difficult access and Spain's relative neglect after the decline of the region's gold production.[27] Most notable among them were the palenques of Guamal and Palizada, on the Cauca River, which in the 1780s, according to Joseph Palacios de la Vega, comprised zambos and blacks with a few mulattoes who lived off fishing and robbing travelers. Showing no sympathy for those he called "outlaw people," the military friar asserted that many carried firearms, especially the slaves who had run away from their masters, and killed each other for the most trivial reasons. Allegedly, all the men lived in polygamy with several concubines they had kidnapped. Their children were not baptized, and many men and women lived and died without being christened.[28]

THE CHALLENGE OF THE FRONTIER

In sum, until the 1770s, if the tens of thousands of insubordinate Indians in the periphery are added to the estimated 60,000 arrochelados of all racial mixtures and the palenqueros of African descent in the hinterland, those who escaped the control of the government, the church, and the law amounted to some 100,000 persons, or probably one of every two inhabitants in Caribbean New Granada.[29] Rather than a bastion against Indian attacks on the region's interior, colonial authorities saw the frontier as a zone of refuge for misfits and criminals fleeing Spanish civilization. For state and church officials, it symbolized the threat of indigenous and African bar-

barity. It corresponded to the unlimited realm of the infidel, where uncon-quered Indians, arrochelados, and palenqueros, although competing among themselves for control of the land and resources, coincided in their oppo-sition to colonial power. Similarly, for Spain, rochelas and palenques were epitomes of social, racial, and family disorder. They were redoubts where free and slave, Indians, blacks, and peoples of all "racial mixes" of both sexes amalgamated in unsanctified and polygamous unions and gave birth to children of even more unverifiable racial categories. Like the sovereign Indians, but in different ways, Caribbean New Granada's frontier commu-nities subverted the colonial order: they challenged the moral norms im-posed by the Catholic Church, ignored the law, had no respect for Spanish racial categories and hierarchies, and displayed some proscribed forms of collectivism, especially in family matters. Apparently, however, they did not question gender hierarchies but kept women and children in subordinate positions and exhibited patriarchal family patterns. Moreover, Spanish offi-cials reported a few white males but no white females among the arroche-lados, which left the alleged virtue of Spanish and white creole women (thus their family honor) intact.[30] Nevertheless, state and church percep-tion of the interconnected threat posed by unconquered indigenous com-munities and illegal settlements led the colonial authorities to conclude that, in order to bring the entire Caribbean region under the king's rule, military action was necessary against both the sovereign Indians and the arrochelados.

From the 1740s to the 1780s the viceroys promoted a series of expeditions of conquest and forced resettlement against Indians on the periphery and arrochelados and palenqueros within the Caribbean region. Unlike most processes of frontier incorporation, attempts in the Caribbean region did not represent the "opening" of an allegedly uninhabited frontier to "white" settlers but the rounding up of its existing dwellers of color and their re-location in newly founded or repositioned towns and villages. Spain's task was complicated by the vastness of the region's fringes and their difficult access; the violent resistance of the seminomadic Indian nations; the con-tinuing option of flight chosen by many black, mulatto, zambo, mestizo, and white runaways and illegal settlers; and the viceroyalty's lack of mili-tary forces and colonial personnel. Although by the end of the eighteenth century several thousand fringe peoples had been relocated to new colonial settlements, their "civilization" and Christianization proved elusive. More-over, the indigenous communities on the periphery remained unconquered and continued to challenge the state.

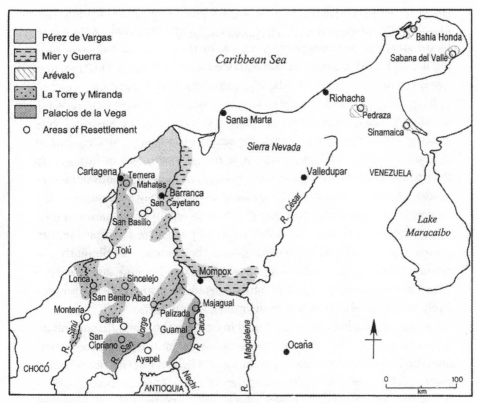

MAP 3. Campaigns of forced resettlement in Caribbean New Granada, 1740s–1780s

SPAIN VERSUS THE INDIAN NATIONS

Until the 1770s, Spain combined military intervention and missionary expansion to impose royal authority on the "barbarous" Indians on the frontier. The military campaigns cost a lot in men and money. Soldiers faced an elusive indigenous enemy who knew the terrain well and subjected them to deadly attacks. Many soldiers also succumbed to disease, malnutrition, and exhaustion. When Spanish authorities managed to build new settlements, few people came from the interior to live on the periphery, and the indigenous population rapidly retook control of most areas.[31] The Catholic missions sent in all directions to evangelize Indians lacked propagandists and adequate teaching methods and often failed to awaken indigenous interest in Christianity. Yet, in the east of Santa Marta Province, the Chimila and the Motilón began to accept their vassalage to the Spanish monarchy. Located closer to colonial settlements than other unconquered groups, they were progressively weakened by the frequent campaigns launched against them by the army and local landlords as well as by their own raids against existing haciendas. This situation benefited the missions of Spanish Capuchins, newly established on their lands, who consolidated their position. The Chimila, in particular, had already suffered a major setback in the 1740s, when *maestre de campo* José Fernando Mier y Guerra was appointed to colonize the lower Magdalena Valley. He seized their lands and forced them to settle in newly founded pueblos or to retreat to the eastern frontier. By the late 1780s the viceroy's secretary, Francisco Silvestre, reported that unsubdued Chimila "had several pueblos from which they come and go, but now without committing hostilities."[32] The Capuchin missionaries did not claim victory over the infidel, as they repeatedly asked for additional help to prevent converted Chimila from escaping to the mountains.[33] Similarly, beginning in the 1770s, the Zenú in the area between the Sinú and San Jorge Rivers faced intense colonization of their lands by cattle rangers, progressively losing the ability to live in their own communities.

In contrast, Catholic missions failed to conquer the more distant indigenous nations. On the Guajira Peninsula, since the early eighteenth century, the Capuchin administered missions to "civilize" the Wayúu with little success. The king entrusted a campaign of pacification to Spanish slave-trader Bernardo Ruiz de Noriega, who in 1760 reported having conquered 15,650 Wayúu Indians whom he resettled in new pueblos placed under indigenous captains (two of whom were women), but the Indians rapidly returned to their way of life.[34] In 1769 the Wayúu rebelled against the Capuchin, destroyed the missions, and massacred their settlers. Unable to repress them militarily, the viceroyalty initiated a policy of pacification and colonization based on the establishment of fortified settlements at strategic locations. Between 1772 and 1775 military engineer Antonio Arévalo successively founded Bahía Honda, Sinamaica, and Pedraza in the peninsula, comprising colonist farmers and some missionaries protected by military forces, but the Wayúu defeated his troops when they attempted to establish a fourth settlement in Sabana del Valle. By 1779 Bahía Honda was also abandoned, leaving only two settlements actively protected. The Wayúu thus continued to live autonomously and to trade with the British and the Dutch. The Crown's policy was even more disastrous in the Darién. Whereas in 1712 several thousand settlers were scattered in small villages throughout the vast region of the isthmus, less than seventy years later their number had shrunk to one thousand as a result of Indian and buccaneer attacks and abandonment. In addition, the Kuna, firmly established on the Caribbean side of the isthmus, repeatedly carried raids into the Sinú Valley, in Cartagena Province. To respond to the threat, in the 1760s and 1770s colonial authorities built forts garrisoned by regulars from Panama and local pardo militiamen and formed militia units in Lorica. But the Kuna resumed their attacks and killed several Spanish boatmen and travelers on the Atrato River, which forced Spain to temporarily close the river to ships.[35]

Starting in 1776 with the appointment of the uncompromising reformer José de Gálvez as minister of the Indies, throughout its American dominions the Crown increasingly relied on the army to pacify and colonize the still sovereign indigenous nations. In New Granada, this new frontier policy targeted the Darién and, to a lesser extent, the Guajira Peninsula. It envisioned the launching of military expeditions and the reduction of indigenous communities into pueblos de indios under the authority of Indian caciques controlled by Spain. But attempts to pacify Caribbean New Granada's western frontier failed. Although an increasing number of Kuna caciques accepted the royal titles of salaried captainships, they still openly rejected vassalage to the king of Spain and traded with the British.[36] Moreover, in 1782 the Kuna killed 140 shipwrecked men of the Crown's regiment, which prompted the king's order to colonize the area of the Darién straddling the two oceans. As a result, Archbishop-Viceroy Antonio Caballero y Góngora sent the regular army and the militias of Cartagena and Panama to build and equip several fortified settlements destined to be inhabited by migrants from Cartagena Province. He also ordered Palacios de la Vega to conquer the Darién Indians with the help of pacified Indians and one hundred troops. After learning that the Kuna had murdered a Spanish officer, the men rebelled and attempted to poison the officer-friar, abruptly ending his mission.[37]

Although in 1787 several Kuna chiefs officially surrendered and agreed to allow colonial settlements in their territory, the viceroy's endeavor rapidly proved to be a costly disaster.[38] Most forts were directly exposed to indigenous attacks and were abandoned. In the words of a Spanish engineer, people could not live in the settlements "due to the complete lack of safety for their persons and plantations, until the extermination of the Indian enemies is verified."[39] The fort of Caimán was the only one built in an area relatively free of Indians, but there, too, settlers failed to arrive in significant numbers, while many soldiers died of disease and malnutrition. According to the diary of expedition commander Luis Arguedas, those who survived and stayed in the tropical jungle lived a "seminude" life of inaction and dissoluteness very unlike the model of "civilization" they were supposed to demonstrate for the Kuna.[40] The operation drained Cartagena's resources of soldiers, militiamen, sailors, and river rowers as well as its food supply, at the expense of Caribbean New Granada's agriculture and navigation. In the 1790s Viceroys Francisco Gil y Lemos and Josef de Ezpeleta ordered the desertion and destruction of the settlements, leaving the entire region between the south of the Sinú River and Portobelo in Panama (including the Atrato River, the primary means of access to the Chocó gold mines) without a Spanish military presence.[41] Although by then their numbers in the Darién had been cut in half to about five thousand as a result of the previous decades of war and epidemics, the Kuna continued to trade with Jamaica and to attack haciendas in Panama and east of the Atrato; in 1803 Viceroy Mendinueta declared their "subjugation . . . an almost desperate matter."[42]

After 1776 the Emberá also resisted aggressively Spain's attempts at conquest. They regularly attacked the few settlements in the Gulf of Urabá and the Sinú Valley to steal their crops and burned Montería in 1782. They hampered the fluvial trade in the region by attacking canoes and peoples. In 1809, for example, they robbed and killed several traders who were transporting products from the Chocó to the coast. Although Cartagena merchants estimated the number of Emberá at less than three thousand in 1810, they believed that the only way to pacify them was through the foundation and relocation of new settlements that would be forcibly populated by the "idles and vagrants" from the province's principal cities, a project that disintegrated with the beginning of the independence process.[43]

The Wayúu in the Guajira Peninsula continued, unsubdued, their contraband trade with foreigners, but they now refrained from attacking New Granada's Spaniards and creoles. Their goodwill was not caused by new military interventions, but "because of the obsequiousness that the governors use with them as a result of H. M.'s orders to maintain good harmony."[44] A governor of Riohacha had first attempted such a policy in 1776 by allegedly diverting the royal budget destined for a military campaign against the Wayúu to "give the Indians corn, liquor, linen clothes, meat, and other things so that they do not rebel."[45] More to the point, the Wayúu's apparent submission resulted principally from their adaptive sense of business. Industrious cultivators, ranchers, salt collectors, and traders, they practically held the city of Riohacha at their mercy. According to military explorer Joaquín Francisco Fidalgo, "extremely insolent and unruly, entering the City and even the houses carrying arms," they sold meat, poultry, fruits, vegetables, salt, and occasionally pearls, and they bought liquor and tobacco. "Whenever they withdrew for some disagreement, [Riohacha's dwellers] suffered shortages and in the interim had to stock up in Valledupar."[46]

In short, Indians on the periphery of Caribbean New Granada used a variety of strategies to resist Spanish colonization and Christianization, ranging from warfare to alliance with Spain's imperial enemies, flight deeper into the forests, treaty making, and selective accommodation. Much of their success depended on their geographical location rather than internal cohesion or combativeness. By the 1800s the population of the Chimila and the Motilón had dropped to less than one thousand, scattered in villages and small towns as they could not withstand the advance of the hacienda and the rapidly expanding new settlements of free people of color in a frontier area important to legal trade and smuggling. The Zenú endured a similar process as a result of increased cattle ranching near the Sinú and San Jorge Rivers.[47] In contrast, Spain's frontier policy failed in more remote areas. The Kuna and Emberá in the western tropical forests, the Wayúu in the arid Guajira Peninsula, and the Kogi and Arhuaco on the steep slopes of the Sierra Nevada of Santa Marta resisted well, and after 1790 the Crown ceased to send military expeditions against them.[48]

SPAIN'S CAMPAIGNS AGAINST ROCHELAS AND PALENQUES

Concurrently with the attempts to conquer the Indians on the frontier, Spain launched four military campaigns against Caribbean New Granada's rochelas and palenques (see Map 3) that also affected many established villages. The first campaign, entrusted to José Fernando de Mier y Guerra, simultaneously aimed at the Chimila and focused on the east bank of the Magdalena River to secure the main route between the coast and the interior of New Granada. It lasted from 1744 to 1765, during which time Mier founded twenty-two settlements with about eight thousand inhabitants. His troops compelled arrochelados to abandon their huts and lands and live in the new villages. Encouraged by generous grants in land, many whites from Mompox and Santa Marta settled along the Magdalena. The most extensive tracts went to Mier himself and other nobles who significantly increased their holdings in the region.[49]

A second campaign, led by the commissioned judge Francisco Pérez de Vargas in 1745, attempted to bring some colonial order to the triangle region of Tierradentro, between Cartagena, Barranquilla, and Barranca, on the Magdalena River, by reestablishing residential separation between Indians and non-Indians. Pérez allowed select pueblos de indios and villages of free residents to remain as viable units, whereas he destroyed others and founded new ones. In the process he forcibly resettled in villages and towns the free population that unlawfully resided in Indian pueblos, cultivating their *resguardos* (Indian communal lands) and escaping taxation. He redirected people living in hamlets out of the reach of the state and the church to established villages. He reshuffled part of the indigenous population and broke up several communities; he also reduced the aggregated area of resguardos. Although Pérez succeeded in reordering the territory of Tierradentro, his actions prompted the formation of new rochelas in the hinterland.[50]

The third and most extensive campaign was headed by Antonio de la Torre y Miranda, from 1774 to 1778, and focused on the valleys of Sinú and San Jorge as well as on the plains of Tolú. In total, La Torre claimed to have founded or relocated forty-three villages and towns with a total of 43,133 inhabitants (7,383 families), most of them arrochelados of all racial mixes and Indians as well as blacks from illegal palenques near Cartagena, whom he allegedly transformed into industrious and Christian citizens.[51] Unlike Mier, who accumulated lands and access to labor during his campaign, the Spanish official only received a monthly salary of 32 pesos (silver coins), raised to 47 pesos in 1776, and contracted a debt of 6,000 pesos during his expeditions, which he implored the king to pay back in light of his accomplishments.[52]

La Torre's campaign stimulated the development of five regions. The most important was the former *encomiendas* (royal grants of tribute-paying Indian workers) in the Sinú Valley, where he resettled indigenous, black, and racially mixed arrochelados in new villages, among them today's city of Montería. There, he boasted, people now annually produced three crops of fruits, cereals, and vegetables on the plots of land they had received. They also grew cotton to make hammocks and clothes to cover their nakedness. They raised pigs and poultry. As a result of their success, La Torre proudly concluded, the Sinú River now formed a safe waterway for slaves to be transported to the Chocó and for gold to be exported to Spain. Moreover, the area produced enough foodstuffs to supply the Chocó mines. The second region La Torre developed consisted of the rich plains south of Tolú, which formerly belonged to the Zenú Indians and had become an area of cattle ranching partially based on slavery. Among the villages he founded there was the present city of Sincelejo. A third area was the San Jorge

Valley and the lowlands where the San Jorge and the Cauca Rivers meet to flow into the Magdalena. Inhabited by the descendants of indigenous communities and of the thousands of African slaves employed in the placer mines during the seventeenth-century gold boom, the region produced food and illegal liquor for those still working in the mines of the Nechí River and northern Antioquia. There, La Torre founded or relocated several villages to curtail smuggling and to increase the safety of transportation and communications. The fourth region in which he was active was the Canal del Dique and the countryside around Cartagena, where he relocated the scattered black population into several villages so they could produce most of the vegetables, fruits, cassava bread, and fish for the provincial capital. La Torre also established some villages along the route between Cartagena and the Magdalena River to make it safer and more hospitable to travelers. He founded the village of Ternera at the gates of Cartagena, where traders could stay overnight and enter the city at dawn to sell their goods on the market. The fifth and last area colonized by La Torre was the Mountain of María, a stronghold of descendants of runaway slaves, which he claimed to have transformed into the main passage for cattle from the ranches south of Tolú to Cartagena.[53]

Although in his words La Torre went to the Mountain of María with only "twenty-four of these Ethiopians" and his personal servant, "a fourteen- or fifteen-year-old little mulatto," without encountering problems other than those posed by dense vegetation, in most other areas he had the support of troops from Cartagena's Regiment of the Fijo (regular army). When arrochelados and palenqueros refused to move to the new villages, soldiers burned their huts and crops. Once in the new villages, if women resisted the labor discipline imposed on them, such as in Ternera, or if men continued to spend the night fishing in the company of women "in the greatest debauchery," such as in the mangrove swamps near Cartagena, La Torre did not hesitate to use force to make them change their ways.[54]

The fourth and last campaign to establish order in the hinterland was undertaken in 1787–88 by Joseph Palacios de la Vega after the suspension of his mission to subjugate the Kuna in the Darién. This time, Archbishop-Viceroy Caballero y Góngora ordered the Franciscan friar and veteran army officer to destroy rochelas and palenques in the southeast of Cartagena Province, an area notorious for its illegal gold panning, liquor production, and smuggling, and to resettle the Indian, black, and racially mixed inhabitants in Christian villages. Brandishing the sword more often than the cross, Palacios de la Vega is credited with the forced settlement of about two thousand people before he was recalled by Bogotá. He began by resettling the village of San Cipriano, close to the source of the San Jorge River. There he separated the Indians from the whites and the castas (of mixed African ancestry). He forcibly resettled in indigenous pueblos Indians who had arrived two decades earlier from the Chocó, fleeing internal indigenous struggle, together with some Chimila who had escaped from the military campaigns against them, without consideration for their antagonism. Then, backed by one hundred soldiers, Palacios de la Vega launched several expeditions of reconquest from San Cipriano, notably against the black palenque of Carate and the rochelas situated in the region of the San Jorge, Cauca, and Nechí Rivers, south of San Benito Abad.[55]

The Franciscan used a scorched earth policy to force arrochelados and palenqueros off their lands and into the new villages. His strategy was one of surprise to minimize resistance. Once a rochela or palenque was surrounded by his soldiers, he separated the men from the women and children, whom he took to their new place of residence. Under the threat of being sent to work in the fortifications of Cartagena or to build the new colonies in the Darién, the men were forced to burn down huts and crops, to take their tools and belongings, and to build provisional shelters for their families in the new villages. There Palacios de la Vega distributed a piece of land and designed a dwelling for each family according to its size. The officer-friar also subjected arrochelados and palenqueros to a process of spectacular mass evangelization that included processions, impassioned sermons, and public confessions to instill fear and obedience. Within a few weeks, he claimed in his diary, they were "living to the sound of the church bell."[56] However, as Palacios de la Vega's crusade increasingly encroached on the power of local magnates and priests, these potent men were eventually able to stop him. In early 1788 the commandant of Majagual refused him the forty troops he requested to destroy the palenque of Guamal, and on 6 February the archbishop-viceroy ordered him to return to Cartagena without finishing his mission of reconquest.[57]

As further discussed in Chapter 2, the principal outcome of the four campaigns of forced resettlement conducted between 1744 and 1788 was the expansion of landholdings belonging to a few hacendados (large landowners), as the untitled lands and resguardos left vacant in the process became royal property available to the highest bidder or the most deserving subject. At the same time, thousands of small cultivators, arrochelados, palenqueros, and Indians lost the lands they tilled. Although male heads of household received a plot of land, many people were forced to become dependent on haciendas or to go elsewhere.[58] Not surprisingly, with less land available for independent cultivation, tensions among the rural population, especially between free people of color and Indians, increased, which further hindered them from uniting to collectively resist.[59] Palacios de la Vega was particularly adept at building on old animosities between Indians and free blacks to maintain order. In the area of San Cipriano, he created two competing networks of spies that enabled him to control both groups; he alternated between liquor and the whip to make people talk and denounce each other; and he astutely used Indians' and blacks' supernatural beliefs to produce terror and submission. For example, after giving him "a good drink of alcohol," he convinced "my Indian Vette" to name the indigenous murderers of two free blacks who had raped and killed an Indian woman by pretending that his clock would tell him the truth: "I put the clock into my ear . . . I placed it into his ear as well. The Indian got drowsy listening to the beat of the balance wheel, and seeing this I told him that it was talking to me: 'Well you know what it is telling me? *Vette knows, Vette knows.*' Then out of fear the Indian confessed that the father of the deceased, her two brothers and an uncle had killed the two blacks."[60] East of the Magdalena, some hacendados sent their slaves with cattle to intimidate recently settled Chimila Indians and destroy their plots in order to expand their own pasture lands, prompting violence between the two groups.[61] When free people of color in the San Jorge River saw their grazing lands invaded by large cattle ranchers, they too did not hesitate to reduce their losses by encroaching on indigenous lands.[62]

The campaigns of resettlement also produced intense demographic movement and mixing that further blurred racial and ethnic boundaries. Along the Magdalena River, Indians from distinct communities were forcibly resettled together in single pueblos de indios. The extension of their communal lands rapidly diminished under the pressure of hacendados and free people of color. East of the river, some Capuchin priests, in charge of reducing the Chimila, were also accustomed to attracting arrochelado men and families to their pueblos in order to Christianize them, together with the Indians, as well as to use them as personal guards, Spanish teachers of the Chimila, and catchers of runaway Indians. This practice, although in violation of the legislation that excluded non-Indians from residing in pueblos de indios, was supported by the royal *audiencia* (high court) of Santafé de Bogotá.[63] Some subjugated Indians from the Darién and the Chocó were deported to pueblos in the newly colonized regions of the Sinú and San Jorge Rivers. Arrochelados and palenqueros were mixed up to form new villages.

Hacendados, officials, and other men in positions of power contributed to the mestizaje by engaging in sexual intercourse with relocated women.[64]

Indeed, gender weighed heavily in the process of conquest of the Caribbean New Granadan frontier. Most colonial reports portrayed men as most likely to reject colonization and viewed women and children as the primary targets of resettlement campaigns. Joseph Palacios de la Vega and Antonio de la Torre focused on these two groups not only because they were easier to capture than men, but also because they perceived women as the best recipients of their moralization and Christianization. If women and children could be resettled in colonial villages and instilled with the fear of God, they thought, the next generation would become obedient, virtuous, and industrious. Consequently, in the late eighteenth century the hinterland was still predominantly male, whereas many former arrochelado women settled in the new villages with male companions coming from more central regions.

PROTEST

Demographic reshuffling did not go uncontested. Indians and free residents used a variety of means to resist resettlement, from foot-dragging to filing protests, taking to the woods, and openly rebelling.[65] According to the Crown official appointed to defend them, most of the Indians relocated in San Cipriano fled and lived in the forest "stark naked" and ignoring the Catholic faith, because Palacios de la Vega "understood neither their language nor their spirit and apparently maltreated them."[66] After Palacios de la Vega left in 1788, taking with him the sacred ornaments of the little church built by the Indians, the Indians systematically refused to pay the indigenous tribute until a priest was assigned to them. As they told an official, "O great Captain, you say that the priest is coming to San Cipriano . . . deceiving Indian so that [he pays] tribute, and priest doesn't come. . . . Indian marries alone, Indian dies in woodland."[67] By 1792 only about twenty adult male Indians and their families still lived in the settlement, the others having fled. The vicar of Ayapel convinced authorities in Cartagena that these inhabitants were "so rebellious and fond of the freedom of thought . . . living without subordination or religion" that any attempt to reconquer them and to bring the runaways back from the woods would be a waste of money, and the Indians were left alone.[68]

The case of the palenque of San Basilio, close to Cartagena, also demonstrates that the conquerors' triumphant reports should be read critically.

San Basilio escaped La Torre's campaign of destruction and resettlement, but a few years later it became the joint target of Cartagena's new bishop, José Fernández Díaz de Lamadrid, a native of Quito with puritan views, and the principal hacendado of the area, Manuel Josef de Escobar. In 1778 the bishop visited San Basilio and was appalled by the mores of the all-black community. According to him, the palenqueros worked on festive days, they did not attend religious services and neglected their church, and they lived in concubinage and were prone to "drunkenness and other vices." In contrast to his predecessor in 1772, Díaz de Lamadrid claimed that the village was "the refuge of all libertine blacks, and those who run away from their masters." As many palenqueros blamed their lack of compliance with church requirements on their poverty and on the priest's tendency to overcharge them, the bishop lowered the priest's fees. During his visit he also collectively performed 11 marriage ceremonies and 495 confirmations without charge. He remained convinced, however, that at the core of the problem was the fact that a "captain, also black," governed the palenqueros; only a white officer with full powers could contain them, he stated.[69] The bishop's arguments had no effect on the government, which in 1779 granted the palenque the property titles of the "communal lands of San Basilio."[70]

Such a decision angered the hacendado Escobar, who in 1782 filed a complaint to Archbishop-Viceroy Caballero y Góngora against this "population or palenque of black fugitives in its origin." He accused them of "hurting and maltreating his servants and workers" in his haciendas of Torohermoso and El Pital, "with their excesses and disorder, their total lack of subordination to the authorities, [and] the continuing thefts they committed of products and crop lands," but he cautiously avoided to mention that his aggressive encroachment on palenqueros' lands had caused their hostility. He claimed that only the destruction of the palenque and the resettlement of its inhabitants in the newly founded villages of San Cayetano, in the plain east of San Basilio, or Caimán, in the Gulf of Darién, could pacify them.[71] Díaz de Lamadrid backed Escobar's request, and in 1788 military engineer Antonio Arévalo brought additional support, maintaining that the forced resettlement in Caimán of about 120 families from San Basilio would secure the survival of the new fort by bringing in much-needed inhabitants, because they were "men of work" and militiamen.[72] The archbishop-viceroy approved the suppression of San Basilio. Reportedly, the governor of Cartagena Province, Joaquín de Cañaverales, carried out the order in the early 1790s:

[Cañaverales] has done a great service to God and H. M. with the demolition of Palenque de San Basilio. It was a den of vices[,] shelter of criminals and deserters, it comprised more than 600 blacks, arrochelados, and it saw itself destroyed not by the violence of arms but by prudent, opportune and correct measures: their huts and cabins were burned without the slightest damage to their possessions [sic], they were scattered and subjected to live religiously and in society in several villages where they received land that they have cleared of trees and cultivated, for the common benefit and prosperity of this city [Cartagena] and its province.[73]

Whether San Basilio was completely destroyed and its inhabitants displaced remains an open question, as further evidence of its destruction is lacking. According to local historian Basilio Pérez, the palenque was strong during the wars for independence but did not participate because its inhabitants "were already free. [Simón] Bolívar did not enter the village and followed straight ahead."[74] At any rate, by the early 1830s San Basilio had reconstituted itself and counted 1,073 inhabitants.[75]

Although the continued existence of Palenque de San Basilio up to the present is exceptional, the vast hinterland within the frontier of Caribbean New Granada remained far from being conquered by the 1800s. José Fernando de Mier y Guerra was able to pacify the Chimila area east of the Magdalena but not permanently settle its Indians and arrochelados of color, many of whom in the late 1780s still lived "in the wilderness, beyond the sound of the parish bell and in the biggest Christian and political incivility."[76] Palacios de la Vega's aborted campaign left many rochelas and palenques south of Mompox intact. Several illegal settlements situated outside or on the fringes of the areas being colonized still existed. In addition, many people who had been forcibly resettled along the Magdalena, Sinú, and San Jorge Rivers and in Indian pueblos fled individually or in small groups to join or form rochelas farther in the backlands. There, the availability of unconquered lands together with the total absence of security forces made the prospect of becoming a free peasant, and, south of Mompox, of finding gold, all the more possible.[77] Reportedly, in 1790 "many persons and even whole families [continued to live] an entirely barbarian life from the political and Christian standpoint . . . because they recognize[d] neither judge nor priest." According to the bishop of Cartagena and the viceroy, they refused to abandon the hinterlands for the newly founded villages because they feared being punished for past and present crimes. As it was impossible to remove them without mounting a massive military operation, the two men concluded, the only way to secure their resettlement was to grant them amnesty, which the Council of the Indies agreed to do.[78] It is not known whether the royal pardon succeeded in convincing arrochelados to move to established villages.

Because flight offered the safest and most available form of resistance among Caribbean New Granada's free population of color, rebellions were few and isolated. They took place in response to forced resettlement and often were not autonomous movements, but were instigated or led by local magnates. For example, Palacios de la Vega claimed that near Nechí he faced alone three hundred armed men and "a troop, in my opinion, of over two hundred concubines [armed] with lances, machetes and sticks," intending to kill him. All of these rebels were Indian, zambo, mulatto, and black arrochelados who had been told that he was a criminal dressed up as a priest in order to rob them. Their leader was the *"mulato-indio"* Antonio López, acting under the orders of a magnate and a priest who ruled the area unchallenged. "But God omnipotent who protected me did not allow it," and the officer-friar managed to escape death, to arrest the women and children, to turn them in to the judge in Nechí, and to have all their huts destroyed. He was nevertheless unable to defeat the male rebels, who escaped, presumably to found new rochelas in the hinterland.[79] In the plains of Tolú, the destruction of rochelas deprived some powerful hacendados of access to their dwellers' services and products. One landlord did not hesitate to mobilize and arm dozens of lower-class men of color to attempt to chase former arrochelados out of their new settlement and to bring them back into his fief.[80] More often, however, rochelas and palenques owed their survival to their relative isolation and accommodation to the colonial establishments and the magnates' fiefdoms. Therefore, they generally kept to themselves and avoided conflicts and alliances with outsiders, except to protect their territory.[81] According to Viceroy Mendinueta in 1803, the remaining arrochelados were content "with freely vegetating."[82]

In contrast, Mendinueta was far from displaying the same composure regarding New Granada's frontier, where the Wayúu and the Kuna remained sovereign. Still in 1803, he feared that the alleged landing in the Guajira Peninsula of two hundred blacks and mulattoes from Guadeloupe, presumably deportees, would trigger a revolution along Haitian lines in the Caribbean region. A friendly indigenous community routinely rewarded for catching runaway slaves turned three of them in to the governor of Riohacha Province, who then faced a difficult dilemma: if he accepted more captives from the Indians, he told the viceroy, the Guadeloupean prisoners could spread ideas of freedom in the region; if he refused them, "these barbarous [Indians]" could kill them and resume hostilities against Spain.[83] Mendinueta recommended that the governor encourage the pacified Indians to bring as many black and mulatto captives as possible to Riohacha to obtain intelligence about their landing and conditions in the French Caribbean. They should then be rapidly returned to a French colony, despite New Granada's need for additional laborers. A more interventionist policy, such as the sending of troops to capture the Guadeloupeans still hiding in Wayúu territory, could break the fragile truce recently reached between Spain and the "Guajiro" (Wayúu) he argued. Indeed, he dreaded that the mere communication between "a class of people infected with the ideas of freedom, equality and the rest that have been so pernicious and have caused so much devastation and horror in the unfortunate French islands" and the numerous, hardened, and well-armed "Guajiro always ready to hurt and always enemies of the Spanish name" could produce "a terrible and cruel domestic war."[84] However, the viceroy's fear of an alliance between unconquered Indians and other subaltern classes, such as slaves, never materialized.

By the early 1800s the Motilón and the Chimila Indians had lost most of their lands to hacendados and free people of color, but the Kogi and the Arhuaco, in the Sierra Nevada, held firm. Moreover, on the frontier, the Wayúu and the Kuna still represented a threat to the Spanish authorities. Organized and well armed, they continued to stubbornly oppose Spanish colonialism. Yet their struggle was a territorial one, situated on the periphery. And despite the fact that the Wayúu and the Kuna nations shared economic and political interests, the enormous geographical and cultural distance between them and their lack of communication prevented them from waging a joint war against Spain. Simultaneously, thousands of arrochelados and palenqueros had been forcibly resettled in villages. But thousands more had rejected resettlement by retreating farther into the backlands and indigenous territory or by placing themselves in the vassalage of powerful hacendados. Moreover, many rochelas survived because the campaigns of destruction did not reach them. As a result, though pushed farther back, Caribbean New Granada's frontier and backlands continued to constitute a vast zone that the colonial state, the security forces, and the church were unable to control. Power, land, and resources there were still contested and negotiated, often with violence. As before, the hinterland was an area of refuge and of fluid socioracial identities when compared with the more established areas. But because race, ethnicity, religious beliefs, language, economic interests, and long distances separated the inhabitants of the periphery, they were unable to jointly challenge the increasing but competing pressure of colonial authorities, landlords, and new settlers.

In Caribbean New Granada, then, the frontier remained unconquered. The problem was not just one of "closing the frontier" but, more importantly, one of "opening a frontier" with few opportunities for wealth on the fringes of a viceroyalty already marginal in the Spanish imperial project.[85] Moreover, the frontier, to be opened, needed first to be emptied of its "barbarian," dark inhabitants, a costly and risky enterprise for a weak colonial state that did not face, as Argentina for example did, the pressure of a growing white population eager to settle there. With no major legal export resources discovered, the Caribbean frontier continued to escape state and elite control, allowing for the survival of several indigenous and marginal groups. Yet the very marginality and isolation of the frontier also explains its centrality for illegal activities, notably the contraband of New Granadan gold and cattle, and British goods.

The colonization of Caribbean New Granada could not fully succeed also because of a scant church and state presence in the rural areas generally. The Christianization of the newly settled population seldom went beyond the cosmetic evangelization that accompanied the campaigns against the rochelas, and few established villages had sufficient state and ecclesiastical personnel to guarantee their compliance with colonial norms. By the late eighteenth century the hinterland had physically narrowed, but, in fact, by displacing its original dwellers to new villages, the Spanish authorities allowed the backlands' socioracial, cultural, and family "disorder" to influence more central areas.

2 COUNTRYSIDE

In 1789 the viceroy's secretary, Francisco Silvestre, contrasted the area of Bogotá and its growing population of whites and mestizos with the region of Cartagena and Santa Marta, where whites had not increased while "blacks, mulattoes, etc." had grown "because, with haciendas closer to the sea and tilled by slaves, a greater portion of these [slaves] have remained there . . . and, mixed with Indians and with half-castes, have let their black and other derived color stand out or whiten."[1] Ten years later Viceroy Pedro Mendinueta warned that, in light of the Haitian Revolution, the "corruption" of the coastal population of African descent "would be of irreparable consequences" for Spain's colony, particularly if they united with the sovereign Indians on the frontier.[2] However, his fear did not materialize. Despite the fact that free people of color largely outnumbered all other socioracial groups and controlled most of the territory of Caribbean New Granada, they never united forces against the region's small white elite—either as a separate group or in association with Indians and slaves.

Although less autonomous than the Indian nations and the rochelas in the backlands, Caribbean New Granada's villages and countryside were far from being controlled by the colonial state and the Catholic Church. For lack of officials and priests, Spain's domination barely extended beyond the region's principal cities. As a result, most of Caribbean New Granada resembled a patchwork of scattered Indian pueblos and black, mulatto, and zambo villages surrounded by hacendados' fiefdoms on a background of unconquered lands. According to the only general census of the viceroyalty, carried out by Spain in 1777–80, most of the 170,404 inhabitants then officially counted in the three Caribbean provinces were still not fully integrated into the colony, despite the extensive campaigns of forced resettlement ordered during the Bourbon era.[3] Only 20.6 percent of them lived in cities, characterized by a considerable presence of royal officials and church personnel, a *cabildo* (town council), and significant militia or standing military units. Among these cities, Cartagena, Santa Marta, and Riohacha were the administrative centers of colonial power around which the Caribbean provinces were organized. Mompox and Valledupar were important centers for the legal and contraband trade but depended on Cartagena or Santa Marta, respectively, for their administration (see Chapter 3).[4] Elsewhere, most Caribbean New Granadans clustered in villages and small towns along the main rivers and some portions of the coast.

PEOPLES

On the basis of the 1777–80 census, Viceroy Mendinueta's warning of a possible revolution of the nonwhites in the region was not unfounded. With a total of 87,788 out of 135,353, the *libres de todos los colores* (free of all colors) represented two-thirds of the Caribbean New Granadans living outside of the main cities.[5] In the words of one governor of Santa Marta Province, "the mulattoes, zambos, and free blacks, the mestizos, and other mixes [castas] of the country's common people . . . make up almost all of its population."[6] Free people of color represented between 89 and 100 percent of the inhabitants in most villages and small towns located along the Magdalena River (including Barranquilla, then a parish of 2,934), in the plain northeast of Cartagena, along the San Jorge and Cauca Rivers, and near Riohacha. Their gender ratio was balanced, except in areas of recent colonization, such as Lorica, Corozal, and their environs; the banks of the San Jorge and Cauca Rivers; and the coast of the Guajira Peninsula, where men and boys outnumbered women and girls.[7]

Only the census of Riohacha Province distinguished between mulattoes, zambos, negros, and mestizos among the free people of color. The picture it provided was one of a population in which partial and full African ancestry predominated, whereas less than 1 percent of the inhabitants were reported of mixed European and Indian descent, or mestizos.[8] As the censuses of Cartagena and Santa Marta Provinces did not classify the free population of color in distinct racial categories, any attempt to differentiate them has to rely on qualitative sources, such as traveler and official narratives and the historical background of each area.[9] Clearly, the *libres de color* in the entire region between Barranquilla, Cartagena, and Mompox as well as on the riversides of the Magdalena and Cauca Rivers were almost exclusively of mixed and full African ancestry.[10] According to French traveler Gaspard Mollien, in the early 1820s most inhabitants were mulattoes and blacks; "Thus we find in the area that separates Barranca from the sea a territory

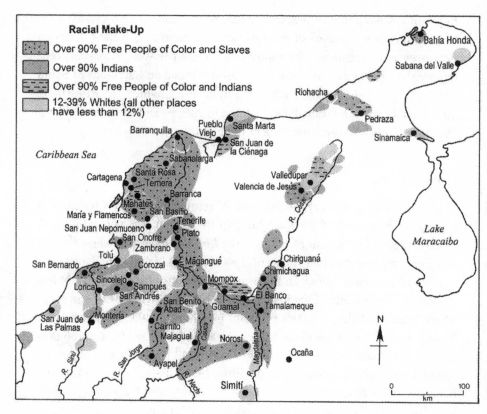

MAP 4. Racial makeup of Caribbean New Granada according to the census of 1777–1780

cultivated and inhabited like the countries I had traveled up and down in Africa."[11] Such an African-derived predominance is not surprising given the fact that between the sixteenth and eighteenth centuries, approximately 120,000 African slaves had been introduced into New Granada through the port of Cartagena, many to be sold as rowers on the Magdalena River or laborers in nearby haciendas.[12] Similarly, the important presence of free people of full or partial African ancestry in the area of the lower Cauca and San Jorge Rivers—people who in the 1950s still referred to themselves as *los libres* to distinguish them from the Emberá—resulted from the existence, since the seventeenth century, of cattle haciendas and from the proximity of the northern Antioquia gold mines, worked by slave labor.[13] The inhabitants of the Sinú River delta and the coastal towns of Tolú and San Bernardo also were mainly of African descent. People in the villages and small towns around Valledupar and Riohacha were mostly zambos, descendants of the

MAP 5. Political Caribbean New Granada

1	Baranoa
2	Usiacurí
3	Malambo
4	Remolino
5	Turbaco
6	María la Baja
7	San Juan del César
8	Chinú

Caribbean Sea

Guajira Peninsula

Riohacha

RIOHACHA PROV.

Santa Marta

Pueblo Viejo

Barranquilla

San Juan de la Ciénaga

Sierra Nevada

VENEZUELA

Sabanalarga

Valledupar

Valencia de Jesús

Cartagena

Ternera

Mahates

Barranca

SANTA MARTA PROV.

R. César

Lake Maracaibo

San Basilio

San Juan Nepomuceno

Tenerife

Plato

Zambrano

San Onofre

Tolú

Magangué

Chimichagua

Chiriguaná

San Bernardo

Sincelejo

Mompox

Guamal

Lorica

San Andrés

Corozal

Sampués

El Banco

Tamalameque

San Benito Abad

San Juan de Las Palmas

Montería

Caimito

Majagual

Norosí

Ocaña

CARTAGENA PROV.

R. San Jorge

Ayapel

Simití

R. Sinú

R. Nechí

R. Cauca

R. Magdalena

CHOCÓ

ANTIOQUIA

N

Provincial Borders

0   100
km

local indigenous population and the many runaway slaves who had formed palenques in the area before its colonization by the Spaniards in the first half of the eighteenth century.[14] Few areas had a substantial mestizo population: Corozal and Sincelejo, where Spain had given grants of land to poor Spanish immigrants during the same period, and a handful of new settlements in the Guajira Peninsula and near Valledupar. In all of these areas white men, bringing few slaves with them, had settled in the proximity of pueblos de indios and had taken indigenous women as common-law wives.[15]

Practically absent from the main cities, the "civilized" Indians in the three provinces numbered about 30,000 according to the census of 1777–80, or a significant 22.1 percent of the rural population.[16] Twenty-five recorded pueblos de indios had over 95 percent of the inhabitants classified as indigenous. These pueblos were located on the margins of the colonized area between Lorica and Corozal, along the Magdalena River south of Tenerife, and around Santa Marta and Valledupar. Although some pueblos de indios had less than 300 inhabitants, others had over 1,000, and San Andrés (east of Lorica) comprised 3,397 Indians, 18 whites, and 10 free persons of color. Seven indigenous pueblos near Barranquilla still held out against the encroachment of free people of African descent, but in four of them Indians were less than 90 percent of the population, which made their status as pueblos de indios tenuous. Similarly, Indians were slowly losing ground to free people of color in San Juan de la Ciénaga on the trail linking Santa Marta to the Magdalena River, in some pueblos near Mompox and Ocaña, and on the coast next to Riohacha. Indians' gender ratio was 107.9 females per 100 males, due to the phenomenon of flight to the frontier and the hinterlands—a means of resistance mainly employed by men.[17]

As indicated by the census of 1777–80, there were no more than 7,708 slaves outside of the six principal cities in the late 1770s, making up 5.7 percent of the nonurban inhabitants of the three provinces.[18] Most of these black, mulatto, zambo, and *cuarterón* (quadroon) slaves lived in the parishes surrounding Cartagena in the east and the south as well as in Santero and San Onofre, on the coast near Tolú, in Caimito, in the vicinity of San Benito Abad, and in Norosí, Ayapel, and Simití, south of Mompox. In each of these locations between 130 and 600 slaves represented between 12 and 73 percent of the local population. In Santa Marta Province, the small towns of Tamalameque, east of Mompox, and Valencia de Jesús, near Valledupar, as well as four villages on the eastern foothills of the Sierra Nevada, comprised over 100 slaves each.[19] These areas were all engaged in sugar and cocoa cultivation, cattle ranching, and gold panning for which slave labor was essential. Indeed, such parishes as María y Flamencos, Santero, and San Onofre shared many characteristics of the sugar plantation societies of the Caribbean islands. In addition, small numbers of slaves were scattered in most villages and in some pueblos de indios, probably in the service of the few white residents. Nevertheless, the presence of slaves in the pueblos de indios near Barranquilla, which counted no whites but some free persons of color, indicates that some libres de color, and perhaps some Indians, owned slaves. A majority of these rural slaves were male (90.1 females per 100 males) and worked in agriculture, ranching, and mining.[20]

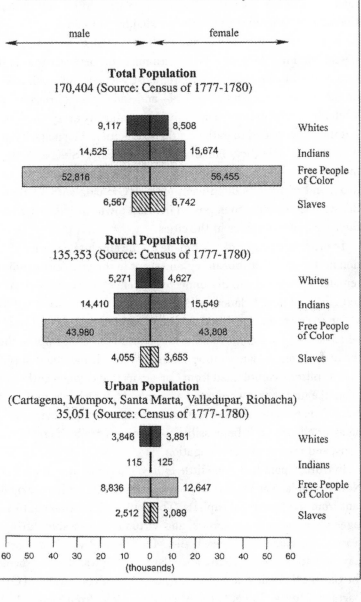

CARIBBEAN NEW GRANADA
POPULATION BY RACE AND GENDER, 1777-1780

male   female

Total Population
170,404 (Source: Census of 1777-1780)

9,117	8,508	Whites
14,525	15,674	Indians
52,816	56,455	Free People of Color
6,567	6,742	Slaves

Rural Population
135,353 (Source: Census of 1777-1780)

5,271	4,627	Whites
14,410	15,549	Indians
43,980	43,808	Free People of Color
4,055	3,653	Slaves

Urban Population
(Cartagena, Mompox, Santa Marta, Valledupar, Riohacha)
35,051 (Source: Census of 1777-1780)

3,846	3,881	Whites
115	125	Indians
8,836	12,647	Free People of Color
2,512	3,089	Slaves

60 50 40 30 20 10 0 10 20 30 40 50 60
(thousands)

Slightly more numerous than slaves, whites residing in the villages and small towns of Caribbean New Granada totaled 9,898, or 7.3 percent of the nonurban population according to the census of 1777–80. This figure included some who were unable to prove *limpieza de sangre* (purity of blood, especially the absence of African, Moorish, Jewish, or heretical ancestry) and *blancos de la tierra*, or local whites, whom Viceroy Mendinueta defined as "mulattoes" whose nonagricultural occupation "lightens the color."[21] Only in the villages founded by Antonio de la Torre y Miranda between Lorica and Corozal, in San Juan de Las Palmas, and in a few small towns around Valledupar did whites make up between 10.0 and 33.0 percent of the inhabitants. Elsewhere, most villages and small towns counted no more than a handful of whites—and some, just a priest or not a single white. In fact, whites were not only in the minority everywhere in the region but they also tended to gather in the main cities. The majority of nonurban whites were male (87.7 females per 100 males).[22] Such a predominance of males in the white population was due to the fact that Spanish officials, soldiers, and merchants often went to New Granada without their wives. At the same time, white men posted in small towns or villages tended to leave their wives and families in the cities.

In brief, free people of color made up the absolute majority of the population in the entire Caribbean region except in the pueblos de indios. Yet they remained scattered and disconnected. In effect, the campaigns of forced resettlement of arrochelados, palenqueros, and Indians were not followed by a plan to create an integrated system of communication and transportation, which would have enabled state and church to better impose their rule on the population. As late as 1807, prominent creole merchant José Ignacio de Pombo bitterly complained from Cartagena that colonial authorities had not taken the first step toward good government, which was to draw "a general map of the Kingdom and of the particularities of the Provinces." Only then, he asserted, would it be possible to open new trails, increase communications, and improve river navigation.[23]

In truth, Spain had done little to develop communications in Caribbean New Granada. The main rivers were extremely difficult to navigate and distant from the provincial capitals. The trails linking colonial towns and villages were narrow, dangerous, and virtually impassable during the rainy season. For example, to reach the Magdalena River from Cartagena, the traveler had to take a trail to Sabanalarga or, if it was not obstructed by sand, the Canal del Dique that linked Barbacoas, south of the Bay of Cartagena, to Barranca Nueva. To get to the Magdalena Delta from Santa Marta one had to follow a trail to Pueblo Viejo, on the Ciénaga Grande, and then to take canoes operated by Indians through fairways and swamps. Santa Marta had no trail leading directly to the interior of the viceroyalty. It had two dangerous tracks to Riohacha—one along the seashore close to some deep water and frightful chasms, the other through the dense forest of the Sierra Nevada, which, according to Spanish brigadier Joaquín Francisco Fidalgo, exposed travelers to "the risks offered by the tigers, leopards, snakes, and still the ferocious Chimila Indians."[24] The safest route between Santa Marta and Riohacha was the long detour by Valledupar.

In general, then, river and land communications were unreliable, hazardous, and extremely slow. Whereas the voyage between Spain and Cartagena lasted about one month, the journey between Cartagena and Bogotá could take one to two months, sometimes longer. A much-dreaded portion of the trip was to row up the Magdalena River in canoes or, more commonly, in champanes—small boats that bogas (rowers) painfully propelled with the help of long poles and ropes.[25] Representative of the difficulty of traveling in the Caribbean region were the ordeals suffered by the bishop of Cartagena, José Fernández Díaz de Lamadrid, during a visit to the diocese in the late 1770s. He faced all kinds of dangers on rough trails, tumultuous rivers, and the unpredictable sea. He had to endure suffocating heat and voracious insects; on several occasions he lacked food and drinking water. Although he survived, both his chaplain and his secretary died of disease and exhaustion during the journey.[26] Even in the most densely populated areas, villages were several hours' walk from each other during the dry season and became completely isolated during the rainy season. Often, only canoes and champanes connected the villages on the banks of the Magdalena River. Farther in the interior, communications between sites generally took days of trekking on narrow trails and navigating canoes.[27]

HACENDADOS

Instead of leading to improved communications, the campaigns of resettlement prompted the creation and consolidation of large landholdings in the hands of a few white proprietors, often the sons of Spanish immigrants residing in Cartagena and Mompox.[28] Facilitated by the scarcity and dispersion of the rural population, this process led to the formation of landholdings that were no less than fiefdoms with little outside interference. Hacendados were able to expand their properties through diverse ways. One was to buy the land that had become the property of the king after the suppression and relocation of several Indian pueblos. The 1767 expulsion of the Jesuits further increased the Crown's lands for sale.[29] Another form of land acquisition was the *composición*, or declaration of ownership and purchase of the property titles to untitled lands cultivated by peasants and arrochelados, who then became landless and a cheap source of labor.[30] Ranchers also increased their holdings by having their cattle invade and destroy the crops of Indians and free people of color in newly established villages, forcing them to take refuge farther in the hinterland or to seek wages.[31] According to Hermes Tovar, the process of land concentration was such that in Cartagena Province, 77 percent of all the land granted by the Crown between 1699 and 1800 benefited fourteen individuals. In Santa Marta Province, 78 percent of the land was awarded to seventeen proprietors. Among them, three families—the Miers, the Madriagas, and that of Micaela de Lanz—managed to accumulate 170,000 hectares between the 1730s and 1770s. Some haciendas, such as those belonging to Andrés de Madriaga or to the marquis of Santa Coa, had their value multiplied by three or four within the same period. Half of the 80,950 head of cattle reported in 1766 in the plains of Tolú and Tierradentro grazed on twelve ranches with 1,000 to 8,000 head each. Not only were the holdings of the magnates managed with no outside interference, they were also parts of larger enterprises involved in legal trade, smuggling, and mining.[32]

The new holdings mainly consisted of cattle ranches in the Tolú plains and near Valledupar as well as along the Magdalena, Sinú, San Jorge, and César Rivers; sugarcane haciendas around Cartagena, Mompox, Ciénaga, and Valledupar; and cacao haciendas south of Mompox.[33] Most of the sugar, cocoa, and cattle was for regional and interregional markets; beef, in particular, was a mainstay of the diet of all classes, due to the scarcity and high price of imported wheat and locally produced corn.[34] Some livestock and hides were smuggled to the British Caribbean. Large estates used a labor force comprised mostly of slaves, who often represented an important portion of estates' total value. In the vicinity of Cartagena, San Onofre, and Valledupar, several cane haciendas had up to one hundred slaves each, organized in gangs under the supervision of an overseer, often himself a highly priced slave.[35] Haciendas and ranches also employed sharecroppers (*arrendatarios* and *terrajeros*), tenants (*colonos*), peons (*matriculados* and *concertados*), and Indians whose labor became increasingly accessible after the campaigns of resettlement.[36] The whip, shackles, stocks, cells, and chains secured the obedience of slaves and free workers.[37] Because they resided in the main cities, the large hacendados were able to build extensive patronage networks beyond the limits of their landholdings, which linked them to the provincial governors in Cartagena and Santa Marta and the viceroy in Bogotá. At the local level, they controlled the men in most royal and ecclesiastical positions. They weighed heavily on the district's justice. The magnates also dominated the population residing in small towns and villages in their areas through various patron-client relations, including labor and land contracts, recruitment in the militia, and access to natural resources.

Hacendados' power could extend to the remaining rochelas and palenques on the fringes of their fiefdoms.[38] As related by friar and army officer Joseph Palacios de la Vega, Don Blas de Otero, a wealthy *patrón* (boss) and his associate, a parish priest who performed the holy sacraments only after payment in goods and specie, autocratically ruled the arrochelados in the area near Nechí. The collusion between the two men was such that when a rochela leader under Otero's patronage committed suicide without having gone to confession, the priest and a local judge claimed that he had received extreme unction in order to bury him in the church cemetery according to the wish of Otero, "who is the God in that place."[39] Apparently, among the few priests serving in the hinterlands, some took advantage of their isolation to live with concubines and to abuse the local population. Others would not administer the sacraments without receiving money, gold, land, or cattle from parishioners, and they became powerful hacendados. According to Palacios de la Vega, a parish priest near Majagual owned one thousand head of cattle but failed to properly attend to his parishioners.[40]

Often hacendados' domination was enhanced by the fact that several of them could buy top royal functions and titles of nobility, which enabled them to put men under their patronage in a multitude of posts. For example, hacendado Manuel Josef de Escobar purchased the positions of *regidor* (town councilor) and *real alférez* (royal ensign) in Cartagena. In these capacities, he managed to expand his sugar plantations at the expense of the palenqueros of San Basilio; by 1786 he petitioned Caballero y Góngora for a special authorization to import three hundred slaves to work on them.[41] From Mompox, hacendado Gonzalo Josef de Hoyos reportedly had "made himself lord of vassals, without having spent any effort or money," after he inherited from his uncle José Fernando Mier y Guerra not only part of the fortune the uncle had accumulated during his campaign of resettlement in the lower Magdalena but also his title of *poblador* (founder) and his absolute jurisdiction in fourteen villages that he founded.[42] Hoyos further increased his wealth in lands, slaves, and cattle through a marriage that related him to the marquises of Valde-Hoyos and Santa Coa. Already colonel of the militia and *alcalde ordinario* (magistrate of the first instance) in Mompox, he purchased the title of marquis of Torre-Hoyos in 1788. As alcalde, he increasingly encroached on the lands of free settlers and Indians. For instance, he imposed on the village of Guamal, on the Magdalena River, don Vicente Olivares as *cabo de justicia* (local magistrate). Olivares illegally lived in a pueblo de indios, destroyed the inhabitants' crops with his cattle, and terrorized the Indians and former arrochelados of the nearby new hamlet of Venero.[43] In Tacamocho, near Magangué, Hoyos decided to forcibly resettle the villagers in the pueblo de indios of Yatí, allegedly to protect them from the Magdalena River floods. When six *vecinos* (members of the local community with full rights and privileges) mobilized the population against the decision, the local priest immediately contacted Hoyos so he could have them arrested.[44] In addition, Hoyos made accusations against other hacendados of lesser stature in an attempt to ruin them and acquire more lands.[45]

The colonial state and the Catholic Church seldom had the means to counter the power of the local magnates. The few authorities established outside the main cities and those serving in small towns and villages were underpaid, thus often incompetent and abusive. Several officials not only mistreated their communities but also defrauded the royal treasury. Many fell under the influence of local bosses and became linked to the patronage networks of large hacendados. Physical abuse and corruption were especially widespread in the pueblos de indios, where captains frequently colluded with priests to exploit the indigenous population.[46] In Peñon, for example, German explorer Alexander von Humboldt witnessed in 1801 an Indian girl in the stocks, half naked with swollen feet; the local *corregidor* (magistrate) had left her there for several days for gossiping about his alleged liaison with his female cook.[47]

The power of the magnates did not go unchallenged. Sometimes priests or local officials successfully defended the poor against hacendados' mistreatment. In 1785 Colonel Agustín de la Sierra, pacificator of a newly founded Chimila pueblo, filed a complaint against the continuing destruction of the Indians' crops by the cattle of a rich hacendado and slavetrader.[48] In the case of Olivares's abuse of the inhabitants of Venero, the Capuchin priest in charge there, Bartolomé de Vinaroz, stood up in defense of his parishioners. Olivares reported these activities to Hoyos, who went directly to the bishop in Santa Marta to have the priest reprimanded. Vinaroz then addressed a complaint to Archbishop-Viceroy Caballero y Góngora, who ruled in his favor.[49] In the 1790s the governor of Santa Marta challenged the marquis of Torre-Hoyos's huge power by appointing alcaldes ordinarios in several small towns east of the Magdalena River. These officials were to dispense justice locally and to select deputies in subsidiary villages, which clashed with Hoyos's inherited prerogatives. Among those appointed, the alcalde ordinario of Tamalameque, cattle hacendado Vicente García, confronted Hoyos's power in a series of lawsuits that lasted from 1794 to 1797, when Hoyos, refusing any limits to his domination, renounced his jurisdiction in the region.[50]

In another case, in 1797, Oleto Marcelino Hatos y Banda, vicar of Simití, near Mompox, saved zamba Dominga Pérez from being returned to slavery after the death of her husband. As the appraised value of the small farm on the banks of the Magdalena, left by the deceased, did not cover the loan he had contracted earlier from the local *cofradía* (religious brotherhood) to buy the freedom of his wife and her mother, Simití authorities auctioned Pérez and her children as slaves to a hacendado in order for the cofradía to recover the value and interest of the loan. The vicar sheltered mother and children before their new master could take possession of them. He organized Pérez's travel to Mompox, where a priest appealed the decision of the judges in Simití on her behalf. Supported by the attorney general and the royal protector of slaves, Dominga Pérez won her case in Bogotá. In June 1799 the royal audiencia ruled that, in accordance with the *Ley de Siete Partidas* regulating slavery, she and her children could not be slaves because her legal marriage had made her and all her offspring free. They were granted certificates of freedom and absolved from any further claim by Simití's cofradía.[51] Nevertheless, these successful challenges to hacendados' power and abuse were the exception rather than the rule.

THE CONFLICTING ISSUES OF AGRICULTURE AND TRADE

Hacendados' fiefdoms stood strong against the colonial state and the church mainly because Caribbean New Granada remained marginal to the economy of the Spanish Empire, despite the Bourbon reforms. After the British capture of Havana in 1762, Spain had promoted a series of reforms to preserve its empire and secure its defense through better control of its American colonies. In particular, the Crown improved tax collection, introduced new royal monopolies, attempted to increase trade between the metropolis and its colonies, strengthened its colonial administration, and expanded its military forces. Yet in New Granada the Crown did not support the cultivation of tropical crops for exportation, as it did in Cuba and Venezuela, nor did it envision that the viceroyalty should produce anything but bullion. The emphasis continued to be on the legal exports of gold from the Pacific Coast and northern Antioquia, which traversed the Caribbean region before being shipped out of the port of Cartagena. In 1778, however, Spain reformed the trade system that had given Cadiz an absolute monopoly of the metropolis's trade and authorized free trade within the empire. Several additional ports were allowed to import and export not only in Spain but in most Spanish American colonies as well. In New Granada, Santa Marta and Riohacha opened to trade, Cartagena ceased to be the only point through which gold legally left the viceroyalty, and textiles, wines, and other goods were officially imported from Spain.[52]

Cartagena-born military engineer Antonio de Narváez y la Torre, who then served as governor of the joint provinces of Santa Marta and Riohacha, hoped that the greater freedom of trade now granted to Santa Marta would be the first step leading to the transformation of the region into a tropical export economy following the model of Cuba. In the detailed report he sent to Spain's minister of the Indies in 1778, he stated that the region, despite its favorable location and fertile lands, "lies in a frightening misery, without agriculture, without haciendas, without wealth, and without trade" because it lacked a large, hardworking population. Allegedly, the unsubdued Indians, many of whom still lived "like wild beasts in the woods," were useless, as they did not produce or consume anything profitable to colonial society. "The remaining whites, reduced Indians, mulattoes, free blacks, and slaves, and other mixes" barely reached 30,000 souls in the province of Santa Marta and 3,780 in that of Riohacha. They were scattered throughout the region, contenting themselves with cultivating just enough for their own subsistence, he reported. Narváez proposed to look to the French colony of Saint-Domingue for a blueprint and to massively import black slaves to cultivate the land. Because Santa Marta Province had no cash, he advocated bartering the region's products for slaves from Jamaica and Curaçao. From now on, Spain would "exchange meat for meat, receiving from [the British] the inestimable [value] of a [slave] man for the depreciable [value] of four to five young bulls, or three mules, or for twenty measures of dyewood offered free by the land." Spain's wealthy merchants would provide the initial cash for such an operation in the form of credit to the "honorable residents" of Santa Marta and Riohacha Provinces who were ready to build haciendas and buy slaves. After a few years, the region would generate enough revenue to continue buying slaves and increase production without Spanish investment. In addition to allowing the region to reach "the degree of splendor and wealth" to which it was destined, such a plan would greatly benefit the royal treasury, develop maritime navigation, and hamper contraband, Governor Narváez concluded.[53]

As a result of Narváez's proposal, Spain temporarily authorized Riohacha Province to export cattle, mules, horses, and dyewood to allied and neutral colonies in exchange not only for "Blacks, tools, and machinery for agricultural work" but also for "all kinds of knicknacks to maintain trade with the infidel and unsubjected Guajiro Indians."[54] Whether Narváez's plan to have plantations tilled by African slaves against a backdrop of sovereign Indians was feasible and could have increased the royal treasury is doubtful; it certainly would have deprived many inhabitants of their lands, making them dependent on the planters. In any case, rapidly changing conditions prevented the realization of the project. In 1781 the Comunero Revolt in Andean New Granada and the war with Britain redirected the attention of colonial authorities to more urgent questions than the growth of the Caribbean region. Not until 1787 did Archbishop-Viceroy Caballero y Góngora turn his attention to Santa Marta and Riohacha Provinces, where he successfully promoted the cutting and export of dyewood, an industry that required little investment. Operated through a state monopoly, the wood was shipped from Santa Marta and directly traded with the United States to finance the military campaign for and the colonization of the Darién. From its initiation, the dyewood monopoly provided cutters with good wages paid by intermediaries and merchants. However, Spain ended it in 1789.[55]

Meanwhile, Santa Marta's governors continued to advocate for new imports of slaves. In 1789 the Crown did not include New Granada in the two-year trial period of free trade in slavery that it conceded to Cuba, Santo Domingo, Puerto Rico, and Venezuela. Two years later, despite the outbreak of massive slave rebellions in the French Caribbean, it extended the free trade of slaves to these colonies for another six years and opened it to other ports, this time adding New Granada to the enterprise. Viceroy Josef de Ezpeleta quickly resisted the decision, arguing that it would only stimulate contraband. But Santa Marta's new governor, José de Astigárraga, repeated Narváez's recommendation to import slaves to promote agriculture in the province. After planters increasingly fled violence in Saint Domingue, he also proposed that refugees arriving with their slaves colonize certain areas, as in Cuba and Louisiana. New Granada's viceroy claimed that this would bring in "the pernicious maxims" of the French National Assembly. Still undeterred, Astigárraga then asked for permission to accept French refugee families that he would settle separately in distant places on the coast, but Ezpeleta only authorized him to allocate a few to the islands of

San Andrés and Providencia, off Nicaragua's seashore, provided that they swore to vassalage.[56] After war broke out again with Great Britain in 1796, the Crown renewed restrictions on the importation of slaves to New Granada, which Santa Marta's authorities protested.[57] In 1804 former governor Narváez complained that, as a result of this ban, "not a single *bozal* [African-born] slave has entered in seven years," to the detriment of the region's agriculture.[58]

As for Cartagena Province, greater freedom of trade within the Spanish Empire allowed for some diversification of its tropical farming. For a few years after 1778, cotton production and export increased sharply, raising hopes among some elite creoles that their province could become a major agricultural exporter. In several villages and towns near Cartagena, people cultivated cotton and transported it to the port city, from which it was shipped to Spain.[59] Some of the cacao produced on the banks of the Magdalena River south of Mompox was also exported. Concurrently, however, sugarcane cultivation suffered from Spain's 1789 decision to authorize the free importation of brandy from Catalonia and Cuba, as it hampered the local production of molasses and liquor. Particularly affected by these imports were the hacendados residing in Cartagena whose slave plantations south and east of the city were the largest in Caribbean New Granada. Added to a tax increase, the importation of foreign alcohol forced several haciendas to shift to extensive cattle ranching and to dramatically reduce their slave labor force. The excess slaves were sold to the mines of the Pacific region or relocated in Cartagena. The cane planters, supported by the governor of Cartagena, warned that the ruin of their haciendas would bring about the ruin of the entire province, but Spain refused to limit the import of foreign liquor.[60]

With the renewal of the war against Britain in 1796, New Granada's legal trade swiftly declined as Viceroy Mendinueta prohibited the commerce with allied and neutral colonies. His successor in 1803, Antonio Amar y Borbón, reopened the free trade with neutral ports but restricted it to Spanish ships and Spanish merchants, prompting protests from Cartagena's *consulado de comercio* (merchant guild).[61] The consulado's spokesman, José Ignacio de Pombo, stated that the primary brake on economic expansion was Spain's system of taxes and state monopolies, which hampered agricultural production and legal trade while stimulating contraband. Measuring the province of Cartagena against the United States and prerevolutionary Saint Domingue, Pombo argued that such a tax system prevented the production of an exportable surplus and condemned the region to recession.

Like Narváez previously, in the 1800s he repeatedly asked that New Granada be granted the same privileges as Cuba and Venezuela, whose economies had prospered since the suppression of some monopolies and taxes. But, unlike Narváez, he did not see expansion of African slavery as the key to success. On the contrary, he envisioned agriculture as the "principal and general occupation of the citizens" in a region he thought unfit for manufacturing, and he relegated slaves to "domestic service." According to him, two products were particularly suitable: cotton and tobacco, the latter being "the cultivation of the poor, because one man alone, without other help than a machete, is capable of planting and benefiting from 2,000 to 3,000 plants every year."[62] Yet, in the turmoil of the 1800s, the consulado's request for free trade and support for cotton and tobacco production, like Santa Marta's earlier demands for slave imports, fell on deaf ears in Spain.

STATE PRESENCE

In New Granada, unlike in some of the other Spanish American colonies, the Bourbon reforms prioritized bullion, tax revenues, and military defense, not agricultural production or modernization. This prevented the viceroys from envisioning the economic expansion of the colony, to the chagrin of some elite creoles. For sure, Caballero y Góngora briefly promoted new exports from the coast. In 1783 he sponsored the Botanical Expedition, in which Spanish scientist José Celestino Mutis undertook the study of New Granada's flora, fauna, and environment. But the expedition did not explore the three Caribbean provinces.[63] Although Spain decreed the establishment of elementary schools in all of its colonies' villages and towns, it did not follow through with funding. In the Caribbean region, notably, most villages remained without schools, and most parents were too poor to send their children to the few that existed.[64] In fact, New Granada's viceroys had two major tasks: to collect taxes and to protect the vast frontier from indigenous and foreign attacks, which became harder as the European wars drained Spain's financial and military resources while simultaneously rendering the frontier more vulnerable.

To the general population of New Granada, therefore, colonial rule manifested itself mostly through increased taxes and military recruitment. However, these two impositions did not affect everyone equally, especially in the Caribbean provinces, as those living in the countryside were more likely to escape them than those residing in towns. The fiscal plan drafted for New Granada by visitor general Juan Francisco Gutiérrez de Piñeres in 1778–83 sought to carry out in the viceroyalty the Bourbon reforms designed for the Spanish American empire in general. As elsewhere, among the measures to improve the management and collection of royal taxes were the organization of the tobacco and liquor monopolies, the revision of the *alcabala* (sales tax), and the revival of the Armada de Barlovento tax, which had become confused with the alcabala. Another empirewide measure introduced by the visitor general in 1780 was an increase in the prices of tobacco and liquor that state monopolies sold. He also planned to impose to New Granadans the temporary head tax on adult males (*donativo*) introduced in some other colonies to contribute to the financing of Spain's war with Britain; through the donativo, each Indian and casta man had to pay the Crown one peso, each Spanish and noble man two pesos. In addition, the visitor general applied to New Granada the new system of registering the goods that merchants traded within each viceroyalty. Finally, he planned to install the new class of royal servants, the intendants, that had been established in Peru and Mexico to locally supervise implementation of the reforms.

The Bourbon fiscal reforms were less successful in New Granada than in Peru and Mexico, notably because in New Granada the system of intendants could never be put into effect. Although the reforms led to an increase in the amount of taxes collected in the viceroyalty, they could not be fully enforced in areas of difficult access and with limited royal personnel, which characterized much of the Caribbean provinces. Moreover, Gutiérrez de Piñeres, who wanted immediate fiscal results, rejected the proposal of New Granada's viceroy, Manuel Antonio Flores, to impose the new taxes gradually to avoid alienating the population and to simultaneously create disciplined militias in the interior as a means of controlling possible disorder. In August 1779, after the outbreak of war with Britain, a frustrated Flores delegated most of his authority to Gutiérrez de Piñeres and left Bogotá for Cartagena to focus on the defense of the viceroyalty. Quite likely he did little there to support the visitor general's reforms in the Caribbean region.[65]

In matters of military recruitment, New Granada's system of defense, which had been based on coastal strongholds and fortified cities defended by a very small army, was profoundly modified in 1773. Presided over by Field Marshal Alejandro O'Reilly, who had just reformed the army in Cuba, the military reorganization began with the Caribbean provinces and Panama. Its most important result was the creation of a disciplined militia in many towns and villages of the Caribbean region. Single and married men from fifteen to forty-five years of age were recruited by lottery from census rolls. Only clergymen, medical doctors, lawyers, merchants and their dependents, teachers, notaries, and other public servants were exempted from service. By 1779 the militia in the Caribbean provinces (excluding Panama) numbered 7,500 men in 2 battalions and 58 companies of infantry, 2 companies and 1 brigade of artillery, and 2 companies of cavalry. In contrast, the same Caribbean provinces counted a regular army of only 1,737 men (a minority of them Spanish), and in the Andean region, where the majority of New Granada's population lived, militiamen totaled no more than 1,400.[66]

Most of this massive recruitment had been the work of the special commander, José Pérez Dávila, who as a reward was appointed governor of Panama. And many militiamen had been enlisted in the villages and rural areas around Lorica and along the Magdalena River. But militia recruitment did not mean an increased state presence in these areas. Rather, it strengthened the power of some regional white elites, mostly hacendados, who used the enlistment of peasant soldiers to acquire officerships. Nor did the militia bring colonial order to small towns, villages, and the countryside. Often led by officers without military backgrounds, whose rank corresponded to their wealth and influence, not their competence, the militiamen generally were poorly trained. Most of them were day laborers, peasants, sharecroppers, and artisans. They had few guns, no uniforms, and no shoes. Their training was often limited to a weekly drill after the Sunday mass armed with sticks. In some cases, enlistment was fictitious and consisted of the rural laborers of a given officer who then refused to send them to perform their military duty. Or the officer in charge accepted bribes from landholders to exempt their enlisted workers from active service. Moreover, when militia companies were actually formed, there was no way they could replicate the separate colonial racial categories of blancos, pardos, zambos, and *morenos* (blacks) in their organization, as stipulated by the 1773 reform. Indeed, most villages and small towns did not contain enough whites to form separate units, and generally the company of white militiamen comprised mulattoes, zambos, and mestizos. As a result, the formation of the militia failed to replicate the colonial ideal of racial order and, instead, strengthened patronage. By 1784 the militia system was phased down and thoroughly reorganized around the principal cities and a few frontier settlements threatened by sovereign Indians. With fewer enlisted men than in 1779, pressure on the rural population decreased, and service in the militia became more professional. In the process, everywhere except in Cartagena the fiction of the racially distinct companies was ended and the new units were renamed, tellingly, *milicias de todos los colores* (of all colors).[67]

The Catholic Church was in no better condition to exercise strict control than the state. Santa Marta and Riohacha Provinces were so poor that some bishops refused to serve there. The priests were few and often ignorant in religious matters, as Santa Marta lacked a seminary for their training. Most existing churches were shabby, and several villages had neither church nor priest.[68] Conditions in Cartagena Province were no better, as shown by the report of its bishop, José Fernández Díaz de Lamadrid. During the dry seasons from 1778 to 1781, he braved the hardships of travel in the Caribbean region to bring some Christian order to his diocese. By his count, Díaz de Lamadrid visited a total of 2 cities, 4 towns, 49 sites of all classes of people, 25 Indian pueblos, and 16 new villages and administered confirmation to 38,255 souls.[69] His report repeatedly lamented "the universal relaxation and corruption of the mores of the faithful; the infidelity, misery, and disgrace of many neighborhoods, the lack of spiritual nourishment of a great number of old and modern parishes in need of priests."[70] He found that a handful of parishes lacked both a priest and a church building. Some villages, such as Ternera and Santa Rosa, mostly inhabited by free blacks and mulattoes in the vicinity of Cartagena, or the more indigenous and zambo San Benito de Abad on the San Jorge River, were too poor to afford a minister. In some needy parishes, priests lived in total indigence and could not even offer bread to the visiting bishop. Several villages were attended only occasionally by a priest established in a nearby town whose mission was hampered by the difficulty of transportation.[71]

Few priests met the expectations of the bishop in terms of devotion, virtue, and excellence. Several failed to keep parish registers and to make annual census lists of parishioners. Others neglected the teaching of the Catholic doctrine, and in some villages the bishop found adults as well as children completely ignorant of their religion.[72] Few parishes could afford the church of stone and wood with a tile roof that the bishop considered "decent." Almost everywhere, the temple, its decoration, and the sacred ornaments were in poor condition or missing altogether. According to Díaz de Lamadrid, some churches consisted of an "arbor" unfit for "the most despicable slaves."[73] Some lacked the most basic liturgical objects. Still others were inappropriately decorated with sacred images made of straw or so misshapen that "they induce[d] laughter, not devotion."[74] The morality and religious compliance of Caribbean New Granada's parishioners did not impress Bishop Díaz de Lamadrid favorably, either. Fulfilling the sacrament of marriage meant learning the rudiments of the Catholic doctrine, providing a set of official documents (such as baptismal certificates and evidence that there was no impediment to the marriage), and paying a five-peso fee that few could afford. Therefore, to the bishop's despair, most people chose to live "in concubinage, whose vice inundate[d] that region." With few priests and inadequate transportation, many parents were unable to have their children baptized within eight days of birth, as prescribed; some waited until they were toddlers or even older. Nor were the Catholic rituals of death and burial possible to accomplish in many places. Only a few individuals were close enough to a priest to be able to do penance and receive extreme unction before they died. For lack of a church nearby, many parishioners did not attend mass, make their annual confessions, or send their children to catechism. At the root of the problem, in the bishop's eyes, were the endemic shortage of priests and the immense poverty of the majority of inhabitants, who lacked the means to support a minister and a church. Consequently, few priests were willing to serve outside of major cities, and among those who did, many were unfit or immoral and misused their authority.[75]

The bishop provided some quick, if momentary, solutions to the region's religious deficiencies. During his journey, he celebrated mass followed by group confirmations in all towns, villages of free people of color, and Indian pueblos. He also reprimanded unscrupulous priests. But, given the scarcity of religious vocations in the Caribbean region, only when negligence was coupled with misuse of power and concubinage did the bishop remove priests from their parishes and punish them.[76] On a few occasions, he remedied problems with his own money. Notably, in Sampués, a former encomienda of Zenú Indians, "noticing the indecency and nakedness of the dress of the women who went to church," he offered four large pieces of cotton fabric to the priest to have shirts and underskirts made for them.[77] Of course, such solutions could not genuinely evangelize Caribbean New Granada's population.

Moreover, the church and the state were often at odds with each other. In the 1790s, for example, the Vatican and the Council of the Indies lifted the five-peso marriage fee for contracting parties and the additional paperwork required for vagrants and foreigners in an attempt to curb concubinage, but the diocese of Cartagena's priests, backed by the bishopric, continued to request them.[78] Conversely, in many places the church found no support from civil authorities who were supposed to ensure respect for ecclesiastical law. Thus, parishioners usually disobeyed the priests and ignored the threat of excommunication, knowing that royal authorities would not intervene.[79]

Emblematic of the lack of state endorsement of church precepts were the two campaigns initiated by two bishops of Cartagena: Diego de Peredo's endeavor to "moralize" popular dancing and José Díaz de Lamadrid's attempt to force hacendados to Christianize their slaves.

In December 1768 Peredo issued a diocesan edict, endorsed by the governor of Cartagena Province, banning, under penalty of excommunication, *bundes* (popular dances) on the eve of religious celebrations. According to the bishop, those who participated in the bundes were "Indians, mestizos, mulattoes, blacks and zambos, and other people of the lower class: all congregate together without order or separation of the sexes, the men mixed with the women, some play an instrument, others dance, and all sing lascivious verses, making indecent movements with their bodies." These activities, performed under cover of darkness, were accompanied by heavy drinking and resulted "in the fatal consequences that can be deduced." Furthermore, they left participants so exhausted that they could not attend mass the next morning.[80] The *fiscal* (Crown attorney) of the audiencia of New Granada reversed the bishop's edict, stating that people would ignore or violently protest the ban of such an established custom as the bundes. As noted by Guy Bensusan, the fiscal believed that matters of public welfare and tranquility, linked with public enjoyment and festive social interaction, were more important than attendance at mass. The Spanish Council of the Indies upheld the fiscal's reversal. It also reprimanded Peredo for usurping the jurisdiction of the secular authority and admonished the governor for supporting the bishop's decision and assuming canonical jurisdiction. Tension between religious and civil authorities continued during the bishopric of Díaz de Lamadrid, who made another unsuccessful attempt to ban bundes.[81]

In a less blatant but equally significant fashion, colonial authorities failed in the 1780s to back Díaz de Lamadrid's drastic measures to bring Catholicism to rural slaves. During his visit to the coast's haciendas and ranches, the bishop found that few owners fed, dressed, protected, and instructed their slaves in the Catholic doctrine as prescribed by law. Most haciendas, he reported, depended on parishes whose temples lacked a solid structure, ornaments, and basic liturgical objects. The hacienda of Majagual had the worst church of all those he visited in the province: it was "an indecent and illegally shaped arbor, where all the animals could take shelter."[82] Moreover, few masters and overseers gave days of rest to their slaves or allowed them to attend mass on Sundays and holidays. Whereas in some cases church attendance was made difficult by long and impassable trails, it often was prevented by masters who required that slaves work on Sunday "in order to buy their own clothes."[83] Had the bishop visited the isolated mines near Ayapel, he would have found that owners, sometimes priests themselves, kept their slaves in a state of utter neglect.[84] Rural slaves and servants generally ignored church doctrine, and the bishop worried about their spiritual salvation.

To remedy this situation, Díaz de Lamadrid reminded all parishioners — masters, overseers, free individuals, as well as male and female slaves and servants — of their duty to go to mass. He ordered several slaveowners to build decent churches for their dependents and to yearly entrust their slaves to priests for basic religious instruction so they could confess at Easter. He prohibited priests from administrating extreme unction to the dying in haciendas until the landowners paid for a reliquary to carry the transubstantiated Christ. To prevent masters from forcing their slaves to work on days of compulsory church attendance, the bishop instructed priests to explain to slaves that "their owners were compelled to give them the necessary sustenance and clothing as well as to teach them the Christian doctrine."[85] Finally, in 1782 he imposed the penalty of excommunication on masters who, after three admonitions, continued to force slaves to work on religious days. In response, Cartagena's cathedral chapter (*cabildo eclesiástico*), a stronghold of slaveowners, petitioned to have the 1782 decree nullified. The Council of the Indies validated it but, instead of ordering the penalty of excommunication, ruled that disobedient slaveowners be brought before the royal magistrates (*jueces reales*).[86] Little change followed, and in 1805 Viceroy Antonio Amar accused hacendados of running plantations that were "the prison and grave of the slaves and blacks, because they do not give them their daily maintenance but leave it to what [slaves] can earn with their unhappy work during their weekly day off."[87]

REVOLT

Despite weak state and church control, hacendados' domination of much of the rural population did not produce major rebellions in Caribbean New Granada. When, in 1799, Viceroy Mendinueta warned that, in the context of the Haitian Revolution, the "corruption" of free and enslaved blacks, mulattoes, and zambos of the region "would be of irreparable consequences" for New Granada, he also accurately recalled that the anti-Bourbon Comunero Revolt of 1781 had been an urban and an Andean affair in which the "very numerous class of people of color in [the Caribbean region] . . . ha[d] not belied their loyalty."[88]

The Comunero Revolt deeply shook Spain's rule in New Granada. It began in the tobacco-producing area of Socorro, in the eastern cordillera of the Andes, prompted by the implementation of the visitor general's fiscal reforms. There, a regional coalition of peasants and local creole elites rose up in arms and marched to the gates of Bogotá to defend the traditional contract between them and the king against new, economically straining taxes that they blamed on the "tyranny" of new peninsular officials, such as the visitor general and his local delegates.[89] Their movement sent shock waves through southern New Granada as well as through the Llanos de Casanare, east of Tunja, where the mostly indigenous population launched a large-scale revolt.[90] It inspired a group of slaves in Antioquia to have all the slaves in the province march on its capital, claiming that the king had released a *cédula* (decree) freeing them, but they were betrayed before the plan was carried out. Also, as the lower-class Comunero leader José Antonio Galán led his men into northern Antioquia, he recruited among the landless free people of color and slaves and freed eighty-one slaves in a Spanish-owned gold mine.[91] Yet Galán's movement remained small and did not reach the mines south of Ayapel. More importantly, the Comunero Revolt did not spread to the Caribbean region.[92]

Several factors explain this. First, as shown by John Phelan, in the area of Socorro the changes in sales taxes and royal monopolies introduced by visitor general Gutiérrez de Piñeres hurt a multitude of small tobacco farmers simultaneously as producers and consumers, whereas they penalized Caribbean New Granadans as consumers of tobacco and liquor but not as producers of sugarcane.[93] In addition, the state's weaker presence in the Caribbean region prevented a strict application of the Bourbon tax reforms, and thus people there did not share the same level of outrage as the *socorranos*. Spain made no attempt to reestablish the tribute of the castas in the region, as it did without success in Guatemala or Nicaragua. In Caribbean New Granada, more than in any other Spanish continental colony except Venezuela, the Council of the Indies admitted that, as the restoration of the casta tribute "opposed an almost immemorial peaceful custom," it was likely to "have fatal results" and provoke rebellion.[94] With few Spanish soldiers available, any revolt there would be disastrous to Spain in the context of renewed war with Britain, as it would annihilate the defense of the coast and the frontier against naval attack and invasion. To keep Caribbean New Granada safe, Spain needed the military participation and support of the region's male population, which was mostly of African descent. Thus, tax collection was not a priority.

Second, the dispersion of the population, the slowness and difficulty of communications, and the resulting isolation of many communities made participation in any revolt difficult. Moreover, the social fabric of Caribbean New Granada had been profoundly affected by the Spanish campaigns to resettle the rural population and the ensuing concentration of lands in the hands of a few hacendados. This contrasted with the Socorro area, for which Anthony McFarlane stresses the importance—previous to 1781— of political life in the villages and small towns, "where alliances bonded by kin and clientage gave form and substance to political life in a ruralized world. Such politics reflected a sense of local identity and separateness," expressed in the Comuneros' claim that creoles should have preference over Spaniards in local office.[95] Indeed, in 1781 few Caribbean small towns shared the socorranos' "lively political life" and aspirations, making a regional crossclass alliance against the central power all the more difficult. As pueblo Indians, arrochelados, palenqueros, and isolated peasants had been forcibly relocated in the 1770s, they had to create new roots and ties of kinship in an environment of relative land scarcity. Longtime residents in established towns and villages had to accommodate to reduced access to land and resources. Simultaneously, the expansion of large landholdings deprived thousands of small cultivators of the land they once tilled, compelling them to become peons on haciendas or to look elsewhere for a living. Tensions among the rural population and between free people of color, slaves, and Indians increased as available lands diminished, hampering any alliance between these groups.[96] In particular, the large cattle ranches, as they spread along the major rivers and on the plains between Tolú, Lorica, and San Benito Abad, employed increasing numbers of young free and slave cowboys, often of African and indigenous descent. Haciendas temporarily hired additional cowboys and helpers to round up cattle, drive herds from pastures to urban slaughterhouses, and move thousands of heads from one ranch to another to avoid floods and draughts. Underpaid, the free cowboys could not save up enough money to buy their own land. Nor were the many slaves among them able to manumit themselves. They could seldom have a family, and they lost their jobs when they became old or were injured. Yet these men played a crucial, if not always conscious, role in the rapid expansion of the magnates' herds and grazing lands by participating in the takeover of individual plots from squatters and peasants and of communal lands from villages and pueblos de indios. Tied to the big hacendados through domination and patronage, the cowboys often clashed with local communities and small cultivators, destroying their crops or abusing them and their families. As a result, the rural population was further fragmented.[97]

Third, few demands of the Socorro insurgents addressed the specific needs of free people of color, Indians, and slaves, which would have helped spread the movement to the Caribbean provinces. Among the thirty-five clauses of the Comuneros' *plan de capitulaciones*, only one mentioned free blacks, demanding a reduction by half of their tribute, the *requinto*, which in reality had never been collected. Other clauses mentioned Indians but many aimed at restoring community lands in the form of individual properties, which ultimately would make these available for purchase by non-Indians. The Comuneros were notably silent on slavery: not a single clause referred to slaves.[98] The Comunero Revolt's failure to spread to Caribbean New Granada probably was also due to the region's history of weak solidarity with the Andean interior.[99]

Neither did the Haitian Revolution echo in rebellions of free people of color and slaves against whites in the Caribbean New Granadan countryside—notwithstanding that most haciendas were relatively isolated and often had more slaves than free persons on their land. In fact, the resurgence of slave conflicts, rebellions, and escapes in late-eighteenth-century New Granada noted by Jaime Jaramillo was limited to the Cauca region, with its numerous slave plantations. In the Caribbean, Jaramillo identifies only one unsuccessful occurrence in a hacienda in the jurisdiction of Mompox, where in 1799 slaves rebelled against the takeover of the property by their owner's heirs and refused, arms in hand, to serve any white. Slaves stayed in their workplace but rejected the new authority over them, acting as if the hacienda had become theirs at the death of their master. They resisted until 1802, when some slaves betrayed the others.[100] Closer to the reality, Hermes Tovar argues that in New Granada there were several *rumors* of slave rebellions but no major uprisings. Rather, slaves struggled "to enter the world of the legitimacy of slavery to break it from within."[101] To gain their freedom, they individually used various legal means—self-purchase, manumission for loyal services or sexual favors, the denunciation of their master for mistreatment, and the purchase of their freedom by paying their owner their appraised value—as well as illegal means—above all, flight.[102]

After 1791, Caribbean New Granadan slaves' preference for methods of resistance other than rebellion did not mean that they ignored the Haitian Revolution but had a deep understanding of local conditions. Even in the Caribbean islands and the Circum Caribbean, few large-scale slave uprisings occurred after 1791.[103] In New Granada, slaves were simply not numerous enough to launch a forceful revolt, except perhaps in a few plantation areas near Cartagena. Elsewhere, communication among haciendas and mines was difficult. For instance, it took four days of canoeing and trekking, including passing through a prominent pueblo of Emberá, to travel between the two most important gold mines south of Ayapel—La Soledad, owned by the marquis of Santa Coa, which employed over one hundred slaves and laborers, and the mine of Uré "with an abundance of blacks."[104] In haciendas close to pueblos de indios, such as those along the Magdalena River, owners often entrusted their slaves with the task of harassing Indians or driving out free squatters of color. This pitted the slaves against the other groups, thus preventing any alliance between them. At the same time it probably allowed unruly slaves to take out their aggression on the victims of their masters.[105] And as suggested by David Geggus, the existence of sanctuaries for runaway slaves in frontier areas, something so characteristic of Caribbean New Granada, helped decrease the likelihood of rebellion. Arguably, some slaveowners could have tacitly accepted the individual escape of especially indomitable slaves as a way to protect their holdings from potential ringleaders.[106]

Although they comprised a majority of the population, rural free people of color in Caribbean New Granada were too scattered, too distant from the centers of direct colonial power, and too linked to hacendados and officials through complex relationships of patronage, mutual protection, and labor to form strong autonomous movements. Extensive and variegated sexual mixing with whites and Indians also hampered collective mobilization against the whites in power. Moreover, in areas with few or no whites, distinctions were generally drawn vis-à-vis Indians and slaves.

RESISTANCE

Such conditions and characteristics also guided the actions of the two most powerful groups among the free people of color—the militiamen and the Magdalena bogas. Most of the men who resisted forced enlistment in the militia or who opposed military orders fled rather than rebelled. Desertion was sometimes collective, as in the case of two Riohacha dragoon companies with a good record when ordered to serve against the Comunero Revolt and in the distant Darién.[107] No doubt, as much as these peasants and laborers accepted the responsibility of defending their area from indigenous attacks, sometimes at a high cost to their own production, the prospect of leaving their families for a faraway campaign against Andean peasants or unknown Indians was intolerable. Conversely, the militia offered avenues of advancement to rural free men of color who could move to the city and find new opportunities there. According to one militia captain, by 1807 Spain's involvement in the European war had increased the number of enlisted men to the point where there were insufficient agricultural workers in the countryside, "being well-known that the laborer who takes part in the royal [military] service either deserts his profession forever or returns to it with little fervor, and worse is the fact that as these hands do not perform farm work, they increase the number of consumers in the city where many of their relatives go with them, despite the Government's vigilance."[108] In villages and towns the militia strengthened class subordination and patronage, as often it brought peons, day laborers, and sharecroppers under the military leadership of their hacendados and overseers.

The rowers who monopolized transportation on the main rivers, especially the black, zambo, and mulatto bogas of the Magdalena, resorted to a wide range of strategies to render their hardworking conditions more human, short of uniting to stop the navigation on the only route linking the Caribbean Coast to the Andean interior. Neither did the bogas customarily commit violence against their passengers by robbing, harming, or killing them, despite the fact that they largely outnumbered the passengers and navigated for weeks in areas with little human contact.[109] No doubt, several travelers, such as Spanish brigadier Fidalgo, denigrated the bogas for allegedly being so inclined to "insolence, theft, rapine, intoxication, and other iniquities suggested by the amorality and relaxation of customs so familiar to them that one can say that they distinguish[ed] themselves from the rest of the human species."[110] Other voyagers showed some empathy for these hard workers.[111] In effect, the bogas, clad only in underwear and large straw hats, propelled longboats upstream, with levers propped up against their chests, for up to thirteen hours a day in a hot and humid environment—a task that required endurance, extraordinary muscular strength, precise rhythm, and coordination, as Alexander von Humboldt observed.[112] To secure the work of the bogas, boat owners needed to pay their salaries partly or fully in advance and to provide them with abundant liquor and food for the duration of the trip.

Even with such incentives, bogas sometimes vanished with the advanced pay, showed up late and intoxicated at departure, or did not complete the journey. Once on the way, to the great displeasure of their passengers, "they stopped as often as they [could]" to fish or gather eggs, or to drink or have sex with the riverside population.[113] Whereas Frenchman Mollien under-

Bogas on the Magdalena River. (Alcide Dessalines d' Orbigny, *Voyage pittoresque dans les deux Amériques* [Paris: L. Tenré, 1836])

stood the bogas' delays as a means of reducing the fatigue of the journey, Humboldt, traveling in 1801, felt no "compassion" for these men who, "despite being badly paid (their food and a daily wage of one and a half reales) are free men, and at the same time very insolent, unruly, and happy." Most irritating to Humboldt was "the barbarous, lustful, ululating, and furious clamor, at times pitiful, at times joyful, some other times with blasphemous expressions, through which these men try to alleviate the muscular effort."[114] At the complete mercy of the bogas, travelers could either bear their suffering with patience or protest and endure reprisals from the crew; such reprisals could range from longer delays to abandoning passengers and goods on the champanes or the riverbanks. French diplomat Auguste Le Moyne, who lived in New Granada from 1828 to 1839, observed that passengers would be wise to avoid maltreating the bogas and give them tips, cigars, and liquor at the end of each day; with these gifts passengers "will spare themselves many tribulations."[115]

Indeed, until the advent of steamboats in the mid-nineteenth century, bogas had exclusive control of Magdalena transportation. Yet their very independence and means of coping with hardship explain why they did not organize across the profession. Although seldom owners of champanes, they were able to impose their profoundly independent way of life on employers and passengers. Commonly denigrated for their alleged African-derived savagery, in the loneliness of the river the bogas knew how to build on their white passengers' vulnerability and stereotyped fears to induce indulgence and temporary respect. In fact, most continued in the transportation industry until their health or old age forced them to adopt a more sedentary life, but many then chose not to give up their independence and became squatters along the Magdalena River.[116]

Most other groups among free people of color outside the main cities faced conditions that often forced them to find individual, rather than collective, solutions. With the best lands monopolized by the magnates, peasants' holdings tended to be exposed to river flooding or to be very distant from the trade routes. Most did not have their own means of transporting their corn, bananas, beans, tubers, fruits, or cocoa to markets and depended on intermediaries who overcharged for their services, leaving them little or no profit. Even in the villages and small towns near Cartagena, where in the early 1790s "many men, women, and children were employed and subsisted ... in the tasks of sowing, harvesting, ginning, transporting, pressing, and bringing" cotton to the port city for export to Spain, the cotton boom was too modest and too short-lived to allow for the formation of an independent peasantry.[117] As a result, many producers accumulated debts that made them even more dependent on the big hacendados. For example, as his small farm on the banks of the Magdalena could never thrive due to seasonal flooding, pardo Francisco Rojas was unable to repay the loan of 300 pesos he contracted from the cofradía in Simití to buy the freedom of his wife, zambo slave Dominga Pérez, and her mother in 1782. When Rojas died in 1795, the net worth of his farm was only 186 pesos and 3 reales, including all the family's belongings: 660 decrepit cocoa trees, a dwelling, a cane field, a small boat, some tools, axes, and machetes, some old iron, grinding stones and pots, 4 hens and 2 roosters, some salt, 1 hide, and 5 calabash trees.[118] Other cultivators gave up and became part of a floating population in search of legal and illegal opportunities.[119]

Thus, in the changing context of the late colonial period, most Caribbean villages bore little resemblance to those made up of independent tobacco producers as in the Socorro region in 1781. Nor did they resemble the native Andean peasant communities with a long tradition of rebellion and resistant accommodation that, according to Steve J. Stern, enabled them to build a common ethnic (or racial) identity to respond to change.[120] Yet, with time, some began to display the "village consciousness and feelings of social distance from the world beyond" identified by William B. Taylor as the main source of rebellion in rural Mexico. As in Mexico, however, villagers tended to see their major enemies in abusive local rulers or neighboring villages, rather than in the higher colonial authorities, and therefore peasants did not unite in regional movements of resistance.[121]

Symptomatic of this situation was the attitude of the inhabitants in the area of Tamalameque, on the banks of the Magdalena, who in the 1790s were involved in the conflict of jurisdiction between Gonzalo Josef de Hoyos, marquis of Torre-Hoyos and heir of José Fernando Mier y Guerra's title of poblador, and Vicente García, recently appointed alcalde ordinario of Tamalameque by the governor of Santa Marta. Rather than taking advantage of the vacuum created by the conflict between the two hacendados to assert their autonomy, the residents of Tamalameque defended García, the owner of large herds in the area, because "he has behaved with all [of them] like Father." "His authority was respected by nobles and plebeians alike." He "did not spare his efforts and personal money" to improve the town. Charitable, he fed the beggars every Saturday.[122] In contrast, the villagers in El Banco, Guamal, Chimichagua, and Plato generally supported Hoyos, a large landholder there. According to his enemies, the marquis never visited the villages but ruled through deputies, often "of lowly birth, who could not read and write," such as zambo Pedro Juan Tinoco in Guamal. The deputies made "these poor rustics, zambos and blacks, vecinos" believe that "they cannot accept or obey any judges" other than them and Hoyos. At the latter's incitement, "the zambos and blacks [have] disobeyed even the governor [of Santa Marta]. . . . They have . . . insulted . . . the very judges of the territory, to the point of breaking their heads and arresting them, making riots just for this."[123] According to their representatives, the people supported Hoyos's absolute power for good reason—it was "the immemorial custom in which they have lived." Since the villages' foundation by Mier and as a reward for their struggle against the Chimila, they had "been assigned adequate land for cattle raising and farming" and had lived peacefully. The appointment of new alcaldes by Santa Marta's governor would jeopardize these achievements, they believed, because the alcaldes would compete with each other and "seek to oppress these poor residents (moradores) so that their sweat would pay for the cost of the [alcaldes'] titles and other expenses."[124] Although they did not state it publicly, the villagers probably also opted for the lesser of two evils with the existing system of domination, because the marquis neglected to collect the royal taxes, "to the detriment of the royal treasury" but to their own benefit.[125]

People outside of the principal cities did not overtly rebel against the colonial order also because they could live on its legal or geographical margins—either by smuggling or by surviving semiautonomously in the backlands. Throughout the colonial period, contraband was a major activity in Caribbean New Granada, and colonial authorities were incapable of curbing it.[126] Thanks to a weak state presence, smuggling was carried out through difficult, complex routes that linked the Chocó and the most productive areas of the coastal provinces to the British Caribbean islands and Curaçao. These paths followed the Magdalena and other rivers, crossed through remote rochelas in the backlands, and reached the sea through Tolú, Sabanilla, or the sovereign Indian nations in the Guajira Peninsula and the Darién. Gold from the Chocó, northern Antioquia, and the area of Ayapel was the most lucrative, but not the only product to be illegally exported. Cattle, mules, hides, brazilwood, and cotton were also smuggled out from the plains near the Magdalena River and the wooded areas near Santa Marta and Riohacha. In return, British sailors illegally brought in fabrics, tools, arms—and, occasionally, slaves.[127]

Spain officially imposed a yearly fixed tax of four pesos on the *mazamorreros* (independent prospectors) panning for gold in the Sinú, San Jorge, and Cauca Rivers and their tributaries. "As the gold extracted by these unhappy men is subjected to the same *quinto* fees as that produced by mine owners, but the latter are exempted from the yearly fixed tax, the injustice of their treatment is obvious," reported creole merchant José Ignacio de Pombo.[128] The only alternative for them was to pan gold illegally, which represented a minimal risk in areas characterized by isolation and lack of state control. Mazamorreros sold the gold dust for cash or smuggled merchandise to small intermediaries, who in turn sold the dust to miners, merchants, or state and church officials involved in contraband. Although royal smelters bought the gold dust at higher prices than smugglers, the former generally involved several days of trekking and canoeing away from the placer mines. As a result, most mazamorreros preferred to deal with illegal intermediaries—and to avoid registering with the royal authorities. Despite laws imposing harsh punishments on unregistered miners and smugglers, few were ever caught, especially if they belonged to networks headed by high officials. In fact, as shown by William Sharp for the Chocó, the few who did fall in the hands of authorities were likely to have been framed or informed on by rivals.[129]

Contraband offered an alternative to many in the Caribbean rural population, not only for mazamorreros, but also for small cattle ranchers, tanners, woodcutters, porters, muleteers, rowers, retailers, peddlers, and market sellers. Many also participated in the illegal production of liquor and tobacco for local consumption. Far from diminishing during the years of free trade within the empire from 1783 to 1796, when Spain was not at war with Britain, contraband exploded, as the taxes on imports and exports remained high. In the early 1790s, when Spain liberalized the importation of slaves from other Caribbean colonies, many vessels from Jamaica and Curaçao, after anchoring in Cartagena "under the pretext of the slave trade," dropped prohibited merchandise along the coast, especially near Tolú, Sabanilla, Santa Marta, and Riohacha to return with New Granada's gold, brazilwood, and cattle. Smugglers carried illegal imports and exports on boats and canoes between the foreign ships and Cartagena Bay or the Magdalena River and Mompox. Similarly, muleteers and porters transported them on trails to diverse destinations.[130] After the war with Britain resumed in 1796, bringing legal trade almost to a standstill, contraband appeared uncontrollable. In vain, Viceroy Ezpeleta attempted to resolve the problem by sending repeated messages to the king, then "letters to the priests [in the Magdalena region] imploring them to use the confessional and the pulpit to make people understand that contraband and crime are inseparable."[131]

These threats had no effect, and several years later cartagenero Manuel Trinidad Noriega denounced the fact that in Barranca, on the Magdalena River, everyone, including the village's current captain, participated in the illegal trade. When navigating upstream, the contraband boats stopped four leagues before Barranca and waited for a message allowing them to continue; they then passed behind an island that hid them from the village. "Once there was no chance to see them, an order was given to send the tax pirogue [piragua de rentas] downstream to check and reconnoiter" the river.[132] Indeed, by 1803 Viceroy Mendinueta gave up the struggle against contraband, for both the region's geography and the lack of funds made it impossible.[133] Several leading cartageneros, notably Field Marshal Antonio de Narváez y la Torre, the former governor of Santa Marta, argued that the only way to limit contraband was to open up free trade to other nations and reduce import taxes. Otherwise, Narváez asked rhetorically, how could even "an Army of Guards like that of Xerxes composed only of men like Argos" control an extended seashore with only four cities but a multitude of secret anchoring places and a vast territory crossed by deserted trails on which smugglers had no chance of being noticed?[134] One official claimed that "only the persons who dedicate themselves [to the scandalous illegal traffic] are well-to-do."[135] According to the consulado de comercio of Cartagena, in 1810 between 75 and 80 percent of the merchandise entering Caribbean New Granada was smuggled in by contrabandists, and most gold exports left the country through contraband trails; at least two-thirds of the liquor consumed locally was produced illegally, outside of the state monopolies.[136] Contraband had indeed become an alternative way of life for elites as well as for free people of color and Indians in the periphery. It was a powerful challenge to the colonial order but one that benefited from the status quo and created networks that crossed class, race, and local distinctions.

SQUATTING AND FLIGHT

The contraband trade did not provide opportunities for everyone, especially the rural poor. In fact, it coexisted with other options of resistance, notably vagrancy, mendicity, flight, and squatting on unclaimed marginal lands. As accurately noted by Archbishop-Viceroy Caballero y Góngora in 1789, in the absence of measures to limit land concentration, "Most of the free population compose a vagrant and unsettled population that, forced by the landowners' tyranny, transmigrate with the facility granted by the light weight of their furniture, the small value of their hut, and their lack of love for the font where they were baptized. . . . This comes from [their] old and deeply rooted freedom to avoid each other in order to be able to live as they please without fearing being noticed for their infamous and vile behavior."[137] In addition to the difficulty of finding vacant lands near villages and towns, the daily wages of laborers had remained stagnant since the 1750s. This contrasted with the rapid rise of hacendados' profits and the increased prices of goods and fabrics, especially after the suspension of legal trade with Britain in 1796. Because sometimes begging paid more than working, some chose to beg.[138] In Viceroy Mendinueta's words, "When the job is big and hard and is badly and scarcely paid, dedication weakens. The lack of remuneration is an insult that the poor day laborer receives from the more powerful who employs him or requests [his services], and he takes revenge from [the rich] by refusing to contribute to the latter's profits."[139]

People settled in the hinterland and squatted on vacant lands beyond the reach of royal and church authorities often to escape indebtedness, coercive labor, enrollment in the militia, prosecution, prison, or death. The fact that rochelas and palenques still existed in the early nineteenth century shows that, despite the campaigns of resettlement, squatting continued to be a significant phenomenon. Some people scattered in nuclear families along the rivers. According to Mollien, those on the Magdalena's banks busily grew tubers, vegetables, corn, and fruit; their principal interaction with the outside world was to sell their surplus to travelers, "but one has to give so many bananas for one *piastre* that these people do not have enough to buy clothes." If their isolated life allowed for autonomy, it also implied strenuous work and hardship.[140]

Although there are no figures for actual slave runaways, mines and haciendas often counted fugitives among their slave workforce, showing that flight was an important means of resistance to slavery. Indeed, the lack of security forces in most of the region increased slaves' chances of successfully running away.[141] For example, zambo slave Eusebio Robles escaped from Mompox to the mining area of Zaragosa, where he spent months unmolested until his master was accused of mortally punishing him; that charge led to his capture and return to Mompox heavily chained.[142] Moreover, it was not impossible to become a self-sufficient farmer in the backlands or to find gold dust south of Mompox. Some runaway slaves took refuge in other provinces or in cities, where they hoped to find protection from relatives or the authorities. In 1797 José Teodoro fled from a hacienda near Guamal all the way to Cartagena, where he denounced his master for mistreatment. To avoid a lengthy and costly legal dispute, the master sold the slave to the first buyer. Although unable to gain his freedom, José Teodoro was rid of the master he hated.[143] Similarly, in 1803 the slave Melchor de los Reyes traveled some five hundred miles from Chiriguaná to Honda, in another province, to escape from his new owner, who refused to sell him to a master of Melchor's choice for the 50 pesos he had been appraised at after he lost an arm in a sugar mill. Melchor took refuge in the estate of his first owner, and, through his work and his relatives' help, he managed to save the 50 pesos with which he hoped to buy his certificate of freedom from his master.[144] In 1805 Melchor was still near Honda, his fate undecided. His case and that of José Teodoro show that flight was an option not only to gain freedom but also to improve slaves' conditions.

COUNTERCULTURE

In sum, poor rural people turned to a variety of individual strategies to cope with hardship. Taken together, these strategies helped to undermine an already weak colonial order. More collectively, rural folks created particular spheres of popular autonomy, notably by resisting the imposition of

Catholic norms. Many times when Bishop Díaz de Lamadrid attributed the limited impact of the Catholic Church on Caribbean New Granada to the want of priests and the parishioners' poverty, he avoided acknowledging the existence of an active counterculture opposed to clerical interference with local practices. No doubt, the lack of churches in remote areas, rather than alternative beliefs, explained some of the "sins" denounced by the bishop. This was the case when relatives in some haciendas near Nechí, for example, administered baptismal rites to newborns themselves or when some isolated communities buried their dead in the woods without informing religious and civil authorities.[145] Often, however, people refused to comply with the church's precepts even when a priest was accessible. Confession was almost universally rejected, no doubt because the Catholic concept of sin did not correspond to folks' view of good and evil.[146]

Not even the threat of excommunication was enough to inspire parishioners to use the confessional or to go to church. Some people escaped religious obligations by claiming that they were attending services and making their confessions in another parish. In several villages, parents resisted sending their children to be catechized, "giving as an excuse that they are not Indians who have to attend the [Christian] doctrine."[147] Reportedly, "free blacks" in several villages and hamlets did "not recognize priests and [did] not comply with any precept of the Church, thus living without law or subordination and in total debauchery."[148] In Sincelejo, the community declined to finance an on-site priest less for lack of funds than for being "so little devout," prompting Bishop Díaz de Lamadrid to pay for a minister with his own money.[149]

Resistance to the Catholic Church was even more obvious in the ways people celebrated holidays. The bundes stand out as the best example of how free people of color, Indians, and slaves succeeded in transforming religious celebrations into occasions for interracial and intersexual dance and enjoyment. Such popular festivities were so deeply rooted in the culture of the Caribbean provinces that royal authorities admonished bishops for having tried to prohibit them, correctly foreseeing that their ban could lead to violent protest. Indeed, in September 1785 the parishioners of Ayapel rebelled against their captain, Rafael Gómez, who threatened them with flogging and called the men "rotten zambos" and one woman "bitch" for rejoicing in a bunde for which they had not previously requested authorization. The rebels drove away "this white" and selected their own captain. After Mompox sent militiamen to suppress the revolt, the rebels threatened to burn Ayapel; when the authorities sent a new captain, the rebels abandoned the town en masse. Eventually, their priest intervened on their behalf and in December obtained their pardon on condition that they would accept the new captain and indemnify Gómez.[150]

Other forms of merrymaking equally defied church regulations. Some villagers left their church open at night during the feast of Our Lady of the Candelaria, allowing "that there individuals from both sexes mix without proper separation." In other villages, parishioners displayed tables with card games and raffles in front of the church during Holy Week, which generated shouting, fights, and drunken binges. Díaz de Lamadrid banned such displays on the grounds that they prevented people from meditating on the passion and death of Christ. But quite likely, with limited ecclesiastical supervision, villagers continued to enjoy religious holidays drinking, dancing, and playing.[151] In some parishes, people misspent the funds of cofradías for their own enjoyment. In Barranquilla, the contributions to the cofradía of the Holy Sacrament were used on "liquor, wine, cakes, tobacco, diverse dances and masquerades on the day of Corpus Christi and its octave." Furthermore, according to Díaz de Lamadrid, the members of the cofradía were accustomed to transforming their meetings in the sacristy, meant to prepare the Holy Sacrament's celebration, into orgies, in which they "drank alcohol, smoked tobacco and carried our several irreligious acts."[152]

In villages founded during the campaigns of forced resettlement, people often openly resisted church norms of behavior. In Corozal, a town of 2,823 parishioners on the plains of Tolú, the whole community made noise and prompted disorder during mass, which they transformed into an opportunity for gathering and fun rather than worship. Not far away, in San Juan Nepomuceno, many villagers preferred to work on holy days rather than attend mass.[153] Observance of the Catholic discipline was no better in several Indian pueblos placed under the authority of a captain and a priest. Although often subjected to the priest's exploitation and to land encroachment, intra-Indian ethnic mixing, and, more rarely, Indian women's union with free men of color, some indigenous communities still retained distinct cultural and religious practices. Several Chimila pueblos along the Magdalena River were particularly resistant to Christianity. In some of them, Indians held on to their tradition of face painting.[154] Other communities, such as Zambrano, continued their habit of digging up skulls to expose them to the people's "derision and mockery." In Tetón, Chimila Indians secretly worshiped two heads made of ashes in a temple hidden in the mountains. The local priest discovered their alleged idolatry, destroyed the temple, and imprisoned the entire community. When Díaz de Lamadrid visited Tetón, he released all prisoners, except those believed to be the leaders of the cult, and required a full investigation of the case. He also ordered the erection of a cross and the singing of a mass at the mountain site of the indigenous worship.[155] The bishop's attempts to instill Catholic precepts and to reform the mores of Caribbean New Granada's rural population were unsuccessful, as shown in the following decades by the reports of his successors, who repeatedly lamented the parishioners' failure to attend church services and their immoral ways of life.[156]

Women appear to have been particularly resistant to the submissive role envisioned for them by the Catholic Church. The bishops routinely portrayed them as immodest, extroverted, strong-willed. Throughout the region they participated in bundes, dances, drinking, and other forms of merrymaking. In several villages in the plains of Tolú or along the Magdalena River, women reportedly entered the church talking loudly and "without any modesty." They wore only two pieces of cloth that left most of their bodies exposed and refused to cover their "dishonesty and nakedness," even when attending mass.[157] Some women approached pregnancy out of wedlock and the baptism of their newborns in their own ways. According to Bishop Peredo, in the countryside where men often sired children, then fled to escape their duties as fathers, the abandoned mothers asked their godfathers, friends, or kin to officiate as priests and to baptize their illegitimate children in order to avoid a church reprimand. Another means for women to "hide their fragility" that blatantly opposed Catholic notions of sin, reported Díaz de Lamadrid, was the "very customary . . . execrable crime of seeking abortion."[158]

Overall, the picture of the counterculture of rural Caribbean New Granadans left by their bishops is one of limited libertarianism but not idleness. For sure, drinking, dancing, playing, and having fun seem to have been important to men, women, and children. Yet they also worked hard, often on days of compulsory church attendance. They tended to form sexual relationships and families without respect for the regulations of Catholic marriage, as the high incidence of free unions demonstrates. Although male companions could abandon their common-law wives and children more easily, women appeared ready to take control of their lives if necessary. Moreover, Mollien's portrait of the nuclear peasant families on the banks of the Magdalena River shows long-lasting commitment between spouses. Even though people seem to have accepted the Catholic precepts of baptism and burial more than marriage, they still obeyed them loosely, as shown by the delay in having their newborns baptized by a priest as well as by their occasional readiness to perform this sacrament themselves. Perhaps most indicative of rural Caribbean New Granadans' libertarianism was their rejection of confession and their ignorance of the priests' threat of excommunication for their alleged sins both in their private lives and for their participation in smuggling.[159]

Nevertheless, limited libertarianism also meant individualism. Despite being the absolute majority, free people of color did not collectively rebel against white domination; neither did "civilized" Indians and slaves. Nor were the few whites living in the countryside individually threatened. In fact, in 1796 Viceroy Ezpeleta could rightly claim that in New Granada "one can travel with a security that other more refined and populated kingdoms would envy."[160] People did not revolt because state and church control was weak or nonexistent, and hacendados exerted their domination through patronage as well as oppression. As these three sources of authority were often at odds with one another, they made it easier to slip through the cracks of power. At the same time, they were all the more difficult to oppose since the population was dispersed and entangled in clientele networks headed by hacendados, priests, and government officials. In addition, the campaigns of resettlement conducted from 1744 to 1788 reduced access to fertile lands, increasing tensions among free people of color, slaves, and Indians.

Yet individually, in small groups, and occasionally as local communities, people challenged the colonial order. Despite the costly campaigns of reconquest, the frontier and the hinterland continued to shelter fugitives and runaway slaves. Due to the scarcity of whites and the complexity of racial mixing, the racially distinct militia companies were transformed into milicias de todos los colores. With their monopoly of communications, the bogas managed to impose their rhythm on travelers and shipments. Smuggling remained a strong alternative to the legal trade for people regardless of their class, race, or gender. More broadly, the occupants of villages and small towns continuously refused to follow the moral norms of the Catholic Church in important aspects of their lives. Dancing, in particular, became inseparable from religious celebrations. And some rural Caribbean New Granadans in search of better opportunities found that migration to the principal cities was their best option. Cities became the haven of ambitious militiamen, young women, and single mothers.

3
CITIES

In 1800 Viceroy Mendinueta expressed his fear that, from the frontier and the countryside, a revolution inspired by Saint Domingue could easily spread in Caribbean New Granada's principal cities, where "there is an abundance of black slaves who are in the majority foreigners, and a people of color who are fond of and supportive of them."[1] Indeed, although most Spaniards and white creoles lived in these cities, there too the majority of the population was of African descent. Not only did slaves represent an important proportion of the cities' inhabitants, but almost all the militiamen in charge of defense were of color. Yet during the Bourbon era Spanish authorities discovered only one urban conspiracy in the entire region—in 1799, in Cartagena, led by slaves from Saint Domingue who were able to recruit bozal and creole slaves and a black militia officer. Denounced by a pardo corporal, the conspiracy was nipped in the bud, with no resistance.[2]

Lack of revolt, however, did not mean that the free and enslaved urban population of African descent conformed passively to the colonial order. This chapter shows that men and women employed a myriad of strategies to pursue the primary goals of the revolutionary era—equality and freedom. Moreover, by their sheer numbers as well as their military and economic importance, the libres de color hindered the full application of Spain's demeaning policies toward them. In the words of Mendinueta, the "corruption" of the "very numerous class of people of color . . . would be of irreparable consequence" to New Granada.[3] Thus, viceroys and governors avoided decisions that could stir up urban protest.

FIVE CITIES

Cartagena, Mompox, Santa Marta, Valledupar, and Riohacha were the centers of political power in the Caribbean region. They were the major settings for social interaction, the primary focus of political identity, and the locus of the first references to "el pueblo" as public opinion.[4] Yet, with an average of 136.5 women and girls for 100.0 males, the majority of the urban population was female, and most of the surplus of females could be found among the free population of color and the slaves (see fig. 1).[5]

In the late 1770s the provincial capital of Cartagena was by far the most important city in Caribbean New Granada, with 13,396 inhabitants according to the 1777–80 census. It was also the city with the highest proportion of whites (27.0 percent), due to its largest concentration of royal officials and military and religious personnel. Among its remaining inhabitants, 56.8 percent were free persons of color and 15.7 percent were slaves. Cartagena also had the highest ratio of women over men among the free people of color (190.3 — almost two women or female children for every man).[6] Cartagena's population grew to 15,887 in the late 1780s and to an estimated 17,600 by 1809.[7] Located on a large, magnificent bay, the fortified city of Cartagena consisted of four racially mixed barrios: Santa Catalina, where most civil and church buildings were located, and Nuestra Señora de la Merced, where most of the army was garrisoned, both the preferred residence of wealthy whites; San Sebastián, the city's commercial center; and Santo Toribio, the workplace and residence of most artisans and slaves. The island of the suburb of Getsemaní housed primarily free blacks, mulattoes, and zambos — either laborers or artisans. Also protected by walls, Getsemaní was linked to the city's main gate by a bridge.[8]

By the 1770s the economy of Cartagena had shifted away from slave trading, on which many elite cartageneros had built their fortunes. Like other Caribbean cities, Cartagena expanded around both its military role in the defense of the Spanish Empire and its central position in the legal trade of New Granada. Since the military reform of 1773, it had garrisoned an infantry battalion, two artillery companies, and a fixed battalion known as the Fijo, formed by men from the Caribbean region and the interior of New Granada. Soldiers and officers required food, housing, clothing, and services, which prompted economic and demographic growth. The 1770s were also a decade of major investments in the fortifications and channels of Cartagena and its bay. These projects brought employment to hundreds of local workers and artisans but also recruited numerous slaves.[9] As Cartagena Province produced little for exportation, its revenues were grossly insufficient to pay for the maintenance of its capital, which was partly financed by revenues from Quito and other New Granadan provinces.[10]

In the 1780s, as the cumulative effect of military reform and the 1778

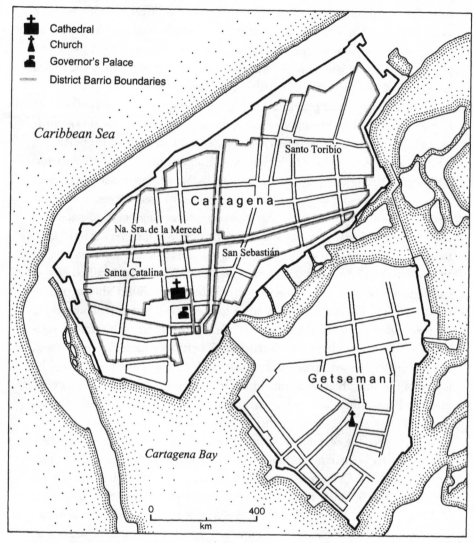

Legend:
- ✝ Cathedral
- ⛪ Church
- ♟ Governor's Palace
- ⌇⌇ District Barrio Boundaries

Caribbean Sea

Santo Toribio

C a r t a g e n a

Na. Sra. de la Merced

San Sebastián

Santa Catalina

G e t s e m a n í

Cartagena Bay

0   400

km

MAP 6. Cartagena and Getsemaní, 1808

royal decision to allow free trade within the empire, the city's legal trade was revitalized. Cartagena was the most important port not only for the coast, but also for the Andean interior as far as Quito. Through its port, manufactured goods, cloth, and wheat entered New Granada, and precious metals, tropical agricultural products, brazilwood, and emeralds were sent overseas. Although most of Cartagena's elite were occupied in sugar production, cattle raising, government, and the Catholic Church, the number of Spanish and white creole merchants increased rapidly and gained economic as well as political power in the city's cabildo.[11] The free population of color autonomously produced most of Cartagena's food, goods, and services, thus also benefiting from the expansion. Getsemaní's inhabitants and independent peasants and sharecroppers cultivated fruits and vegetables near the capital; others fished in the bay and delivered their catches to the city. Women of color transported and sold goods on the streets and at the local markets; others sold food and ran boardinghouses, while still others worked as domestics, laundresses, and seamstresses. Black, pardo, and zambo artisans made tools and clothing in small family shops and larger units, employing free and slave labor. Black and mulatto masons, carpenters, and cabinetmakers provided the city with buildings and furniture. Although some artisans prospered, they could not attain elite status. Their skin color and African origin prohibited most of them from entering the professions, the church, and many positions in the army and state bureaucracy. Slave men, women, and children worked in domestic service as well as in construction, small trade, transportation, port activities, and agriculture in the vicinity of the city.[12] However, by 1790 Cartagena's economic growth came to a halt. Due to financial constraints, the Crown suspended Cartagena's fortification works and reduced its military force. The 1789 decree authorizing the free importation of brandies from Catalonia and Cuba interrupted the production of molasses and liquors by the city's hacendados.[13] Fear of the influence of the French and Haitian Revolutions on its dominions prompted Spain to again restrict trade and slave imports. This economic deterioration, in the Caribbean context of revolution and social upheaval, affected all classes of society.

Although many elite creoles envied the privileges of the Spanish-born, the two groups were brought closer together by their common economic interests. Simultaneously, the philosophy of the Enlightenment and economic liberalism had made their way into the younger generation trained in Bogotá. The economic crisis also affected the free population of color as state and elite demand for labor, services, and goods decreased. As the material benefits of the previous boom vanished, the limitations due to their race seemed all the more unfair, particularly in light of the events in Saint Domingue and other parts of the Caribbean.[14] Slaves who lived separately from their masters, to whom they paid a fixed amount of their wages, also saw their earnings decrease. At the same time, they learned about the major local and international movements happening around them, above all, the Haitian Revolution. As the viceroy of New Granada in 1800 observed, "Slaves don't need much incentive to conceive ideas of freedom in view of the pernicious example of those from the French colonies."[15]

Next in size after Cartagena was the interior town of Mompox, stretching along the west bank of the Magdalena River. With 7,197 inhabitants according to the 1777–80 census, Mompox was the Caribbean New Granadan city with the largest proportion (74.3 percent) of free people of color. Whites comprised no more than 12.9 percent of its inhabitants and slaves, 11.7 percent.[16] Mompox shared several socioracial characteristics with Cartagena, notably an elite of Spanish and white creole hacendados and merchants, and a large, mostly female, population of free people of color. There were fewer royal and church personnel in Mompox, resulting in a lower proportion of whites and slaves among its population. Still, several large cattle hacendados who had built their fiefdoms after the campaigns of forced resettlement, such as the marquises of Torre-Hoyos and of Santa Coa, resided in Mompox. Some of them also owned gold mines south of Nechí. With the development of commerce in the 1770s, more merchants and smugglers settled in Mompox, which had become the major center for legal and illegal trade and communications between the Caribbean Coast, the Andean provinces, and the eastern province of Riohacha. In this obligatory stopover, free men and women of color busily worked as bogas, porters, muleteers, peddlers, street and market vendors, artisans, innkeepers, laundresses, and food retailers, among other occupations.

In the 1790s and early 1800s, Mompox, more than any other New Granadan city, blossomed from increased legal and especially contraband trade. As more people from the nearby countryside, other cities in the viceroyalty, and Spain settled there, the city's population grew rapidly and, according to Alexander von Humboldt, by 1801 numbered 14,000 inhabitants—twice as many as in the 1770s. Humboldt noted Mompox's "nice squares, many churches, 3 convents, among them San Juan de Dios, with assistance to the sick."[17] It had a well-kept dock, a cane liquor factory, a prison, and a town hall, as well as offices for customs, the treasury, the mail service, and the Inquisition. All testified to the city's economic and political importance. Although dependent on the diocese of Cartagena, it sheltered more religious personnel than Santa Marta, Valledupar, and Riohacha combined. The river city also had a hospital and was an important cultural center with several schools, and, after 1808, a university.[18]

In contrast to Mompox and Cartagena, Santa Marta, capital of the province of the same name, remained isolated, small, and poor up to the early

1800s. The 1777–80 census recorded no more than 3,598 inhabitants—69.2 percent of them free people of color, 15.9 percent slaves, and 14.3 percent whites. According to the same census, the largest city in Santa Marta Province was Ocaña, in the Andean northeast, with 5,668 inhabitants.[19] Located on a beautiful bay surrounded by mountains, the city of Santa Marta had no adequate fortifications against maritime attack and no reliable communications with the rest of New Granada. Because its port had no wharf, ships' merchandise had to be carried by rowboat to the beach, where porters awaited. Its only two-story buildings were the cabildo house and one private dwelling. Despite being the see of the diocese of Santa Marta, it had no cathedral and no bishop in residence during much of the late colonial period. Although a cathedral was eventually completed in 1796, it was not served by a bishop until 1809. There was no specific residence for the province's governors, who until 1809 lived illegally in the vacant episcopal house. Santa Marta had a few elementary classrooms but no college or seminary, no official jail, and no military barracks.[20] Apart from some Spanish high-ranking officials, merchants, and ecclesiastics, the small minority of white *samarios* (residents of Santa Marta) included few wealthy people. According to Steinar Saether, a total of six families enjoyed noble status, monopolized practically all important positions, and owned the province's largest sugar and cattle haciendas. The category of whites also included Spanish commoners, such as sailors, as well as creoles in nonprestigious professions.[21] With little legal trade entering or leaving its port, Santa Marta lacked an active merchant class, limiting economic opportunities for lower-class men and women.[22] Slightly more numerous than whites, the city's slaves were generally employed in domestic service. Indicative of its scarce resources, most of Santa Marta's revenue came from its slaughterhouse.[23]

The greater freedom of trade granted by Spain in 1778 allowed Santa Marta to enjoy limited growth in the late 1780s, when Archbishop-Viceroy Caballero y Góngora promoted the cutting of dyewood and its export from the port. However, between 1792 and 1796, when city merchants were briefly authorized to barter products for slaves from neutral colonies, they legally imported only seventy-four bozales.[24] No doubt smugglers brought in additional slaves but in small numbers, as Santa Marta's merchants could not compete for their acquisition in a declining international slave trade in which Cuban planters had the lion's share. Several samarios found in contraband a way to make up for the lack of legal trade and agricultural ventures. To avoid a major scandal in the 1790s, Viceroy Mendinueta chose

Dining room in Santa Marta. (Alcide Dessalines d' Orbigny, *Voyage pittoresque dans les deux Amériques* [Paris: L. Tenré, 1836])

to ignore the fact that Santa Marta's governor, some officials of the treasury, and eminent white families and free people of color traded illegally and defrauded the royal coffers. At the end of the decade, smuggling received a new boost from Spain's suspension of free trade. By the same token, the detention of foreign ships in illegal waters and the confiscation of their cargo became a regular source of revenue for the city.[25]

Situated in a valley at the foot of the snow-covered Sierra Nevada, Valledupar developed late, after the mid-eighteenth-century campaigns of forced resettlement of arrochelados, palenqueros, and Chimila Indians who dominated the area. Following these campaigns, several whites received grants of land and founded cattle ranches and sugar haciendas using slave labor. According to the 1777–80 census, Valledupar's population of 3,677 exceeded that of Santa Marta. Two out of ten inhabitants were white, as many were slaves, and free people of color formed the remaining 58.2 percent.[26] One of Santa Marta's few bishops, as well as several hacendados linked to elite families in Santa Marta lived in Valledupar, attracted by the city's cooler climate, its crucial location on the viceroyalty's contraband route between Mompox and Riohacha, and its proximity to sugarcane, cattle ranching, and dyewood areas. Free people of color, largely zambos descendants of the palenqueros and the Chimila, also seized such opportunities, and the number of artisans and laborers grew steadily in the following decades. In addition to domestic service, transportation, street and market vending, and skilled trades, many worked in sugar production, particularly legal and illegal distillery, while others produced dry meat, lard, cheese, and hides.[27]

Finally, the port of Riohacha, on the Caribbean Sea, for which the 1777–80 census reported 1,515 inhabitants, was little more than a large village of low houses made of plaited cane and mud, covered with palm-leaf roofs. Few buildings reminded the visitor of Riohacha's previous opulence, when merchants and jewelers lived off the pearls gathered by Indian divers, with the exception of three run-down forts built in the late seventeenth century to protect the city from corsair attacks. As in Santa Marta, the port had no wharf, so ships had to cast anchor in the open sea. Local bogas transported passengers and merchandise from the ships to the city in small boats and canoes. Surrounded by mountains, notably the Sierra Nevada to the west and the south, and the desert Guajira Peninsula to the east, Riohacha had no safe route to Santa Marta except by sea or via Valledupar, its only door to the rest of the viceroyalty. Moreover, Riohacha's sandy soil proved inadequate for farming, which made its population dependent on the Wayúu Indians or on the city of Valledupar for food. The few whites residing in Riohacha (12.7 percent of the total inhabitants) were mostly men—sailors, merchants, smugglers, state and army officials, and a handful of priests—some of them with families. Blacks, mulattoes, and zambos largely outnumbered this white minority in a town where in the late 1770s as many as two out of three residents were free people of color, one out of four was a slave. Riohacha's slaves worked in domestic service and transportation, whereas the free population of color consisted of sailors, bogas, fishermen, muleteers, artisans, peddlers, and market vendors, among others, often linked to the illegal trade.[28]

Not surprisingly, the economy of Riohacha principally depended on contraband with the Caribbean islands, notably Curaçao and Jamaica. In fact, the illegal trade reached such high proportions that in 1789, in an attempt to curtail it, Spain again separated the provinces of Riohacha and Santa Marta and appointed a governor of Riohacha who was independent of the governor of Santa Marta. The new governor zealously seized foreign ships and cargoes, and persecuted smugglers and Indians. His actions antagonized everyone in the city, leading to his removal three years later. His successor, José Medina Galindo, took the opposite approach and closed his eyes to contraband. During the years of free trade, smuggling increased, as sailors, after unloading their legal cargo, secretly anchored near the port to discharge foreign products and to load dyewood, dry meat, horses, and mules. After war with Britain suspended free trade in 1796, contraband continued to expand. In reality, Riohacha's survival depended on maintaining both the illegal trade and the truce with the Wayúu, as the two were interdependent. By 1808 Governor Medina had become so blatantly involved in smuggling that Viceroy Amar suspended him and launched a full investigation into his activities.[29]

Caribbean New Granada's five major cities not only differed in their development, they also actively competed with each other. Since the sixteenth century, Santa Marta had resented Cartagena's monopoly of the Atlantic legal trade and its importance in the Crown's budget. As a result of Spain's neglect, Santa Marta turned to smuggling.[30] Santa Marta and Riohacha vied for both control of smuggling and Spain's extension of legal trade. Tensions between the two cities were further exacerbated by Riohacha's changing status as the Crown's means of eradicating contraband. In effect, from 1777 to 1789 Riohacha Province was united with Santa Marta Province and administered from Santa Marta's distant capital. After 1789, Riohacha returned to its former status as a separate province with its own governor.[31] Santa Marta was also challenged in its attempt to dominate the province by the more dynamic cities of Valledupar and Ocaña in the Andean interior. Similarly, Cartagena resented Mompox's late colonial growth and attempted by every possible means to keep the river city under its rule. In particular, when in 1776 the king approved the creation of a distinct province of Mompox, independent from Cartagena, and elevated Mompox to be its capital, rivalries between the governor of Cartagena and Mompox's corregidor and between the corregidor and the city's cabildo ruined the project.[32] Like Santa Marta, Mompox also complained about Cartagena's monopoly of the Atlantic trade. Moreover, it resented Cartagena's inability to keep the Canal del Dique navigable, to the detriment of the fluvial city's commerce.[33]

WHITE ELITES

In each city, the white elite remained far from united. Generally, relationships between Spanish authorities and local merchants and hacendados depended on Spain's trade policies and the governors' willingness to turn a blind eye to smuggling. When antagonized, local interests quickly responded with insulting broadsides and slanderous accusations.[34] Intra-elite divisions cut deeper in Cartagena and Mompox than in Santa Marta, Valledupar, and Riohacha, which were dominated by a few related families. Also, from the latter three cities only eleven creole sons of the elite studied at the Colegios Mayores de San Bartolomé and del Rosario in Bogotá after 1792, when the French and American Revolutions began to be debated. This was far less than the number from Cartagena and Mompox. No doubt, those who studied in Bogotá shied away from openly embracing the egalitarian principles of the French Assembly, the abolition of slavery, and racial equality. Yet some began to favor reform within the established system and to clash with the more traditional elite. In addition, the Declaration of the Rights of Man and Citizen, illegally translated in 1793 by *bogotano* Antonio Nariño, made its way to Cartagena and Mompox but did not reach the other cities.[35] *Momposinos* and cartageneros had more access than residents of the other cities to modern ideas and revolutionary news from Bogotá, the Caribbean, and Europe reported by free and slave sailors, bogas, merchants, or members of the elite. These ideas also had a stronger impact due to the presence of a local intelligentsia.[36] Elementary education was more available in Cartagena and Mompox than elsewhere. In fact, few residents of Santa Marta, Valledupar, and Riohacha could read and write, and fewer had higher training. According to the bishops who sporadically served Santa Marta, priests were remarkably ignorant. These cities had no printing presses, and few books and newspapers circulated.[37]

In Cartagena after 1789, differences between creoles and the more privileged Spanish-born tended to give way to differences founded on economic interests, as merchants and hacendados did not share common solutions to the economic crisis. Sugar producers hit hard by the importation of foreign liquor wanted protectionism in order to continue their monopoly on the production of cane alcohol for local markets. Only then, they argued, could they be wealthy enough to pay high taxes, finance the work of the church, give employment to the poor, and buy the luxurious goods legally imported from Spain—all to the great benefit of the royal treasury.[38] For their part, Cartagena's merchants, represented by the city's consulado de comercio, founded in 1795 with Spanish approval, stated that the chief brake on economic expansion was Spain's resistance to free trade and its system of taxes and state monopolies that hampered agricultural production and legal trade while stimulating contraband. Increasingly, some linked free trade to the broader issue of the province's economic and domestic autonomy from both Spain and Bogotá. In the 1800s the consulado's spokesman, José Ignacio de Pombo, repeatedly asked that New Granada be granted the same privileges as Cuba and Venezuela, whose economies had prospered since the diminution of monopolies and taxes. But such demands fell on deaf ears in Spain and elicited the opposition of the owners of slave haciendas. Moreover, the consulado antagonized New Granada's viceroy when it acquired a printing press to publicize its views without his authorization at a time when Spain was attempting to prevent the diffusion of new ideas.[39]

Similarly, in Mompox a new generation of slave-owning hacendados with interests in legal trade and smuggling, often the creole sons of noble Spaniards of recent immigration, began to gain power over the traditional landowning class represented by the marquis of Torre-Hoyos that had built its fortune on the campaigns of forced resettlement (see Chapter 2). Headed by Spanish merchant Pedro Martínez de Pinillos, they comprised such hacendados and merchants as Vicente Celedonio Gutiérrez de Piñeres and Pantaleón Germán Ribón, both lawyers trained in Bogotá. They bypassed the Sociedad Económica de Amigos del País (economic society of friends of the country), founded in Mompox by Spanish officials in 1784, which attempted to promote cotton growing with little success, and they established in 1796 a local deputation of Cartagena's consulado de comercio. This new generation of hacendados played a major role in politics by progressively controlling Mompox's cabildo and top royal positions. They reformed the city's culture by establishing a university college, several elementary schools, and charity institutions. In this endeavor, they found help from the city's new vicar, Juan Fernández de Sotomayor, and its new parish priest, Manuel Benito Revollo, both from Cartagena.[40]

Competition within the elite of Cartagena and Mompox often took the form of costly litigation. According to Governor Joaquín de Cañaverales, in the province of Cartagena "reside inequity, imposture, and calumny, where neither positions nor ranks have been respected."[41] In Mompox, the marquis of Torre-Hoyos (d. 1805) and cattle hacendados Pablo and Vicente García, father and son, repeatedly sued each other during the last decades of the colonial period. In 1798 the cabildo, then controlled by members of Mompox's newly established consulado de comercio, went so far as to challenge Gonzalo Josef de Hoyos's title of marquis of Torre-Hoyos on technical grounds.[42]

The overall effect of these political and personal disputes, clashing economic interests, and intercity rivalries was to hinder the small, urban, white elite class from dominating Caribbean New Granada, despite a weak church and state presence. Comparison with the white export planter class in Cuba and most of the Caribbean, which was able to impose some of its socioeconomic views on the metropolis, shows the limits of hacendados' and merchants' power in the provinces of Cartagena and Santa Marta. Furthermore, their correspondence to the Crown demonstrates their inability or unwillingness to articulate a racial ideology as a means of oppressing both slaves and free people of African descent, as their peers in several Caribbean islands and Venezuela did.[43] No doubt, racial divisions could have sharpened along Cuba's lines (whites versus people of color) had Madrid supported the creole governor of Santa Marta, Antonio de Narváez, in his promotion of tropical plantations based on massive imports of African slaves (see Chapter 2). Yet the waning of slavery in the region only partially explains the absence of clear-cut racial boundaries.

RACE AND STATUS

After the first decades of conquest, Spain experienced great difficulties in transferring the metropolis's three estates—nobles, clerics, and the large majority of commoners—and in establishing clear racial categories in its American colonies. More specifically in Caribbean New Granada, with scant Spanish immigration, non-noble whites had tended to assume a noble status on arriving in America. The mass inflow of African slaves and the decline of the original indigenous population in the early seventeenth century had resulted in the rapid growth of castas, among whom mixed African ancestry predominated. For demographic and cultural reasons, the castas had tended to form alternative sexual unions rather than marriages sanctioned by the church.

The Council of the Indies continuously attempted to clarify the blurred racial boundaries of Spanish Americans and to bring order to their sexual arrangements. The racial paradigm on which colonial society was founded credited whites, Indians, and their mestizo offspring with purity but attributed a permanent "depraved origin" to African slaves and their mixed or unmixed descendants. Also hereditarily degrading were illegitimate birth and the exercise of manual professions.[44] By law, proof of limpieza de sangre and legitimate birth were required for appointment to most civil, military, and church positions; for admission to secondary and higher education; for the legal exercise of some arts and crafts; and for all kinds of grants and honors.[45] A candidate of uncertain background had to produce various documents and provide numerous witnesses declaring that he or she was "considered white, honorable, clean of the bad races of blacks, Moors, Jews, newly converted to our holy faith, and punished by the holy office of the Inquisition and other courts."[46] Marriage was regulated by the 1778 Royal Pragmatic, which prohibited the alliance of partners of unequal class and status under age twenty-five without parental consent, making legal unions between whites and castas difficult. However, in line with Spain's treatment of people of African descent as "a very inferior species," the Royal Pragmatic did not apply to marriages among blacks, mulattoes, and zambos, considered depraved by nature, unless they were officers in the militia or had distinguished themselves by their excellent reputation and service.[47] In the early 1800s new regulations made marriages between castas and whites of noble status and/or legitimate birth contingent on licenses issued by the viceroyalties.[48]

In 1795 Madrid offered a way out of "the stain of slavery" to well-to-do individuals of mixed African ancestry by extending the sale of *gracias al sacar* (legitimations of status change) to pardos and *quinterones* (offspring of a quadroon and a white) seeking the status of whites. As shown by Ann Twinam, this decision did not reflect a change in Bourbon socioracial policy, but probably was the by-product of an attempt by royal accounting officers to improve revenue collection by putting together a price list of gracias al sacar based on recent practice.[49] Yet the decision threatened to destroy the racial paradigm on which colonial society was founded and was immediately opposed by some white creoles, notably in Venezuela, on the grounds that it would lead to "scandalous and subversive movements" and possibly a revolution led by pardo militiamen.[50] A growing number of dissatisfied whites protested that if many pardos began to apply for gracias al sacar, "believing that [these gracias] make them equal to whites without any other difference than the accident of their color," they would feel qualified for all positions and marriages with legitimate whites.

The Council of the Indies reacted with empathy and in 1806, in the context of Caribbean upheaval, agreed that to preserve "the political order," it was necessary to keep people of African descent in an inferior position. In an argument that racialized culture and politics, the council turned down the recommendation by a high religious dignitary in Guatemala that the Crown declare the free castas "equal to the class of Spanish commoners" in order to create new opportunities for them and free them from their "vices and disorders." In effect, the council ruled, it was not "color" that separated people of African descent from whites, Indians, and mestizos but the "stain of slavery" as well as their "corrupt customs, being most of them bastard, adulterous, and illegitimate." In addition, "because of their perverse character, their pride, and inclination to liberty, they have been and they are not fond of our government and nation."[51] Similarly, in 1807 the council refused to extend to its colonies an 1803 cédula that encouraged industry in Spain by declaring certain trades, such as that of blacksmith, tailor, shoemaker, and carpenter, "honest and honorable" and not degrading to artisans and their families. It argued that, because in the Americas most artisans were of mixed African ancestry, the cédula would encourage disorder and make the castas believe that they were free of their evil and infamous roots.[52] Paradoxically, these opinions were not followed by changes in the Spanish American defense system, which relied heavily on militiamen of African descent. Still, the 1806 ruling agreed to examine a few requests for gracias al sacar by castas with orderly behavior, fidelity to the king, and extraordinary merit and services, in view of their whitening. It also concluded that blacks and mulattoes who could rigorously document four generations of legitimate birth and freedom qualified for any trade or office open to commoners in Spain.[53] Thus, by singling out for royal privileges a small number of individuals of African ancestry who could prove exceptional merit and/or legitimate birth, the Crown thinned the upper strata of the urban population of color and demonstrated its fundamental opposition to the new principles of liberty, equality, and fraternity proclaimed by the French and the French Caribbean Revolutions.

Of course, Council of the Indies rulings on race and birth status could not be fully obeyed in Caribbean New Granada, where the pool of whites able to prove limpieza de sangre and legitimate birth was simply too small. In the countryside the population was overwhelmingly of African descent, illegal sexual unions were plentiful, and state and church officials were too few to implement Spain's policies; in villages with few or no whites, men of African descent were destined to hold higher positions. In the principal cities, not only did blacks, mulattoes, and zambos constitute the majority, but also this majority comprised many more women than men.[54] Consequently, the chances of women of color finding a partner in their own socioracial category were limited, leading to a high frequency of single motherhood and illegitimate unions. In Cartagena, especially, in the late 1770s, one mother out of five was a single parent.[55] Thus, many children of African descent suffered from the double handicap of "bad race" and illegitimacy, whereas a majority of white children had legally married parents.[56] Over time, Indians, Spaniards, and Africans had mixed to such an extent that it was often impossible to differentiate a "pure" mestizo from a "depraved" mulatto, zambo, or quadroon on the basis of "the signs of color, hair, and physiognomy," as recommended by the Council of the Indies.[57] Moreover, obedience to these rulings in a region where military defense and economic production depended almost entirely on people of African descent could prove dangerous. Elite whites were so conscious of this reality that, unlike their peers in Venezuela, they did not challenge the 1795 extension of gracias al sacar to pardos and seldom questioned the tenure of offices or grants by mulattoes solely on account of their race.[58]

Classification by race and birth status therefore proved fuzzy in Caribbean New Granada's cities. According to Adolfo Meisel Roca and María Aguilera Díaz, in Cartagena's 1777 census 1,080 individuals were called *don* or *doña*, a title usually reserved for whites of legitimate birth. Among them, 241 (22.3 percent) were free persons of color, all residents of the artisan barrio of Santo Toribio.[59] Such a high proportion demonstrates that well before the 1795 royal decision on gracias al sacar, there existed pardos of higher status in Cartagena and other Caribbean New Granadan cities. Quite likely, these individuals, who otherwise could have provided leadership for "scandalous and subversive movements," ceased to identify with common libres de color.[60]

In reality, in every city in the region some light-skinned libres de color passed for white (blancos de la tierra), a phenomenon already highlighted in the mid-eighteenth century by Spanish travelers Jorge Juan and Antonio de Ulloa, who explained that some of Cartagena's white families were "intertwined with [families] of castas or originated from them."[61] Moreover, there were mulatto or zambo clerks, notaries, and captains of justice.[62] Until the late eighteenth century Spain viewed professions such as surgeon or teacher degrading, enabling some pardos to get the appropriate training and to work in these occupations.[63] For example, Manuel Antonio Gasterbondo and his sons were medical doctors. A few pardos, like Laureano Faris, owner of three slaves, were merchants.[64] Given the scarcity of religious vocations in Caribbean Colombia, some quadroons and mulattoes could overcome their "bad race" to become lower servants of the church. According to Bishop Díaz de Lamadrid, "one can see in the streets [of Cartagena] dark-skinned mulattoes and blacks professed in the religion of Saint Francis."[65] This was one of the reasons he gave in 1794 for accepting María Juliana as a lay nun in the city's convent of Santa Clara, despite the fact that her mother was a mulatto and her father was unknown. Other reasons cited by the bishop for pardoning the young woman's color and illegitimacy were that her sponsors offered a dowry of one thousand pesos and three prominent witnesses testified to her excellent behavior and habits. Moreover, he probably took into account that allegedly a cleric had fathered her.[66] As most mulattoes in positions legally reserved for whites had been sponsored by white aristocrats, they generally became part of the latter's patronage network and did not directly challenge white power. Moreover, they had little in common with the numerous free blacks and mulattoes who worked as day laborers, porters, peddlers, or washerwomen, for example, and whose harsh lives resembled those of slaves.

The bishops of Caribbean New Granada were unable to force their flocks to respect the Royal Pragmatic. In the early 1800s one bishop campaigned against "the frequent abuse among minors of contracting unequal marriages without waiting for paternal consent." He claimed to know of seven documented cases in Cartagena and more to come. Arguing that such marriages threatened parental authority, public tranquility, and the order of the state as well as the spirit of the church, he requested that Madrid authorize monetary penalties and prison terms for offenders, "because people pay very little attention to the ... penalty of excommunication." Madrid refused, simply recommending increased church vigilance.[67] Although the bishop did not refer explicitly to interracial marriage, his claim shows that, even among the white elite, marriage norms were not always respected.

Nevertheless, that some individuals of partial African ancestry and illegitimate birth could pass for white or gain positions of higher status did not mean that in the region's cities there were no sharp distinctions between whites and nonwhites and between legitimate and illegitimate children or that prejudice did not exist. Quadroon nun María Juliana paid a high personal price for the bishop's favor. Although welcomed by the convent's mother superior and her entourage, she became the scapegoat of other nuns who accused her of destroying the convent's good reputation for being "the bastard daughter of a cleric who had taken vows of chastity and a mulatto mother." The nuns repeatedly petitioned the governor and the royal audiencia for her removal. Although in 1797 the Council of the Indies ruled in María Juliana's favor and recommended that the rebel nuns learn to live in Christian peace, it is unlikely that her suffering ended there.[68] Those pardos and zambos who became notaries, clerks, or justices were often stigmatized for their race and, when it applied, their illegitimate birth.[69]

The racial and birth origins of prospective students and professors at Cartagena's College and Seminary of San Carlos, established in 1786, were strictly scrutinized. In 1801, for example, the request of don Josef Noble, a white cartagenero, that his sons from his legitimate marriage to a quadroon be declared octoroon (*octavones*), thus "free of the origin of pardos," and admitted to the college was not granted until he had documented his wife's legitimacy and racial status.[70] In the same year a conflict broke out at the seminary when a new professor of philosophy was to be selected from a pool of four applicants, among them Pedro Carracedo, a mulatto whose mother was the illegitimate daughter of a black woman. Interestingly, Carracedo's race had not prevented him from graduating from the Seminary of San Bartolomé and the Thomistic University in Bogotá. Also, his father had become an attorney (*procurador*) despite being a "reputed mulatto." Carracedo's candidacy was approved by the bishop of Cartagena, who thought his titles and qualifications sufficient. But it was vigorously opposed by Juan Fernández de Sotomayor, who briefly taught at San Carlos before becoming the vicar of Mompox, on the grounds of Carracedo's "impure" birth.[71] Sometimes illegitimacy was pardoned but race was not. When the bishop opened a small orphanage in Cartagena in 1791, the king granted his request that all foundlings be presumed to be of legitimate birth—a pioneer decision that was extended to other Spanish colonies by a royal cédula in 1794. However, the bishop stipulated different dowries for those foundlings who later legally married—300 pesos for the pardos and 500 pesos for the whites—and only if they married partners in the same racial category.[72]

In the cities of Caribbean New Granada, race, class, and birth status clearly mattered. The 1777–80 census shows that whites and free people of color lived side by side in the same streets and often in the same residential units, but it also exhibits a socioracial hierarchy corresponding to residence.[73] In Cartagena, for example, the closer the unit was to the Plaza Mayor, the Governor's Palace, and the Cathedral, the more likely it was to be headed by a white man living with numerous slaves and his close family members. In contrast, the farther they lived from the city center, the darker the residents.[74] For Getsemaní, it is possible to extrapolate from the limited number of slaves (5 percent of its population) and of persons identified as don or doña that primarily lower-class free persons of color inhabited the suburb.[75]

In Cartagena, people showed a preference for endogamous legal marriages. Whites tended to marry whites; quadroons, quadroons; pardos, pardos; zambos, zambos; blacks, blacks; free, free; and slaves, slaves. In fact, a few decades earlier Juan and Ulloa noted that castas attached much importance to racial hierarchy—for example, they considered it an insult to treat a quinterón as a cuarterón.[76] Analyzing Santa Marta's marriage registers, Saether also observes endogamy among samario whites. Among the elite, race, class, and birth status counted in the selection of a partner, whereas among non-noble whites, race seemed to matter most, as several creole women married Spaniards of lower economic status. However, among free people of color, he notes that several pardo women married poor Spanish newcomers, a fact probably linked to the excess of females in the population of African descent.[77]

Furthermore, racial categories often came with certain economic attributes, indicating a clear hierarchy of occupations corresponding with the color hierarchy. According to the returns of the 1777 census for Cartagena, some jobs involving hard manual labor, such as mason and carpenter, were overwhelmingly held by black men; such work was also performed by some men of mixed ancestry but no whites. More skilled professions, such as those of barber and tailor, were predominantly the province of mulattoes and a few whites, but no blacks, whereas storekeepers and bakers were usually white or in a few cases men of mixed ancestry but, again, not black. Slave ownership was not the privilege of any racial group, but the whiter the head of household, the more likely he or she was to own slaves. Whites tended to own more slaves than persons of mixed African ancestry, whereas there were only a handful of black slaveowners and these had no more than one or two slaves. Yet the mere fact that in the popular barrio of Santo Toribio, for example, one out of seven households of color included slaves shows the complexity of a socioracial hierarchy in which race, status, and class did not always overlap.

Ethnicity also mattered. Despite the waning of the slave trade after the 1640s, the African-born were still noticeable in the city: the Loangos, Ararás, Jojós, Minas, Karabalís, Lucumís, and Chalás all had *cabildos de nación* where they met. These mutual aid societies, originally supported by Spain to promote Christianity while maintaining divisions among the African slaves, allowed descendants of distinct African ethnic identity to perpetuate part of their cultural heritage. In the late 1770s a dispute between the Bibi and the Briche Karabalí cabildos, in which members, many of them bozales working on the fortifications, accused one another of disturbing the public order, prompted the governor to close all of them temporarily. African presence in the cabildos probably increased in the 1790s, when hundreds of bozales were legally imported to Cartagena, where some of them made their home.[78]

According to the childhood memories of General Joaquín Posada Gutié-rrez (b. 1797), several patterns displayed by the 1777 census still prevailed in early-nineteenth-century Cartagena. In February, during the carnival of the Virgin of the Candelaria, patroness of the city, each racial category occu-pied a specific space and celebrated the virgin in a particular way. Wealthy whites, pardos, mulattoes, zambos, and blacks went to Pie de la Popa at the foot of the hill where the convent venerating the virgin stood. Poor whites and quadroons remained in Cartagena. The aristocracy and free people of color of some means organized dances in a ballroom in Pie de la Popa, in which whites from Castile, pardos, and blacks took turns, without mixing. "The poor and shoeless, free and slave, pardo or black," danced outside, beneath the sky, "to the sound of the African drum." Indians participated with their own dances, which they performed to the sound of *gaitas* (long flutes). Within the city walls, poor whites and blancos de la tierra of some means, such as physicians, pharmacists, painters, silversmiths, and shop-keepers, organized separate dances in their homes, a tradition also followed by the "very poor quadroons" who made up most of the city's dressmakers, seamstresses, and cigar makers.[79] Class thus divided people within the same racial category.

Posada's reminiscences indicate that those whose economic circum-stances clearly questioned the sociracial hierarchy—poor whites and light-skinned mulattoes of some means—segregated themselves or were segre-gated from the main festivities. Only poor people of color, free and slave, seemed to intermingle. However, African-born slaves and some of their off-spring generally organized along ethnic lines in their cabildos de nación, wearing traditional ceremonial costumes and body paint. Sometimes hier-archies momentarily vanished. During the celebration of the Virgin of the Candelaria, since not everyone could fit into the churches to say the novena, the wealthy who had oratories in their homes welcomed rich and poor alike without color or status restrictions. On the last day of the carnival, people of all races and classes met in Pie de la Popa—the wealthy richly dressed, the poor clothed with "meticulous neatness," and slaves wearing some of their masters' garments and jewelry—to attend mass and climb in an orderly pro-cession up to the convent. The members of the African cabildos de nación danced all the way, headed by their elected kings and queens with magnifi-cent umbrellas. Then each returned to his or her own group to celebrate and dance until dawn, when all hierarchies were reestablished, and the slaves returned the borrowed clothing and jewels to their masters.[80] No doubt, on this festive day the free and the slave, the poor and the more affluent could forget their hardships and envision equality.

Similar commemorations occasionally brought people closer together while still respecting the socioracial hierarchy, notably on a city's patron day or during Holy Week. In Mompox, the hooded penitents who carried the ceremonial floats and led the processions were rich whites and poor men of color drawn from numerous racially inclusive cofradías.[81] Santa Marta observed the birthday of the Spanish king, Spain's declaration of war against France in 1808, and a significant Spanish victory over Napoleon's troops the following year with huge, popular celebrations including a Te Deum mass, fireworks, and a procession.[82] In Mompox in 1808, the milicia de todos los colores, church and royal officials, and the wealthy honored Spain with a banquet, while all of the town's vecinos and inhabitants showed their love of Spain. "Even the youngsters distinguished themselves with enthusiasm, and each woman wore on her left arm and on her head a red bow with . . . an emblem in the center that sai[d] 'Long live Ferdinand VII!' imitating the men who put it on their hats."[83] Beyond expressing fidelity to the king, these observances strengthened the hierarchical bonds of each urban community.

In addition, racial mixing was frequent. Churches were not segregated. According to Mollien, this often put mulatto women in competition with white women, because, unlike in the United States, "all pray to God together, regardless of color, and people would not be long to rise up if the authority posted on a church door: *Today instruction for the men of colour.*"[84] During religious and patriotic celebrations, the guilds of the merchants, the artisans, the navy register (matrícula de mar), cofradías, arsenal workers (*maestranzas*), and militiamen attended mass and marched in processions. Although the merchant guild comprised almost exclusively Spaniards and white creoles, the other associations were racially mixed.[85] For example, in Santo Toribio in 1777 the navy register included members of all racial categories.[86] As a result, crossracial and crossclass relations were multiple, though not egalitarian.

Nevertheless, the urban population had some mundane opportunities to challenge socioracial hierarchies. When a wealthy person died, the family displayed the body for at least twenty-four hours; during this time relatives, neighbors, and employees of the dead, rich and poor, visited the departed and consumed food and liquor. Dressed in black, groups of lower-class women of color came, one after the other, to mourn and drink, alternately weeping and shouting furiously, to which the audience responded by calling the name of the deceased. According to Juan and Ulloa, "They continued to refer to all of his or her good and bad qualities when he or she was alive, without changing their tone and placidness, and without excepting from this lamentable report those impure customs or weaknesses which they knew with all the details and circumstances so that one could not be more personal even in a general confession." When no more mourners came from the street, the house's female slaves and servants continued the mourning and shouting until dawn.[87] Such ceremonies allowed not only for intense socioracial mixing but also for lower-class and slave women to express their love, hate, anger, or disrespect toward a rich individual or the wealthy in general. More commonly, carnivals and celebrations were emblematic of the complexity of race relations in Caribbean New Granada. On the one hand, they created and reinforced hierarchy and division, and bonded the community. On the other hand, they did not clearly separate the population along racial and class lines and offered temporary outlets for criticism and nonconformity.

MILITIAMEN OF COLOR

Another institution exemplifying the fuzziness of the socioracial hierarchy in the cities was the urban disciplined militia formed in the 1770s. The militia comprised mostly free men of color, as many among the minority of Spanish and white creole residents belonged to the professions exempted from recruitment or avoided service. Although service in the militia could imply sacrifice, especially when it entailed missions away from the city, it also gave men of African descent a higher status in the community, because only able and self-supporting men could enlist. Moreover, the Crown extended to militiamen the military *fuero* (judicial prerogative allowing officers and enlisted men to present causes before military tribunals rather than before royal or ordinary tribunals) and some corporate privileges that limited the authority that the cabildo and alcaldes ordinarios had over them.[88] The extension of military privileges to men of color was prompted by Spain's need to entrust part of the defense of the Caribbean Coast and its frontier to its African-derived population (rather than the result of new colonial social policies challenging the inferior status of castas). However, full equality did not exist among whites and men of color. By law, pardo officers could not be promoted to positions higher than captain, though after 1800 with Spain's increasing reliance on them, some advanced further.[89] Nevertheless, extension of the military fuero, which occurred with the reorganization of racially based militias into companies of all colors everywhere except in Cartagena, further blurred racial boundaries.

Not surprisingly, Cartagena was the only city where racial distinctions were maintained in the militia until the end of the colonial period. Moreover, only Cartagena garrisoned a substantial regular army to reinforce its militia. In 1789, for example, the militia consisted of one infantry regiment of whites, one infantry battalion of pardos, and two artillery companies— one of pardos, the other of morenos. The Crown had difficulty recruiting Spaniards and white creoles for Cartagena's white regiment, because many were legally exempted or avoided the militia by enlisting in the less demanding navy register, created by Spain in 1775 to organize a coast guard. By law, all men earning their living from the sea had to register in order to legally pursue their industry, but people from other professions, such as silversmiths, bakers, and grocers, also enlisted in the navy register, which in 1781 claimed over three thousand men for Cartagena and the surrounding area.[90] The city's militia thus did not correspond to a strict racial segregation but to a color continuum, from the lighter militia of whites, the mostly mixed militia of pardos, and the darker moreno militia of artillery. According to the 1780 census of the city's artisans, the militia of whites included Spaniards and white creoles as well as some quadroons, mulattoes, pardos, zambos, and a handful of blacks, whereas the militia of pardos comprised quadroons, mulattoes, pardos, zambos, and blacks. The militia of artillery included darker-skinned people—predominantly blacks, together with some mulattoes and pardos.[91] Cartagena was the only city in Caribbean New Granada where the formation of the militia reflected the racial and class hierarchy within the population of African descent already exhibited by the 1777 census. For the men of color who managed to belong to the militia of whites, new opportunities, perhaps also a modification of their racial classification and a new white identity, could result from such enlistment.

In contrast, the cities of Santa Marta and Riohacha counted solely on a poorly armed and trained militia for their defense, whereas Valledupar and Mompox had no militia units of their own until the late 1790s. In Santa Marta and Valledupar, where the white minority comprised mostly men in the professions exempted from enlistment, the division into white and pardo units proved illusory. As most militiamen were zambos, mulattoes, and blacks, in 1784 the militia was reformed into companies of all colors. After the resumption of war with Britain in 1796, Madrid requested that

Uniform of the mulatto and black militiamen of the artillery of Cartagena de Indias. (Courtesy of the Archivo General de Indias, Seville)

New Granada's immense Caribbean Coast be protected from possible British invasion by native troops. However, since the Haitian Revolution was raging, it opposed the enlistment of more men of African descent, despite Viceroy Mendinueta's assurance that, with the exception of a few "perverse spirits," these New Granadans were more loyal to Spain than those from the Andean interior. By 1799 the Crown recognized that its only option was to accept the viceroy's plan to form two militia units of all colors in the defenseless cities of Valledupar and Mompox, on the only route between the vulnerable port of Riohacha and Andean New Granada.[92]

Caribbean New Granada's free men of color agreed to enlist in the militia—despite the risks and drain on personal income caused by military expeditions—for complex reasons. In a society that legally excluded men of African descent from the most distinguished professions and positions, the militia offered one of the few avenues of social advancement. It enabled some men from the countryside and small towns to settle, often with their families, in a city offering greater opportunities. Given the flexibility of racial categories, a few light-skinned artisans registered in Cartagena's white militia may eventually have passed for white. In addition, a limited number of them were promoted to officer rank with some benefits. Although the "stain of slavery" prohibited pardo militiamen from ascending to ranks higher than captain, after many years of impeccable service, lower-ranking officers of African descent received a monthly pension. Fifteen years of duty yielded between 6 and 9 silver reales monthly; twenty-five years, up to 90 reales—more than the average income of a silversmith.[93] Promotion was not easily gained, as shown by the career of Ignacio Xavier de Castro, a house painter from Mompox, who described himself as "color trigueño" (literally, wheat-colored).[94] In 1773, at age twenty-five, Castro enlisted for eight years in the militia, for which he received 20 pesos. Three years later he was promoted successively to corporal, first sergeant, and second sergeant within six months but was then prevented from receiving higher promotions because of his race. In 1784, however, for some unknown reason, Castro was indicted, stripped of his rank, and returned to the position of ordinary soldier. In 1787, in a new reversal of fortune, he was promoted to corporal again, then to sergeant, and finally, in 1794, to first sergeant in the staff of Cartagena's battalion of free pardos. In 1798, "with robustness and agility to continue in the armed service," he successfully requested a monthly allowance of 90 reales after twenty-five years of duty.[95] But few men of African descent became lower-ranking officers. As indicated by the service records of Cartagena's pardo militia, most noncommissioned officers were Spanish or white creole; less than 25 percent were "plebeian" or "common" and possibly of color.[96]

A greater incentive for enlistment was the royal grant of the military fuero to militiamen regardless of race, because men of African descent could expect to be treated more fairly by corporate military courts than by ordinary courts enforcing racially biased criminal codes. The fuero also exempted militiamen of African descent from paying the casta tribute, but the exemption had no effect in New Granada, where this tribute was not collected.[97] In fact, when Viceroy Mendinueta advocated the formation of a milicia de todos los colores in Mompox, he went so far as to state that these casta militiamen, like those in Valledupar, should be granted the military fuero, because "without this distinction and incentive they will not submit to the instruction and order necessary to serve with usefulness should the opportunity arise." Eventually, Spain agreed.[98] Moreover, since the militia was considerably bigger in the Caribbean region than in Andean New Granada, it gave militiamen of African origin a sense of importance compared to the mostly mestizo militia in the interior, which the Cartagena militiamen acknowledged by agreeing to participate in the repression of the Comunero

Revolt in 1781. Belonging to the urban militia put free men of color in a position of power vis-à-vis the lowest strata of society: the free destitute, slaves, and Indians.[99] Solidarity with the lower classes could also be hampered by the fact that many militiamen were artisans with small businesses that tied them to white contractors and customers, making them part of vertical crossracial patronage networks.[100]

Awareness of their special status in colonial society also forged a corporate identity among militiamen of all colors and diminished their sense of subordination to whites. Indeed, with the scant presence of Spanish soldiers and white resistance to enlistment, the defense of the Caribbean Coast depended on the goodwill of militiamen of African descent. This put them in a unique position of relative power in Spanish America, one they shared only with Venezuelan pardo militiamen. Caribbean New Granada's governors knew that, in the context of the Haitian Revolution, any provocation could transform militiamen's goodwill into urban revolt. Thus, many of Spain's humiliating regulations aimed at disallowing "the typical arrogance that these pardos usually demonstrate," such as the obligation to wear particular ribbons and belts to be distinguishable from slaves, as in Mexico, were not enforced in the Caribbean region. Viceroy Mendinueta and Anastasio Zejudo, the governor of Cartagena Province, were so conscious of the fact that unnecessary discrimination could threaten the security of New Granada that, when in 1794 Madrid suspended the right of pardo, but not white, officers to wear the same insignia as veteran officers, they neglected to apply it to the officers of African descent in Cartagena's pardo battalion, despite the protest of the war secretary.[101] In 1799 the viceroy and the governor renewed their tactful concern for the pride of militiamen of color in the wake of the alleged slave conspiracy in Cartagena by publicly rewarding Manuel Yturen, the pardo corporal who had denounced it, with a promotion to sergeant. They asked Madrid to award him a Merit Medal and grant him a permanent salary even when he was no longer in active service. Zejudo thought that with such a "dignified example," the love for and gratitude to the king of all pardo militiamen would be "strengthened and stimulated," which were keys to "the conservation of these dominions."[102] Mendinueta believed that such a generous gesture would have an incommensurable effect on "this very numerous class of people of color in that province who so far have not belied their loyalty, and whose corruption would be of irreparable consequence." He added that the privilege of a permanent salary would be economical, because Yturen's race excluded him from higher promotion and because he would almost always be on active duty.[103] Spain granted Yturen the medal and the permanent salary.[104]

In sum, although militiamen of African descent were still not equal to whites, their legal status challenged the racial order and gave them more privileges than other castas. At the same time, they had a stake in colonial society that, despite the concerns of Zejudo and Mendinueta, made it unlikely that they would autonomously revolt.

WOMEN OF COLOR

Colonial hierarchies were also challenged by the preponderance of black and mulatto women in the urban population. Most travelers to Caribbean New Granada's cities noticed the activity of slave and free women of African descent in the streets and markets. At the same time, they stressed that white women seldom left their homes except to go to mass accompanied by a female slave—a habit Frenchman Mollien attributed to their desire for entertainment rather than to their devotion.[105] Indeed, women of color contributed in extensive and diverse ways to the economy of cities. The gender imbalance in the urban population characterized by the prevalence of women of working age, notably of African descent, was not unique to Caribbean New Granada but was manifest in other cities of the Americas. Despite the scarcity of sources documenting motivations, several factors seem to explain female migration to urban areas. Cities offered women greater security, autonomy, and economic opportunities in domestic service and the markets than small towns and villages. Some rural parents placed their teenaged daughters as servants for urban families. Masters sometimes shifted urban male slaves to their haciendas and rural female slaves to their urban residences when individuals in both groups reached their teenage years. This enhanced slave women's possibilities to manumit themselves.

Young urban free men of color tended to follow the opposite path, as they went to small towns and the countryside looking for employment in trades, clerical work, mining, ranching, and agriculture.[106] Other men in search of greater independence left for the vast uncontrolled hinterland.[107] Urban men also tended to express their nonconformity and rebelliousness by individually escaping to the unconquered frontier and the Caribbean Sea, notably through enlistment on ships.[108] In other words, urban gender imbalance was the result of two processes: female immigration and male departure.

Market in Mompox. (Alcide Dessalines d' Orbigny, *Voyage pittoresque dans les deux Amériques* [Paris: L. Tenré, 1836])

The predominance of women in the urban labor force probably increased the traditional gap between male and female income levels. Lower incomes particularly affected women heads of household, such as single mothers and widows. Discriminated against on the basis of race, gender, and in many cases marital status, women of color developed adaptive strategies to make ends meet. Some rented rooms or beds in their homes, sold meals, or took in relatives from the countryside. A handful prospered, such as sixty-year-old mulatto Barthola Vallesteros, whose large household in Cartagena included the two daughters she was raising as a single mother, a tenant family, and eleven slaves.[109] Some women of color deliberately conducted their lives autonomously, ignoring the norms of the Catholic Church that prized marriage and subordination to patriarchy. Others showed resilience and an acute understanding of the complexities of their society. Such was the case of María Gervasia Guillén, caught in 1796, during a crackdown on illegal trade, with a *negrito* who carried a large quantity of fabrics and yarn presumed to be contraband. The black boy escaped, but she declared that the package was hers and was jailed. In her words, she was "free, born in Guinea, status single, occupation before cook and washerwoman and now because of her poor eyesight selling goods in the streets." About forty years old, she was the single mother of a daughter. Although her record does not mention how she gained her freedom, it provides a portrait of a woman with skills and determination. To all police questions beyond her identity, Guillén responded that she did not know the answer. After twelve days in jail, she obtained a release on account of sickness on the bail of a white man. As most of the fabrics seized at her arrest proved to be imported legally, she argued that "because of my sex and natural stupidity as a black woman of pure blood (*negra de casta*), I have to be believed ignorant of the nature of the articles prohibited from trade and of the laws and royal dispositions against those who buy and sell them, and if I am considered deserving some penalty, the imprisonment I have suffered with no few hardships and awareness should be sufficient." The court acknowledged her innocence but refused to return the legally imported fabrics seized from her. Not content with this ruling, Guillén unsuccessfully appealed to the royal audiencia for the recovery of her goods.[110] Although she probably acted on the advice of the defender of the poor (*defensor de los pobres*), she showed not only her astuteness but also her ability to protect by silence her business network, from the sailors who sold her the fabrics to her clients and protectors.

Like male artisans, many free and slave women of color cultivated, through their businesses, relationships with members of the elite, who could offer patronage, become the godparents of their children, and help them in difficult moments. In addition, women of color were often protected by kinsfolk. Godmothers and godfathers not only sponsored the baptized child but also provided a supportive network for the child's parents. Although godparents tended to be of the same status as the child's parents or the child's aunts or uncles, in other cases they belonged to the elite, probably as a means of securing employment or business relationships. According to Cartagena's baptismal records, the godparents of slave children were sometimes slaves in the same household, or other slaves, but more frequently free persons of color. Occasionally, some were whites of higher status but never the children's owners. Reflecting the importance of women in urban society, when baptisms were sponsored by a single godparent, the godparent was more likely to be a woman than a man.[111]

Kinship and extended family also probably accounted for the low incidence of child abandonment among the population of color in Caribbean

New Granada's cities—apparently less than 5 percent of the baptisms were of foundlings.[112] In contrast, during the same period Spanish, French, and Italian cities had rates of 20 to 43 percent of child abandonment.[113] If we accept John Boswell's conclusion that child abandonment increased in Europe not only because of famine, plagues, and war, but also because of the rigid sexual restrictions and purity of lineage imposed by the Catholic Church, we can hypothesize that the lesser impact of Catholic marriage norms on the population of African descent fostered a more generous acceptance of children regardless of the conditions of their birth.[114] In 1791 Cartagena's first royal orphanage registered only nineteen babies, both whites and castas, who were cared for by wet nurses for a monthly salary of seven pesos.[115] Women of color were reputedly charitable, and the number of destitutes in city streets declined thanks to their initiative. Mid-eighteenth-century Spanish travelers Juan and Ulloa admired the disinterest of "the free black and mulatto women . . . who pick up, take to their homes, and assist" newly arrived fugitive and vagrant Spaniards, who were left to sleep under the squares' arcades because merchants would not hire them and the hospital for the poor refused them shelter. Although some women may have acted out of hope of becoming their wives, Juan and Ulloa thought, most considered these men too miserable to marry and worked hard through their networks to find them employment outside of the city.[116] Nevertheless, because free and slave women of African descent largely outnumbered men in each socioracial category, some of them formed liaisons and had children with white men, which contributed to racial fuzziness. Women of African descent's sexual unions with white men, reliance on white patronage, and kinship relations, together with charity, reoriented overall urban mobilization toward strategies of protest and resistance that were not overtly confrontational.

SLAVES

Caribbean cities comprised numerous slaves who toiled in numerous jobs. In the late 1770s, on average one out of six urban inhabitants was a slave. In all households of some means, slaves performed domestic tasks that were considered degrading and unsuitable for whites and prominent persons of color.[117] As cartagenera doña Michaela Sánchez expressed it in 1788, she needed her black slave Rafaela de Genes released from jail "because as I am not made to cook, wash, or [do] other servile jobs, I see myself forced to beg for someone to charitably do it for me."[118] Transportation,

to which [these slaves] were accustomed."[122] Despite prompt security measures, two slave conspirators managed to escape capture and burned a hacienda in the vicinity of Cartagena. One week after the discovery of the alleged plot, Zejudo proudly informed Viceroy Mendinueta that the arrest of the French blacks and other suspects "has not caused the slightest sign of unreasonableness or discontent among the remaining Blacks . . . entertained [sic] in their respective occupations."[123] Nevertheless, Zejudo asked for additional troops from Spain to reinforce the military presence along the Caribbean Coast, so far mostly comprised of "dull" natives who could easily "become corrupted by the detestable maxims of liberty and disobedience."[124]

Most annoying to the governor was the fact that the black artillery sergeant and the slave sailors implicated in the alleged conspiracy requested the military fuero in order to be prosecuted by military justice. Zejudo predicted a lengthy process in which some defendants would be sentenced by military judges, others by civil judges, when swift and exemplary justice in a single trial was necessary. His opinion was countered by the viceroy, who favored letting justice follow its normal course.[125] In the end, Zejudo prevailed. The black artillery sergeant and slave sailors received no mercy. Their alleged conspiracy was linked to a plot discovered on 19 May 1799 in Maracaibo, on the Caribbean Coast of Venezuela. This plot involved two mulatto French captains, their black and mulatto crew, and the pardo second lieutenant of the city's pardo militia who allegedly intended to "introduce in [the city of Maracaibo] the same system of freedom and equality that has reduced to total ruin . . . the French ports of the island of Saint Domingue."[126] As a result, the Council of War in Madrid denied the defendants in Cartagena the military fuero and demanded their prompt condemnation and execution. Arguing that these slaves "were from the French colonies, where in past disturbances they learned false ideas of freedom," the council also ordered strict obedience to the royal decree of 1791 prohibiting the importation of foreign slaves not born in Africa to prevent the ideological "contamination" of Spanish American ports. Such slaves already in the Spanish colonies should be isolated from others of similar origin and subjected to the special vigilance of their masters, who should report suspicious slaves and relinquish them to the authorities if necessary.[127]

Aside from the alleged conspiracy in Cartagena, there is no indication of the collective mobilization of slaves in Caribbean New Granada's cities. In 1793 a series of fires destroyed more than four hundred houses in Mompox, which Orlando Fals Borda has attributed to runaway slaves attempting to prevent punitive expeditions against them or to slaves from noble mom-posino families taking revenge against their masters, or to a combination of the two. Fals, however, provides no evidence of slave agency except that the arsons were named "the fires of Juan Santiago" for the slave who reported them to his master; the culprit could never be determined, despite the efforts of the city's alcalde, the marquis of Torre-Hoyos.[128] In reality, urban slaves were scattered throughout the cities, making concerted action difficult. Many lived separately from their masters, sometimes in couples; although they were required to make fixed payments to their owners, they enjoyed a certain degree of independence that they would probably have hesitated to risk.[129]

That urban slaves did not collectively rebel does not mean that they did not struggle against bondage individually, in families, or in small groups, like their peers in the countryside. The main difference between urban and rural slaves was that flight was less risky in the countryside, whereas legal means such as self-purchase and the denouncement of abusive masters were more feasible in cities, where slaves were less isolated and earned higher wages.[130] Traditionally, manumission, especially *coartación* (self-purchase), had been relatively available to slaves, contributing to the rapid growth of the free population of color in Caribbean New Granada during the colonial period. In cities, many slave men and women obtained daily wages for their hard work, of which they paid a certain amount to their owners and supported themselves with the rest. Some were able to save enough money to purchase their freedom at their appraised price.[131] On average, urban slaves on wages had to save for ten to fifteen years to buy their freedom — half the amount of time required for rural slaves. According to Dolcey Romero, in the city of Santa Marta, which recorded 571 slaves in the late 1770s, a total of 32 men, 64 women, and 16 children were manumitted from 1791 to 1810, 84.8 percent of them through purchase, the remaining as a result of their masters' goodwill. In the first group about two-thirds of the slaves bought their own freedom, and most of the others were manumitted by their enslaved or free mother. Although manumission figures for other Caribbean New Granadan cities are currently unavailable, data for other Spanish American cities indicate a similar pattern, with slave women who bought their own freedom comprising the majority of the manumissions (a trend consistent with women outnumbering men in urban slavery).[132] A setback in the process occurred in 1788, when Spain ruled that the children of mothers who had bought their own freedom (*coartadas*) must remain in bondage.[133] Then, a revision of the alcabala ordered by the visitor general in the late 1770s, which imposed a tax on the sale of slaves, as José Ignacio de Pombo put it, "made it harder, and even impossible, for many unhappy slaves not only to be able to acquire their freedom but also to get out from under the power of cruel and tyrannical masters."[134]

Pombo alluded to the option of slaves to legally denounce their master or mistress for maltreatment in order to be appraised and sold to another master. Short of bringing freedom, this action, if successful, allowed slaves to get out of situations of unbearable abuse. However, it required the slaves first to escape their master's vigilance and then to have some savings or sponsorship, since no legal action was free of charge.[135] In the city of Cartagena in 1781, in a case of extreme cruelty, slave Gertrudis Subisa obtained a rare outcome when Governor Juan Pimienta ordered her owner, doña Juana María Sáenz de Maza, to grant her freedom and a small pension. For some time, Sáenz de Maza had subjected Subisa to such torture that she had scars and purulent wounds all over her body. Subisa's last punishment had been "so extreme that it was publicized in the whole city and put her at serious risk of death." She was transported, "all covered with blood," to a neighbor's house, where the governor saw her "prostrated and so disfigured that he did not recognize her."[136] This incident convinced him that limits to owner abuse had to be set, especially in a case that had become so "public and notorious." Ignoring the witnesses produced by Sáenz de Maza, he issued a summary sentence mostly based on Subisa's medical report and public knowledge of her mistreatment. To the slave's horror, her mistress successfully appealed the sentence in Bogotá on procedural grounds. The royal audiencia ordered the governor to reopen the case, permitting the presentation of Sáenz de Maza's witnesses. Although the ultimate fate of Subisa is unknown, it is unlikely that she eventually obtained freedom from the Crown, a grace it reserved for slaves who had accomplished acts of extraordinary heroism.[137]

As difficult as it was, the possibility for slaves to challenge their masters for abuse was confirmed by the royal cédula of May 1789, which gave "instruction on the education, treatment, and occupation of the slaves," better known as the Código Negro. Following a decree that deregulated the slave trade in the Spanish colonies, in no way did the Código question slavery or serve as an antidote to a nonexistent Spanish or Spanish American version of the late 1780s incipient abolitionist movements, such as the popular mobilization in Britain, the Quakers in Anglo-America, and France's prerevolutionary Amis des Noirs.[138] Rather, the Código Negro compiled former legislation on the rights and duties of masters and slaves in an attempt to reconcile Christian and human principles with state needs and public order. The long list of slaveowners' duties included the provision of religious education and services, adequate food and clothing comparable to what was "commonly given to free day laborers," medical care, decent accommodations allowing for the sexual separation of the nonmarried, and supervised recreation divided along gender lines. In addition, the cédula stipulated that the principal occupation of slaves be in agriculture, not domestic service, and that owners could make them work only from dawn to dusk, during which time two hours should be reserved daily for slaves to labor for their own profit. Owners should prevent promiscuity and encourage Catholic marriages between slaves. When newlyweds belonged to different slaveowners, one master, preferably the bride's owner, was to sell his or her slave to the owner of the other spouse, so that the couple could consummate the marriage. The cédula also prohibited masters from escaping their duties to the elderly and the sick or to slaves' children. In contrast, its list of slaves' duties was limited: "to obey and respect their masters and overseers, to fulfill the tasks and jobs that are assigned to them in conformity with their means, and to venerate their owners as heads of the family."

Among the most controversial provisions of the Código Negro were those strictly defining the physical punishment that owners and overseers could inflict on careless or disrespectful slaves: a maximum of twenty-five lashes "with a soft instrument that does not cause them serious contusion or spilling of blood." If masters believed that slaves deserved harsher punishment, they should turn them over to the justice system. Owners and overseers who did not take good care of their slaves would be fined. Those exceeding their right to punish would be prosecuted and incur "the penalty corresponding to the crime, as if the injured were free, and the slave would be confiscated to be sold to another master." If the injured slave was permanently disabled, he or she would be free and receive a life pension from the guilty owner. In all court cases, the city's attorney would defend the slaves. To prevent the concealment of slaves' violent deaths, hacendados were required to provide annual lists of their slaves and to report and document escapes and deaths within three days. To ensure the good treatment of slaves, owners were subjected to the confidential supervision of the local priest and to three visits yearly by a special commissioner.[139] However, the relative leniency of the Código Negro did not apply to punishment by the courts: for example, Caribbean New Granada's slaves convicted of robbery were routinely condemned to be "put on a donkey with a packsaddle [and paraded] through the streets, with his crime announced publicly by the town crier, and to receive 200 lashes from the hand of the executioner." This torture was equated with the death penalty by defenders of slaves; it was often followed, for those who survived, by years of forced labor.[140]

Although the 1789 royal cédula did not break legal ground, it did resemble a slaves' bill of rights. Slaveowners and Spanish officials in the rapidly developing plantation economies of Cuba and Venezuela immediately protested, claiming that if they obeyed its provisions, they would no longer be able to produce crops or goods. In response, Spain issued a decree in 1794 that discreetly nullified the Código, a change also prompted by fear of the spread of the French Caribbean revolutions to Spanish America.[141] Yet in Caribbean New Granada, where the prospects of a rising plantation economy never materialized, the 1789 cédula continued to serve as a yardstick of owners' duties and rights. The 1794 decree went unnoticed, and in 1805 Cartagena's slaveowners still protested the three annual inspections of haciendas stipulated by the Código Negro.[142] Moreover, the Código Negro encouraged slaves, especially in cities, to protest their master's ownership following mistreatment. Some slaves began to view the change of master because of abuse as a right. Such was the 1791 case of Petrona Pabla Bernal, in Cartagena, who had been beaten repeatedly by her mistress, Ana Isabel Rodríguez, after Rodríguez discovered that, lured by a promise of freedom, Bernal had prostituted herself to Rodríguez's husband, Juan Vivanco, and given birth to his child. According to Bernal's declaration, her mistress had given her "blows with a stick, lashes, and wounds without allowing me the freedom that is conceded by right to the unhappy [beings] who like me are born subjected to servitude, which is to change owner when we are maltreated with the cruelty my mistress does to me." Bernal stated that her right was to be bought by the new master she had found. The governor of Cartagena, Joaquín de Cañaverales, ordered Vivanco to sell Bernal to protect her from continuing physical and sexual abuse.[143]

Although Bernal took action against her mistress, it is likely that some slaveowners exceeded the authorized punishment with impunity, especially in the countryside. Yet her case and others show that masters challenged by slaves' legal actions did not dispute the limits fixed by the 1789 cédula. In Mompox, where intra-elite conflict was acute, some aristocrats even used these limits to prosecute other hacendados for alleged slave abuse. When there was little proof of culpability, masters and their witnesses used the very language of the Código Negro to declare that they treated their slaves well.[144] If there was evidence of physical abuse, owners questioned the veracity of the medical reports supporting slaves' claims. They also portrayed slaves as fundamentally evil and untrustworthy. Bernal's owner, Vivanco, went so far as to accuse her of self-mutilation to achieve her goal. Masters argued, most effectively, that if claims of abuse were allowed to multiply, slaves would transform the most benign correction into cruelty, and "there would not be a slave who soon would not be free; neither would the master have the assurance of their services, particularly in Cartagena."[145] Yet no one stood up to defend slaveowners' absolute rights over their human property.

In contrast with the governors in Caribbean New Granada, who in the above cases opted to protect slaves, the audiencia in Bogotá displayed growing nervousness in the face of slaves' attempts to improve their condition. Both coartación and the accusation of owner abuse questioned the essence of slavery and threatened its permanence. In 1782, in the case of flagrant torture of slave Gertrudis Subisa, the Crown attorney criticized Governor Pimienta for having ordered her mistress to grant her freedom without hearing the arguments of the defense. Such a decision, he feared, would prompt "a chaos of confusion and continuing disorder." Slaves would routinely "insult their Masters in the hope that as a result of their punishment they could change Owners or gain freedom." According to the Crown attorney, the governor's decision was particularly ill-advised "in Cartagena where the Blacks are famous for their perversity and where, in order to restrain them and receive basic service, one is compelled to raise one's hand all the time and not to allow them even the most trivial defects. Hard is, to tell the truth, the condition of the Slaves, but so is that of their Masters, who are forced to serve themselves with a caste of men of a nature opposed to them who view them as irreconcilable enemies," he concluded.[146] A decade later, another Crown attorney in Bogotá also revoked the ruling of Governor Cañaverales granting Petrona Pabla Bernal the right to be sold to another master. The royal audiencia ruled that Vivanco could keep Bernal provided that he would treat her charitably. The Crown attorney used the same argument for the preservation of slavery and public order as his predecessor. No doubt thinking of the revolutions in France and the French Caribbean, he blamed slaves' "pride and arrogance."[147]

By 1800, after the thwarting of the alleged slave conspiracy in Cartagena, fears of a Haitian-like revolution in the Caribbean provinces increased in Bogotá.[148] In Cartagena and Mompox, however, no similar atmosphere of fear existed. Slaves individually challenging their masters continued to find support not only from governors but also from a few merchants and hacendados. Some alcaldes ordinarios, who also served as official protectors of slaves, tended to defend abused slaves by positing the superiority of natural law, "in which slaves also participate, which is common to all human beings without difference in status, quality, condition, or person," over human law, "which made slaves inferior to their masters." Citing Seneca, Justiciano, and the Bible, they stated that "there are limits to what masters can do, because life is God's domain." Masters who killed or mutilated their slaves should be punished as if they had committed these crimes against free persons. Another argument was that slaveowners who misused their authority were unworthy of dominating and should lose their slave property.[149] Some protectors of slaves began to move away from the notion of public order supported by the Crown attorneys and to openly include slaves as participants in and beneficiaries of the common good. Gertrudis Subisa's defender repeatedly stated that her lengthy torture had been "publicized in the whole city"; it "scandalized the People, and distressed the pious hearts." To protect the "republic" [sic], it was necessary to take into account public opinion and punish the "tyranny and barbarism" of abusive masters.[150]

Progressively, arguments defending abused slaves added the notion of their individual rights and freedom to natural law and Christian charity, notably in a case opposing two masters over the split ownership of a married slave couple in Cartagena in 1808. Wrongly accused of theft, slave Cristino Valverde had claimed publicly that the wife of his former master, Juan Chacón, was an alcoholic. Chacón demanded that he be allowed to buy Valverde back from his new owner, María de los Angeles Barraza, in order to sell him and his slave wife, still Chacón's property, out of Cartagena. Only this, Chacón alleged, would restore the honor of his family, which had been undermined by Valverde, given the "most enormous difference between the offender who is a vile Person and Me, who is a white and honorable man." In Chacón's mind, honor was a complex mix of qualities that included the virtue of his family, his ability to control the behavior of his wife, and his status as a privileged white male inherently distinct from and superior to the common people.[151] To this argument, Barraza's attorney responded that Valverde had mentioned the alcoholism of Chacón's wife only to defend himself against Chacón's accusation that he was a "wicked thief and many other insults that would have been much more offensive to any man of honor." It was not because Valverde was a "slave and of inferior status . . . that he lack[ed] feeling and natural understanding," the attorney continued. Neither did the status of Chacón's wife excuse her from the fragilities of human weakness.[152] Without saying that Valverde, too, could have honor, the attorney subtly challenged Chacón's belief that only race and status mattered. Far from presenting Valverde as an equal man, he added the dimension of gender to the balance by contrasting the male slave's feelings and natural intelligence with the weaknesses of Chacón's wife. Eventually, Barraza offered to buy Valverde's wife from Chacón so that he could escape revenge from his former master and the two could live and work together. The audiencia in Bogotá approved this solution, which did not undermine slavery and respected the Código Negro's gender hierarchy according to which a slave wife should follow her slave husband.[153]

It was in Mompox, however, that the defense of slaves came closest to an antislavery discourse. In 1805-7, during a legal dispute with hacendado and brickmaker Francisco de la Barcena Posada, the alcalde ordinario and protector of slaves, Melchor Sáenz Ortiz, eloquently denounced the treatment of slaves like animals when nature had never approved such humiliation. "I could easily demonstrate that no human beings are slaves except in the laws and the . . . insensibility of other free men," he added. "And, God willing, death will not prevent one of my biggest wishes: it is to see the vile and insulting words of Serfs and Servitude, Slave, Slavery banished from the laws."[154] Whether Sáenz, who sold slaves to miners in northern Antioquia in the 1790s, still owned slaves after 1800 is unknown.[155] However, when he indicted Francisco de la Barcena for cruelty against his slaves in 1805, he incarcerated six of them so that they could more easily testify against their master. Although he denied the defense's charge that he promised the slaves freedom in exchange for their testimony, it is likely that he exposed them to the ideas of freedom and natural equality while they were in jail. Reportedly, after their release the slaves paid a high price for Sáenz's protection, as Barcena greeted them with shackles and chains and paraded them in Mompox before severely whipping them. Probably as a result of both Barcena's mistreatment and Sáenz's ideas, the slaves then "became insolent in terms that they wanted to kill the overseer don José Eslavas and a free lad . . . while . . . the rumor lasted that they were going to be free, they did not comply with their duties, and their lack of respect and insubordination increased."[156] If Barcena recovered the property of his slaves, he and his overseer were unable to fully control them again.

Whereas some elite whites left written documentation protesting slavery, few people of African descent were literate and in a position to do so. The case of slave José de Castro is unique. While still in Mompox in 1805, Castro claimed in a brief—probably written by a lawyer—that all human beings had a common divine origin and that slavery was opposed to nature and was the work of human wickedness.[157] In fact, the artisans, overseers, servants, and slaves who left testimony on slave treatment most often served as witnesses for masters and, connected to their patronage networks, denied the existence of abuse. But a few free men of color helped prominent whites to denounce slaveowners' alleged excesses. Among them, in 1796, was Pedro Juan Tinoco, a supposedly illiterate zambo captain of justice in Guamal who gathered false evidence on behalf of the marquis of Torre-Hoyos that hacendado Pablo García had whipped a slave to death.[158] Similarly, when Sáenz charged Barcena with cruelty against his slaves, several hacendados and merchants claimed that Sáenz was "directed" by José Luis Muñoz, "of intrepid influence, of the dark pardo class, and of perverse condition," who specialized in legal cases pitting the "principal subjects" of the city against each other. Little more is known about Muñoz, except that he then declared himself to be a merchant from Mompox and that in 1810 he was one of the two leaders of a popular uprising against Spanish authorities (see Chapter 4).[159] Although Tinoco's action was probably guided by his client relationship with the marquis of Torre-Hoyos, Muñoz seems to have acted on his own initiative. Unfortunately, the two men's ideas and beliefs on equality and slavery were not recorded. Also, so far there is no documentation of the treatment of slaves owned by free persons of color.

The alleged slave rebellion of Cartagena in 1799 is a good illustration of the role of color, ethnicity, and status in dividing free and slave people of full and partial African descent. Among its leaders and followers, the conspiracy included several French and African-born slaves who could not speak Spanish or communicate effectively with most of the city's slave population.[160] The handful of creole and African-born slaves, as well as the only officer that the "Black French slaves" had been able to "attract" to the conspiracy, were "of the same color as they were."[161] Also crucial in the failure of the conspiracy was its denouncement by pardo militia corporal Manuel Yturen, who identified with the colonial order and was placed in a position of power regarding the black slaves. The subsequent arrest of the alleged conspirators had no impact on other blacks in the city, and free and slave peoples of mixed African descent stayed out of the conspiracy.[162]

Nevertheless, to overemphasize the absence of massive revolt in Caribbean New Granada's cities would be misleading. As pointed out by Victor M. Uribe-Urán, most urban insurgencies discovered in Latin America after 1789 "were relatively small-scale, harmless, regional, or local incidents" led by a handful of individuals and often blown out of proportion by authorities fearing the spread of the French and Haitian Revolutions.[163] This chapter has shown that even in cities, where the church and state presence was stronger and whites were more numerous than in the countryside, free people and slaves used multiple strategies to improve their situation. Of course, they exhibited profound socioeconomic, cultural, and ideological differences among themselves. Even the pardos, as noted by Matthias Röhrig Assunção for Brazil and Venezuela, did not constitute a "class in itself," autonomously representing their interests.[164] Most lower-class actions were individual, nonviolent, and often legal, thus not an overt threat. But taken together, these actions challenged the colonial order. Some free women of color achieved economic autonomy, and a few, wealth, despite defying the Catholic norms in their private lives. Some men of color attained positions legally reserved for whites; probably others were able to pass for white. Even some slaves managed to buy their own freedom through hard work and savings, whereas others confronted abusive masters in the courtroom, notably on the basis of the Código Negro.

Simultaneously, however, the urban white elite remained at the top of the socioracial hierarchy, although it was far from hegemonic. Unlike their peers in Cuba and Venezuela, Spanish and creole whites were too few and too divided by economic interests to challenge the extension of gracias al sacar to pardos and to reject the Código Negro. As a result, the Crown's small legal improvements regarding free people of African descent and slaves did have some impact in Caribbean New Granada, at least in the cities. Moreover, the white elite, to maintain its position, needed to compromise with the lower classes. At the same time, it was often elite patronage, in addition to kinship, that made lower-class actions viable. More collectively, crossracial and crossclass clientage mitigated tensions between the local aristocracy and the free and enslaved blacks, mulattoes, and zambos. Patronage had the dual effect of individually helping the lower classes of color but collectively dividing them and making their joint challenge more difficult.[165] In addition, as women largely outnumbered men within the population of color, some of them formed temporary unions with white men that added to the complexity of social relations. Moreover, urban communities were regularly brought together by carnivals and fiestas that both replicated and blurred the socioracial hierarchy.

If the inhabitants of Cartagena, Mompox, Santa Marta, Valledupar, and Riohacha displayed a sense of community, they also developed strong rivalries among themselves. The mutual grievances these cities accumulated were so great that at times they overshadowed domination by Bogotá or Madrid. Moreover, the shock waves of the American, French, and Haitian

Revolutions did not reach the five cities equally. Some were more exposed than others to outside revolutionary news and ideas. Local conditions, such as the balance of power between whites, people of African descent, and Indians in the proximity, or the economic effects of Bourbon reforms launched in 1778, shaped the impact of new concepts. This partially explains the cities' distinct position in regard to independence in 1810: Cartagena, Mompox, and briefly Valledupar, in favor of it; Santa Marta and Riohacha, against it. Ultimately, as foreseen by Viceroy Mendinueta, those who held the balance of power in the cities were the militiamen of color on whom the defense of the Caribbean region depended. As long as these soldiers supported the king, Spanish authorities could guarantee the fidelity of New Granada to the Crown. However, when in 1810 the militiamen switched allegiance to the reformist elites in Mompox and Cartagena, they sealed the fate of Spain in the region.

THE FIRST

INDEPENDENCE

In 1816 creole hacendado, merchant, and lawyer José María García de Toledo attempted to escape execution by a Spanish firing squad by arguing that if he had not played a leading role in Cartagena's early independence, Caribbean New Granada would have followed the deadly path of the Haitian Revolution. He claimed that in 1810 he had supported the removal of the province's Spanish governor by Cartagena's cabildo because the populace threatened to kill him: "Once the person of Mr. Governor [would have been] knocked down, the heads of the wealthy, the nobles, all the whites would have followed, and the scene of Santo Domingo would have repeated itself." The fact that blacks and mulattoes greatly outnumbered whites, that many slaves were gaining their freedom, that people were making a connection between independence and equality, and that some leaders were ambitious made a revolution similar to the Haitian one very likely. García de Toledo further stated that he had opposed Cartagena's declaration of independence in November 1811 but was forced to accept it for fear of being murdered.[1] Not only did García de Toledo's arguments fail to save his life, but also they grossly misrepresented Caribbean New Granada's First Independence and his role in achieving it.

INDEPENDENT CITIES

The abduction of King Ferdinand VII by Napoleon in 1808 and the subsequent formation of regional juntas in Spain created a new context for widening the options of Spanish American colonies. The juntas introduced the principle of popular sovereignty, and in some colonies, such as Venezuela and New Granada, prominent creoles began to think of their region as an autonomous province within the Spanish kingdom: not only did they form juntas, but also in 1810 they rejected the authority of the Council of the Regency established on the Isle of León to rule for the king.[2] However, New Granada's embrace of autonomy, and later independence, was far from countrywide. Rather, it was a fragmented and conflictive elite-led movement limited to some cities and areas, whereas other cities and villages remained faithful to Spain.[3]

In 1809 the Cartagena cabildo, comprised of Spanish and creole merchants, hacendados, and lawyers, began to resist Spanish rule by continuing to trade with the United States despite a ban by colonial authorities.[4] The arrival later that year of a new Spanish governor for the province, Brigadier General Francisco Montes, who intended to regain the power assumed by the cabildo, only increased tensions between the city on the one hand and Bogotá and Spain on the other. Rumors spread of a possible popular uprising in Cartagena, and in May 1810 Montes seized the arms in the workshop of a powerful pardo gunsmith, Pedro Romero, allegedly to distribute them to Spanish residents. In response, the cabildo accused Montes of conspiring with France and threatening the region's security by favoring Spaniards over creoles, and it placed Montes under the supervision of two elected deputies, one a creole and the other a Spaniard.[5]

Meanwhile, cabildo member José María García de Toledo capitalized on popular discontent to organize a force able to neutralize, if necessary, the pro-Spanish Fijo and other troops garrisoned in the city. He entrusted Pedro Romero with the mobilization of "a large number of men of worth and resolution" from the black and mulatto neighborhood of Getsemaní, "who would be ready at García de Toledo's first call." García de Toledo assigned the same task to others in the barrios of Santo Toribio and La Catedral.[6] At first, Romero resisted the call. Born in Matanzas, Cuba, in the 1740s, he had been posted as a master blacksmith in Cartagena's arsenal. He now successfully operated his own foundry at the entrance of Getsemaní, where he worked with his brother and sons, numerous laborers, and, possibly, some slaves. His wealth depended on contracts from the Spanish army. Although legally a pardo, he was rich and influential enough to marry off several of his children to well-to-do whites, and in early 1810 he petitioned the king for a license that would allow one of his sons to study philosophy and theology, "excusing his condition of mulatto."[7] Despite his power and affluence under Spanish rule, Romero "became convinced of the justice of [García de Toledo's] plan" and rapidly rallied "all the neighborhood of Getsemaní" behind García de Toledo in the new unit called the Patriot Lancers of Getsemaní.[8]

On 14 June 1810 men from Getsemaní, Santo Toribio, and Santa Catalina, armed with machetes and backed by a huge crowd, stood in front of the Governor's Palace, where the cabildo was meeting. The cabildo then unanimously voted to depose the governor, who was deported to Havana. Impressed by such a display of popular resolution, the commanders of all the military corps, including the fixed battalion of the Fijo, solemnly approved the cabildo's decision.[9] To prevent clashes between Spaniards and white creoles, the cabildo stressed the two groups' "ties of fraternal union and fidelity to Spain," their common religion, rights, and duties, and mobilized them in a white battalion of "patriot volunteers to conserve the august rights of Ferdinand VII." Confirming the Spanish colonial divisions along racial lines, it organized a separate battalion of pardos.[10]

In Mompox, discontent against Spanish authority also erupted in early 1809, when Spanish lieutenant colonel and engineer Vicente Talledo y Rivera arrived as the city's new military commander. The cabildo of Mompox immediately opposed Talledo's appointment and accused him of collusion with the French.[11] As in Cartagena, the elite sought to rally the population of color. By May 1810 a fearful Talledo urged his few supporters to "gain the zambo José Luis Muñoz (one of the directors of the town councilors) because we cannot afford to have him against us, given the following he has among some mulattoes and zambos," but in vain.[12] The majority of the cabildo, the city's vicar, Juan Fernández de Sotomayor, most leading families, the "numerous relatives [of the recently deceased Pedro Martínez de Pinillos] with the many slaves who served them," and Muñoz and his mulatto and zambo followers all united against Talledo.[13] Some residents remained neutral, and the few members of the cabildo still supporting Spain withdrew to their haciendas. According to Talledo, on 24 June the "conspirators" spread the rumor that he had sold all the inhabitants of Mompox as slaves to Napoleon, which prompted a great uproar. Talledo's enemies gathered men in the streets, telling them that they were going to free them from their new slavery, and locked them up in the liquor factory for the night with plenty of rum to drink. The next day many more joined them, "among them all the slaves of the house of the [Martínez de] Pinillos, armed under the leadership of their owner, don Pedro Manuel de Nájera." As Mompox's cabildo debated whether to approve Cartagena's deposition of General Montes, the insurgents, led by zambo José Luis Muñoz and black Luis Gonzaga Galván, occupied the small squares and streets around Talledo's house to prevent him from mobilizing the troops against them. In Talledo's words, they turned "the place . . . into a labyrinth and into the greatest turmoil: blacks, zambos and mulattoes, and on top each one was doing what he wanted." On 2 July before dawn, Talledo escaped to Bogotá, with the hope of returning with troops to suppress the rebellion, but Viceroy Antonio Amar ignored his request, sending him instead to Cartagena where he was put under house arrest.[14]

Mompox and Cartagena followed similar paths until the revolution of 20 July 1810 in Bogotá established a Supreme Junta to govern New Granada in the name of Ferdinand VII. The Supreme Junta was to be autonomous from the Council of the Regency but, much to Cartagena's chagrin, kept the viceroyalty's power structure centralized in Bogotá. When the Supreme Junta summoned the provinces to send delegates to Bogotá for a General Congress that would form a centralist government, Cartagena refused, proposing instead that a congress be held in Medellín to establish a federalist government.[15] In contrast, people in Mompox exulted. On the night of 5 August they took to the streets, shouting "Long Life to Freedom and Independence! To the Supreme Junta of Santafé [de Bogotá]! To Our Municipal Council!"[16] Broadsides proclaimed that Mompox was in a "state of perfect and holy anarchy," and some people began to wear red cockades adorned with the tree of freedom and the slogan "God and Independence."[17] An open cabildo ousted two pro-Spanish councilmen and replaced them with two young lawyers from rich creole families in the Andean interior, José María Salazar and José María Gutiérrez de Caviedes, both professors at Mompox's newly founded university.[18] The next day Mompox's cabildo formally recognized the Supreme Junta of Bogotá and signed the city's Act of Independence from Spain, which was sent to the juntas of Cartagena and Bogotá for approval. In addition, hacendado and cabildo member Vicente Celedonio Gutiérrez de Piñeres, the creole son of a noble and wealthy Sevillan established in Mompox, freed his slaves, an act reportedly imitated by a few other patriots.[19]

On 7 August 1810 the cabildo and the people of Mompox attended a Te Deum mass celebrated by Vicar Fernández de Sotomayor to thank God for their new "redemption." Then, following a well-established tradition in the region, the principal leaders of the city opened their houses to the lower classes, offering them drinks, food, and music. Shortly afterward, the cabildo organized two battalions of volunteers to defend the city: one for whites under Colonel Nicolás Valest y Valencia, a former Royal Navy officer and the son of Spanish immigrants, the other for pardos under Pantaleón Germán Ribón, a rich merchant and a magistrate, the son of white elite momposinos.[20] Whereas in the 1790s the viceroy could only form militia units of all colors, apparently in 1810 enough whites were willing to join to create a separate battalion; as in Cartagena, the measure aimed to prevent distinctions between white creoles and Spaniards. To equip these units, the cabildo imposed new taxes on salt, grain, and boats; it also forced some supporters of Talledo to pay high contributions. As a result, several royalists fled to Santa Marta. In the cabildo, pressure to ignore Cartagena's opposition and send a delegate to represent the interests of Mompox at the congress in Bogotá increased.[21]

Meanwhile, in August 1810 Cartagena's cabildo established its own Supreme Junta as a means of overshadowing Bogotá's 20 July revolution while securing Cartagena's prerogatives in the province established by the Crown.[22] Presided over by García de Toledo, the Supreme Junta of the city and province of Cartagena comprised the twelve members of Cartagena's cabildo, a vice president, six deputies chosen by the people of Cartagena, and five delegates representing the rest of the province. The new junta made two significant steps toward democracy. First, the free adult men of Cartagena, regardless of color, were called to select their city's six deputies. The inclusion of the lower classes of color in the selection process was a major sociopolitical change, even if the selection was done through public demonstrations that could easily be manipulated and produced only white elite creole deputies.[23] Second, the interests of the rest of the province were given limited recognition with five delegates representing the areas of Mompox, Tolú, Simití, and San Benito Abad. In the new context created by the 20 July revolution in Bogotá, however, such an overture was too modest to satisfy Mompox's radicals, who saw it as a way for Cartagena to keep Mompox under its control.[24]

Tensions between Mompox and Cartagena heightened. In September Cartagena issued a manifesto against holding a General Congress in Bogotá and, in an open affront to the momposinos, released military commander Talledo. Antioquia joined Cartagena in its opposition, sealing the failure of the congress.[25] In response, Mompox's cabildo voted to separate the city from the jurisdiction of Cartagena and to proclaim it capital of the new Mompox Province, a decision ratified by an open cabildo on 11 October 1810. The self-proclaimed independent province of Mompox formed a Patriotic Junta presided over by Vicente Celedonio Gutiérrez de Piñeres and promulgated a provisional republican and democratic constitution. It was reportedly drafted after consultation with "all classes of persons and [it] took into special consideration the Indians of the territory, an unhappy and unfairly despised portion of society, who . . . merits the indemnification of their usurped rights," but its position on slavery remains unknown.[26]

Following the example of Mompox, Simití also seceded from Cartagena to form its own province.[27]

Although still officially tied to the king of Spain, Cartagena, too, was progressively breaking away. In October 1810 the consulado de comercio sent to the city's Supreme Junta a report on the state of the province and the means to develop its economy. Written by José Ignacio de Pombo, the report was nothing short of an indictment of the colonial government, which it characterized as "barbarian, impolitic, and antisocial." Approved by the Supreme Junta, it framed, in December 1810, the junta's economic reforms, which opened trade with all countries except France but banned or over-taxed foreign goods competing with the region's agriculture and industry.[28] Concurrently, free cartageneros of African descent expressed growing anti-Spanish feelings. When, in November 1810, the Council of the Regency sent a new governor to replace the deposed Montes, the lower classes randomly attacked Spaniards and pro-Spanish creoles, and a crowd surrounded the Governor's Palace, ensuring that the cabildo would not allow the new governor to disembark. Several Spaniards took refuge in Santa Marta, which was becoming a royalist stronghold.[29]

As a gesture toward the popular classes, in December 1810 the Supreme Junta of Cartagena approved an electoral system of indirect representation. All male citizens, "whites, Indians, mestizos, mulattoes, zambos, and blacks who were heads of a family or a household, or lived off their own labor" could participate in the election of parish electors. "Only vagrants, those who had committed a crime leading to infamy, those who are in actual bondage salaried [*los que estén en actual servidumbre asalariados*], and slaves will be excluded from [elections]."[30] In turn, parish electors chose the districts' grand electors; and the grand electors elected the deputies to the Supreme Junta. Indians were granted full rights of citizenship. There were no requirements regarding the race, place of birth, property, or education of the people's representatives, but only character requirements. However, the secession of Mompox and Simití made the election impossible.

Moreover, the junta of Cartagena declared war against Mompox, initiating a long-lasting policy of military attack to resolve political challenges. In January 1811 aristocrat Antonio José de Ayos led four hundred well-equipped veterans of the Fijo against Mompox's battalions of pardo and white volunteers.[31] Under the banner of "God and Independence," but with few arms and little ammunition, the momposinos resisted the attack for three days. On 23 January, when they ran out of bullets, Mompox's junta ordered the evacuation of the city.[32] Cartagena's troops occupied Mompox and ruthlessly destroyed its revolutionary institutions. Ayos swore in a new cabildo and new authorities, many of whom were Spaniards or firm supporters of Spanish rule. He reinstated the Inquisition, which the radicals had abolished. Dozens of revolutionary leaders, such as Vicente Celedonio Gutiérrez de Piñeres, Pantaleón Germán Ribón, Nicolás Valest, Pedro Manuel de Nájera, and José Luis Muñoz, fled to other provinces. Many others were captured and imprisoned in Cartagena, among them Luis Gonzaga Galván and Vicar Sotomayor. The occupying forces confiscated the property of prisoners and fugitives.[33]

Ayos's brutal repression of revolutionary Mompox fed hopes among Cartagena's pro-Spanish inhabitants that they could still turn the tide of events. On 4 February 1811, a few days after returning from the war against Mompox, the Fijo, backed by supporters of the Regency, attempted to take over the Governor's Palace. Denounced by lower-ranking officers, the conspiracy collapsed before any shots were fired.[34] García de Toledo personally arrested its leaders, and the elderly Field Marshal Antonio Narváez y la Torre stepped in to prevent a clash between pro-Spanish troops and new patriot units. Nevertheless, the incident strengthened the power of the lower classes. As rumors spread that the conspirators, allegedly including all the Spanish-born, planned to "destroy the Junta, arrest [its members] and embark them on a ship to Spain, install D. Blas de Soria as the governor and begin to hang, quarter [the people]," the spirit of revenge soared. A mob of armed blacks, mulattoes, and zambos attacked Spanish homes; they arrested Spanish men and imprisoned them in the barracks of the Pardo Patriots. According to a lieutenant of the Pardo Patriots, "The whole night [of 4 February] was of revolution: over 3,000 souls were patrolling and walking in the streets. . . . Day 5 was of horror and fright. The streets were filled with people looking for the accomplices of the revolt of the 'Fijo,' whom they said were all Europeans. . . . During days 6, 7, 8, 9, and today 10, the imprisonment and movements continued, but now slower because the chiefs were locked up and because Mr. García Toledo was prosecuting them for insurrection and *lèse-patrie*."[35] Despite the destruction of property and physical abuse, these days of popular anger reportedly left no deaths.[36] Nevertheless, more pro-Spanish elite families left for Santa Marta and the Caribbean islands. As stated by two merchants on their way to Kingston, "With [this junta] nobody was safe in his or her home because of the impudence of the zambo, black and mulatto loafers . . . and because the property of the honorable people was always exposed to the endless needs of the Junta."[37]

Indeed, after thwarting the conspiracy of the Fijo, the Supreme Junta of Cartagena had growing difficulty in justifying its loyalty to Spain now that the popular classes had shown their capacity to act against the will of their leaders. Ahead of the rest of New Granada, a radical portion of the elite began to demand that the province declare full independence from Spain. Ideology intertwined with family ties, as momposino lawyers and government officials Gabriel and Germán Gutiérrez de Piñeres headed the movement for independence and simultaneously denounced the junta's fierce repression of the revolution their brother, Vicente Celedonio, had led in Mompox.[38] The weekly newspaper *El Argos Americano* helped to inform and mobilize the population. It reproduced the debates in the Cortes of Cadiz (the Spanish worldwide royal parliament) and presented peninsular deputies' denial of parity in representation to Americans as proof of Spain's continuing despotism. Indeed, the Cortes agreed to limit apportionment and suffrage to Europeans, Indians, and those of mixed European-indigenous descent, excluding from both Africans and their "pure" or mixed progeny. Such a decision implied that, unlike Andean New Granada, Cartagena Province, with its overwhelmingly pardo, zambo, and black population, probably would not have its own deputy to promote its interests in the next Cortes.[39] Consequently, in April 1811, *El Argos Americano* published an anonymous open letter, signed "the Reformer," demanding a republican constitution and independence from the Spanish Cortes.[40] In June several radicals handed García de Toledo a petition, written by Germán Gutiérrez Piñeres and signed by 479 vecinos from Cartagena, containing identical demands. The junta refused to declare independence, arguing that the petition did not represent the general will of the province and that broader consultation was necessary.[41]

Eventually, on 11 November 1811, the radicals launched a coup that compelled Cartagena's Supreme Junta to declare independence. The Patriot Lancers of Getsemaní and the Pardo Patriots took positions on the city's walls and turned its artillery on the barracks of the Fijo and the White Patriots to prevent them from intervening. Gabriel Gutiérrez de Piñeres and Pedro Romero assembled lower-class men and artisans in front of the church of Getsemaní. The crowd entered the city, forced open the doors of the arsenal to seize arms, and, according to a supporter, "armed some with guns, others with lances and still others with daggers, they all went to the front of the [Governor's] Palace."[42] The rebels sent white lawyer Ignacio Muñoz, Romero's son-in-law, and bogotano priest Nicolás Mauricio de Omaña to the junta to demand absolute independence from Spain, "the equal rights of all the classes of citizens," a government divided into three branches, the placement of the army command under the executive, the opening of legislative sessions to the public, the appointment of pardo and black commanders in the battalion of pardos and the artillery, the abolition of the Inquisition, and the exclusion of "unpatriotic Europeans" from public office.[43] Then the armed populace invaded the palace, assaulted García de Toledo, and forced the junta to sign the province's Act of Independence, putting Cartagena at the vanguard of all New Granada's provinces.[44]

Like *El Argos Americano* and the June 1811 petition, the act argued that the Spanish Cortes's failure to grant Americans equal representation had compelled the province to declare its independence. In the following days, all members of the military corps, public officials, and ecclesiastical authorities, with the exception of the bishop, swore fidelity to the Act of Independence (instead of the king).[45] As for the Inquisition, it was forced to shut down, and its officials moved the Holy Office to Santa Marta. On 11 November the demonstrators in Cartagena also successfully demanded an end to the occupation and repression of Mompox. Ayos was recalled from Mompox and placed under house arrest for several months for complicity with the royalists in Santa Marta. The Spaniards and pro-Spanish creoles residing in Mompox left for Santa Marta, whereas Vicente Celedonio Gutiérrez de Piñeres and Pantaleón Germán Ribón returned to power, abandoning their plan to form an independent province of Mompox.[46] As Cartagena Province declared its independence from Spain, delegates in Bogotá representing the provinces of Cartagena, Antioquia, Neiva, Pamplona, and Tunja signed an act creating the Federation of the United Provinces of New Granada, inspired by the loose federalism of the U.S. Articles of Confederation of 1776 and going along with each area's tradition of provincialism. Centralist Cundinamarca opposed the act of federation, forcing the congress of the United Provinces to move to Tunja and provoking several armed conflicts between federalist and centralist areas until the Spanish reconquest in 1815.[47]

In early 1812 Cartagena Province's male heads of family, regardless of race, as stipulated by the December 1810 electoral law, designated the electors who chose the deputies to a constituent convention. The radicals led by the Gutiérrez de Piñeres brothers won a majority of the thirty-six elected deputies. A sign of the new times, at least one of them, Pedro Romero, was of partial African descent. The 1812 constitution of the State of Cartagena de Indias, approved by the deputies, developed the principles put forward by the 1811 Act of Independence. It was representative, republican, and lib-

Title page of the 1812 constitution of the State of Cartagena. (*Boletín Historial: Organo de la Academia de la Historia de Cartagena de Indias* 1 [May 1915])

eral and stressed the fundamental rights of free individuals. It granted suffrage to any free man, regardless of race, who was a "vecino, father or head of a family, or head of a household, who lives off his rents or labor, without depending on another person [for a wage]." It sealed the reorganization of the royal Fijo and militias into a state army composed of racially inclusive battalions of veterans and militiamen. The constitution stated the importance of the Catholic religion in preserving public morality, seen as a necessary complement to the people's freedom. It was concerned with slaves' well-being and banned the import of new slaves but did not mention abolition.[48] Inapplicable to the conditions of war and upheaval that followed its adoption, it was rapidly superseded by a series of regulations that gave extraordinary powers to the executive branch.

ROYALIST STRONGHOLDS

In contrast with Cartagena, Santa Marta became a stronghold of Spanish rule. The city's royalist stand, however, was not a foregone conclusion. To begin with, in 1810 Santa Marta's control over its province fell apart as several cities and villages rebelled against their capital. In Valledupar, on 21 May, according to a royalist, over four hundred vecinos rose up against the royal authorities, "screaming 'Down with the [alcalde] mayor marquis of Valde-Hoyos and the most excellent viceroy!' and 'Death to H. M. Ferdinand VII!' The lower people are governing, and all the public servants are fleeing, hoping to come back with public forces to restore authority."[49] Although the royalist perhaps exaggerated the events to move Viceroy Antonio Amar into action, the abuses committed by the marquis of Valde-Hoyos against all classes in Valledupar, with the viceroy's tacit backing, largely explained the revolt. Still, one month after Caracas's declaration of autonomy, Valledupar was the first New Granadan city to launch a movement against Spain, preceding Mompox, Cartagena, and Bogotá. It was the only place where the popular classes of color apparently acted independently of the elite. And only in Valledupar did the people allegedly also wish for the death of Ferdinand VII, whereas all the autonomous juntas created later in 1810 were initially faithful to the king.[50] Few details are known of Valledupar's movement, except that it was rapidly neutralized. In the wake of Bogotá's 20 July 1810 revolution, more villages in Santa Marta Province rebelled, such as Chiriguaná, whose few local whites, pressured by a crowd of free men of color, proclaimed the village's independence from the jurisdiction of the city of Tamalameque; but there was no coordination.[51] Not surprisingly, Santa Marta counterattacked and eventually reconquered Valledupar and the rebel villages.

In Santa Marta itself, as in several other New Granadan cities, a portion of the creole elite, backed by a popular crowd, demanded in August 1810 that a junta rule the province autonomously from the Council of the Regency. However, the Spanish governor, Víctor de Salcedo, responded masterfully to the popular pressure. He met with the city's cabildo, and together they agreed to entrust the male heads of households, regardless of race, with the selection of a junta over which he would preside. As elsewhere, only white elite men were selected. The junta included autonomists (Colonel of Militia José Munive, Lieutenant Governor Antonio Viana, four members of the wealthy Díaz Granados hacendado family, and militia officers with family ties to prominent members of Cartagena's Supreme Junta) as well as strong supporters of the Regency (notably powerful merchant and ship-owner José María Martínez de Aparicio, also commander of the city's militia and administrator of the royal taxes). Most lower-class people of color backed Munive's push for a government similar to Cartagena's and repeatedly demonstrated in the public square to force reform on the junta. However, the governor limited Munive's power over the militia by forming new units under pro-Regency officers. As an increasing number of Spanish and creole royalists took refuge in Santa Marta to escape from the revolutions in Venezuela and New Granada, the balance of power shifted to the supporters of the Regency.[52]

On 22 December 1810 a crowd headed by mulatto contractor Narciso Vicente Crespo made a last attempt to impose an autonomous junta.[53] Massed in front of the building where the junta was in session, the throng demanded that the people of Santa Marta be allowed to immediately elect their own representatives to the junta, as in Cartagena, and that Munive be elected as the province's deputy to the Spanish Cortes. The junta responded that such an election on the spot would be "invalid because a great part of the noble people and other plebeians were absent from the crowd," but it agreed to have "the vecinos heads of family, nobles as well as plebeians" orderly elect six deputies to a new junta. Simultaneously, the junta declared its president, the Spanish governor, "perpetual" and thus not on the ballot.[54] With Munive elected representative at the Cortes, the new junta tipped toward the royalists. Spain sent a new Spanish governor, Tomás de Acosta, to the city. The voices for change were silenced definitively in June 1811, when, following pro-Spanish demonstrations and an expeditious vote in which only some sectors of the capital were consulted, the junta was abolished and replaced with the old form of government comprising the governor, his lieutenant, and the cabildo. An edict strictly prohibited "all commotion, tumult, or reunion of many persons, under the pretext of representing and demanding what they judge convenient to their right."[55]

Support of the Regency in Santa Marta was further strengthened by Cartagena's attempt to maintain its exclusive rights to Atlantic trade and political superiority over lesser Caribbean New Granadan cities, which alienated many samarios regardless of their political leanings. While waging a war against Mompox, Cartagena's Supreme Junta decided to heavily tax all imports from other provinces, including Santa Marta. It also warned Santa Marta's junta to withdraw allegiance to the Regency or face an embargo.[56] In this heated context, Guáimaro, Remolino, and Sitionuevo, three villages on the east bank of the Magdalena River, seceded from Santa Marta Province, which they accused of despotism, and placed themselves under the jurisdiction of the Supreme Junta of Cartagena.[57] Cartagena sent troops to protect the secessionist villages from retaliation by Santa Marta. In July 1811 the Supreme Junta, still in the name of Ferdinand VII, threatened Santa Marta with war unless it followed Cartagena's model of government.[58] The long-standing tensions between Santa Marta and Cartagena turned into armed conflict, not only over the issue of Spanish rule versus independence, but also over political and commercial control of the region.[59]

Royalist sentiments in Santa Marta increased. Isolated from the rest of the country and defended only by its militia of all colors, Santa Marta had no ally other than Riohacha, which also remained faithful to Spain partly due to its inhabitants' fear of the Wayúu Indians. Yet the defense of Riohacha also rested only on its militia of all colors, which could not be diverted to Santa Marta, across the Sierra Nevada, without major risk. Since the suspension of its governor, José Medina Galindo, for engaging in contraband activities in 1808, Riohacha had been ruled by the alcalde ordinario, Pedro Pérez Prieto, who opposed illegal trade. Like most other cities, in September 1810 Riohacha had formed a junta headed by Pérez. Similar to Santa Marta, it refused to disallow the Regency, which provoked economic reprisals from Cartagena. However, a coalition of free people of color, merchants, smugglers, and hacendados, displeased with Pérez's rule, mobilized in favor of Medina's return as governor of the province. In early August 1811 Medina arrived from Honda with an armed escort of supporters who shouted, "Death to the traitors in the cabildo." Backed by a large crowd, they forced the cabildo to approve Medina as the new governor. Pérez fled to Maracaibo, which paved the way for a general reconciliation. In an open meeting, all men regardless of race swore allegiance to Ferdinand VII and the Council of the Regency and proclaimed Medina governor of the province, an act that was followed by church and street celebrations. Not surprisingly, in the context of general revolt in its empire, Spain forgot its accusations against Medina and welcomed the loyalty of Riohacha.[60] Nonetheless, if isolation protected Riohacha from Cartagena's attacks, it likewise prevented that city from rescuing Santa Marta.

As in the case of Riohacha, Santa Marta's allegiance to the Regency was also motivated by the existence of important unsubdued Indian communities in its hinterland and the presence of a large indigenous population in its vicinity, notably in Ciénaga. The samarios knew that these Indians could take advantage of any breakdown of the colonial order to rebel. As for the Indians, they realized that the Spanish king was their best protector and showed no interest in provincial autonomy or independence. With time, they revealed themselves among the strongest defenders of Spanish rule in the area.[61]

ORDER AND REVOLUTION

Taken together, the popular movements of 1810–11 in Caribbean New Granada blended elements of traditional order with social revolution. In all the principal cities they gave electoral rights to adult men regardless of race but did not destroy the colonial socioracial hierarchy and corporatist order. The movements' intellectual leaders were all hacendados, merchants, lawyers, and clergymen. Powerful black, mulatto, and zambo professionals and contractors of some means linked them to the lower classes of color, whom they mobilized and organized in mass demonstrations to pressure for change. In all the cities, the popular mobilization in 1810 was bloodless. Yet its outcome varied. In Cartagena and Mompox, mobilization led to the eviction of Spanish officials and independence. In Santa Marta, the small autonomist elite and its followers in the population of color were rapidly silenced by the growing number of royalists. In Riohacha, a crossclass and crossracial coalition ousted an unpopular governor and replaced him with one who had well served the majority's interests in the past. The only city in which the proindependence movement may have been genuinely lower class is Valledupar, but the evidence is too scanty to develop this hypothesis. At any rate, the movement there did not last, probably for lack of organization and elite support.

Important factors explain the different outcome in each city. First, in Santa Marta, Riohacha, and Valledupar the influence of New Granada's currents of enlightenment and economic liberalism was limited. The cities' elite was small and, except for a handful of priests, comprised few men of letters. Those who supported autonomy were rapidly marginalized by wealthy royalists seeking refuge in these cities and were forced either to embrace the cause of Spain or to leave. In contrast, several reformist elite leaders in Cartagena and Mompox had earned law or theology degrees in Bogotá, where they had taken part in political discussions, built long-lasting relations with the intellectual elite of Andean New Granada, and closely followed the debates of the Spanish Cortes. In addition to the three Gutiérrez de Piñeres brothers linking Cartagena and Mompox, many shared family ties.[62] Second, whereas in 1809 both Governor Montes in Cartagena and Commander Talledo in Mompox were new to the region and lacked the experience to handle the creole challenge, from the beginning Víctor de Salcedo, who had governed Santa Marta Province since 1805, managed the situation with an expert hand, seeming to give in to the popular will while retaining absolute power for himself as president of the junta. In Riohacha, the governmental crisis was resolved by recalling the popular Spanish governor, José Medina Galindo. Finally, only in Cartagena and Mompox did the elite and the intermediate leaders organize lower-class men of color into militias and distribute arms. This armed mobilization, given the demography of these cities, inevitably neutralized the royalist minority. In contrast, in Santa Marta the population of color opposed to Spain remained amorphous and unarmed, and the men in the colonial militia of all colors did not take advantage of being the city's only military force to challenge their officers—all of them white and members of the junta. Independence thus established roots only when a powerful nucleus of the local elite was committed to reform and when, together with leaders of African descent, they mobilized and armed lower-class men of color.

Yet even in Cartagena and Mompox the creole elite failed to unite. At the beginning, the forces in favor of change were dramatically diminished by Cartagena's occupation of Mompox in early 1811. After November 1811, when Cartagena also declared independence and withdrew its forces from Mompox, the conflict between *toledistas* (partisans of José María Gracía de Toledo) and *piñeristas* (partisans of the Gutiérrez de Piñeres brothers) continued to weaken the independence movement by shaping Cartagena's politics until the Spanish reconquest. From 1812 to 1814 the piñeristas controlled politics in these two cities and the government of the sovereign state, with Bogotá-trained lawyer Manuel Rodríguez Torices as its president and Gabriel Gutiérrez de Piñeres as its vice president. Now in power, the piñeristas kept the capital's black and mulatto lower classes in check. Still, the toledistas strongly resisted piñerista rule. Several of them, notably García de Toledo, retreated to their estates in the countryside. Through their network of haciendas and patronage in such towns as Barranquilla, Mahates, and Sabanalarga, they progressively built up an important opposition movement. The conflict between piñeristas and toledistas reached a point in 1813 when President Rodríguez Torices publicly warned that "in the midst of so many calamities, in the midst of so much suffering, civil war raises its head in the very heart of the state."[63] This "civil war" was all the more deplorable in that it was less a conflict of fundamental views than one of personal enmity between the two parties. Indeed, García de Toledo's claim (cited at the beginning of this chapter) that all of his actions since 1809 aimed at preventing a piñerista revolution inspired by Haiti was at odds with the events themselves. It was also contradicted by the fact that the two parties shared similar ideas on most issues, notably slavery and elite control.

Surprisingly, the distinction between the traditional hacendados and the more enlightened aristocrats interested in freedom of trade (examined in Chapter 3) did not evolve into a division between royalists and autonomists, respectively, or, after 1810, between toledistas and piñeristas. Nor did members of the elite who had taken an antislavery stand in the past necessarily support independence. As could be expected, José Ignacio de Pombo became the toledista economist of Cartagena's Supreme Junta. In Mompox, however, among those who supported Spain were Melchor Sáenz Ortiz, a critic of slavery; Mateo de Epalza, the heir of the marquis of Torre-Hoyos; and Vicente García, a long-time opponent of the marquis. All three men opposed the city's declaration of independence, and Sáenz and García were members of the toledista cabildo imposed by Ayos after Cartagena's occupation of the city.[64] Conversely, the leaders of the revolution of August 1810, Pantaleón Germán Ribón and Vicente Celedonio Gutiérrez de Piñeres, had shown no previous interest in social reform or in the fate of slaves.[65]

In reality, in addition to the timing of the declaration of independence in 1811, piñeristas and toledistas principally disagreed on the nature of the relationship their province should have with Bogotá. The toledistas advocated strong federalism and rejected the leadership of the New Granadan capital, whereas the piñeristas, often themselves not native cartageneros, did not oppose some centralization in Bogotá in order to secure victory against Spain.[66] Beyond these differences, both groups supported racial equality among the free but were anxious to keep in check the people of African descent who had brought them to power. In a pattern that was in many ways a precursor of the two-party system Colombia adopted in the 1840s, the ideological similarities between piñeristas and toledistas prevented the polarization of the movement into two opposing views of society—one of social revolution empowering the lower classes and the other conservative and socially exclusive. At the same time, like the Conservative and Liberal leaders, both the piñeristas and the toledistas were able to channel lower-class men of color into their movement, thus neutralizing their autonomous socioracial challenge.

The concern with keeping free people of color in check had already appeared during the 1810 debate on suffrage between two members of Mompox's cabildo. Using a Jacobinic discourse, José María Gutiérrez de Caviedes supported full independence, alignment on Bogotá, and legal equality. Since the people of Mompox had risked their lives for the freedom of their homeland during the joyful and bloodless night of 5 August 1810, he claimed, they had severed their bonds with "the tyrannical Council of the Regency" and "stood with no other sovereign than themselves." On this ground, Gutiérrez de Caviedes asked the cabildo to hold an open meeting so that Mompox's free men could elect the city's delegate to the General Congress called by Bogotá:

> Gentlemen! . . . Let's help the Capital [Bogotá] to sanction a legitimate and indestructible Government. . . . Let's not have the weakness to deny that we are in anarchy nor the arrogance to assert that our will contains the will of the whole people of Mompox. Let's convene this valiant people, let's not abuse their political ignorance . . . and their confidence. . . . Let's teach them briefly the Rights of Man; let's offer them at least for one instant the chalice of freedom, let's bring it to their lips so that they can taste it, savor it, so that their bodies fill up with the virtuous and exalted spirit that freedom begets, and let's receive it promptly from their liberal hands to put it on the sanctuary erected by the heroic *santafereños* [bogotanos] in the capital of the Nation.[67]

Although appearing to support universal male suffrage, Gutiérrez de Caviedes actually was proposing to give men of color a onetime opportunity to endorse the reformist elite's candidate. Such a proposal was still considered too dangerous by Councilman José María Salazar, who argued that an open meeting was unnecessary because the people had already demonstrated their commitment to independence on 5 August. Moreover, it would arouse their anger against the already neutralized supporters of Spain. To Salazar, an open meeting also raised the delicate matter of who would be qualified to participate in it: "If it is a question that the nobility attends, the inferior class will take offense for not participating in the session. If some individuals of this class are admitted, others, jealous of this honor, will complain about such preference: if those pardos who have fame and faculties are included, others will say that poverty is not a crime." Salazar warned of the fatal effects of demagoguery, anarchy, and lack of control of the popular classes: "It's one thing for the people to be free, another to misuse freedom," he concluded.[68] Two months after this exchange, in October 1810, Mompox declared its independence in an open cabildo well supervised by the elite, and in the ensuing years top-down democracy was replaced with military discipline.

From the beginning, both toledista and piñerista leaders in Cartagena were committed to the idea of racial equality of the free adult male population. This position had been adopted by Cartagena's cabildo in 1810 in response to the decision by the Cortes of Cadiz to exclude from apportionment and citizenship free Africans and those with full or partial African ancestry—that is, the great majority of the population in Cartagena Province. As argued by the anonymous letter of "a Creole" to *El Argos Americano*, the free "castas" deserved the right to be represented as much as the "ignorant Indians obedient to the priests."[69]

Both the toledista electoral law of 1810 and the piñerista-sponsored constitution of 1812 extended suffrage to all men regardless of race except slaves, vagrants, and criminals. But the constitution was less egalitarian than the electoral law: it excluded from suffrage "the salaried" [*asalariados*], a larger category than "those who are in actual bondage salaried [*los que estén en actual servidumbre asalariados*]" stipulated in 1810; it also included property and educational qualifications for state electors and representatives, in contrast with the 1810 law, which only mentioned qualifications regarding character.[70] Little was decided, however, to effectively promote equality and eradicate the remains of the colonial caste system. The 1812 constitution advocated "the diffusion of the learning and knowledge useful to all the classes of the State" and maintained that "public enlightenment" was what "best equalize[d] all citizens."[71] But the war prevented the implementation of any educational policy.

Although some toledistas, such as Ayos and Manuel del Castillo, made no secret of their racism and contempt for the lower classes, they did not oppose legal racial equality.[72] Indeed, once Cartagena's cabildo encouraged the show of force of free men of color against the Spanish governor and recognized them as citizens with electoral rights in 1810, the elite could not back out.[73] Therefore, when Gabriel Gutiérrez de Piñeres astutely accused García de Toledo of haughtiness in order to attract his popular following, García de Toledo took pains to publicly claim his good relations with the lower classes:

In my house I have given seats to all classes when they have come, and on amusement days they have been down to its most remote corners without me opening my mouth. I have danced in my house and in many other parts with women from all classes; I have acted in private relations with the greatest affability, so that I don't think that anyone could say that I have offended him or her in words or acts, attending every place I was invited to, and not accepting preferential seats except in church celebrations.[74]

Even when court-martialed by Spain in 1816, García de Toledo used the fact that the piñeristas had accused him of being "an aristocrat, enemy of independence and equality" as an argument to prove his innocence, but, unlike Ayos, he did not assert anti-egalitarian beliefs. He simply stated that, for fear of another Haiti, he favored autonomy over independence, an option that vanished in Cartagena with the influx of foreigners and refugees from Caracas and the exile of "the peaceful and fond-of-order vecinos."[75]

Surely in 1811 the piñeristas' demands were more radical than their opponents', such as for a republican government that separated the legislative, judicial, and executive branches.[76] Also on the piñerista agenda was "a constitution that secures the people's benefit of the precious rights they snatched from their tyrants with so many risks and sacrifices" and a body of "laws that prescribe the obligations and rights of man toward man."[77] Yet their radicalism, inspired by the French Revolution, was mostly rhetorical and avoided specifically addressing issues of race. Their strategy to gain power was the same as the toledistas'. The Gutiérrez de Piñeres brothers organized and armed the lower classes of color but kept tight control over them during most of the process leading to 11 November 1811 and their accession to power. Once in power, they did not hesitate to prevent popular challenge. During the convention's debates to draft the constitution in February 1812, in particular, the populace and the Patriot Lancers of Getsemaní began to organize armed demonstrations to influence the deputies' decisions. Rodríguez Torices erected gallows at the city's entrance and arrested a few officers, which convinced the Lancers to return the cannons they had seized on 11 November and abstain from further demonstrations.[78] If the toledista and piñerista leaders of the First Independence avoided referring to the race question, they were explicitly silent on the issue of gender. As true of other revolutions at the time, their discourse and reforms centered on men. But unlike the French revolutionaries, they did not even make peripheral or secondary references to women—for example, to exclude them from citizenship or to prohibit them from organizing. In particular, the 1812 constitution contains only one indirect reference to women: that "schools for both sexes" be founded.[79]

Not only did the piñeristas and toledistas agree on the key issue of free men's equality, they also concurred on the matter of slavery. Neither side perceived slavery as a colonial institution that needed to be ended in order to achieve democracy.[80] Although in mobilizing free people against Spain, advocates of both parties repeatedly referred to colonialism as slavery, most of them did not acknowledge that they themselves maintained other human beings in true slavery on the grounds of their race and birth. With the exception of Vicente Celedonio Gutiérrez de Piñeres and perhaps a few others in Mompox, masters are not said to have voluntarily freed their slaves to show their commitment to independence. Pombo's 1810 report to the Supreme Junta did not question slavery; it merely criticized the royal sales tax (*alcabala*) imposed on slaves who attempted to manumit themselves or to be bought by a less cruel master.[81] The 1812 constitution sponsored by the piñeristas did not free the slaves or extend citizenship to them but only contemplated the decline of slavery by prohibiting the "importation of slaves into the state, as objects of trade." This measure, also decreed by other new Spanish American nations, followed the British ban of the slave trade in 1807 and was partly intended to secure British support for independence.[82] The constitution announced the possible creation of a manumission fund, but it specified that in no case would slaves be emancipated without the consent or indemnification of their masters. Like the colonial laws, it protected slaves from maltreatment and neglect by their owners.[83] Yet it did not open new avenues to freedom. In contrast, in 1814 Antioquia (where some slaves had planned a protest during the Comunero Revolt) adopted a "free womb" law that gave freedom to the newborn babies of slave women, a significant measure in a region where gold mining depended on slave labor.[84]

Not surprisingly, toledistas and piñeristas showed more willingness to bring remote Indians into the free community than the slaves who worked as their property in their houses and haciendas. Pombo's 1810 report to the Supreme Junta advocated the abolition of the Indian tribute because it degraded the indigenous population.[85] Seen as victims of past colonial oppression as well as obstacles to a united republic and competitive agriculture, the Indians were the focus of an edict signed by García de Toledo in May 1811. The edict blamed indigenous misery and degradation on the "unjust personal tribute," the priests in charge of the pueblos de indios, and colonial authorities. It revoked the tutelage instituted by the old regime, promoted Indians to "the class of free citizens," and designed a program of integration of the pueblos de indios to dilute their ethnic identity. Schools were to be established in each pueblo. Indian women were encouraged to marry "the citizens of other castes," who could settle in their pueblos with the same land privileges as Indians. Indians were also allowed to leave their communities and engage in any legal activity. As citizens, they lost their special colonial status and would now have to pay the same taxes as other residents. And they could be drafted into the army—the edict assigned them to white battalions following the Spanish Cortes's decision that made Indians equal to whites.[86]

Another point on which toledistas and piñeristas agreed was that the Catholic religion should continue to be the moral guardian of the new society. All of the major phases in the independence process were celebrated with masses and processions. Moreover, several priests were patriot leaders —among them, Nicolás Mauricio de Omaña, Juan Marimón, Juan Fernández de Sotomayor, and Manuel Benito Revollo. Some priests were elected as the people's deputies. Together with lawyers, these clergymen had been trained in Bogotá, where they had become acquainted with new philosophical ideas and gained a broader view of New Granada. They saw independence as an opportunity for a distinct, creole church to regain some of its power, which had been curtailed by the Bourbon reforms. Yet they were the exception, as most priests in villages and small towns did not actively support independence. Many remained neutral and attempted to continue to rule their parishes and run their businesses in the turmoil of the war. Some priests firmly supported Spain and mobilized their parishioners against independence, especially in the area around Sincelejo and Corozal. A few took refuge in royalist bastions.[87]

No anticlericalism characterized the region's First Independence. No doubt patriots criticized the colonial priests who supported the Crown and kept their parishioners in ignorance in order to dominate and exploit them. But given the small number of teachers and literate persons in Caribbean New Granada, clergymen were among the few existing authorities at the local level and to bar them from the process of independence would have been costly. In addition, the patriot priests played an important role in the formulation of the First Republic's laws, which explains their continuing insistence on the social necessity of Catholicism. The Electoral Law of 1811 gave political responsibilities to priests. It recognized the parish as the electoral district and the list of parishioners compiled by the priest as the official source from which to draw the electoral register. Elections were to take place after mass and to be presided over by the local priest and judge.[88] The 1812 constitution, of which Father Revollo was the primary author, stated that religion was the strongest bond of society. It made Catholicism the official and only authorized religion in the province, and it prohibited anti-religious publications. Despite the growing influence of French deism and Freemasonry in Cartagena, only the preamble of the constitution, which thanked the "Supreme Legislator" and "Arbiter of the Universe" for allowing the inhabitants of the province to govern themselves, showed some distance from Catholicism.[89] Although the law abolished racial privileges, priests were not asked to apply these new egalitarian principles in parish records, which continued to register births, marriages, and deaths of whites separately from those of blacks and mulattoes.

The absence of anticlericalism in the region also resulted from the weakness of the Catholic Church and the limited observance of Catholic principles by society—thus, the relative indifference to religious matters among the population. In Mompox, however, people did revolt against the Inquisition, which they perceived as a colonial institution of terror. The cartageneros forced their bishop into exile in late 1811 because, in his words, "despite their threats, outrage, and degrading expressions, in the midst of the clamor of the armed blacks and mulattoes, in the midst of the insulting voices of the leaders of the insurrection . . . I duly refused to swear independence from the mother country."[90] Clearly, the reason for the cartageneros' actions against the bishop was not religious but his fidelity to Spain and the Crown.

Finally, neither the toledistas nor the piñeristas envisioned the end of Cartagena's colonial prerogatives and privileges in Caribbean New Granada. Like most other proindependence leaders in Spanish America, they did not question the territorial organization inherited from Spain or imagine the new nation with different boundaries. In early 1811 Cartagena's creole leaders waged a war to reimpose colonial subordination on the secessionist Mompox. Throughout the period, they fought for Cartagena's hegemony over Santa Marta. They exercised domination over the villages, towns, and territory they considered to be in Cartagena's jurisdiction, alienating many communities in the process. These leaders were unable to visualize new, less centralized relations of power in order to forge broad regional support for the cause they championed. Therefore, they failed to unite Caribbean New Granada as a whole behind a regional project strong enough to compel a renegotiation of the region's place in the new political configuration slowly emerging in the struggle against Spanish colonialism.

Indeed, Cartagena could not prevent its own province from disintegrating. In September 1812, in a move coordinated by their priests, the small towns and villages in the area of Sincelejo and Corozal, all the way to Tolú and Ayapel, rebelled against Ignacio Muñoz—the corregidor imposed by Cartagena—and declared their allegiance to Ferdinand VII.[91] Troops from Santa Marta entered Cartagena Province to assist them and inflicted heavy losses on Cartagena's army, which was already hampered by "desertions and insubordination." Some villages avoided destruction by helping the samarios attack pro-Cartagena communities. This lack of popular support for the cause of independence revolted Gabriel Gutiérrez de Piñeres. "I thought that 300 years were enough to come out of ignorance and for men to understand their rights, but unfortunately I was wrong. I see that the people are as on the first day of their conquest, because they continually work and fight to be slaves," he complained.[92] Surrounded by hostile villages, Cartagena could not secure its food supply and exhausted its treasury. It began to issue paper money, making its government even more unpopular in the province. The military fate of Cartagena only briefly improved at the end of 1812, after the arrival of as many as four hundred Venezuelan (and some French) refugees from the proindependence army of Venezuela that Spain had just defeated. Many were officers and soldiers eager to continue to fight. Among them was Simón Bolívar, who during his brief stay in Cartagena established a lifelong friendship with Gabriel and Germán Gutiérrez de Piñeres. Bolívar, then a colonel, regained most of the Magdalena region south of Barranca for Cartagena. According to a royalist source, in January 1813, after the victory of the proindependent forces in Chiriguaná, Bolívar allegedly promised to "end oppression and free all slaves and blacks." Whether true or false, this report no doubt raised concerns among the local elite.[93]

Among Cartagena's military refugees was French professional officer Pedro Labatut, who led the province's proindependence troops in the reconquest of most of the lower Magdalena region and the triumphal occupation of Santa Marta in January 1813. Santa Marta's royalists were compelled to flee by boat to Riohacha, Panama, and some Caribbean islands.

Four hundred and fifty-one residents of Santa Marta took refuge in Panama alone.[94] But rather than building support for independence among the remaining samarios, Labatut humiliated them, forcing them to approve the constitution of Cartagena Province, imposing exorbitant contributions to help finance the war, and pillaging the city and its surroundings. As a result, he alienated the city's entire population, including the proindependence sectors that still existed among the lower classes of color. In March 1813 the indigenous villages around Santa Marta, reinforced by samario escapees, attacked the city. The residents welcomed them with the cry of "Long live Ferdinand VII!" and Labatut and his men rapidly fled to Cartagena. Two months later Cartagena made a last attempt to conquer Santa Marta. About 600 troops disembarked near Ciénaga, commanded by another French officer. Mulatto Narciso Vicente Crespo, now with the royalists, mobilized the local population and, masterfully directing his 200 men, imposed a bloody defeat on the cartageneros, who lost more than half of their forces, including their commander, in the battle. This royalist victory earned Crespo the personal sword of Santa Marta's governor, and the city once again became Spain's stronghold in the region.[95] During his two-month occupation of Santa Marta, Labatut had threatened the inhabitants of Riohacha and Valledupar with mass slaughter if they did not swear obedience to the constitution of Cartagena. Yet the people of Riohacha, regardless of class and race, never withdrew their support for Governor Medina and Spain.[96] Although isolated and unable to count on outside reinforcements, Riohacha's royalists were protected by the Wayúu Indians surrounding them, whom even Bolívar thought it unwise to attack.[97]

In Valledupar, it was not Labatut's threats but the persuasive work of Bolívar, then campaigning in the Magdalena region, that resulted in the city's brief embrace of independence. Bolívar was aware of Valledupar's popular support for independence in May 1810. In January 1813, he met with proindependence members of the city's cabildo, including María Concepción Loperena de Fernández de Castro, the wealthy widow of a militia colonel and the owner of cattle and horse haciendas, in Chiriguaná, where they all accepted his leadership. Shortly afterward, they sent a delegation to Cartagena to discuss with the authorities the details of Valledupar's declaration of independence; however, with Bolívar heading back to Venezuela, they could not agree on a plan to defend the city after his departure. In effect, royalist refugees from both Labatut's occupation of Santa Marta and Bolívar's campaign in the Magdalena region flocked to Valledupar, outnumbering the patriots. Nevertheless, in a public celebration on 4 February

1813, María Loperena, acting for the cabildo, proclaimed the independence of Valledupar and promised to personally deliver three hundred of her own horses to Bolívar to help him in the war. She then set fire to the portrait and coat of arms of Ferdinand VII and allegedly freed some of her haciendas' slaves. Not surprisingly, Valledupar's independence was short-lived. After the March 1813 defeat of Cartagena's troops in Ciénaga and the departure of Bolívar's army for Venezuela, the city returned to royalist control.[98]

With Valledupar's failure to secure its independence, Cartagena's hopes for establishing a proindependence stronghold in Santa Marta Province were dashed. In reality, however, the patriots did little to convince the province's residents that they would be better off ruled by the patriots than by Spain. Not only did the samarios suffer under Labatut, but in May 1813, after the royalist reconquest of Santa Marta, Gabriel Gutiérrez de Piñeres issued a decree promising the free plunder of the city to those who volunteered to bring it back to Cartagena.[99] Alarmed by such extremism, the government of the Federation of the United Provinces warned Cartagena that this would only further decrease patriotism at a time when Cartagena already lacked reliable troops.[100] To make matters worse, in June 1813 Captain General Francisco de Montalvo arrived from Spain to become Santa Marta's new governor and prepare the groundwork for Spain's reconquest of New Granada. Unlike Labatut, Montalvo avoided acting like a ruthless conqueror but still imposed on individuals and communities a levy for money, goods, cattle, and conscripts to sustain the war. He also purged several villages and cities of active partisans of independence. Yet he could not fully restore order in the province. In particular, he was unable to clear out the bands of Chimila and free people of color, often deserters of one or the other army, who since 1810 had controlled some rural areas and pillaged farms and haciendas.[101]

In Cartagena Province itself, support for independence outside of the port capital was vanishing. Most villages and towns had paid a high price for the war against Santa Marta, as they had been repeatedly occupied, pillaged, burned, and subjected to recruitment and contributions.[102] Cartagena's position was further weakened by the conflict between Bolívar and toledista Colonel Manuel del Castillo y Rada, sealed in mid-1813, when Bolívar demoted Castillo because he refused to allot some of his troops to the campaign to liberate Venezuela. Furthermore, the Venezuelan campaign, despite its military achievements, failed to defeat Spain and led to Bolívar's desperate decree of war to the death, as a result of which large portions of the population were cruelly massacred on the basis of their birth—the patriots killing Spaniards, the royalists slaying creoles.[103] As news of the deadly campaign reached Cartagena, Venezuelans again took refuge in the fortified city under the protection of the Gutiérrez de Piñeres brothers, prompting fears among many, especially the toledistas, that Bolívar's war to the death would spread into Caribbean New Granada.[104]

In late 1814 new conditions created a possibility that the toledistas would return to power. The appointment of Governor Manuel Rodríguez Torices to a top position in the government of the Federation of the United Provinces gave them the opportunity to present García de Toledo as a candidate for the governorship of the state of Cartagena. Building on his regional network and perhaps manipulating votes, García de Toledo defeated his opponent, Gabriel Gutiérrez de Piñeres. The piñeristas refused to accept the results of the election and, returning to the political practices of 1810–11, staged a coup d'état on 17 December. Headed by the deputy, Ignacio Muñoz, a group of armed men of color locked the legislators in their chamber and threatened them with death unless they chose Gabriel Gutiérrez as governor. The city's security forces, controlled by the piñeristas, did nothing to rescue the representatives. Although no deaths were reported, anarchy prevailed in Cartagena until 5 January 1815, when a governor of compromise, Venezuelan Dr. Pedro Gual, was elected to prevent a direct confrontation between the two parties. In the meantime, the toledistas had called to the rescue Manuel del Castillo, now commander of the army of the Magdalena Line.[105] For their part, the piñeristas sent word to Bolívar, now in Honda, to bring troops to assist them.[106] Before Bolívar responded, Castillo withdrew his forces from the war against the royalists, besieged and took Cartagena, and imposed a drastic punishment on the piñeristas: seizure of property and banishment of sixty men and two women—among them, Gabriel and Germán Gutiérrez de Piñeres and Ignacio Muñoz. Several more were sentenced to remain in the United States for six years to study "the true principles of political and civil liberty."[107]

Against this backdrop, the Federation of the United Provinces authorized Bolívar, who had just won a campaign to force Cundinamarca to join the Federation, to evict the royalists from Santa Marta, and to reconquer Venezuela. In addition, Bolívar received the command of the army of the Magdalena Line, which Castillo had used to defeat the piñeristas in Cartagena. Such a decision, taken by the federal government without consulting the new authorities in Cartagena, infuriated the toledistas, who interpreted it as a piñerista maneuver to launch a war to the death in Caribbean New Granada. In late January 1815 all the corporations and "all the subjects of the first rank and of the most notable part of [Cartagena's] community" petitioned against the federal government's decision in favor of "Bolívar [the] exterminator." To fend off the Venezuelan general, Castillo demobilized the army of the Magdalena Line to bring it home and ordered villages and towns in the region not to obey Bolívar—all of which strengthened the royalist position.[108] Despite various orders from the government of the Federation, from February to April 1815 Cartagena refused to supply Bolívar with men, arms, and ammunition and prevented him from attacking Santa Marta by sea. With Cartagena's piñeristas in exile, Bolívar's only prominent supporters in Caribbean New Granada were Vicente Celedonio Gutiérrez de Piñeres and Juan Pantaleón Ribón in Mompox, where Bolívar's 4,000-man army was immobilized, decimated by disease and desertion. Meanwhile, in 1814 Ferdinand VII had returned to the throne in Spain. He abolished the 1812 constitution of the monarchy, restored royal absolutism, and ordered the reconquest of his rebellious South American colonies.

FREE MEN OF COLOR

Neither during events leading to the First Independence nor during the war up to Spanish reconquest did free men of color, women, slaves, and Indians lastingly challenge the elite leaders or upset the colonial socioracial order. In the major cities, in effect, the white elite's alliance with free men of color, unlike the French revolutionary clubs, remained highly hierarchical. In 1810–11 the popular sectors in Cartagena and Mompox conformed to the elite's decision to organize the urban defense along racial lines. Although in Cartagena such an organization corresponded to the racial separations established by Spain in the militia, in Mompox, where the colonial militia included soldiers "of all colors," it introduced a new division between whites and those of African descent. In neither place did men of color oppose this organization, nor did the momposinos question the command of their pardo unit by white aristocrat Pantaleón Germán Ribón. This reluctance to directly challenge the role of race in the militia may have reflected the fact that under Spain the institution granted men of color equality by extending the military fuero and some corporate privileges to all militiamen, regardless of race.[109] In the new independent units formed in 1810, those traditionally subordinated because of their race and birth gained further consciousness of their equality, grounded in their political, economic, and military participation in the struggle against Spain, which led to the acquisition of their political rights as citizens.

Yet these racially based military units did not transform themselves into autonomous political organizations. Although they were armed and comprised the majority of the male population, in 1810–12 the free men of color in Cartagena and Mompox continued to entrust their political representation to the white reformist elite. This was partly due to their mobilization by leaders of African descent, such as Pedro Romero and Luis Gonzaga Galván, who were too entangled in vertical patronage networks headed by white aristocrats to become ideologically independent. The only exception was perhaps zambo José Luis Muñoz in Mompox, already described as "director" of the city's alcalde ordinario in 1805, but unfortunately his ideas were never recorded.[110] This pattern of white patronage with intermediate leaders of African descent also explains why in Santa Marta the only armed unit in the city, the militia of all colors, did not rebel. There, as the influx of numerous royalists forced the pro-autonomy elite to switch their allegiance to Spain, the dependency of the leaders of color on them prompted dramatic political realignments: whereas some left for Cartagena, Narciso Vicente Crespo, for example, became a commander in Santa Marta's royalist army and led his lower-class followers to fight victoriously against Cartagena's proindependence troops.

These hierarchical alliances did not evolve into autonomous political organizations also because for free men of color they represented a major step toward their much desired integration into the new political system. In the scornful words of toledista Antonio José de Ayos, "The supposed rights of equality . . . were all that the scum of the people were interested in and the origin of their fanaticism."[111] From equality within their military units under Spain, the militiamen of color obtained individual equality for all men who shared the burden of their city's defense, regardless of their skin color. Furthermore, racial equality became part of the electoral law of December 1810 that gave suffrage to male citizens in all of the colonial racial categories who were economically self-sufficient or heads of a household. In other words, officially economic and paternalistic criteria replaced racial ones, even if some racial groups were more likely to be enfranchised than others. In such a legal context, any discourse on equality required silence on the question of race, and demands for equality were not made on the grounds of one's color, but of one's personal value and services to society. As a result, qualifying free men of color dissociated their cause from that of further disenfranchised members of society such as indigents, slaves, servants, women, and Indians. Moreover, by participating in some organizations, such as the militias, that supported the new social order against anarchy, the citizens of color helped prevent unwelcome movements and slave unrest. Although many dark-skinned piñerista supporters united behind their leaders' message of independence and equality, they did not question the significance that racial categories such as negro, pardo, zambo, or cuarterón had in defining one's socioeconomic status and identity. Distinctions between free persons of partial and full African ancestry continued to manifest themselves in a hierarchy in which "full" blacks were assigned to the lower stratum.[112] Thus, no racial consciousness uniting the free and slave populations of full or partial African ancestry in political action emerged in this process.

Nevertheless, these hierarchical political alliances were not exempt from ideology. Notably, when García de Toledo began to resist a process he found too rapid, the Gutiérrez de Piñeres brothers understood and capitalized on the popular classes of color's desire for independence and equality to rally their support. Yet the piñeristas were never able to attract all of them. When their ally Simón Bolívar returned to Cartagena in 1814, according to a royalist source, "some military and lower-class leaders" opposed his presence, prompting him to take matters to the Federation in Tunja.[113] Mulatto Pedro Romero and his followers, who had switched their support from García de Toledo to the Gutiérrez de Piñeres brothers in mid-1811, then reverted back to the toledistas, and Romero was elected as a representative in early 1815, after Castillo's overthrow of the piñeristas.[114]

Still, by not forming their own political movement in 1810–11, the free people of color missed a unique chance to make demands beyond what the elite was ready to concede. Although they briefly showed their capacity to act independently from the white leadership in the revolt against the conspiracy of the Fijo in February 1811, afterward they returned to their homes and barracks. When in November 1811 they were able to directly influence the Supreme Junta, their demand for equality of all citizens regardless of race was a repetition of what had already been granted to them in 1810. Their request that "the battalion of pardos have its commander from the same class and the faculty to name its adjutants," and that "the militia of artillery have the same terms as the battalion of pardos, with officers from their class," confirmed their acceptance of the colonial corporatist society and racial categories.[115] Apparently they did nothing then to promote the end of slavery. By the time of the debates to draft the constitution in February 1812, piñerista leaders had managed to halt armed demonstrations by the populace and the Patriot Lancers of Getsemaní to force decisions on the deputies. Later that year, the influx into Cartagena of hundreds of Venezuelans and some Frenchmen who took many positions of command previously held by cartageneros completed the political subordination of the city's free population of color. In 1812, as the war with Santa Marta intensified, the separate units of men of African descent were dissolved and their soldiers were absorbed into racially and regionally inclusive armies. They had definitively lost the possibility of organizing autonomously around a distinct agenda.

Beyond the main cities, free people of color in several villages and small towns took advantage of the breakdown of Spanish authority and of their demographic superiority to momentarily seize power in 1810. In some places, their detractors in neighboring villages claimed, the "frail remnants of subordination that contained the people" rapidly vanished under the pressure of the lower classes of color, and "the evils of anarchy" reigned.[116] In Santa Marta Province, in addition to Valledupar where in 1810 the common people reportedly declared independence from the elite, several villages on the east bank of the Magdalena River defied their provincial capital. In Chiriguaná, in particular, some vecinos informed the governor of Santa Marta that "in junta the people of the lower populace summoned the whites to the municipal house, and there they all proclaimed absolute independence from the town of Tamalameque," on which they depended.[117] However, lacking coordination, leadership, and arms, the lower classes in these villages could not resist the elite's response and the forces sent by Santa Marta, and their movements were rapidly subdued.

WOMEN

Women's exclusion from suffrage and many aspects of equality does not signify that the First Independence made no change in their lives. Although they did not struggle for new rights as wives, widows, and single heads of household, in Cartagena women, regardless of race, valued the term *ciudadanas* (citizens) to define themselves, as shown by many baptismal certificates.[118]

The case of patriot hacendado widow María Concepción Loperena, in Valledupar, sheds light on the role of some elite women as leaders, organizers, suppliers, and fund-raisers. As the president of the independent state of Cundinamarca commented in his praise of Loperena, "If a fair number of these types of perfect women could be found in the other provinces, what couldn't we do of the hard task we have imposed on ourselves?"[119] A Spaniard, for his part, characterized her as "unrestrainable and impetuous."[120]

In her February 1813 declaration of independence, Loperena described herself as "a free woman of royalist origin but today a republican."[121] In fact, her sister-in-law in Cartagena and Anita Lenoit, Bolívar's French mistress in a village on the Magdalena River, who both belonged to a network of proindependence women in the region, convinced her to support Bolívar. In her will of 1835, Loperena stated that the Spaniards made her pay dearly for "aspiring to a better, noble and great fatherland, full of progress" and for her early "material and moral help [to Bolívar] . . . when he was called the insurgent, when nobody knew him, when he lacked sufficient means." Royalists seized most of her property, and she was forced to flee to escape execution, but she kept "alive a consciousness of freedom."[122]

Royalist female owners of haciendas played a similar role among the defenders of Spain. When Mompox declared its independence in 1810, Marquise María Josefa Isabel de Torre-Hoyos sent her husband, Mateo de Epalza, with a considerable sum of money to a pro-Spanish village where the family had haciendas. She also relocated herds of horses and cattle to safe places in Santa Marta, then requested troops from Santa Marta to overthrow Mompox's revolutionary government; however, patriots intercepted her letter and threatened to seize all of her properties. The arrival of the Fijo to restore Cartagena's authority in Mompox in January 1811 and Ayos's rule prevented confiscation, but the marquise was unable to continue to collect levies on the riverine communities previously dominated by her deceased father, the marquis of Torre-Hoyos. After 11 November 1811 she managed to stay in Mompox by keeping a low profile until the reconquest of General Morillo allowed her to recover much of her wealth and privileges — and sent many momposinos to death, prison, and exile, among the latter the wives and families of the patriot aristocracy. When the proindependence army liberated Mompox in 1820, the marquise did lose her haciendas and went into exile in Jamaica, just as the patriot deportees returned.[123]

Although more difficult to document, lower-class women also took part in mobilizing communities for or against Spain, contributed their scant jewelry to the war effort, and sometimes accompanied the troops. Some served as messengers, spies, and healers or protected fugitives. Some women participated in the defense and evacuation of Mompox against Cartagena's attack in 1811. They also skillfully struggled against disease and hunger during the 1815 and 1820–21 sieges of Cartagena (see below), no doubt limiting casualties through their ingenuity. But in both Cartagena and Mompox, they did not go as far as mobilizing in favor of surrender, which was a lost cause in cities with numerous militias and armies. Elsewhere, women were instrumental in the protection of villages and small towns that were repeatedly occupied by both sides in the war. Others chose flight rather than abuse by the enemy, taking to the woods with children and the elderly. Yet women, regardless of race and class, did not gain much from the First Independence. Many died in the 1815 siege of Cartagena; others lost sons, husbands, and lovers to the competing armies. Free women of color in small trades, businesses, and agriculture suffered from the economic crisis. Slave women did not see new opportunities to achieve freedom opening to them, in contrast to slave men who occasionally could join the military to become free.[124] Because they did not organize and press for more rights for themselves, they generally did not make long-lasting gains.

SLAVES

Similarly, slavery did not become a major issue in Caribbean New Granada partly because slaves maintained themselves at the margin of the independence process, and few, if any, took advantage of the breakdown of the colonial order to organize movements to gain their freedom and equality. Neither did the free population of color or the "blacks from Haiti," whose presence in Cartagena allegedly terrified the toledista Castillo, promote an abolitionist movement in the city or in the province. If kinship and similar labor conditions sometimes linked slaves and poor free people of color, no racial or class consciousness united them to produce a common movement. As a result, the reformist elite was free to draft social policies that promoted their own interests as hacendados, merchants, miners, and slaveowners.

Nevertheless, census figures reveal that after 1810 the number of slaves dropped sharply in the three Caribbean provinces: from 14,067 in 1777–80 to 6,827 slaves in 1835.[125] Much of this decline was due to factors unrelated to the war, such as natural death, the end of the slave trade, the low birthrate among slave women, self-purchase, and flight. But the general lack of order and the crisis produced by the war accelerated the process. On the one hand, flight increased dramatically. Slaves (and free people of color) escaped from their workplaces and the army. Owners and administrators abandoned haciendas and ranches to take refuge in the city or serve in the army. In some cases, slaves apparently remained on haciendas to continue working for their absent masters.[126] More often, they seized the opportunity to run away and vanish individually or join other fugitives to re-create rochelas, sometimes in the vicinity of Cartagena. When the war was over, they quietly joined the ranks of the free population of color.[127] On the other hand, the war caused the departure or death of many slaves. Some slaves emigrated with their masters. In 1813, for example, out of 194 refugees from Santa Marta residing in Portobelo, Panama, 55 were slaves.[128] Others were exported to Cuba or Panama, especially patriot conscripts captured by royalists, or appropriated as payment for fines and war contributions; still others were sold by impoverished hacendados.[129] In Santa Marta, transactions involving slaves increased threefold in the 1810s compared with the previous two decades, as the royalist city became a center for the export of slaves, including small children taken from their mothers.[130] The number of slaves also declined because those residing in cities were the victims of wartime hunger and epidemics. The most dramatic case was that of Cartagena's slaves during the 1815 siege. Since they were the least likely to get food and medical care, they figured prominently among the six thousand cartageneros who died of hunger and disease.[131]

Enlistment in the fighting armies did not represent a major avenue to freedom for male slaves in Caribbean New Granada. The drafting of slaves was limited. For instance, Pedro Nájera did not free the slaves he armed and mobilized against Spanish commander Talledo in Mompox in June 1810, and when some of them were taken prisoner by Spain in 1812, they were sold to Cuba as "black slaves."[132] Except for the liberation of several slaves by Vicente Celedonio Gutiérrez de Piñeres and some other patriots to be integrated into Mompox's pardo battalion in August 1810, there is no evidence of substantial manumission during the First Independence of Cartagena Province.[133] Nor is it clear whether the slaves allegedly freed by María Concepción Loperena in Valledupar in 1813 were enlisted in Bolívar's troops or whether the royalist hacendados who participated in the war with their slaves granted them freedom.[134] Even the forced mobilization of men by Manuel del Castillo to fight against Spain's reconquest included sharecroppers, day laborers, and temporary residents but not slaves.[135]

INDIANS

In contrast to slaves, several Indian communities attempted to seize the opportunity of war to protect or improve their position locally, indicating that they were not as "strangely and absurdly royalist" as some of the existing literature portrays them.[136] Obviously, the unsubdued Wayúu in the Guajira Peninsula, as well as the Emberá and the Kuna in the west, benefited from the colonial status quo and had little to gain from Cartagena's republican project, which pursued their disappearance as separate nations.

In contrast, it is likely that the equality and citizenship granted to Indians by the Cortes of Cadiz and the 1812 constitution of the Spanish monarchy as well as the abolition of all Indian personal services decreed by the Council of the Regency in late 1812 fostered support for the royalists among the pueblos de indios that heard of these decisions.[137]

At any rate, indigenous support for Spain was far from being blind. Although the Indian villages around Santa Marta played a crucial role in the suppression of Labatut's brutal dictatorship in March 1813, two months earlier these communities had done little to prevent his occupation of the city. In Ciénaga, in particular, the indigenous population had resisted forced incorporation into the royalist troops. When a Spanish officer ordered them to clear a path in the forest for his soldiers, "these people did nothing but cut some branches and posts without showing up to work again, hiding in the woods," forcing the troops to complete the job. Shortly after that, two priests convinced 250 members of this community to join the royalist force, "reinforcing them with 60 black slaves sent and armed by the owner of the hacienda 'Papares.'" But, when the commander ordered "the Indians [to] march at the vanguard of the commune, in order to control them better . . . they mutinied." They took a cash box, killed a few soldiers, and escaped to the woods again, preventing the royalist troops from rescuing Santa Marta.[138] Clearly, Indians mobilized against the proindependence army only after they had experienced Labatut's abuse. This could work the other way around. Near Valledupar, the tyranny of the royalist marquis of Valde-Hoyos prompted some Chimila communities, such as the pueblo of Villanueva headed by the cacique Canopán, to support Valledupar's declaration of independence in 1813.[139] Yet, except for the Emberá and the Kuna, who remained isolated from the war, Indian communities did not unite in their resistance. Death, destruction of their pueblos, forced conscription, and flight left them weaker and fewer in number than in 1810.

VILLAGES AND SMALL TOWNS

Likewise, small towns, villages, and hacendados' fiefdoms reacted without regional vision or coordination. Allegiance to one or the other side often depended more on specific circumstances than on ideology. In 1810 several villages and small towns momentarily fell under the control of their free inhabitants of color, who managed to displace the local elite and reject Santa Marta's jurisdiction until military intervention returned them to elite rule. Other villages along the Magdalena River took a different path but still were unable to sever colonial ties. For example, in July 1811 the "honorable vecinos" of the villages of Guáimaro, Remolino, and Sitionuevo, under the jurisdiction of Santa Marta, petitioned the Supreme Junta of Cartagena for annexation to Cartagena Province. Probably led by an opponent of the royalist takeover in Santa Marta, they claimed that Santa Marta obstructed their industry, free trade, and liberty. Its despotic government was corrupt and denied people the right to be represented by freely elected deputies who would have their interests at heart. From the "fair, enlightened, and beneficent government of Cartagena" they expected schools and jails, protection from the floods of the Magdalena River, and an end to Santa Marta's yearly forced recruitment of two hundred villagers into the militia, which destroyed their families and the area's agriculture. In their words, they acted as much to preserve trade and close family ties with residents in Cartagena Province as to avoid the "evils of anarchy" that had seized the communities in which the populace refused any subordination to a superior government.[140] Although Cartagena's junta welcomed these villages, it was unable to fulfill their demands and adequately protect them from Santa Marta's reprisals. Even the villages and towns in the plains of Corozal and Sincelejo, which in 1812 rejected the jurisdiction of Cartagena and proclaimed allegiance to royalist Santa Marta, did not become strongholds of support for the Crown. Reportedly, the Spanish commander in the area, Antonio Rebustillo, was no better than his predecessor, piñerista lawyer Ignacio Muñoz. Rebustillo forced the people of Corozal to pay heavy levies, but "he only entertained himself in dance, games, and big parties, embezzling funds, deflowering maidens, and persecuting widows and married women." The inhabitants eventually drove him out, and Corozal returned to the bosom of Cartagena.[141]

Throughout the First Independence, then, neither royalists nor patriots were able to consistently rally Caribbean New Granada's communities to their cause. In 1814 piñerista vicar Juan Fernández de Sotomayor recognized that Cartagena authorities had failed to convince the region's population of the rightfulness of independence. In a belated and vain attempt to remedy the situation, he published a brief *Catecismo o instrucción popular*. Written in a question-and-answer format, the *Catecismo* denied that the war for independence was incompatible with the Catholic faith, as the royalists maintained. It was the conquest of America and the slave trade that had been immoral, Fernández de Sotomayor claimed, because the goal never had been the evangelization of Indians and Africans, but gold mining and agricultural production. In contrast, the present conflict was a just war of self-defense to preserve life, freedom, and individual property—a war that would create a new society and elevate the country to the rank of nation, he concluded.[142]

In fact, people struggled merely to survive. As the war went on, villagers increasingly abandoned their dwellings and crops to the invaders, taking refuge in the woods to avoid abuse and conscription. Both sides attempted to prevent disaffection by awarding glorious titles of fidelity to villages and towns that supported the fight. For example, Guamal, the old fief of the deceased marquis of Torre-Hoyos, was praised by the governor of Santa Marta for having always been faithful to the Crown under the rule of zambo Pedro Juan Tinoco, now its alcalde.[143] Cartagena promoted Barranquilla and Carmen, notably, to "towns" (villas) and departmental capitals in reward for continuing to provide men and goods to the cause of independence.[144] But as misery, havoc, and conscription increased, more and more communities missed the loose domination that had characterized Spain's rule before 1810.

SPAIN'S RECONQUEST

In 1815 Spain's royal army began its reconquest of Caribbean New Granada from Santa Marta, under the command of Captain General Montalvo. Exhausted by four years of war and abuse, many communities welcomed the royal army. Progressively, those villages and towns still supporting independence fell into Spanish hands, including Mompox in late April. Even these developments did not persuade Manuel del Castillo and his followers in Cartagena of the necessity to unite with Bolívar. With his army crumbling and the cause of New Granada's independence provisionally lost, a hopeless Bolívar offered his resignation to the government of the Federation and left for a Jamaican exile in May. In the meantime, Ferdinand VII had sent Spanish general Pablo Morillo with a massive expeditionary force to reconquer northern South America. Morillo's army rapidly regained much of Venezuela to the Crown. In July 1815 he established his headquarters in Santa Marta, from which he carried on the reconquest of New Granada.

Quickly Cartagena and its surroundings remained the only bastion of resistance against Spain in the region. On 1 September Morillo initiated its siege. In despair, the cartagenero authorities allowed the piñeristas to return from exile to help defend the city. In mid-October, as the siege tightened and the neighboring villages welcomed the Spaniards, people in Cartagena began to blame the tragedy on Castillo, who was deposed by Venezuelan officers.[145] Hunger and disease took over. The poor ate "rotten meat and flours . . . dogs, rats, crows," while the wealthy consumed "meager rations of rice with dry prawns and chocolate" bought with jewels and silver from speculators.[146] Many residents were walking skeletons, and bodies were left to the buzzards, unburied. The authorities ordered all cartageneros who were unfit for military defense to leave the city in order to save some food for 3,600 enlisted men. About 2,000 women, children, and elderly people left to surrender to the Spaniards, many succumbing on the way. Conditions did not improve with their departure. On 4 December alone, 300 inhabitants expired in the streets of Cartagena. In view of the disaster, the government ordered the evacuation of the city. Gathered on thirteen crowded corsair boats, 2,000 to 3,000 exhausted men, women, and children fled, many to die or never return.[147]

On 6 December 1815 General Morillo's troops entered Cartagena. In the words of one of them, "bodies [lay] in the streets and the houses. . . . It smelled so terribly bad that it was almost impossible to breathe. Nothing, in sum, was noticeable among these unfortunate inhabitants except weeping and grief."[148] Appalled by the sight and smell of death, disease, and desolation, the troops did not massacre the remaining residents. However, one colonel spread terror in Cartagena Bay, killing all the lepers in its lazaretto and most of the inhabitants in the black fishermen's village of Bocachica. Morillo's 106-day siege cost Cartagena perhaps as many as one-third of its approximately 18,000 inhabitants, who died of hunger and disease.[149]

Those who managed to escape when the Spanish troops were about to enter the city suffered new ordeals. Many of them died at sea from hunger, thirst, and exhaustion. Some were abandoned on isolated beaches by deceitful sailors. Others ended up in Cuba, only to be imprisoned. The most fortunate ones landed in Haiti and Jamaica, among them the three Gutiérrez de Piñeres brothers, the priests Juan Fernández de Sotomayor and Manuel Benito Revollo, and Ignacio Muñoz. Pedro Romero, however, succumbed just as he set foot on Haitian soil.[150]

Reconquest after 1815 was so brutal that Spain could not rebuild support for colonial government, even among those communities that had welcomed it.[151] The Spanish governor of Cartagena Province, Brigadier Gabriel Torres y Velazco, witnessed with growing powerlessness the "general dissolution and the loss of the New Kingdom of Granada" due to Spanish oppression. He sent alarming messages to the viceroy in Bogotá and to the king in Madrid demanding constructive policies—but all in vain. Weakened by war, occupation, and economic crisis, Spain lacked the will and the means to enact policies that could benefit Caribbean New Granada's population.

On the contrary, it burdened with exorbitant taxes and demands a people already exhausted by five years of war and destruction, "reducing villages and towns to refuges of beggars." In this context, agriculture, cattle raising, and artisan enterprise could not recover. Spain ordered the seizure of all circulating paper money and prohibited its use, hampering the little trade that had survived. Madrid restored the royal monopolies and high import and export taxes, making contraband the only viable alternative.[152] With the few literate men in the Caribbean provinces suspected of sympathizing with the cause of independence, public administration lacked qualified personnel.[153] The scant educational and health facilities that had existed in the region were severely impaired.[154] Given the key role played by militiamen of color in the revolution in Cartagena and Mompox, Spain withdrew the confidence it had in them for the defense of Caribbean New Granada before 1810. Notably, the governor prohibited the reestablishment of Cartagena's battalion of free pardos "because of the pernicious impressions the revolution left on them, until time rectifies them and they can be trusted again." Whereas in 1781 Spain had not hesitated to send this pardo battalion to repress the Comunero Revolt, now it ordered recruits from Socorro, cradle of the revolt, with the specification that "all be white" to make up for the shortage of troops in Cartagena, no doubt relying on the coast's history of weak solidarity with the Andean interior.[155]

In 1815–16 Morillo established military courts to eradicate the independence movement. These courts arbitrarily and swiftly executed prisoners, promoting, in the words of Spanish officials, "scenes of blood and terror" to subjugate the population.[156] Morillo's public executions, often followed by the display of severed heads, also decimated the tiny enlightened elite and the leadership of African descent. Men such as toledistas José María García de Toledo, Antonio José de Ayos, and Manuel del Castillo and piñerista Juan Pantaleón Ribón were caught and in early 1816 court-martialed and executed for high treason, together with five others. Luis Gonzaga Galván was also publicly shot. More were exiled, and others, such as the Gutiérrez de Piñeres brothers, died in combat.[157]

After 1816 the military continued to terrify and repress the local population and to undermine the governor's efforts to instill confidence in the government, prompting men and women to address numerous complaints to him.[158] The Catholic Church added to people's misery, as shown by an increasing number of letters sent to bishops by the vecinos of villages and small towns to report priests' abuses and misconduct. According to Bishop Gregorio José Rodríguez of Cartagena, certain priests practiced usury and "wholly devoted themselves with their greed to Satan's hands." Clergymen punished their parishioners "with their own hands, with shackles, slaps in the face, blows with a stick, lashes, and other means that are reprehensible and indecent. . . . Adding to these abuses the horrible one of servitude understood according to their own caprice."[159] Although not new, in the context of war and occupation, all of these practices, which violated the canonical law, further eroded popular support for church and Crown.

As aptly shown by Gustavo Bell Lemus, war and reconquest erased much of the limited order the colonial authorities had been able to foster before 1810. Men resisting enlistment escaped to the woods. Desertion and lack of discipline hampered the existing armies. Slaves continued to run away from the haciendas that were still operating. Together with deserters, fugitives, vagrants, and people who had lost everything in the war, they roamed the countryside and formed new rochelas in the backlands. The war, with its many casualties, disrupted colonial networks of patronage, whereas new ones formed in the armies. Farther away on the frontier, unsubdued indigenous people regained the little terrain they had lost in the late eighteenth century. The war also nullified the limited progress achieved by the church to make people live according to Catholic norms. According to Governor Torres, "the horrible vices of concubinage, adultery, and scandalous dissolution of the language" prevailed with new strength in several areas, notably the Mountain of María and Mahates. In the cities, especially Cartagena, prostitution and "shocking behaviors" were on the rise.[160]

By 1819 Simón Bolívar and Francisco de Paula Santander, a law student from Cúcuta, had begun to retake control of Andean New Granada. Through pastorals to be read in all churches, Cartagena's bishop attempted to mobilize the population against independence. He warned them that Bolívar "ha[d] sold your blood to the black gentiles from Santo Domingo" and would establish in Caribbean New Granada the model of monstrous dictatorship he had learned in Haiti from Dessalines, Christophe, and Pétion.[161] Bishop Rodríguez promised a plenary indulgence to those who remained faithful to the Crown but God's worst punishment to those who joined the cause of Bolívar. However, in a region mostly inhabited by people of African descent, his tactic of raising the fear that the Caribbean provinces would become other Haitis only convinced some whites.

As a new war for control of Caribbean New Granada began in 1819, few communities participated in the patriot advance or the royalist resistance. Many peasants, laborers, and bogas again rejected recruitment by escaping to the woods, and desertions plagued the armies on both sides.

Villages were abandoned to the enemy. Only a few communities, such as Barranquilla and Soledad, volunteered men and goods to the proindependence army. Still, backed by attacks from the sea, patriot ground troops slowly overcame the Spaniards in the region. Like their Spanish predecessors, the patriot troops sometimes insulted, assaulted, robbed, and raped the population.[162] When in October 1819 an Irish patriot commander allowed his men to sack Riohacha and abuse its inhabitants, the residents, helped by the Wayúu, massacred the occupiers. Eight months later, the Irish unit was back; it took Riohacha and burned it to the ground. After tenacious resistance from neighboring Indians and royalist forces, Santa Marta surrendered in November 1820. As during Morillo's reconquest, Cartagena, under Spanish rule since December 1815, was the last city in the region to resist. In June 1820 news of the restoration of the 1812 constitution of the monarchy in Spain after a Liberal revolution produced divisions among Cartagena's royal authorities and disorder among the troops, but still the city adopted the Spanish constitution in great pomp.[163] There is no evidence of protest by the free men of color, despite the fact that the constitution was a major step backward: it excluded from suffrage free men of full or mixed African descent (except the wealthy sons of legally married parents who had distinguished themselves through acts of patriotism or talent).[164] In September 1821 the republican army began to surround Cartagena. It nevertheless took fourteen months of siege for the port city to surrender.

Coming after the Haitian Revolution, the crossclass and crossracial movement of Cartagena and Mompox against Spain in 1810 had few equivalents in other Latin American cities with large populations of African descent. Yet, as elite leaders and the popular classes joined forces, they did not upset the colonial socioracial order. Each group pursued different goals behind a common republican discourse: freedom from the restrictions imposed by the metropolis for the elite and racial equality for the lower classes. Although this multilayered movement failed to take root and to radically transform society, class and race were not meaningless categories in the war in Caribbean New Granada. In Cartagena, the piñeristas in 1811 advocated more radical reforms than the toledistas, and the line separating them tended to correspond with the color line—people of full or partial African ancestry versus whites—and the class line—the poor versus the wealthy. Still, after 1811, once the piñeristas were in power, their ideology and policies resembled those of their opponents. Moreover, both parties competed for control of Cartagena's free people of color, using patronage networks that crossed class and color lines. In the process, the population of African descent remained divided along status, color, class, and gender lines.

It is impossible to infer from the case of Cartagena that in the rest of the Caribbean provinces whites tended to favor autonomy or Spain's continuing colonialism, and free people of color, independence. In reality, the abduction of the Spanish king by Napoleon prompted the inhabitants of some cities, towns, and villages to rise up against their provincial capital; others rebelled against an abusive local government, and still others protested Spanish direct government. In the process, some localities stood up for independence, others supported autonomy, and still others were loyal to the Spanish monarchy. Several aligned themselves with one or the other side according to changing circumstances. Neither did Indian pueblos support the royalist cause if they did not see major benefits for them. Nor did slaves or lower-class women gain much status during these years, although the turmoil created new opportunities for slaves to escape to freedom. In most of the region, however, as material conditions worsened with the war, enthusiasm for independence dissolved. After 1815, although Spanish reconquest was increasingly resisted, it did not transform into general support for the advancing patriot troops.

Cartagena Province was the first province in New Granada to declare independence and to grant equality and full citizenship to people of African descent, but it became one of the last provinces to regain independence in 1821.[165] Fragmentation, division, and competition between cities and among the elite, as well as the inability of the lower classes of color to challenge the white elite, frustrated the Caribbean region's unique opportunity to lead the movement of independence in New Granada—or its chance to form a separate Caribbean nation. As a result, the Andean elite could blame much of the failure of the First Independence on Cartagena's opposition to the General Congress called by Bogotá in 1810 and to the leadership of Simón Bolívar. When in the early 1820s Caribbean New Granada became part of Gran Colombia (composed of Venezuela, New Granada, and Ecuador), its economy was more damaged than that of Andean New Granada, and two sieges had initiated Cartagena's rapid decline. The region had lost its leadership. Moreover, in 1821 continuing Spanish rule prevented Cartagena from selecting its own representatives to the assembly—the Congress of Cúcuta—that formulated the nation's first constitution.

5
EQUALITY AND
FREEDOM UNDER
THE REPUBLIC

In July 1823, after rumors spread that Haiti had sent three hundred secret agents to destabilize Venezuela and after two alleged conspiracies to exterminate whites were discovered there, Gran Colombia's minister of the interior, *antioqueño* José Manuel Restrepo, noted in his diary: "The situation in [Gran] Colombia is very critical regarding the pardos. . . . These days, in the province of Cartagena too, seeds of disunion with the pardos are noticeable. They are reportedly promoted by the senator Remigio Márquez, who has been ordered to come to the capital [Bogotá]. If we don't have a strong foreign immigration soon, the republic runs a high risk of an intestine civil war with the negros and mulatos, and Venezuela is promptly lost."[1]

Following the adoption by the Congress of Cúcuta of Gran Colombia's first constitution in 1821, Restrepo's fear of a revolution along Haitian lines in Caribbean New Granada contrasted with the reality of relentless attacks by Indian rebels in this region. As in the southern province of Pasto, in Riohacha and Santa Marta Provinces royalist guerrillas, backed by pro-Spanish forces from Maracaibo, fought against independence until late 1823. The continuing presence of the unsubdued Wayúu on the frontier added to the instability of the region. Isolated in Santa Marta and Riohacha, patriot units under Venezuelan aristocrat General Mariano Montilla suffered from desertion and the lack of food. In 1821 several villages on the Guajira Peninsula and around Valledupar and Santa Marta rebelled in the name of the Spanish king. The next year the "civilized" Indians in Ciénaga and villages near Santa Marta resumed their struggle against independence. By January 1823, 350 of them occupied Santa Marta for eighteen days and sacked part of the city. Guamal and other villages on the east bank of the Magdalena River and south of Valledupar also rose up against the new government. Only after Admiral José Padilla, a pardo from Riohacha, led a successful maritime attack against the Spaniards in Maracaibo could the patriots overcome the royalist rebels in Caribbean New Granada. Many supporters of Spain were killed; others fled to Venezuela. Still others, especially among the Indians, were forcibly drafted into the army and sent far away to fight with Simón Bolívar for the independence of Peru.[2] Nevertheless, Gran Colombia's leaders clung to the view that Indians were pitiable and backward but docile, whereas they believed that any gathering of individuals of African descent could degenerate into a rebellion against the white minority.

THE CONSTITUTION OF 1821

Racial equality had been at the core of the First Independence of Cartagena and Mompox. After Gran Colombia won its independence in 1821, equality continued to be a mobilizing idea, but, as the war receded, the concept of individual equality for all men who could demonstrate "civilization" and economic independence displaced military achievement. Like other republican charters in the 1820s, the constitution adopted by the Congress of Cúcuta in 1821 stressed its protection of Colombians' "liberty, security, property, and equality." It established a system of indirect representation that limited suffrage: electors were chosen by adult males who owned 100 pesos in real property or earned their living "without depending on another person as a day laborer or a servant." Because colonial Spain had not provided public education, literacy would not be required to vote until 1840. In turn, the electors (one for every 4,000 "souls") who chose the president, vice president, senators, and representatives must be able to read and write and to possess real property valued at 500 pesos or an annual income of 300 pesos. Thus, suffrage in the 1821 constitution resembled Cartagena's constitution of 1812, when it was guaranteed to all male heads of household who lived independently off their rents or labor. It was, however, more limited than for the election of the Congress of Cúcuta, which gave suffrage to soldiers regardless of their economic status, although in practice unqualified military men were allowed to vote until 1827.[3]

Slaves were the focus of the Law of 21 July 1821, which progressively abolished slavery while attempting to reconcile the contradictory constitutional rights to freedom, equality, and property. This law banned the importation of new slaves into the country and directed that henceforth all children born of slave mothers would be free but would have to work for the mothers' masters without pay until age eighteen—theoretically as compensation for their upbringing.[4] The equality of Indians was approved by the Congress of Cúcuta in its Law of 11 October 1821, which also laid the groundwork for the liquidation of their resguardos.[5] In the eyes of Minister of the Interior Restrepo, these two laws were crucial to the future of the nation. He told the congress: "Within fifty or sixty years at the latest, Colombia will be inhabited only by free men, the Indians will have mixed with the European and the African races, and a third race will result, which according to experience does not have the defects of the indigenes; finally the racial mixes (castas) will progressively disappear from our soil."[6] Anticipating the cosmic race imagined a century later by Mexican José Vasconcelos, Restrepo foresaw a nation of free and increasingly white people.

The principle of equality prevailed in the law, censuses, legal documents, and even notices of fugitives, which all abolished the colonial racial categories with the exception of Indians and slaves.[7] Equality was also the long-term goal behind the promotion of education. Education, the legislators believed, would eradicate colonial ignorance and prepare Colombians to become full citizens. Consequently, legislation in 1821 gave priority to male education and decreed the establishment of an elementary school for boys in each town and village, with a teacher on the community's payroll to teach them reading, writing, arithmetic, religion, and "the rights and duties of man in society." Because "girls and young women . . . ought to make a portion so considerable and of such influence in society," the government also hoped to promote their instruction but, in the wake of the postwar crisis, entrusted female education to women's convents and vecinos' initiatives.[8] In the mid-1820s new legislation addressed specific aspects of equality. With time and in response to individual challenges, the colonial requirements of limpieza de sangre and legitimate birth faded away. The government opposed the exclusion of pardos (but said nothing of blacks) from higher education. Similarly, an 1825 law established that on the grounds of the equality of all Colombians, illegitimate birth could not prevent individuals from graduating from universities and becoming lawyers. The legislators, however, did not pronounce illegitimate individuals equal to legitimate ones, on the grounds that such equality would tarnish the international image of Colombia and promote "incontinence" among Colombians.[9] To boost church-sanctified unions, viewed as sources of demographic growth and moral improvement, all colonial restrictions on interracial and crossclass marriages were lifted, and legally parents could only oppose the marriage of their minor children (under twenty-one years for men, under eighteen for women).[10] Gender equality was recognized only for entering convents and monasteries. "Youngsters of either sex" were to be at least twenty-five years old to take orders.[11]

TABLE I. POPULATION OF GRAN COLOMBIA, BY COUNTRY AND CASTE

	Venezuela	New Granada	Ecuador	Total
Whites	200,000	877,000	157,000	1,234,000
Indians	207,000	313,000	393,000	913,000
Free pardos	433,000	140,000	42,000	615,000
Slaves	60,000	70,000	8,000	138,000
Total	900,000	1,400,000	600,000	2,900,000

Source: See note 12.

Although these measures aimed at dismantling the colonial caste system, the congress passed them when, simultaneously, some leaders of Gran Colombia worried about the influence the Haitian Revolution might have on free people of color in Venezuela and Caribbean New Granada. Not fortuitously, in 1825, José Manuel Restrepo completed his imposing *Historia de la revolución de la república de Colombia*, which portrayed New Granada as Andean and white, in contrast to Venezuela, where "free pardos" dominated, and Ecuador, where Indians were the absolute majority. He included a table with estimates of Gran Colombia's population by country and "caste," despite the fact that the census of 1825, which he directed as minister of the interior, did not include racial information (table 1).[12] To whiten New Granada's population, Restrepo simply eliminated the category of mestizos and assimilated them into whites. Andean New Granada thus appeared as the white, civilized center of Gran Colombia as opposed to pardo Venezuela and Indian Ecuador. Yet Restrepo still attributed 140,000 free pardos to New Granada, mostly in the Caribbean region, where he feared the same "seeds of disunion with the pardos" as in Venezuela.[13]

The leader most concerned with the alleged pardo threat was the liberator and president of the republic, Simón Bolívar. Bolívar believed that this threat, which he called "pardocracia," would lead to the extermination of whites in Venezuela and Caribbean New Granada.[14] His apprehension dated back to his firsthand experience with the racial violence that characterized the first phase of Venezuela's anticolonial struggle, often referred to as a race war, when in 1814 royalist José Tomás Boves led an army of pardos and manumitted or fugitive slaves against the white creoles.[15] Fundamentally, Bolívar doubted the motives of the pardos fighting for the independence of Venezuela and New Granada; for many of them, he thought, race was more important than the nation. This doubt, added to Bolívar's thirst for absolute leadership, could turn deadly for those who stood in his way—as in 1817, when he had pardo Manuel Piar executed for challenging his supremacy. On the other hand, he then tamed with rapid military advancement his two other challengers, white aristocrat Santiago Mariño and the rough but reportedly white *llanero* (horseman of the tropical plains) José Antonio Páez.[16] Despite the fact that Bolívar was in Peru and Bolivia from September 1823 to August 1826, he continued to worry about the possibility of pardocracia and a race war in Venezuela and New Granada. By June 1826, after he received alarming letters on this matter from his sister in Venezuela and he unveiled in Peru an alleged plot by Spain to invade Venezuela and the Caribbean Coast, Bolívar's concerns became obsessive.[17] In contrast, Gran Colombia's vice president, Francisco de Paula Santander, had no direct experience with Boves's race war or with the black republic of Haiti but was not insensitive to the possibility of pardocracia. In 1825 he referred to Venezuela's problems as follows: "There are federalists and there are Spaniards [*godos*], but this would not count much if there weren't the castas."[18] A few months earlier Santander had backed the controversial execution in Bogotá of a well-known officer of African descent, Venezuelan llanero Colonel Leonardo Infante, for a murder he probably did not commit, to teach both the military and the blacks a lesson.[19]

Gran Colombia's uneasy relations with Haiti added to the government's preoccupation with its population of African descent. In 1816 Bolívar had welcomed Haiti's money, arms, and ammunition in return for the abolition of slavery in Venezuela but had only partially fulfilled his promise, as the 1821 constitution of Gran Colombia did not free the slaves. Some leaders feared that, in retaliation, Haiti would try to incite Afro-Caribbean New Granadans to rebel. When in 1824 a representative from Haiti landed in Santa Marta to negotiate the establishment of diplomatic relations with Bogotá, the British consul in Cartagena commented:

> The mixed population of Colombia, especially on her extensive coasts upon the Atlantic, renders any contact of whatever nature it may be, with the island of Haiti, a matter of most serious and deep consideration. The executive government I believe to be fully aware of this vulnerable part of her present weakness, and I conclude the mission [of the Haitian emissary] will meet with very doubtful reception at Bogotá, although in the course of the late struggle for independence, the Colombians may have been bound by many obligations toward the people of Haiti.[20]

As the consul predicted, the government in Bogotá declined to establish relations with Haiti, arguing that such an alliance could prevent the European nations from recognizing Gran Colombia.[21] All the more offensive, Haiti was the only American nation that neither President Bolívar nor Vice President Santander invited to the Inter-American Congress in Panama in 1826.[22] Taken together, the fear of a revolution inspired by Haiti and the measures discriminating against Haiti did not augur well for the application of Gran Colombia's new principle of equality under the law.

Even discounting the fear of pardocracia, the government had limited means to reform society and achieve equality. There was an acute lack of trained personnel in all domains. War debts and maintaining the army drained much of the small national budget. Foreign exports still consisted primarily of gold, and the high cost and slowness of transportation precluded the development of new exports, which translated into low state revenues from trade. The population of Gran Colombia traditionally resisted taxation and labor levies, placing constraints on the state's ability to raise revenues. The government thus dealt with the most urgent matters and left others unresolved.[23]

POSTWAR SOCIETY

As a whole, the people of Caribbean New Granada had suffered greatly from the war. From 20.5 percent (162,272) of 792,468 inhabitants in New Granada in the late 1770s, the population of the three Caribbean provinces had dropped to 14.2 percent in 1835, with 239,269 inhabitants out of 1,686,038 nationwide.[24] The subregions around Cartagena and Mompox were losing residents to the triangle formed by Barranquilla, Soledad, and Sabanalarga, in the lower Magdalena region, and to the area situated between Corozal, Lorica, and Chinú, east of the Sinú River.[25] Although the absence of racial categories in New Granada's postcolonial censuses renders any analysis of the racial makeup of the population after 1821 impossible, some trends can be identified.[26] The number of whites in the Caribbean provinces' total population decreased as a result of exile, death, and the departure of most Spaniards following independence.[27] The urban Spanish and white creole elite who had exercised leadership in the royalist strongholds and the proindependence areas had largely disappeared. The war also had taken a heavy toll on people of African descent, who had provided most of the troops and many lower-ranking officers. Like the white elite, black, pardo, and zambo artisans and leaders in towns and cities had been decimated by war, exile, and repression.[28] According to an anonymous British officer in the Colombian military, black participation in the war had a profound impact on the region's economy because "the injury sustained has been greater in the quality than in the number of those who have been thus swept away, for the Negroes and their descendants, whether slaves or free, were by far the most active and industrious of the laboring population; but as they likewise formed the best soldiers, and were always taken for the service in preference to the Indians, a much greater proportion of this race than of any other has been destroyed during the revolution."[29] Not only were free people of color decimated by the war, they also lost their most active members with a potential for leadership.

After 1821 the top political and military positions in Caribbean New Granada were filled by whites. Traveling up the Magdalena River in the early 1820s, Frenchman Gaspard Mollien noted that despite people of African descent comprising the great majority of the population, "I saw everywhere the authority in the hands of whites or of people who claim this title without having the very real right to bear it."[30] Since many elite regional leaders had died in the war, the government, rather than turning to native men of color, appointed Venezuelan elite whites, notably Generals Carlos Soublette and Mariano Montilla who successively became governors of the newly formed department of Magdalena (comprising the provinces of Cartagena, Santa Marta, and Riohacha). Venezuelan officers also commanded some towns and villages, and Europeans and North Americans assumed important positions in trade.[31] At the lower levels of administration, however, some men of African descent gained power, despite the actions of local whites to prevent their appointment. The nomination of blacks as government officials in small villages with an overwhelmingly black population, which continued a colonial practice, met with little resistance. For example, U.S. traveler Richard Bache noted that the well-accepted alcalde of Nare, inhabited by "blacks and castas" on the bank of the Magdalena River, was "a man of colour."[32]

Caribbean New Granada thus slowly moved away from the loose socioracial restrictions that had prevailed under Spain. More people of color were able to exercise professions traditionally restricted to elite whites. Travelers on the Magdalena River noted a handful of mulatto merchants and doctors, as well as a black hacendado running a cocoa plantation, apparently with a few slaves.[33] Yet the republican avoidance of racial categories in government documents renders any in-depth analysis of race in postindependence society speculative. With no budget appropriation to implement most laws, it is likely that racial discrimination continued in several domains and was seldom challenged in the courts.[34] Furthermore, until the mid-1830s the baptism and marriage records of the Catholic Church, which had the force of civil registry, continued to list whites separately from pardos, blacks, and zambos; afterward they continued to indicate whether an individual was of legitimate or illegitimate birth. Among the baptism records of foundlings, several included notes specifying that the baby's parents were white, probably to enhance his or her chances for a good life.[35]

The series of laws passed in 1821 to secure constitutional equality had limited effects. Education only exceptionally accomplished its mission of leveling cultural differences and preparing a new generation of literate citizens to comply with the constitutional provision stipulating that by 1840 literacy would be required, in addition to property ownership or an independent occupation, to exercise suffrage. Due to the lack of teachers as well as the general poverty of the population, few schools functioned and education often depended on the goodwill of the local priest, if there was one. The government's decision to turn to British pedagogue Joseph Lancaster's method of mutual education for a less costly substitute to regular schools changed little. Consequently, most villages had no schools, and mostly the children of parents with some income in cities and small towns received a formal education.[36] Only in a few places where economic and demographic growth created new opportunities, such as Sabanalarga and Sincelejo, did elementary education become available to boys and girls from a less fortunate background.[37] After independence, in addition to patronage, formal schooling and professional experience became imperative to qualify for important positions; consequently, the poor, regardless of race, suffered from the continuing lack of access to education. Because in Caribbean New Granada class lines tended to overlap with racial lines, this deficiency reproduced some of the colonial patterns of exclusion.

POLICIES TOWARD SLAVES

The manumission law of 21 July 1821 only foresaw abolition in the long term. Until the late 1830s, the law changed little for most slaves due to the resistance of slaveowners and the state's inability to enforce it. Most importantly, the principle of "free womb" included in the law signified that no children born of slave mothers would really be free before they reached the age of eighteen, that is, before the end of 1839, unless someone was willing to pay their estimated value to their mothers' owners. Slaves' children born after 1821 could still be sold. For instance, Jacinto and Manuel Salvador, born in Barranquilla in 1834, were sold to the same master as their mother for twenty-five pesos each in compensation "for their education and subsistence."[38] Moreover, freedom at age eighteen was conditional to receipt of a certificate of good conduct and working habits issued by the master. A slave who was denied such a certificate by his or her master would be destined by the government to perform useful work, thus becoming a kind of public slave.[39] At the same time, few masters fulfilled the requirement of educating their slaves' sons and daughters beyond quickly exposing them to the rudiments of the Catholic doctrine, despite the fact that these children worked for them without pay.[40]

The creation by the 1821 law of manumission funds to compensate owners for the freedom of the most "honest and industrious" adult slaves, financed by a portion of the value of bequests, encountered major problems.[41] Several cities and capitals of cantons were slow to form a manumission junta. For example, the junta of the city of Santa Marta carried out its first manumission only in March 1825 by paying 150 pesos to José González Rubio for the freedom of Ana Raquel. As a result of foot-dragging and evasion, many local juntas collected so little in inheritance taxes that at best they could purchase the freedom of only a handful of slaves per year.[42] The juntas of some towns never raised enough money to manumit a single slave. Between 1826 and 1832 the junta of Mompox manumitted a total of twenty-three slaves, twenty of whom were men.[43] Although no figures for the same period are available for Cartagena—the Caribbean New Granadan city with the highest potential to collect inheritance taxes—its junta manumitted six men and four women in December 1826 and about thirty slaves of both sexes and all ages in 1829.[44] In each city the junta performed these manumissions together, on 25 December, in one annual public ceremony on the main square during the celebration of independence. The theatrical dimensions of the ceremonies of manumission masked the small number of slaves emancipated by the juntas and showed the remaining slaves that freedom rewarded loyalty and patience.

If the 1821 law prohibited the importation of new slaves into the country, it also allowed all kinds of transactions within Gran Colombia, except the sale of children below "the age of puberty" outside of the province in which their parents resided.[45] Newspaper ads of slave sales continued unabated. An 1826 article in Cartagena's weekly *El Mundo Observador* denounced the practice by "some inhuman masters" in the Caribbean region of selling slaves for more than their purchase price to residents of the interior of New Granada, presumably the gold miners of the Cauca.[46] The article also protested the fact that higher sale prices jeopardized slaves' option to buy their own freedom. Indeed, given the insufficient funds collected by the juntas of manumission, self-purchase continued to be the principal legal means by which slaves gained their freedom; however, as shown by Dolcey Romero for Santa Marta Province, in the 1820s the average price of self-manumission exceeded by 40 percent slaves' average market price.[47] Moreover, after the war of independence, slaves lost the option of joining the army to get out of bondage. New regulations limited conscription to slaves who had the authorization of their masters and specified that the state would compensate the owners.[48] No promise of freedom was attached to enlistment. Regarding the slaves emancipated during the war, the Congress of Cúcuta agreed that "all slaves and newborn children of slave women who, having obtained their freedom by means of the laws and decrees of the different republican governments, were later reduced again to slavery by the Spanish government, will be declared perpetually and irrevocably free."[49] The slaves freed by the Spaniards "out of hatred of [the cause of] the independence" were excluded from this measure.[50] The delegates in Cúcuta also rejected a proposal to distribute national lands to the most deserving freedmen because they were "not the best class of people."[51] No postindependence legislation aimed at easing the conditions of the existing slave population beyond the norms established by the Código Negro in 1789. Finally, as slaves continued to run away to gain freedom, new departmental ordinances focused on the repression of flight and of assistance to fugitive slaves.[52]

By 1835 the number of slaves registered in Caribbean New Granada was 6,827, or 2.9 percent of the region's total population, in contrast to 14,067 slaves, or 8.7 percent, in the late 1770s.[53] Many small towns and villages now had less than a dozen slaves. Slavery had almost disappeared from Mompox Province and along the Magdalena River, where shortly after independence foreign travelers had noted slave haciendas.[54] However, census figures did not tell the full story of slave labor, because they did not include the children of slaves who provided unpaid labor to the owners of their mothers until age eighteen.[55] Moreover, some areas remained committed to slavery: in 1835 one-third of the inhabitants in the sugarcane-producing canton of María y Flamencos and 17 percent of those in San Onofre were slaves. Slaves were also numerous on sugar and cattle haciendas in Tolú, Santa Marta, and south of Valledupar. The urban elite still depended on slaves, especially women, for domestic service. The wealthy barrio of La

Catedral in Cartagena had the highest ratio of urban slavery in Caribbean New Granada: one out of ten inhabitants in 1835.[56] Although the number of slaves rapidly declined, existing data challenge the well-established image of an aging and mostly female slave population after independence.[57] In 1842 a majority of the adult slaves registered in Santa Marta Province were between twenty-one and thirty-five years old, indicating that self-purchase and manumission tended to occur after the most productive period of slaves' lives.[58] In Caribbean New Granada as a whole, the gender ratio among slaves had not changed profoundly: 103.6 women to 100 men in 1835, in contrast to 102.7 women to 100 men in the 1770s. As in the late colonial period, most slave women worked in cities, and most slave men performed agricultural labor in the countryside.[59]

INDIGENOUS POLICIES

Regarding the "civilized" Indians already living in legal pueblos, the Congress of Cúcuta considered their misery and "backwardness" to be the result of colonial exploitation as well as their racial heritage. Therefore, they hoped that Indians—now euphemistically called "indigenes"—would achieve the equality that the 1821 constitution had granted them through the legal suppression of the tribute and personal services, the prohibition of public whippings, the division and privatization of their resguardos, the establishment of elementary schools in their pueblos and the admission of a few young Indians to colleges and seminaries, and "the example of the other classes of the State [and] the mixture that will happen with them as a result of marriages."[60] In reality, however, Native Americans did not become more equal after independence; they merely became less visible and less numerous as a result of several processes. Many men in Santa Marta Province were deported to serve under Simón Bolívar in Peru. The pressure of free people of color and whites on community lands prompted the dispersion of pueblo Indians. Mestizaje tended to reclassify the descendants of one indigenous parent as zambos or mestizos. Finally, the legal equality gained by Indians in 1821 was tenuous. In October 1828 Bolívar temporarily reestablished the indigenous tribute under the name of "personal contribution of indigenes," fixed at 3 pesos 4 reales per adult per year; at the same time he reintroduced the colonial protection of Indians as well as their exemption from some taxes and military service.[61] In violation of the law, the state, the church, and some hacendados continued to demand personal services from Indians and to use the whip against them.[62] Due to the lack of state funding and the poverty of indigenous parents, education was seldom available to them.

As for the independent indigenous communities living in Caribbean New Granada's vast, unconquered periphery, there was hardly anything the government could do to bring them into the nation as equal citizens. The few pueblos founded on the frontier during the Bourbon era to "reduce" the Indians to "civilization" had vanished with the departure of the missionaries during the war of independence.[63] Although on several occasions the government discussed how to proceed with the "barbarous Indians" engaged in smuggling in the Guajira Peninsula and the Darién, it opted for the status quo and not just for lack of funding. On the one hand, Colombian authorities feared that any action against the Indians would incite them to launch a war armed by Spain. On the other hand, the government could not afford to displease Great Britain by attempting to curb the contraband trade between the British Caribbean islands and the Wayúu and Kuna Indians. Thus, in 1822 the government decided to simply request foreign ships to purchase a license in an official Colombian port prior to trading with the indigenous "independent nations." To the displeasure of Jamaican merchants, it confirmed this policy two years later and stipulated that no arms or ammunition could be sold to the Indians.[64]

If such a renouncement of sovereignty over a vast portion of the so-called national territory was the only practical option available to Colombia's new rulers, they still held to the Spanish colonial dream of having missionaries civilize the Indians.[65] When in 1824 Colonel Mauricio Encinoso petitioned to buy and colonize land in the Guajira Peninsula, arguing that he would use "soft means" with the "savage Indians," the government, after some hesitation regarding Gran Colombia's rights over the territories of "independent nations," agreed to sell him land "not indispensable" to the Indians at the price of two pesos per *fanega* (1.59 acres). Whether Encinoso succeeded in his endeavor is unknown.[66] By 1826, in an illusory gesture of sovereignty, a law determined that the indigenous population of the Guajira and the Darién should be protected by the government as other Colombians were and be "civilized" through the establishment of settlements, but no action followed.[67]

RURAL POLICIES

For the immense majority of Caribbean New Granadans living in the countryside, the early republican government did little to promote more equal relations and to modify the prewar patterns of land tenure. After 1821 the *baldíos* (vacant lands) that had belonged to the Spanish Crown became national lands. However, the government inherited no records of what lands were actually in the public domain, nor did it have the skilled personnel and financial means to conduct a national land survey. To complicate matters, in most of the Caribbean region public lands interfused with private properties, resguardos, church-owned lands, and municipal common lands, few of which had clear boundaries.[68] Thus, until the mid-nineteenth century, when the government began to issue certificates of public debt redeemable in public lands to back the national debt, land tenure was relatively open. Ten years of war had impoverished the region. Several of the largest haciendas, notably those belonging to the Epalza-Hoyos (heirs of the marquis of Torre-Hoyos), Gutiérrez de Piñeres, García de Toledo, and Díaz Granados families, had endured repeated military occupation and confiscation. Most horses and mules had been taken by the armies, and thousands of cows had been slaughtered to feed the troops. Some sugar mills had been destroyed and had lost part of their slave workforce. Hacendados rarely had the necessary capital to prosper as they had before independence.[69] Several villages along the Magdalena River, especially those that had supported the royalist cause, had been burned. Many inhabitants had fled repeated conscriptions and abuses by taking refuge in the hinterlands.[70] Many soldiers never returned from the war. As Eduardo Posada-Carbó argues, during the first decades of the republic Caribbean New Granada's social institutions became even looser than they had been under Spanish colonialism, and "what was striking for those who visited the region in the mid-nineteenth century was the lack of control that any *hacendado* possessed over a scant and dispersed labour population."[71]

Insufficient data for the first half of the nineteenth century have prevented thorough study of the evolution of land tenure in the Caribbean region before the 1850s. However, three major trends, leading to the rapid development of vast cattle haciendas in the second part of the century, can be drawn from the existing literature: first, the slow recovery of late-eighteenth-century estates; second, the increase of small ranches (often also producing grains and vegetables) along the Magdalena River up to Simití and around Sincelejo and Corozal; and third, the displacement of peasants, tenants, and squatters from these areas farther into the hinterlands south of María y Flamencos, south of Sincelejo, and along the Cauca River, where some marginal communities subsisted, several of which had been originally founded by runaway slaves.[72]

In the 1820s the republican government's chief agrarian policy was to develop agriculture through generous land distribution to European immigrants who would at the same time reinforce the white minority. Secretly debated in the context of government fear of alleged pardo and Haitian-backed conspiracies, the colonization law of 1823 targeted areas considered particularly at risk, such as the Venezuelan *llanos* (tropical plains) and the coastal provinces. The law granted large tracts of land to companies founded specifically to attract immigrants. If only a few European settlers ever materialized, several members of the postcolonial elite took part in the colonization scheme.[73]

In the Magdalena department, Venezuelan patriot General Mariano Montilla received large grants of land for colonization. He also obtained an "enormous plantation" near Sabanalarga and the large hacienda of Aguas Vivas in Turbaco, fifteen miles from Cartagena, among others. German Juan Bernardo Elbers was compensated for his attempts to establish steam navigation on the Magdalena River with vast holdings on the banks of the lower river, where he cultivated tobacco with mixed success. Some former royalists got a share in the land distribution, such as Juan de Francisco, a rich merchant of Spanish origin deported from Cartagena for his involvement in the 1811 Conspiracy of the Fijo.[74] Similarly, the heirs of colonial hacendados were able to reconstitute part of their domains. As shown by Orlando Fals, in 1825 the Epalza-Hoyos family returned from their Jamaican exile to reclaim their holdings. Through the help of their allies in the proindependence aristocracy and the marriage of one daughter with the son of patriot and rich merchant Juan Pantaleón Ribón, executed by Spain in 1816, they managed to have their royalist past overlooked and the confiscation of several of their haciendas nullified. Likewise, the heirs of the Gutiérrez de Piñeres brothers, who died for the cause of independence, managed to recover the seized properties of a royalist relative.[75]

In contrast, the government did not help the rural poor. No land grants were awarded to returning rank-and-file veterans as a means of paying their war wages and recognizing their services to the homeland. The most veterans could expect were vouchers, which they generally had to sell below their value to speculators.[76] Far from aiding peasants and laborers, after 1821 the state showed its face outside the main cities principally through its arbitrary and brutal recruitment of many of them into the army. The constitution established the service and defense of the homeland as a duty of all Colombian men, but those conscripted were mostly the rural poor of African and indigenous descent. In addition, the government punished the defeated royalists and Indians in Santa Marta Province by drafting them into the army and sending them to fight for the independence of Peru. Criminals and vagrants were drafted in lieu of punishment, and political opponents were taken away as soldiers.[77] In mid-1822 Bolívar requested that Santander send 3,000 trained men from Venezuela and Caribbean New Granada to fight the Spaniards and the royalists in Peru. By late 1823 he demanded a total of 12,000 men: 6,000 more from Venezuela, among them 1,000 llaneros, and 3,000 from Caribbean New Granada.[78] Passed down to provincial authorities and local officials, this order resulted in the violent recruitment of poor villagers. Forced conscription did not end with the war but became a pattern in New Granada; laborers and peasants developed a long-lasting distrust of the state and its institutions. In 1826 the U.S. consul in Cartagena reported with dismay:

> The system of impressing, or rather kidnapping for the army and navy (and by the way men were never procured otherwise since I knew the Country) is a source of discontent, calculated to drive those exposed to it to desperation. The men are brought from the most distant parts, tied or handcuffed together. In this way they are now manning one or two ships; for seamen are out of the question. None can be found to enter the service, as they receive little or no pay. Afraid of being torn thus from their homes, the Indian population abandon the cultivation of the soil, and take to the woods.[79]

According to Frenchman Auguste Le Moyne, in the late 1820s groups of recruits were shipped from the Caribbean region on champanes from which they could not escape for fear of drowning in the Magdalena River or being eaten by alligators, and many died during the ordeal.[80]

Beyond forced recruitment for the army, the government had little involvement in the countryside. In the one domain singled out by foreign observers as crucial to the development of agriculture and trade in Caribbean New Granada—transportation—few concrete measures were taken. As noted by a British officer, the high cost of transport and the great distances involved prevented the export of most agricultural products from the region and made even the exploitation of the natural forests of dyewood near Riohacha and Valledupar unprofitable.[81] Moreover, the Caribbean Coast's deficient connections with Andean New Granada and Venezuela hampered not only the export trade from central New Granada but also the integration of the Caribbean region into the nation. Transportation continued to rely on bogas and muleteers, as it did under Spain. Legally, the maintenance of roads, trails, rivers, canals, and bridges depended on the taxes that municipalities collected on the goods and cattle transiting through their areas as well as on the "personal service" of their male residents (or their servants) who had to yearly provide up to four days of free labor.[82] But neither the taxes collected nor the labor conscripted met the region's needs. Although in 1823 the German Elbers was granted the monopoly on steam navigation on the Magdalena River, all of his attempts to promote it failed, partly due to the difficult nature of the river.[83]

Lacking the funds to build roads and to make rivers more navigable, the government enacted legislation to enforce security. In May 1826 a new law imposed harsh sentences for theft and robbery and repressed vagrants.[84] Another measure aimed at regulating navigation on the Magdalena River and policing bogas, whose unruliness and unpredictability were blamed for the weak trade. All boats had to be under the command of a patrón, and all bogas were required to be experts in navigation and to have a known residence, a certificate of good conduct from the mayor of their community, and a labor contract. The law divided the Magdalena River into four districts in which inspectors would collect taxes on foreign goods and control boats, crews, and trip provisions. Inspectors were also expected to resolve disputes between passengers, bosses, and bogas and to apprehend fugitive bogas, who could be sentenced to up to two years of service on warships.[85] Given the state's weak presence in the region, it is doubtful that this law was fully implemented, yet Le Moyne, who traveled upstream from Santa Marta to Honda from November 1828 to January 1829, reported at the beginning of his trip the desertion of only three bogas in Pueblo Viejo; the remaining crew reliably performed exhausting work for over two months on the perilous Magdalena River.[86] The problem with Colombia's transportation, however, was not its insecurity or the bogas' capriciousness, but its slowness, seasonal variation, discomfort, and high cost—drawbacks that could be corrected only by a new, expensive infrastructure not within the government's reach.

THE CHURCH'S APPROACH

The influence of the Catholic Church was even weaker than before independence. Caribbean New Granada's two dioceses of Cartagena and Santa Marta were without bishops until 1828. Most Spanish priests and missionaries had abandoned the country, leaving many parishes unattended. Among the remaining clergymen, several ignored their vows of chastity and openly lived with their concubines and offspring. Such was the case of José María Berástegui, who owned a large cattle hacienda south of Sincelejo, run by slaves, and fathered five children with María Josefa Burgos but nevertheless was a member of Cartagena Province's electoral college.[87] The Congress of Cúcuta's decision in 1821 to nationalize convents with less than eight members and transform them into secondary schools worsened relations with the Vatican, already strained by Spain's defeat. In 1824 the congress went even further and approved a law of *patronato*, which, as under Spain, gave state control of clerical appointments. Yet, despite being resented in Rome, the law did not prevent the pope from agreeing in 1827 to name bishops for Gran Colombia's vacant dioceses.[88]

In reality, the Colombian early republic was far from being anticlerical. Like the independent province of Cartagena in 1811–15, and like all Spanish American constitutions in the 1820s, it viewed Catholicism as essential to public order and as the nation's official religion.[89] For example, in 1826 the national congress approved funding to build a church in Riohacha, a city destroyed by the war, because it considered it "a duty of the Congress to support religion and the cult that ought to be offered to the Divinity."[90] There was no question, however, that the government would support the church only as long as it would help to build the new nation. In fact, many clergymen had actively supported independence.[91] As during Cartagena's First Independence, in the 1820s several priests were members of electoral colleges, provincial assemblies, and municipal councils. Among them was Berástegui, whose life had more in common with that of a magnate than a virtuous servant of God. Others were more involved in politics than in their religious mission, which further weakened the role of the church.[92] This was notably the case with Santa Marta's new bishop, José María Estévez, who took possession of his see in May 1828. A native of Bucaramanga and a close ally of General Santander, Estévez had distinguished himself for introducing applied sciences into the curriculum of the College-Seminary of San Bartolomé in Bogotá. There he had belonged to the Biblical Society founded by an Englishman to disseminate Protestantism in the country. Thus, Estévez greatly differed from the former royalist bishops of Santa Marta, and he quickly disagreed with the city's pro-Bolívar military authorities. In fact, he excused himself from performing the funeral mass after Bolívar died in Santa Marta in December 1830, claiming to be sick. Elected a representative to the constitutional congress in 1830, he spent most of the last four years of his life in Bogotá rather than in Santa Marta.[93]

The tour that the bishop of Cartagena, Juan Hermenegildo de León, made of his diocese in 1838 illustrates the difficulties encountered by the church in the early republic. Like his predecessor, José Fernández Díaz de Lamadrid, in 1781, León singled out the endemic shortage of priests and the misery of the majority of the population as the key problems, but he did not share Díaz de Lamadrid's spirit of crusade and simply offered realistic solutions whenever possible.[94] Most church buildings, already in poor condition under Spanish rule, were in a state of decay, either as a result of the war or, according to León, "the indifference of the community."[95] Few cofradías had survived the war, and those that had were in decline. Some temples lacked decoration and indispensable sacred ornaments. When a church had no altar, the bishop authorized worshipers to use a board instead.

With few new vocations in New Granada, especially in the Caribbean region (in 1826 Cartagena's college and seminary had to suspend religious training for lack of students),[96] and few active priests willing to settle in the Caribbean Coast's hot, unhealthy, and poor parishes, the bishop made the best of the scant clergy at his disposal. Many priests simultaneously served several parishes that were far apart and could not attend them adequately, particularly in areas inhabited predominantly by blacks, such as María y Flamencos, Norosí, Simití, and Loba, south of Mompox. A few villages were not assigned any priest. The bishop had no alternative but to confirm the priests' multiple assignments, and in some cases he even entrusted them with an additional parish. Some priests fulfilled their mission poorly, only serving the parishes where they resided. Several did not properly register baptisms, marriages, and burials. And many gave little attention to preaching and catechism. Without taking any punitive action, the bishop reminded priests of their duties, emphasizing the need to teach children the Christian doctrine. He also insisted that the priests were obliged to baptize and bury their parishioners, even if they were too poor to pay for these sacraments. However, the relationship had to be reciprocal, and the bishop assigned priests only to communities that took "part in feeding [the priest] and give him what is his fair share," which he set at 80 pesos (640 reales) per year.[97]

Bishop León's principal concern, besides ensuring that available priests were assigned to solvent parishes, was that the dead be properly buried. He struggled against the immemorial practice of peasants and squatters in remote areas to secretly inter their kin on their own land. Also, in implementing an 1827 decree, he tried to secure obedience to a much-resisted 1789 royal cédula that banned the practice of burying bodies under a church, authorizing burials only in fenced-in cemeteries outside villages and towns.[98]

Major problems existed in southern villages located in the vast area from Norosí to San Pablo that lacked both graveyards and priests. Relatives of the deceased lived too far from the parish equipped with a cemetery, and owners of canoes refused to transport bodies. Inhabitants of these remote areas strongly preferred to continue burying their dead under churches and chapels, arguing, "There are the ashes of their ancestors and of their descendants."[99] In small parishes with no priests and only a smattering of Catholicism, there was no way to stop them from doing so.

Conditions were no better in the diocese of Santa Marta, including Riohacha Province, where the number of parishes had dropped from 72 before the end of the war to 65 in 1833. There were a total of 57 clergymen, counting canons and sacristans, when Bishop Estévez estimated that 88 were needed.[100] Many priests were immoral and ignorant of the doctrine, and some could not read Latin, Estévez complained.[101] Several parishes simply disappeared as people abandoned them "to form many hamlets so that the day will come when one will find only roaming hordes since at this rate they will lack civilization and ignore their rights and duties." The want of priests was particularly serious for newly founded *pueblos de indígenas*, such as Soldado, established in 1826, where the Wayúu had helped to build a church but had withdrawn to the Guajira Peninsula after failing to obtain a clergyman.[102] Given the small size of most parishes and the misery of their inhabitants, both the bishop of Santa Marta and the governor of Riohacha recognized that the region would not attract regular priests and demanded without success that the government in Bogotá send religious missionaries from the interior of New Granada.[103]

PARDO EXPECTATIONS AND DIFFICULTIES

The limited intervention of state and church did not prevent people from valuing political change. Although few lower-class men and women left records of their feelings, no doubt some expected that their lives would improve in the republic with the legal equality guaranteed by the 1821 constitution. Some laborers, peasants, and artisans understood the fair balance between their rights and duties as opposed to the high contributions the state, the military, and the church sometimes required from them. Moreover, as the colonial administration had been unable to systematically collect taxes, the zeal of some republican officials could seem abusive. Harsh new requirements for militia service, which were imposed without the royal military fuero, could prove intolerable, as asserted by carpenter José Francisco Escudero in Cartagena. Escudero agreed to the principle of "serv[ing] the government because as citizens we are all obliged to this," but he opposed being drafted time and again because the navy needed his skills. He bitterly compared the republican navy register, which "imprisoned [him] with chains" like a "slave of the Navy," with the register of "the old Spanish monarchy," joined by his father, which provided a "privileged fuero."[104] Those most likely to publicly demand republican equality in racial terms were the newly promoted officials of African descent facing "prejudice and partiality" or "contempt" from the local white elites. As the lawyer of one of them asked, "Is it not a crime, in a government whose corner stone is the citizens' equality, prescribed and defended by the constitution, . . . to want to deprive of public office a certain class of men who out of their conduct deserve everything?"[105] Two cases, which local elites transformed into pardo threats, illustrate the difficult position of these men.

The first incident attributed to pardo unrest occurred in 1823 in Mompox. The city's military commander, Carlos Robledo, reported a brief protest early that year when he replaced pardo lieutenant colonel Remigio Márquez, who had been elected to the senate, after which "the divisions of classes had disappeared." Every night since Márquez's return to Mompox in May 1823, Robledo claimed, there were broadsides, fights, and unrest, leading to the death of a boga.[106] Reportedly, Márquez was "attracting the pardos and the rabble with binges, dances of blacks, and these kinds of parties, and as he hands money over to them and opens the liquor case, they are devoted to him."[107] The broadside that most preoccupied Robledo—and not just because it mentioned him—read:

> Mr. Political judge: Won't you tell me why the broadsides have not continued? Then I will tell you. It is because the mean little whites knew that when you, Commander Robledo, and the mayor Trespalacios took over, the people wanted Mr. Márquez, and they fear that the machete swings, damn it! You don't want that Mr. Márquez be Political Judge because that takes from you what you sponge from [the distillery] of the *aguardiente* (rum). Mr. Robledo doesn't want to give up command because it would take the theft of the troops away from him; and mayor Trespalacios because he remembers that he depends on the Marquis [of Epalza-Hoyos] and that other one; and at the end you'll be fucked up because blood will flow like in Saint Domingue.[108]

Fulfilling the demand of "the sane part of the people," the intendant in Cartagena, José Ucros, accused Remigio Márquez of conspiracy and gave him twenty-four hours to leave Mompox. Simultaneously, he ordered the momposino authorities to promptly arrest the authors of the broadside and to show fearless vigilance. Márquez was excluded from public office and faced charges in Bogotá.[109] In 1824, however, he was able to prove all the accusations false. Six "white and notable persons" testified that "there [had been] no division of pardos against the whites, that they [had] never heard [Márquez] say any word that could relate to such ideas." Moreover, the authors of the broadside and the instigators of the unrest were none other than Márquez's accusers themselves, a fact confirmed by General Mariano Montilla.[110] Their hatred of the pardo officer dated back to 1822, when, as Mompox's political judge, Márquez had uncovered their corruption and contraband activities and imposed a punishment. They retaliated by organizing "an open cabildo, unknown by the laws of Colombia, or a real tumult" to replace him with a commander who would have a blind eye to their smuggling.[111] As a result of such compelling evidence, Robledo and his allies lost their positions, and Márquez recovered his senate seat. Members of Mompox's white elite had astutely, if unsuccessfully, drawn parallels with the Haitian Revolution to eliminate an authority unfriendly to their illegal interests.

In 1822 a similar incident happened in the village of Majagual, on the Cauca River south of San Benito Abad, but with more serious consequences for the defendant. There, some white officials played upon racial fears to remove the thirty-one-year-old literate pardo carpenter Valentín Arcía from the elected position of magistrate [alcalde ordinario de segunda nominación]. They accused him of "declaiming against the class of white individuals, without reflecting that we are all individuals of the Society" and of "dividing the union in which this quiet vicinity has rested, inspiring a criminal aversion against the whites." Reportedly, Arcía had said that now that the war against the Spaniards was over, "it was necessary to awaken at once the bloodiest [war] against the whites as it occurred in Guarico [Haiti], and that he longed for this moment to join [the fight] against them."[112] To substantiate their accusations, the plaintiffs mentioned a dialogue that Arcía had written and read to them; they also produced a proclamation by Arcía that ordered the inhabitants of Majagual to "wake up" rather than "escape to the woods to not serve Colombia."[113] On these grounds, in June 1822 Arcía was arrested and imprisoned in Cartagena for conspiracy against the whites.

From the beginning, Arcía claimed it was all pure calumny invented by his political enemies: "Because as I belong to the pardo class they got annoyed to see me as a judge and that they would be under my authority." He had issued the proclamation to stir up the population because he was able to "collect only twenty men and not the fifty he was asked to provide for the army of Mompox because the others were running away."[114] As for the incriminating dialogue, it was never found in the possession of either Arcía or the man to whom he sent it. Arcía did not deny having written the piece, but he refuted his accusers' interpretation of its meaning. According to him, he merely told a friend that after being magistrate he would become a laborer, but the friend advised him against it because workers were enlisted in the army and had to contribute labor to the church and the government. Arcía also alluded to his difficult relations with the "administratorship of a certain master in his jurisdiction." At the end of the dialogue, referring to his persecutors in Majagual, he stated: "If everywhere in Colombia those of his quality [of pardo] were treated with similar contempt, God would not want another war of those [pardos] against the whites."[115] But he asserted that nowhere had he said that he longed for this war and would take part in it.

Despite the fact that several witnesses, including priests, testified to Arcía's good and peaceful conduct, he remained in jail. Moreover, after a report reached Cartagena that he had almost killed a black servant in the village of Algarrobo, near Majagual, he was accused of conspiracy and high treason and transferred to a Bogotá prison in 1823. Arcía was eventually tried in April 1825. Fortunately for him, the judge accepted the argument of the defense and ruled that the incident with the servant occurred because the villagers "scandalously resisted" providing men for the army. New information showed that Algarrobo's priest, heading "the *pueblo* in arms," had insulted Arcía and provoked the riot. As for the accusation that Arcía had promoted a race war, the judge concluded that it was groundless and motivated by personal enmity: in fact, there were "no parties based on color" in Majagual, and Arcía's proclamation had been a patriotic effort to enlist men for the army. The judge ruled that Arcía had fully paid for his mistakes during his custody. However, no charges were filed against Arcía's accusers, who had achieved their goal. For having been elected alcalde ordinario and having attempted to perform his duties "despite being a pardo," Arcía had spent three years in prison, where he became seriously ill; his wife and children endured misery, and his carpenter business was ruined.[116]

The cases of Remigio Márquez and Valentín Arcía show that the local white elite did not hesitate to build on the well-established fear of a revolution along Haitian lines to obtain the removal of pardos from public office, particularly if these officials attempted to destroy long-standing privileges.

By doing so, the local gentry was sure to strike a sympathetic chord among the leaders of Gran Colombia preoccupied by pardo power. Yet in the 1820s Caribbean New Granada's majority of free people of color was no more able to establish pardocracia—that is, according to Bolívar, to organize autonomously, seize power from and eliminate the white elite minority, and maybe also liberate the slaves—than it had been previous to 1810. No doubt, as the cases of Márquez and Arcía indicate, some pardos took their new equality literally and tried to challenge the primacy of local whites. But they did not mobilize people of African descent against whites.

Nor did pardo military men attempt to stir up the troops. As a British officer noted, the republican army units in the region were "filled with Indians, negroes, and all intermediate races" who irregularly received meager pay. "The mutinies which arose entirely from this cause, in the years 1822 and 1823, at Cartagena and Santa Martha [sic] taught the government how dangerous it would be to trifle in future with a body of men who began to feel their own strength and importance." But according to the same officer, these soldiers "are for the most part in a good state of discipline, and many of the regiments are capable of performing their evolutions with a steadiness and precision which would not disgrace any European regiment."[117] Indeed, when in 1823 General Mariano Montilla jailed all of the sergeants in Cartagena's artillery after a mutiny for lack of food and clothes, the troops did not revolt even though eighteen months later "these poor fellows" still languished in prison.[118] Conditions in the garrisons did not improve with time. Loaded with debt, the government owed the soldiers months'—sometimes years'—worth of wages. Commanders had no money to buy rations for their troops, who endured hunger. As a result, the provincial authorities in Santa Marta and Cartagena continuously feared mutinies; yet after 1823 the troops in the Caribbean region remained peaceful.[119]

STRUGGLING FOR A LIVING

In fact, most people strove to make ends meet, working in their trade and resorting to additional strategies to improve their lot. Many in the countryside produced food for the local markets or, like the farmers along the Sinú River between Lorica and Montería, for Cartagena and the Chocó.[120] When some peasants and hacendados tried to diversify and export, they generally encountered a vicious circle of low international prices, high local transportation costs, and competition with already established foreign products, never making enough profit to invest in better plants and technology. Notably, by the late 1820s the cultivation and production of cotton underwent a brief revival, especially in the area of Barranquilla. In the following decade, some cotton was exported from Cartagena, but the endeavor did not last long due to the low yield of the native plant and because peasants could not afford to clean cotton by any method other than whipping (there was only one cotton gin in the area, located in Barranquilla), which produced poor results.[121] Large-scale attempts to cultivate cacao and tobacco along the Magdalena River and rice in San Onofre failed for similar reasons.[122] Workers, mostly slaves, still cultivated sugarcane near María y Flamencos, San Onofre, Tolú, and Valledupar. According to a U.S. consul, when they boiled the juice extracted from the cane, they used an antiquated method that prevented its transformation into refined sugar through further boiling. Although they produced molasses for rum distilleries and a brown sugar loaf that the consul found "purer, better tasting, more nutritive" than West Indian sugar, Caribbean New Granadan sugar did not match the standards of world demand and only sold locally.[123]

The most common alternatives to working on farms were fishing, working as bogas and muleteers, smuggling, and providing manual skills and services. Some women drove goods to markets. When travelers stopped for a few days, other women sold them food and meals, washed their clothes, or hired themselves out as cooks.[124] Men in the proximity of small towns and cities prepared lumber, worked in construction, or made furniture. In the wooded areas near Santa Marta, Valledupar, and south of Tolú, men cut dyewood and collected balsam of Tolú to be exported from Santa Marta or Cartagena. The villagers in Ternera provided charcoal to Cartagena.[125] As they had under Spanish rule, in the area of Simití, according to British officer John P. Hamilton, "the people wash[ed] the earth for gold-dust, and procure[d] considerable quantities, which [was] sent for sale to Mompox."[126] Evidently, a large portion of the gold dust fed the contraband trade, especially after the imposition of high taxes on gold exports in 1829.[127] Cotton cultivation produced cottage industries, notably in Soledad, Sabanalarga, and Corozal, where women and girls specialized in fine weaving and embroidery.[128] In Turbaco and in villages near Barranquilla and Sabanalarga, women excelled in making baskets, canvas, string, mats, and hats. In Barranquilla and near Cartagena, people made bricks and roof tiles. Inhabitants of the former Indian pueblo of Malambo, near Barranquilla, were renowned in the region for their earthenware. Many workers in Corozal

Women on the bank of the Magdalena River. (Edward Walhouse Mark,
Acuarelas de Mark, 1843–1856. Un testimonio pictórico de la Nueva Granada
[1963; Bogotá: Banco de la República–Litografía Arco, 1976])

extracted oil from a palm that provided much of Cartagena's lighting.[129]
In addition, migration to the cities continued to be appealing, especially to
women.[130]

Despite these myriad activities, as noted in 1839 by Liberal politician
Juan José Nieto, the most successful activity in the region was cattle ranching, which rapidly recovered from the effects of the war. Almost everywhere, pasture for cattle occupied large portions of land. This was especially
true in the plains near Corozal, Sincelejo, San Benito Abad, and Sabanalarga. In addition to supplying the local meat demand, cattle were driven to
the cities' slaughterhouses. Not surprisingly, the only significant regional
export from the port of Cartagena—far behind gold—was cowhides.[131] Yet
until the 1830s the large cattle ranchers only controlled portions of the land.
Whole areas that today symbolize Caribbean New Granada's livestock industry, such as the Sinú Valley around Montería, were densely forested.

Those individuals who wanted to flee or retreat could still find shelter
in the backlands and on the frontier, even though these areas had receded.

Although the 1823 colonization law had granted some of the best lands to contractors, numerous families continued to squat on untitled lands along rivers and in the hinterland, living in semi-autarchy. In the vicinity of Mahates, several communities stood halfway between rochelas and established villages. They were principally inhabited by blacks who claimed to be descendants of runaway slaves and who kept intruders at bay by recounting their ancestors' highway robbery.[132] Farther into the hinterland, one could find individuals who would have met Antonio de la Torre y Miranda's definition of arrochelado more than half a century before, such as the "others" that French engineer Luis Striffler discovered living among unsubdued Indians in the upper Sinú Valley in 1844. These "others" were a dispirited former navy officer; a ruined Italian trader with his common-law wife, herself a runaway slave from Medellín; a male black maroon, "who never took his hands off a gun," and his family; and "an individual of fair color" from Cartagena who, formerly a shipowner trading with Jamaica, had become a simple boga. All lived in close association but were headed by the Italian, whom they called "don Francisco."[133] Many also subsisted as arrochelados in Riohacha Province and in the vast area around Norosí, indicating that survival on the periphery still represented an option.[134]

Despite the generally substandard living conditions in Caribbean New Granada, the inhabitants seldom showed organized discontent.[135] Most rural folks enjoyed a certain degree of autonomy and only occasionally experienced the immediate force of the state, the church, or the hacendado. They felt their survival to be secure as things stood and thus were unwilling to jeopardize the little they had rebuilt since the end of the war. As a result, they did not transform the postindependence lack of institutional order and relative openness in land tenure into opportunities to make lasting collective advances. No doubt, many of the factors that had precluded peasants from organizing in the colonial period, such as the lack of communications and marketable opportunities, had not disappeared after 1821. Also, the Caribbean New Granadan population was growing at a much slower pace than its Andean counterpart, causing no immediate demographic pressure on the land. The region's rural inhabitants thus felt much less compelled than those in Cauca studied by Germán Colmenares, notably, to struggle for the legalization of their settlements.[136] Despite the 1823 colonization law, in the 1820s and 1830s, with a few exceptions such as General Montilla, the hacendados had not recovered their colonial strength (i.e., vast landownership in various areas, control of villages, and key positions in the cities).[137] The rural population could not foresee that the hacendados' relative weakness would be short-lived. Many peasants probably thought that squatting on unclaimed lands, sharecropping, itinerant work, and withdrawal to the hinterland were permanent arrangements and so did not try to protect them from possible action by hacendados and the state. In the eventuality that they had wanted to do so, they would have been discouraged by the magnitude and cost of the task, which involved documenting one's ownership and presenting a legal claim to distant authorities. As a consequence, most of the land remained untitled, if not unoccupied, and ready to be acquired by large ranchers and hacendados in the second half of the century.[138]

In fact, it was forced enlistment in the army—the state's primary manifestation outside the cities—that prompted the fiercest resistance among the rural population. Recruits in Gran Colombia could lose everything in the ordeal—their lives, their families, their land, their work, the little they owned—and they were ready to take major risks to avoid it, even to rebel. Whereas under Spain joining the militia of all colors could represent social advancement for rural men of African descent, during the war of independence enlistment had been increasingly forced on the population. Yet male equality and liberty had been mobilizing ideas among those who fought in the patriot armies: military distinction had sometimes erased the stigma of race and class, and some slave soldiers had been able to gain their freedom. After 1821, however, military service ceased to represent prospects of equality and freedom and became a symbol of state oppression. The draft, though promoting some interregional mix in the units, deepened socioracial inequalities by targeting mostly the poor of African and indigenous descent. However, resistance to enlistment did not become a racial affair fostering racial identity. As shown in the incident in Algarrobo involving pardo Valentín Arcía, recruitment was carried out by black and white authorities alike. Resistance in the form of flight or fight could be embraced by the entire community regardless of race and class, as independent peasants and day laborers dreaded loss, abuse, and death, and hacendados refused to see their workers go. Algarrobo parishioners, led by their priest, "scandalously resisted" providing the number of recruits requested of them during the wave of enlistments ordered by Bolívar for Peru. After an initial setback, Arcía returned there with enough force to "back his authority." But on 13 June 1822

> Marcos López and others set in motion the parish so that its vecinos fled and the levy could not take effect. But [Mayor] Arcía, anxious to fulfill his duties, withdrew . . . so that some would come out of their

hiding place, in order to catch them. . . . The vecinos beg[an] to throw stones that injured some of those who went with the Mayor. In these circumstances natural right demanded defense; the skirmish br[oke] out, the mulato Acosta attack[ed] the Mayor and injure[d] him, the latter recover[ed], r[an] after his aggressor, and cause[d] him some injuries.[139]

No doubt similar incidents happened elsewhere in Caribbean New Granada and Venezuela. In effect, only 3,000 of the 12,000 soldiers requested by Bolívar from these two regions ever materialized. Soldiers who made it to Peru continued to protest with their feet. In late 1823 Bolívar reported the loss of 3,000 Gran Colombian soldiers within a few months through death or desertion.[140] As forced conscription persisted after the end of the war, communities continued to resist and individuals to "take to the woods."[141]

Once in the army, soldiers faced hunger, lack of pay, and mistreatment. Punishment was particularly harsh on the poor. For example, soldiers and officers found guilty of stealing in the barracks could be sentenced to death unless protected by a higher social rank.[142] Yet soldiers seldom rebelled but rather chose individual desertion. For those who accommodated to garrison life, there could be some opportunities of limited promotion. From Cartagena the U.S. consul noted with surprise: "There is a curious practice in the formation of the army of Colombia . . . it is, that the whole body of privates and non commissioned officers are negroes, mulatos and Indians, and that the officers, with very few exceptions, are also of these different colours."[143] What seemed odd to the consul made sense in the New Granadan postwar context, in which the military profession was rapidly losing status, and therefore attractiveness, for the elite and the educated. With low and often unpaid wages and no land distribution program, a career in the army seldom meant socioeconomic mobility.[144] Yet a few men of lower socioracial origin were able to gain rank and power over others. Among the higher army officers, for whom class and—above all—race still mattered, whites predominated. Among the rank and file the mere possibility of individual escape, limited promotion, or simply the prospect of making it safely back home precluded collective revolt.

COUNTERCULTURE

More fruitfully, members of the lower classes took advantage of state and church weaknesses to shape long-term family patterns, religion, and culture according to their own views. They won a major victory regarding sexual unions, which the bishops of the Bourbon era had repeatedly attempted to bring into the Catholic canon. In the 1830s the vicar of Cartagena, Juan Fernández de Sotomayor, censured the "small number of marriages" and the "laxity of the mores." Bishop León kept busy making cemeteries conform to the law, but he gave up on Catholic morality and did not try to eradicate free unions and adultery.[145] People in Caribbean New Granada were also able to impose their views on religious ceremonies. All efforts by church officials in the previous decades to ban drinking, dancing, and gambling had failed. The christening of infants in church, supposedly on the eighth day after birth, was generally followed by a big party at the parents' home with cake, liquor, cigars, and dancing to band music. Funerals were preceded by all-night wakes in which women prayed, wailed, drank, and smoked until morning, when friends and relatives accompanied by a priest would take the body to the church and then to the cemetery. In remote hamlets and villages that had no priest, some families buried their relatives on their land or under a chapel. In addition, people used various means to feel safer. They protected their houses with woven charms made from palms that a priest had sprinkled with consecrated water on Palm Sunday.[146] In Santa Marta, they made syncretic images of Jesus with shells. When John P. Hamilton visited Peñon, its inhabitants struggled to get rid of evil spirits in the village by organizing processions led by an old Indian singer and by making children say prayers three times a day, without the supervision of a priest.[147] According to another traveler, bogas would not leave the riverbank until one of them, "assuming the clerical function, recited a prayer for the prosperity of our voyage"; then the other crew members would name as many saints as possible.[148]

Caribbean New Granada's inhabitants continued to modify religious celebrations based on their own ideas. During Holy Week, penitents, especially women, generally showed much veneration and grief in the processions, whereas men from all classes met every night at the gambling tables erected for the occasion. In Barranquilla, Resurrection Day was celebrated with music, the discharge of firearms, abundant food, and balls.[149] To the displeasure of Bishop León, Mompox parishioners added new prayers for the dead on All Souls Day to extend the processions well into the night.[150] Also in Mompox, the January celebrations of Saint Sebastian were converted into a street party in which participants, especially young women, threw flour on each other's heads. "It was strange and ridiculous to see

Wake of a child. (Alcide Dessalines d' Orbigny, *Voyage pittoresque dans les deux Amériques* [Paris: L. Tenré, 1836])

everywhere black heads covered with white powder, making a dissonant contrast with their obscure physiognomy," noted Swedish traveler Carl August Gosselman in 1825.[151] In Simití, John Hamilton was struck by the African influence in the music and dances performed during the carnival festivities of the Virgin of Candelaria:

> In the evening the village was unusually gay, groups were here of men and women in their holiday clothes, some dancing, others playing at cards for sweetmeats. We here saw the Negro or African dance: the music consists of a small drum, and three girls who clap their hands exactly in time, sometimes fast, sometimes slow, who join in a chorus, whilst another man, an improvisatore, sings verses extempore, and apparently with much readiness. In one patriotic song we caught these words:

Mueran los Espanoles [*sic*] picarones tiranos;
Vivan los Republicanos Americanos![152]

Probably the most altered Catholic celebration was Christmas, which turned into ten days of street dancing and masquerading until dawn and when most economic activities were at a standstill. During all of these celebrations, people from different walks of life mixed together, danced, drank, and gambled. However, each individual kept a sense of his or her alleged place, and fights were not rare.[153]

According to foreign travelers, in the 1820s and 1830s Caribbean New Granadans also performed music and danced simply to conclude the day, regardless of their color, class, and gender and whether they lived in cities or in the countryside. These characteristics have led some foreigners to portray both rich and poor as unconcerned fun lovers interested only in idleness, dancing, and gambling in their fertile tropical environment.[154] A close reading of their descriptions, however, shows that all festivities took place in the evening, on Sunday, or on holidays. According to New Yorker Rensselaer Van Rensselaer, the carnival in Barranquilla was limited to three days because "so many are dependent upon each day's labor."[155] Moreover, travelers conceded that the Caribbean's heat, humidity, voracious mosquitoes, capricious rivers, and destructive rainy season made all human endeavors very difficult. They agreed that the work of the bogas was among the most strenuous they had ever seen. Some recognized that clearing and cultivating land in the region required hard labor, and that fishing and hunting were dangerous and necessitated skill, effort, and patience. French traveler Gaspard Mollien struggled to reconcile his observations with his racism: "The vivacity and exuberance of the [people of color]," he wrote, "contrast singularly with the nonchalance and gentleness of the men whom are called white, so that, despite their laziness, the former seem active and laborious."[156] More to the point, a British officer remarked that much was said about the indolence of the "natives" of African descent to explain why Caribbean New Granada had not developed a tropical export agriculture, but "persons who are acquainted with their habits, and will humor them a little, may procure laborers who will steadily perform at a cheap rate."[157] The core of the problem, he stated, lay in the difficulty and high cost of transportation, which hindered any profitable agricultural undertaking.

Against this backdrop, the recollection of an evening in the village of Plato, on the Magdalena River, by British officer Hamilton in 1823 suggests not only fun but also talent. He and his associates witnessed two black boys playing on violins, a girl on a small drum, and a mulatto-boy on a triangle. We were much surprised to hear these swarthy musicians play some waltzes with great taste, and having expressed a wish to see some dancing, a circle was soon formed and dancers found. My young Secretary waltzed with two or three pretty mulatto girls, and some of the villagers waltzed away for an hour or two. It was quite pleasing to see how gracefully young girls of eight or nine years old waltzed, placing their arms in a variety of elegant attitudes. The Creoles, Indians, and Negroes, have an exceedingly correct ear for music. I have since often thought with pleasure of this evening.[158]

Despite the fear among Gran Colombian leaders that Caribbean New Granada's population of African descent would launch a race war and emulate the Haitian Revolution, in the early 1820s armed resistance came mostly from indigenous villages and unsubdued nations in the provinces of Santa Marta and Riohacha. The few incidents denounced as pardo conspiracies turned out to be made up by local elite whites intending to eliminate mulattoes who threatened their domination and challenged the socioracial order from newly assigned positions of power. In reality, however, although some people of African descent on the frontier, in the countryside, and in small towns expressed frustration at their continuing subordination to whites, they did not protest collectively. Isolation and slow communications as well as localism continued to inhibit a unifying socioracial identity. Although the 1821 constitution guaranteed liberty and equality for all inhabitants, most slaves remained in bondage until death, and the poor and illiterate enjoyed few new opportunities to improve their condition. Nevertheless, after the war rural people strove to produce, make a living, and have some good times, often taking advantage of hacendados' weakness and the scant presence of the postcolonial state and church. In the long term, they were quite successful in resisting the imposition of Catholic cultural norms. Yet they were unable to make permanent gains in employment and land occupation, thus to lay down forms of organization and land tenure that could have limited the rapid growth of large-scale cattle ranching and tropical agriculture in the second half of the nineteenth century.

Political leaders also raised the specter of a pardo takeover at any attempt toward popular mobilization in Cartagena. There, in 1828, personal enmities, a strict socioracial hierarchy, Bolívar's obsession with pardocracia, and the growing conflict between followers of Bolívar and supporters of Santander worked together to drive mulatto general José Padilla—by far the most popular leader in Caribbean New Granada—to the firing squad for a three-day takeover. By 1831 competition between the principal cities of the Caribbean Coast for the control of foreign trade had evolved into war between Cartagena's Bolivarian partisans of strong centralism and Liberals who called on the memory of a raceless Padilla to advocate federalism.

6

THE PARDO AND
LIBERAL CHALLENGES
TO BOLÍVAR'S PROJECT

In November 1824 pardo general José Padilla issued an incendiary broadside "To the Respectable Public of Cartagena" in which he warned that "the sword that I brandished against the king of Spain, this sword with which I gave days of glory to the fatherland, this same sword will support me against anyone who tries to lower my class and degrade my person." He began:

This is not the first attempt by my enemies, the enemies of my class, to discredit me before the government, before my fellow citizens, before the entire world; one can see right away, I don't belong to the *old families*, nor do I draw my origin from . . . the ferocious Spaniards who, through their atrocities against the unfortunate Indians . . . accumulated riches with which they bought new grandparents. . . . Citizens, I lament in my heart to [have to] contemplate that the sacrifices I have made for my Fatherland and that conferred me the high rank I obtained are the motive of the jealousy . . . with which these men look at me, [these men] to whom Colombia owes only treasons and indifference, these men who each day shamelessly increase their attacks and undermine the holy edifice of the people's freedom and equality in order to build on its ruins the foundation of ambition and replace the republican ways with their old privileges and the exclusive domination of a small and miserable portion of families over the great majority of the peoples.[1]

Padilla's declaration not only alarmed elite cartageneros, but it also sent shock waves to Vice President Francisco de Paula Santander, as far away as Bogotá, and to President Simón Bolívar, still waging the war in Peru, prompting in 1825 an exchange of letters between the two white generals about the threat of pardocracia. Bolívar saw Padilla's protest as representative of the disposition that [Padilla] has toward the government and the system. . . . I think that this affair very much deserves the attention of the government, not to thrash but to take measures that spare in the future the horrible disasters that Padilla himself foresees. Legal equality is not enough for the spirit the people have, as they want absolute equality, in the public and the domestic areas alike; and next they will want pardocracia, which is their natural and unique propensity, in order to then exterminate the privileged class. This requires, I say, big measures that I will not tire of recommending.[2]

Bolívar did not define the measures he deemed necessary but expressed his unwavering conviction that equality—and, by extension, the power of prominent pardos—should have limits; otherwise people of African descent would dominate and massacre whites. Far less critical of Padilla, Santander responded to Bolívar: "I don't know how the germ of pardocracia could be destroyed. Nothing pleases [the pardos] and everything annoys them. They want everything exclusively; and I must be fair with Padilla, who until now is among those who least spread scandal."[3]

Less than two months later Bolívar expressed his opposition to a joint Colombian-Mexican expedition to liberate Cuba from Spain, in which Padilla would have played a leading role as head of the navy in Cartagena, on the grounds that it would lead to "the establishment of a new republic of Haiti" in Cuba.[4] Although in 1825 Bolívar did not take disciplinary action against Padilla, when in 1828 Padilla threatened once more to use his sword, this time to defend Santander and the 1821 republican constitution, the Liberator did not hesitate to endorse his execution to eradicate the specter of pardocracia in Caribbean New Granada.

PADILLA'S PARDO CHALLENGE

Padilla issued his broadside of November 1824 in response to an open letter published by an anonymous paterfamilias who vilified the mulatto general's separation from his adulterous wife and his "immoral" cohabitation with Anita Romero, a daughter of deceased pardo artisan Pedro Romero, a pioneer of Cartagena's First Independence. Astutely, the letter writer, by focusing on the illegitimate union of Padilla (who, in addition, had no known children), excluded him from the body of respectable patresfamilias personifying true citizens with full rights without having to mention his race. Padilla was particularly offended by the fact that cartagenero aristocrats had not invited his "virtuous companion" to a private ball at the residence of rich merchant Juan de Francisco, on the grounds that their union had not been sanctified by the Catholic Church. Padilla did not hesitate to denounce the hypocrisy of the white elite men who had mistresses and whose "fertile wives have only awaited the blessing of their wombs to be mothers, prodigiously conceiving and giving birth at the same time." In reality, he asserted, Anita Romero was excluded from the ball not because of the illegitimacy of their union but because of her race: "Everybody knows the class to which she belongs, and the desire to humiliate and degrade this class has been the only intention of the paterfamilias."[5] Padilla also denounced the attempts by aristocrats, such as Francisco, who had been deported during the First Independence for taking part in a royalist conspiracy, to destroy the republic and restore the colonial hierarchies.

Padilla had often been the target of racial discrimination and not only in the private sphere. Born in Riohacha in 1784 (or perhaps 1778) to a black father from Saint Domingue and a Wayúu mother, he had enlisted as a cabin boy at age fourteen and crisscrossed the Caribbean Sea on Spanish ships for several years until the British captured him in the battle of Trafalgar. In November 1811, after returning to Caribbean New Granada, Padilla joined Cartagena's piñerista movement and, from 1812 to 1814, participated in the war against the royalists, supporting Bolívar against Manuel del Castillo, toledista commander of the regional troops. When in early 1815 the toledistas regained power in Cartagena, Padilla continued to follow Bolívar's leadership, which led to his imprisonment by Venezuelan aristocrat General Mariano Montilla, then among Bolívar's foes. After Spain's reconquest, Padilla took refuge in Haiti. He joined Bolívar's expedition from Les Cayes and fought in Venezuela, reportedly witnessing the execution of the pardo Piar. He became a hero in Cartagena for his decisive role in liberating the city from Spain in 1821. In the next two years, together with the newly committed Montilla, Padilla brought independence to Gran Colombia's Caribbean Coast, including Santa Marta. Padilla's military career culminated at Maracaibo Bay in 1823, when he won the naval battle against Spain that sealed the independence of Venezuela. As a result, Padilla gained broad popularity in Caribbean New Granada. However, in a decision partly due to the fear of pardocracia, the government promoted Montilla, not Padilla, to the position of commander-in-chief of the department of Magdalena, despite Montilla's previous opposition to Bolívar. In the process, the personal rivalry between the two men dating back to Padilla's imprisonment in 1815 increased, exacerbated by race and class differences.[6]

General José Padilla.
(*Documentos sobre el proceso de la conspiración del 25 de Septiembre de 1828*, ed. Enrique Ortega Ricaurte [Bogotá: Prensa de la Biblioteca Nacional, 1942])

In his new position, Montilla constantly suspected pardos and radical patriots of stirring up the issue of race. In 1822 he asked Santander several times to remove Padilla from Cartagena, accusing him of backing "the damned people of Santo Domingo," that is, the piñeristas who had been in exile in Haiti after Spain's reconquest in 1815 and returned with broad ideas of equality. Montilla was particularly suspicious of Calixto Noguera, whom he wanted to "judge . . . as a seditious enemy of the whites," of Pedro Romero's son, Mauricio José Romero, and of "a fellow called [Juan Josef] Pita from Les Cayes, [a] grand pirate native son of Bocachica . . . with a lot of influence in Barú and Santa Ana, a big support there for the restless and turbulent spirits." In addition, Montilla complained, "some zambos of Getsemaní" had begun to say that the troops rightfully "requested colonel Padilla as commander."[7] Although Montilla placed all the suspects under the vigilance of the secret police in order to find legal ways to expel them, he managed only to send Padilla out of Cartagena, but Padilla had swiftly returned to light fireworks and hold a ball at his home "without inviting a single white woman," he reported to Santander, no doubt to show Padilla's racial exclusiveness.[8] Montilla could not emphasize enough to Santander "the powerful reasons why that man would be harmful."[9] In February 1823 Montilla again alleged that there was a resurgence of "the tumults about colors [differences]. Padilla who insisted on going [to Cartagena] to see his mistress for eight days, decreed in 'La Popa' death to the nobles, etc., for an alleged rebuff of his mistress who is a *pardita* sister of [Mauricio José] Romero and who publicly lives with him." In addition, Montilla lamented, some prominent creoles had married pardo women, among them man of letters Antonio del Real, "a *mulatica* from the gang"; white Mayor Manuel Marcelino Núñez was "very impregnated with the ideas of Les Cayes, where he has lived many years, and half of the cabildo [was] from the same class." Montilla cautioned Santander to "keep his eyes well open on that city."[10]

Perhaps for that reason, in 1824 the government in Bogotá saw fit to give Padilla only a promotion to general and an annual pension of three thousand pesos for his triumph at Maracaibo. Not fooled, Padilla bitterly compared the high position "other military men" had obtained as a "reward" for their services with his own compensation, which he characterized as "the pay of a mercenary." As an officer, he wanted "to conclude his career with honor," not with a pension.[11] In the end, Padilla was appointed commander of the navy in Cartagena, a position below his expectations and in which he was doomed to clash with Montilla.

Padilla's broadside, "To the Respectable Public of Cartagena," issued in late November 1824, offers a rare insight into his view of equality. As correctly noted by Bolívar, Padilla wanted absolute equality in the public and private spheres, which he did not differentiate. If the republic had banned class and race privileges, only service to the fatherland should matter in the new social hierarchy. And because of his outstanding military achievements, he deserved his superior rank and the corresponding respect, regardless of his lower-class origins and pardo race. Even if he considered himself superior to his fellow citizens, he was, in his view, not only an individual of republican merits but also part of a colonial socioracial category— the pardo class. Any affront to him was an affront to all pardos and by extension to the republic they had helped to build more than the elite whites. Padilla's understanding of equality went further than that of other officeholders of African descent, such as Valentín Arcía in Majagual and Remigio Márquez in Mompox (see Chapter 5). Arcía and Márquez envisioned that the republic would extend equality of rights and duties to all citizens without consideration of race and class. They claimed to have acted against corrupt whites simply as true servants and guardians of the republic's interests. Unlike them, Padilla openly defied the socioracial hierarchy inherited from Spanish colonialism and threatened to rally the pardo class behind him.

In all three cases, a small group of powerful whites, unwilling to renounce their alleged racial superiority at a time of scant resources and low employment, brandished the scarecrow of pardocracia to silence prominent men of color. In the end, they suppressed only Padilla. The governing elite was forced to recognize that Arcía and Márquez addressed equality within the limits set by the constitution and the laws, which had banned all privileges based on race and established the legal equality of all free male citizens. In contrast, Padilla's vision of equality clashed with that of the cartagenero aristocrats surrounding Montilla, who perceived further demands by pardos, such as equal advancement with whites and equality in private relations, as proof of arrogance and a violation of the private sphere. Padilla's vision also exceeded that of many free men of African descent who accepted the official egalitarian discourse. By using the colonial racial category of "pardos" to make democratic claims, he could fairly have been criticized for being a man of the past who clung to the Spanish caste system. Moreover, by announcing that he would use his sword to defend the equal rights and full integration of the pardo class at all levels, Padilla formulated the very scenario that, since the late 1790s, colonial and early independent authorities had predicted would transform Caribbean New Granada into another Haiti. In other words, when Padilla began to use race as a mobilizing idea, his detractors could easily raise the specter of the Haitian Revolution and accuse him of preparing for a race war. Indeed, the legal equality contained in the constitution and the threat of pardocracia prohibited people of African descent in general from making demands as pardos.

Despite Bolívar's concerns, in November 1824 Padilla's broadside did not mobilize Cartagena's free population of color. Neither did it diminish his popularity among enfranchised citizens, who in February 1825 elected him a senator of the republic for the department of Magdalena. In August, as a member of Cartagena's electoral council, Padilla took part in Gran Colombia's presidential election. Like almost all electors in Gran Colombia, he voted to return Bolívar to the presidency. But unlike most of Magdalena's electors, who supported a native cartagenero, Finance Secretary José María Castillo y Rada, Padilla cast his vote for Santander, helping to secure the vice president's more contested reelection.[12] As a result, Santander and Bolívar expressed their renewed confidence in the pardo leader. Santander wrote Bolívar that Padilla was "one of the most enthusiastic friends of the government, who idolizes me but you above all."[13] Bolívar did not hesitate to pronounce Padilla "the most important man of Colombia," adding: "I like him very much for his record of service and his adherence to me. May God keep him in this feeling."[14] With these words, Bolívar probably referred to Padilla's unique position as Gran Colombia's only pardo general and one of its most popular leaders, whose antagonism, he felt, could have enormous consequences.

Indeed, the paterfamilias's anonymous letter denouncing Padilla's so-called immorality convinced few in Cartagena, a city where many lived in free unions.[15] Padilla's attachment to Anita Romero was well accepted, and the show of bigotry of the new elite—among whom some, including Montilla, indulged in gambling, fiestas, and extramarital sex—had little impact.[16] Other aspects of Padilla's private life, which differed from the colonial ways, mattered more. In the words of his advocates, Padilla was unlike Montilla and several others, who had benefited from "graces and favors" that enabled them to acquire "many properties," live in "opulence, pomp and sumptuousness . . . [and] insult the public misery."[17] In contrast with Montilla, who lived in the mansion of the former marquis of Valdehoyos, Padilla had contracted a loan from Santander to buy a two-story house at the entrance of the popular suburb of Getsemaní; nearby he opened a tavern where people went to drink, shoot dice, and discuss politics, to the great displeasure of the elite.[18] He built a large following not only among the popular classes but also among many small contractors and merchants, clerks, officers, and the like. Support for Padilla stretched far beyond Cartagena, and in 1822 and 1825 he was elected senator to the congress in Bogotá.[19] After his second victory, Padilla celebrated with local elites and authorities on his way to the capital. Along the Magdalena River people gathered to see the general of African and indigenous ancestry, like most of them. According to Swedish traveler Carl August Gosselman, who was invited twice to have lunch with Padilla along the way, the guests drank abundantly, first "to the Great Bolívar" and "to the Republic of Colombia," then increasingly to "General Padilla." With all doors open, "the banquet was truly public and blacks and indigenes observed the scene open-mouthed, truly enjoying the spectacle and struggling to enter into the area."[20]

When, in April 1826, General José Antonio Páez defied the Santander government and launched a massive rebellion in Venezuela, many feared that Padilla would emulate him in Cartagena. From Peru, where he had waged a war against the royalists since 1823, Bolívar had become convinced that in Venezuela and Caribbean New Granada the root of the problem was that "pardocracia was gaining ground."[21] He also had grown increasingly pessimistic about the success of a republican government in Gran Colombia and unhappy with the civil administration of Santander. In his view, only strong military leaders—*caudillos*—could prevent the end of Gran Colombia and the rise of a new Haiti. He perceived Páez as Venezuela's lesser evil: although Páez was a rough, lower-class llanero, he was white, popular, and supported by a portion of the aristocracy. However, Bolívar could not find an adequate leader for Caribbean New Granada: Montilla was an elite white without a wide following; Padilla, a lower-class pardo with broad popularity who agitated for racial equality. As Bolívar wrote Santander, "Both seem very devoted to me: the first one cannot [do] anything; the second can [do] everything."[22] Bolívar began to profess that only by adopting the semi-monarchical constitution he had designed for Bolivia could Gran Colombia and Peru cure themselves of all the ills typical of the young, multiracial, and mostly illiterate Spanish American nations. Briefly, Bolívar's pan-Andean constitutional project consisted of a federation of authoritarian republics placed under the supreme authority of a president for life (himself) who would choose his successor, a formula he interestingly borrowed from the 1816 Haitian constitution. The project guaranteed equality and banned all privileges, including slavery, but limited suffrage to those who were literate, paid taxes, and had an occupation. It violated the 1821 constitution, which authorized no revision before 1831.[23]

From Lima, Bolívar sent *caraqueño* Antonio Leocadio Guzmán, well known for his role in Páez's rebellion and his anti-Santander sentiments, to rally the military and civic leaders of several cities behind his constitutional project.[24] Not surprisingly, Guzmán carried two letters of instructions from Bolívar to Cartagena: one for Montilla, the other for Padilla. According to Bolívar, it was essential to have the support of Padilla because, as a pardo and a military hero, he was very popular in Caribbean New Granada. At the same time, however, Bolívar increasingly suspected Padilla of leaning toward pardocracia and sympathizing with Páez. Thus, he began to consider Montilla, for whom he previously had little esteem, as his most dependable ally in the region.[25]

Despite the profound enmity between Montilla and Padilla, both facilitated the task of Guzmán when he arrived in Cartagena in September 1826. Montilla returned from his hacienda in Turbaco to take charge of the security of the city. Padilla invited "the persons of most influence and representation" to his home, to whom Guzmán explained the need for Bolívar's authoritarian constitution and emergency powers. Together Montilla and Padilla decided to call "a meeting of the male heads of household, associations, and leaders" to prevent "the civil war that threaten[s] us."[26] But several of Cartagena's native elite were confused and skeptical. Most vocal among them was rich white creole merchant Manuel Marcelino Núñez, a veteran of the First Independence and a staunch defender of the 1821 constitution and of Santander's legal government. On 25 September he anxiously asked Santander for advice, questioning Bolívar's motives and the legitimacy of his emissary, Guzmán, who was so deeply involved in the rebellion of Páez.[27] Given the slowness of transportation on the Magdalena River, Núñez's letter took over three weeks to reach Bogotá, and when Santander responded, on 21 October, Bolívar's request had long been approved by the cartageneros. The select assembly called by Montilla and Padilla met on 29 September 1826 and voted to "beg that [the liberator president] return to take charge of the Fatherland's destiny and [to] deposit in his hands all the authority necessary for its salvation."[28] Guzmán proudly reported to Bolívar that he could rely on the "complete adherence" to his takeover not only of Montilla and Padilla, but also of the city's consuls and foreign residents.[29]

The correspondence of several cartageneros to Santander immediately after the vote in favor of Bolívar's dictatorship illustrates the deep divisions within the native elite. Their letters also indicate the limits of Padilla's popularity and the restrictions imposed on him by his fear of being accused of promoting a pardocracia. According to one of them, Padilla was "the one who has been most constrained in this affair."[30] In Padilla's own words, the letter from Bolívar left him no choice but to "listen" to his ideas and to trust "the Liberator."[31] He told Santander: "If I had not taken this step, maybe Montilla would have been the cause of the spilling for many torrents of blood, because should he have sought to launch [a rebellion] like Páez in Caracas, I would not have allowed it, and you can see how the action would have gone."[32] With Padilla supporting Guzmán, the skeptics had little hope of being heard. Only Núñez was brave enough to refuse to sign any resolution against the legal government of Santander. The others reported sick or ended up signing the act concocted by Guzmán. Montilla forced the city council into compliance. The next day, on 30 September 1826, the male heads of families were summoned to approve the act in a general meeting, but as not all of them could fit into the room, only one out of twenty was allowed to participate in the vote by a show of hands.[33]

The parody of democracy displayed in September 1826 illustrates how deeply the dynamics of the city of Cartagena had changed since 1810-11. First and foremost, the lower classes—the pardos, zambos, and negros— which had massively pushed for equality and independence, represented no challenge to the civil and military authorities and the elite in 1826. Reportedly, Montilla took military measures to prevent unrest, and Padilla himself helped "calm the spirits, drive away the animosities and, in short, mollify the [public] opinion."[34] As a result, there were no popular street demonstrations of force but rather a docile show of hands confirming the elite's decision. The differences between the ideas expressed in Cartagena's 1812 constitution and those in the public act of 1826 were equally striking. All references to equality and democracy had been replaced with a discourse now centered on Bolívar as the "father of the Fatherland." Implicitly reassuming the position of king of Spain, Bolívar was the "common center" that "united all interests," neutralized all opposition, and irradiated all virtues. To be patriotic was to follow him uncritically.[35]

Meanwhile, Bolívar left Peru in August 1826 and arrived in Bogotá two months later to assume the special powers reserved by the constitution for the president in case of a national crisis. He promulgated extended legislation to replenish the treasury and reduce public services and the armed forces. Most unpopular of these measures was his decision to restore the colonial head tax, which he fixed at three pesos for every male over fourteen years, regardless of status. Also unwelcome was his reestablishment of the alcabala, described by the U.S. consul in Cartagena as "a very oppressive tax . . . not only . . . upon the purse but upon the time of the labouring poor." Discontent grew, and violence broke out against General Páez in Venezuela, prompting Bolívar's departure to negotiate with him. In many regions, federalism was on the rise, and rumors of secession increased, including the story that Cartagena would break away from the government of Bogotá and place itself directly under Bolívar's authority.[36] Although no such plan seems to have existed, Cartagena's unconditional support for the

Liberator was increasingly at odds with the rest of the Magdalena department. Even in Cartagena, pro-Santander sentiments were gaining ground among some officers and many cartageneros despite the vigilance of Montilla. In March 1827 the British consul, a strong advocate of Bolívar, worried about "intrigues to seduce" the four thousand undernourished and unpaid troops garrisoned in Cartagena "to favor views which are called constitutional."[37] At the same time, the U.S. consul commented: "General Padilla is a man of colour (a [z]ambo) uneducated, but said to possess daring courage. His influence among his own cast is unbounded, and as they constitute almost the whole population, it may in truth be declared that if he chose to abuse his power, he could do so with impunity."[38]

Nevertheless, Cartagena's unity behind the Liberator lasted through most of 1827. When in July Bolívar stopped in Cartagena on his way back from Venezuela, he received a warm welcome from the armed forces and residents congregated on city walls, streets, and balconies. Bolívar boasted to Páez: "I have met a very enthusiastic people [and] two excellent friends in Generals Montilla and Padilla."[39] The navy, despite Bolívar's attempts to reduce it, hosted a sumptuous banquet for him at Padilla's cramped home.[40] A satisfied Bolívar claimed to have found in Cartagena "a second Venezuela" and pronounced his famous sentence: "If Caracas gave me birth, you [cartageneros] gave me glory; with you I began the freedom of Colombia."[41]

In Andean New Granada, however, most cities mobilized against Bolívar's constitutional project and passed acts supporting Vice President Santander and the 1821 constitution. In Bogotá, the conflict between the supporters of Bolívar and Santander escalated. In Cartagena, bolivarista publications and broadsides turned increasingly against Santander and his "factious" followers.[42] Since Bolívar had the backing of the armed forces, Santander was forced to confront him on nonmilitary grounds. Ceding to bolivarista pressure, the national congress, controlled by the santanderistas, agreed in August 1827 to hold a convention in Ocaña on 2 March 1828 to revise the 1821 constitution. The election of delegates to the convention was set for November, but the congress, in order to weaken the bolivaristas, decided to strictly enforce the suffrage requirements imposed by the 1821 constitution and disenfranchised soldiers and lower-ranking officers in active service who until then had been discreetly allowed to vote. Consequently, the election produced a minority of delegates in favor of Bolívar, spawning rumors that he would launch a coup d'état.[43]

By late 1827 support for democratic institutions was growing even in Cartagena. Generals Padilla and Montilla resumed their dispute, despite the Liberator's call for order.[44] The bolivaristas showed increasing nervousness, particularly after Montilla, their candidate at the Ocaña convention, failed to be elected. By early February 1828, to men such as General José Padilla, the "salvation of the Fatherland" had ceased to depend on Bolívar and his authoritarian constitution. Padilla now backed the pro-Santander convention delegates who would defend "a freedom guaranteed by a popular representative system."[45] In response, the pro-Bolívar sectors led by Montilla had the military chiefs and many officers in the ground units issue an "Exposición" to the convention in Ocaña that blamed the misery and shrinking prerogatives of the army on Santander's civilian government and backed Bolívar's strong power.[46] Some officers who refused to sign the document were threatened with transfer to remote posts. Padilla stood up for them and, as commander of the navy, prohibited the officers under his authority to sign the manifesto. On 29 February 1828 the two parties clashed in a tavern; the defenders of the civil government called the champions of Bolívar "servile," and Bolívar's supporters called the advocates of Santander "factious." Padilla offered to defend those who had refused to sign with his sword if necessary. Cartagena's acting commander in chief, José Montes, found the situation explosive enough to ask Montilla, who was in his hacienda in Turbaco but whom Bolívar had authorized to assume unlimited power whenever necessary, to intervene. Instead, Montilla chose to let the conflict grow.[47] In the meantime, on 20 February Bolívar had established the first phase of his dictatorship and issued a decree that called for the immediate execution of convicted traitors and conspirators. Three days later he declared the public order disrupted in the provinces of Venezuela and assumed extraordinary powers there. As a result, suspicions among santanderistas that he would cancel the convention escalated.[48]

On 2 March 1828 Padilla rallied some officers of African descent and told them that he "was leading the people" to protect their freedom and the Ocaña convention because if "the crown" [i.e., Bolívar's constitution] was to "become reality," "they would kick us" for being pardos.[49] Padilla also attempted to enlist the support of a lower-ranking pardo officer by asking him "whether he could not see that he had not advanced with so many years of service and that tomorrow they would put above him any little white candidate as officer, as it was happening."[50] Rumors began to spread that

Padilla was arming "a large number of individuals" in Getsemaní, Cartagena's predominantly black and mulatto suburb.[51] On 5 March a new incident increased tensions. Some officers in the pro-Bolívar artillery shouted "Death to General Santander!" Padilla discussed with Montes the best way to prevent a crisis. Montes resigned, and a commission nominated Juan Antonio Gutiérrez to replace him as commander in chief. The acting intendant of Magdalena, Vicente Ucrós, remained in his post. Concurrently, still from Turbaco, Montilla assumed the extraordinary powers given to him by Bolívar to restore the public tranquility threatened by "a spirit of faction."[52] Surprisingly, Montilla ordered all military units to pull out of Cartagena at 2:00 A.M. on 6 March and transfer to Turbaco. By so doing, he lured Padilla into taking charge with the intent of accusing him of launching a coup and promoting the long-awaited race war on the Caribbean Coast.[53]

As Montilla expected, Padilla immediately mobilized the navy and the soldiers who were left in the city and assigned them to guard key posts. When newly appointed commander in chief Gutiérrez recognized Montilla's special powers, Padilla, allegedly responding to popular pressure, assumed military command of the department, a decision he knew was illegal but one he thought necessary to "bring the besieging general [Montilla] to reason."[54] According to Cartagena's municipal council and the British consul, Padilla acted only to secure order in the city, and there were "no thefts or disorders" on 6 March or the following days.[55]

Also on 6 March, all cartagenero men were called to a meeting that focused on the issues of liberty and equality. Padilla declared that Montilla's goal was to destroy the 1821 constitution and to dissolve the Ocaña convention, and he vowed to defend the people's freedom with his sword.[56] Reportedly, he threatened to demand a new loan from merchants to pay the troops. However, Padilla said nothing in favor of slave emancipation or the Haitian Revolution. As recognized by a pro-Bolívar newspaper, he never accepted the "various propositions of plundering, contributions, and extermination" that were made to him.[57] Moreover, according to all the witnesses in the investigation opened by Montilla a few days later, the most vocal activist and Padilla's guide was Ignacio Muñoz, the same white lawyer from Corozal who had played a leading role in the piñerista coup that compelled Cartagena's Supreme Junta to declare independence on 11 November 1811. Muñoz told the assembled men that he wished for the death of Montilla because Montilla wanted to "subjugate the rest of the Colombian population by tyranny, principally by the Bolivian Charter; that the latter would be of no advantage for the second class [the pardos], because they were the ones who had fought on the battlefields to suppress the tyranny; that Muñoz harangued General Padilla that in no way should he yield but carry on the fight until the ultimatum." One witness declared that Muñoz had asked the militiamen whether "they did not recognize [Padilla] as general commander and intendant, whether they wanted to be slave or free." Another person testified that Muñoz had publicly promised Padilla to find twenty thousand pesos to support his cause.[58] Not a single witness stated that Padilla had mobilized the population of color against the whites. But two whites testified that on 6 March pardo Captain Damián Berrío had told them that José Ignacio Ibarra, a "stranger" "of African color," stirred up the racial question, even saying that "one should give the signal to behead the whites." But when Berrío gave his deposition, he said that Ibarra had only expressed his fear of a war against whites, which would force him to escape since his foreign status put him at risk.[59]

On 7 March the municipal council of Cartagena refused to appoint Padilla as the new commander of Magdalena and sent two emissaries to negotiate a settlement with Montilla: the santanderista Muñoz and the bolivarista Juan de Francisco, the aristocrat and former royalist who in 1824 had excluded Padilla's partner from a ball.[60] The mission, however, was unsuccessful. Montilla restated that he had assumed extraordinary powers, but, according to Ucrós, also present at the meeting, he agreed to "an amnesty regarding those involved" and began to redirect the troops to Cartagena.[61] The next day tensions in the city reportedly escalated to the point where some men of African descent were talking about killing whites.[62] Padilla now realized that his supporters had abandoned him. He returned the military command of Cartagena to José Antonio Piñeres and left with Muñoz and a few others on a navy schooner bound for Tolú; from there they rode to Mompox.[63] In a letter to the U.S. consul, Padilla declared that he had left Cartagena to prevent the "spilling of blood" that would have resulted if Montilla had attacked him.[64] When the troops under Montilla reentered Cartagena, Padilla's supporters offered no resistance. Several fled, while others were arrested and imprisoned.[65]

As soon as he reached Mompox, Padilla wrote to Bolívar, blaming the events in Cartagena on Montilla.[66] On the same day he denounced Montilla's misuse of power to the president of the convention in Ocaña, offering to help defend the convention against any attack by bolivaristas.[67] Padilla also sent an insulting letter to Montilla telling him to leave Cartagena in peace and return to Venezuela.[68] Nevertheless, once he arrived in Ocaña,

Padilla only obtained lukewarm support from the pro-Santander delegates and failed to get practical advice from those who backed Bolívar. Disillusioned, he returned to Mompox, but the tight security he encountered, ordered by Montilla, forced him to proceed to Cartagena, where he arrived on 1 April 1828. He was immediately arrested, accused of planning a race war in the city, and imprisoned in Bogotá. There he was fatally entangled in the conspiracy against Bolívar. On 25 September 1828, the night of the attempted murder of the Liberator, conspirators entered Padilla's jail, killed his guard, gave him the guard's sword, and fled with him. After turning himself in, Padilla was swiftly tried and sentenced to death, with thirteen other defendants, for a murder he did not commit and a conspiracy he did not plan. On 2 October a defiant General Padilla was publicly stripped of his rank and shot, his body displayed hanging from the gallows. The presumed leader of the conspiracy, white creole Santander, was reprieved and exiled.[69]

With the execution of Padilla, Bolívar had definitively exorcized his fear of pardocracia in Cartagena and Caribbean New Granada. Yet he quickly realized that his racial biases would weigh on his legacy. As he wrote to Generals Pedro Briceño Méndez and José Antonio Páez one month after Padilla's death:

> Things have reached a point that keeps me wrestling with myself, with my ideas and with my glory. . . . I already repent for the death of Piar, of Padilla and the others who have died for the same cause; in the future there will be no justice to punish the most atrocious murderer, because [by saving] the life of Santander [I have pardoned] the most scandalous impunities. . . . What torments me even more is the just clamor with which those of the class of Piar and Padilla will complain. They will say with more than enough justice that I have only been weak in favor of this infamous white [Santander], who did not have the services of those famous [pardo] servants of the fatherland. This exasperates me, so that I do not know what to do with myself.[70]

Indeed, the tragic conclusion of the life of José Padilla is yet another proof of the double standard that guided the Liberator. Although he executed pardo Padilla for a three-day bloodless coup in Cartagena, Bolívar pardoned and, from 1826 to 1828, negotiated with the white llanero Páez, who headed a full-fledged Venezuelan rebellion against the government in Bogotá.

The terrible fate of Padilla raises important questions. The most immediate one concerns the key role played by Ignacio Muñoz, of dubious pro-Santander credentials, in the radicalization of Padilla's brief coup and ensuing downfall. The year 1828 was not the first time that Muñoz distinguished himself as a popular leader. During the First Independence of Cartagena Province, he mobilized large numbers of Cartagena's free men of color against established authorities on several occasions (see Chapter 4); during the Spanish reconquest he took refuge in Les Cayes and participated with Padilla in an expedition to reliberate Venezuela. Muñoz was a skillful manipulator of crowds, which he harangued like "a preacher."[71] That he seized the opportunity to act again in 1828 behind—or perhaps against— Padilla is thus not surprising. Less understandable is the fact that Padilla accepted Muñoz's support when the two men had a long history of petty quarrels and physical aggression against each other, which Montilla had used to denigrate Padilla. Padilla had repeatedly asked Santander to remove Muñoz, this "very evil man," from Cartagena.[72] As late as February 1827 Padilla had warned Santander that Muñoz was in jail for having attempted to incite Cartagena's troops to rebel against himself and Montilla but that he probably would not be adequately punished.[73] In March 1828 Muñoz not only radicalized and racialized Padilla's movement in Cartagena, he also represented him at the meeting with Montilla, where, according to a pro-Bolívar newspaper, he "sold out Padilla."[74] Yet Muñoz accompanied Padilla in his flight, helped to formulate most of the letters Padilla sent from Mompox, and suggested the steps he took in Ocaña. Finally, in June 1828 Muñoz made a sworn declaration in Cartagena that provided the major evidence against Padilla until his entanglement in the attempted murder of Bolívar. Muñoz accused Padilla of being the leader, together with several delegates to the convention, of a broad armed conspiracy to prevent the adoption of the Bolivian Constitution and to separate New Granada from Gran Colombia. Padilla's intention on leaving Ocaña, Muñoz claimed, was to stir up first Mompox then Getsemaní and the navy in Cartagena, but he failed to find backing.[75]

A fundamental question is why the popular Padilla failed to mobilize Cartagena in early March 1828. Why was the disliked General Montilla able to reestablish his control over the city and to arrest Padilla there? According to the British consul, Padilla plotted to overthrow all the supporters of Bolívar in Magdalena, "confiding in the strength of his own party among the people of colour, 'los Pardos' as he terms them." But they deserted him. The consul added, "It is said that in the paroxysm of his rage, Padilla threw his hat on the ground, stamped on it, and uttered the most bitter imprecation against the faithless people of Cartagena."[76] Other sources confirm that as early as 7 March Padilla accused "of apathy the people he could not move, and of treason the officers who misleadingly had offered him the cooperation of their units."[77] The next day the troops under Montilla met no resistance when they returned to Cartagena, and Padilla's closest partisans chose to escape rather than fight. As a close associate wrote to Bolívar after meeting with Padilla in Ocaña, "Regarding Cartagena, I will say that Your Excellency has formed a very exaggerated idea of the event. Padilla's steps in this city and the behavior he observed with me show, without any doubt, that he has no party at all."[78]

In his memoirs, white conservative general Joaquín Posada Gutiérrez wrote that "General Padilla, because of his color," had hoped that "the people" would support him. But the majority of the population remained indifferent because in Caribbean New Granada and principally in Cartagena, the pardos "who enjoy a complete equality of political and civil rights . . . know that only knowledge and merit are legitimate titles of superiority" and are accessible to all.[79] This explanation spared Posada Gutiérrez an analysis of the limits of the legal equality granted by Gran Colombia's 1821 constitution and the racism prevalent among Cartagena's elite, which Padilla experienced repeatedly. Moreover, contrary to Posada's allegation, in 1828 Padilla attempted to unite the cartageneros behind the constitution of 1821 and the government of Santander rather than behind a pardo identity.

THE OLD AND THE NEW IN PADILLA'S CARTAGENA

A close examination of Cartagena's society and economy in the 1820s will explain the loneliness of Padilla in 1828. In the late 1820s Cartagena still suffered from the effects of the wars for independence and Spanish general Morillo's deadly siege in 1815. According to the census of 1835, Cartagena's population reached only 11,929, in contrast to an estimated 17,600 in 1809—a reduction of about one-third of its inhabitants.[80] North American traveler Richard Bache reported that in 1822 about one-eighth of Cartagena was unoccupied or in ruins, and half of Getsemaní was destroyed when Spain took it over.[81] Cartagena had lost the privileged military status and budget it enjoyed during Spanish colonialism. Already challenged by the opening of the port of Santa Marta to legal trade in the 1790s and by widespread contraband from diverse points on the Caribbean Coast, Cartagena's monopoly of the foreign trade of Colombia came to an end with independence. All attempts by cartagenero authorities and merchants to restore the port's predominant trade rights were hampered by their inability to repair the Canal del Dique leading to the Magdalena River.[82] So few boats anchored in Cartagena that foreign consuls regularly complained about the lack of trade.[83] Still, Cartagena remained the most important city in Caribbean New Granada and therefore became the capital of the department of Magdalena.

Cartagena also continued to be mostly inhabited by people of African descent, as under Spain. In 1825 Gosselman's first impression on landing on the esplanade between the city's entrance and Getsemaní was that of "a multicolor human anthill. The major part were blacks, accompanied by other colors forming a sample of tones that went from the African black, passing by the American yellow-brown, and ending in the European white."[84] Whites still held most positions of economic and political power, but Spaniards had been replaced by British, North Americans, French, and other foreigners in trade, and several Venezuelans served in the administration.[85] Yet, as before independence, complex networks of patronage and kinship linked individuals across class and race. Another lasting and even amplified characteristic of the past was the high ratio of females among the city's inhabitants. One Andean visitor lamented: "The poverty of this city in all senses and the almost absolute want of men have deeply afflicted me."[86] According to the 1835 census, there was an average of 154.4 women over sixteen years of age for every 100.0 men. Although the census does not provide information on race, it divides the city into three barrios—La Catedral, Santo Toribio, and Trinidad (Getsemaní)—that had clear socioracial differences. Whereas women residing in the largely white and elite barrio of La Catedral only slightly outnumbered men, in the popular and more mulatto and black barrios of Santo Toribio and Getsemaní, they were more than twice as numerous as men (respectively, 268.8 and 196.3 women per 100.0 men).[87] Although by 1835 slavery had declined to 5.0 percent of the city's total population (in contrast to 15.7 percent in 1777), the wealthy barrio of La Catedral showed the highest ratio of urban slavery in Caribbean New Granada: one out of ten inhabitants were still slaves, a majority of them female.[88]

If Padilla lived among a population of predominantly African descent, this population was also largely female, thus disenfranchised. Although few available sources provide information on cartageneras generally, none mentions the presence of women in the events of February–March 1828, probably because they had little to do with the issues that mobilized the rival parties, such as military pay, benefits, and suffrage, the Ocaña convention, and the dispute between Bolívar and Santander. This is not to say that women were not active in Cartagena; on the contrary, aside from those working in domestic service, many women sold goods in the streets and the markets; did laundry; ran inns, taverns, and small shops; and drove goods between the city and its surrounding areas. They often were single heads of household. Thus, it is likely that women would have participated in a movement of broader appeal, such as the protest against Bolívar's recent reestablishment of some colonial taxes, which affected most of them. Surely, such a movement would also have rallied more men who were jewelers, tailors, shoemakers, those who worked in construction and small industries, as well as sailors, stevedores, porters, muleteers, fishermen, and day laborers.[89] Yet, in addition to students and professionals, the focus of the dispute on military and political matters made Padilla's appeal mostly relevant to soldiers and officers, who were reputedly loyal to Montilla and whose number shrank after Montilla withdrew most of them from the city.[90]

Besides, the composition of the troops garrisoned in Cartagena in the 1820s greatly differed from that in the late colonial period, which also explains their lack of participation in the movement headed by Padilla in 1828. Spain's extension of the military fuero to Cartagena's militiamen of color had prepared their proindependence activism in 1810–11 by enhancing their status and giving them a sense of importance and equality. After independence, the fuero progressively disappeared and recruitment deepened socioracial inequities. The troops stationed in Cartagena generally comprised black, zambo, mulatto, and Indian peasants and laborers who had been dragged away from their homes and had little interest in disputes concerning urban leadership. With the exception of a mutiny for food and clothes in the artillery, swiftly repressed by Montilla in 1823, the troops in Cartagena did not revolt but, according to a British officer, showed "patient endurance . . . under their many privations."[91] Indeed, in early 1827 Ignacio Muñoz failed to instigate them to rebel against Padilla and Montilla.[92] Later that year General Montilla encountered little opposition when he ordered the officers of every military corps in the city to issue manifestos of support for Bolívar against "the faction of Bogotá" embodied by Santander.[93] Doubtless, many soldiers and officers would have voted for Montilla in the election to the Ocaña convention had their suffrage not been restricted by the congress. Thus, not surprisingly, in February 1828 few resisted his demand that they sign the anti-Santander Exposición to the convention, which protested the violent draft without pay, the exclusion of soldiers from suffrage, and the lengthening of military service through the creation of new intermediate ranks, all issues stressing the inequity between citizens' duties and rights.[94] In early March the troops went along with Montilla when he pulled them out of Cartagena in the middle of the night only to return them two days later.

Like the ground troops, most seamen left in Cartagena in early March 1828 had been enlisted in the navy against their will.[95] Also, the navy's practice of forcing artisans to abandon their shops and perform unpaid work on ships alienated many of them, as exemplified by carpenter José Francisco Escudero. Since 1822 the navy had retained Escudero's services by bodily force and mistreated him repeatedly. In his protest to the intendant, he declared his willingness to fulfill his duties as a citizen, but "I will not consent that, because they need my skills, they want to . . . reduce me to a Slavery more unbearable than the one the Government is trying to extinguish in the territory of the Republic." Although the intendant defended Escudero, in 1824 Padilla ordered his arrest for disobedience and his assignment to a warship, where he was still serving one year later.[96] Such experiences were unlikely to encourage naval personnel to risk their lives in the defense of their commander, Padilla, who until 1827 had sided with Montilla.

Moreover, in 1828 Cartagena lacked the strong native leadership it had in 1810, when a reformist elite of creole hacendados, merchants, lawyers, and priests had organized the free population of color against Spanish rule. José María García de Toledo, the Gutiérrez de Piñeres brothers, and mulatto Pedro Romero—to name a few—had all died during the war. The most outstanding members of the elite born in the region tended to pursue their careers in Bogotá. Whites still held the highest positions of power, but some of them, such as Montilla, were Venezuelan. Others, like Juan de Francisco Martín, had a royalist past. The native survivors of the First Independence of some significance, such as Ignacio Muñoz and rich merchant Manuel Marcelino Núñez, were unable to offer a viable plan for the department of Magdalena and to undermine the domination of Montilla. As for Padilla, despite Bolívar's assertion that he was "the most important man of Colombia," he could not transcend the limits imposed on him by his race.[97] Because he had often boasted of his pardo roots and his determination to defend the pardo class, Padilla had exposed himself to accusations of pardocracia and of envisioning a Haitian-like revolution for New Granada's Caribbean provinces. In a political culture that banned references to blackness and its mixtures (but not whiteness), Padilla had excluded himself from the possibility of becoming a broad-based regional caudillo.[98] Unlike the uneducated but white Páez, whose boldness and resolution had gained Bolívar's support against Santander and had progressively united Venezuelans regardless of race and class against New Granadans, Padilla simultaneously alienated the local aristocracy and courted the national leadership.[99]

By attempting to reconcile Bolívar and Santander after Bolívar initiated his campaign for a semimonarchical constitution, Padilla distanced himself from the native leaders, such as Núñez, who backed Santander.[100] Some even accused him of having "absolutely sold out to the faction [of Bolívar]" and of using seduction and intimidation to silence the lower classes.[101] When in February 1828 Padilla eventually abandoned his attempts to reunite Bolívar and Santander and stood up to defend Santander, no doubt many cartageneros still remembered his role in the celebration of Bolívar's visit eight months earlier and did not take him seriously. More importantly, the pro-Santander delegates in Ocaña acknowledged Padilla's offer to defend the convention but did little to save him. Clearly, though popular in Caribbean New Granada, Padilla lacked national stature and political constancy, which explains the cartageneros' reluctance to follow him. All these factors strengthened the bolivaristas' confidence that the elimination of Padilla would not ignite a protest. Indeed, when in April 1828 his sister, Magdalena Padilla, asked fifteen political and religious notables in Cartagena to testify that he had not disturbed the public order in March, all declined her request.[102] Similarly, the broadside she then issued to refute "the horrible accusations with which they attempt to vilify the glorious prowesses of my brother, the general of division José Padilla" failed to mobilize cartageneros.[103]

Furthermore, the dynamics of race, class, and power in the city had changed since 1810, when the reformist elite realized that it could secure autonomy from Spain only by building an alliance with the free population of color. The leaders then had empowered and armed militiamen of African descent, and aristocrat García de Toledo had felt it necessary to assert that he had danced in his house and elsewhere "with women from all classes."[104] By the 1820s a conservative elite under Montilla dominated Cartagena and sought to keep the lower classes of color in check, not to organize them. The elite did not hesitate to ban General Padilla's pardo partner from a ball, allegedly because of the illegitimacy of their union. Evidently, race still overlapped with class. As observed by a French diplomat, the young men in the upper class tried to find a government job or studied law, and "the mechanical professions were left to the foreigners and the men of color."[105] Yet racial boundaries were loosening. Among the progressive elite opposed to Montilla, a few white men had married *mulatas*.[106] More generally, given the continuing gender imbalance in Cartagena's population, several women of African descent were involved in short-lived or long-term relationships with white men. Among the lower classes, the introduction of legal equality and the elimination of racial divisions in the armed forces and of the mention of race in state (but not church) records had led people to refer to themselves more as "citizens" or "el pueblo" than as "los pardos," "los negros," or "los zambos." Whereas race continued to be meaningful and influential to individuals, it was less so collectively. Thus, when in March 1828 Ignacio Muñoz attempted to revive the rhetoric of 1811 and 1815 and to mobilize the lower classes of color on racial grounds, he had only limited success.

In 1828 people were also unlikely to defend Padilla against Montilla because Cartagena was not a city where political confrontation often turned violent. In October 1829, exactly one year after Padilla's public execution, the U.S. consul in Cartagena disagreed with his European colleagues who still supported Bolívar's authoritarian constitution on the grounds that Colombians needed a strong executive to prevent rebellions. To the consul, neither a government of the wealthy nor a president for life were necessary. "The South Americans are an extremely docile people and very obedient and submissive to the laws. . . . All the insurrections that have disturbed the country within the last two years have been attempts of well informed members of the community; and in no one instance are the low and ignorant classes to be blamed," he claimed.[107] In making this declaration, the consul surely had in mind the events of March 1828, when Cartagena's blacks, mulattoes, and zambos did not back Padilla against the unpopular Montilla. Yet this lack of involvement did not signify that people were indifferent to the form of government that ruled them, as the consul believed.[108] In 1828 the lower classes did not endorse Venezuelan aristocrat Montilla either. They simply did not take part in a dangerous confrontation that was unlikely to yield them much—whatever the outcome.

In reality, the solidarity among the cartageneros, already highlighted by Spanish travelers Juan and Ulloa in the 1740s, did not disappear with independence. One French observer noted that, despite the customary remarks on people's idleness and dissoluteness, Cartagena's inhabitants had some virtues: "Respect for their parents, a strong bond in the families, hospitality, charity toward the poor and the sick, and a lot of politeness: in their sharpest quarrels, they know how to keep up appearances, and they never lack a certain dignity, this being in all classes of society, even the lowest." From the late eighteenth century, literate people tended to express differences of opinion or protests in the form of handwritten pasquinades or printed broadsheets directed against a specific person. This generated responses and counterresponses but, as the same Frenchman reported, consequently "the people of the country . . . only fight with quills."[109] Although few inhabitants could read, the content of posters and newspapers reached the illiterate in the streets, workplaces, and taverns through discussions and improvised speeches. If fierce verbal disputes did arise, such as the one that opposed Padilla to the supporters of Bolívar in February 1828, they seldom led to physical confrontation, manslaughter, or rioting. By all accounts no violence occurred during Padilla's takeover on 6–7 March 1828.

Cartagena's numerous holidays also served to reduce confrontation. Celebrated with public ceremonies, balls, and gaming, they brought all classes and races together without threatening the permanence of the socioracial hierarchy. Notably, the carnival festivities of the Virgin of Candelaria, patroness of the city, had played a mollifying role since the colonial period (see Chapter 3).[110] In the mid-1820s Christmas celebrations began to be combined with the commemoration of independence and the public manumission of slaves. For ten days economic activities were at a standstill. At night, fireworks exploded in the sky. Carrying torches and flags, and playing music, groups of participants strolled around the city, occasionally stopping at houses for drinks. People danced and masqueraded in the streets. According to New Yorker Rensselaer Van Rensselaer, only the rich could afford luxurious costumes and masks and could dance in the central part of the main square "surrounded by the mob. . . . A corner of the same square is appropriated to the slaves for their use during the 'fiestas'; imitating the example of their betters, they have their own fun dancing the monotonous 'fandangos' while the festivities last."[111]

Established by the Manumission Law of 21 July 1821 (see Chapter 5), the public ritual of manumission began to take place in Cartagena on 25 December 1826, less than three months after the city voted its controversial support of the armed forces and of Bolívar's authoritarian constitution. Following songs, processions, parades, and a mass in the cathedral, the local manumission junta emancipated in the main square all the slaves whose freedom it had bought during the year: ten in 1826 and about thirty in 1829, of both sexes and all ages. Rensselaer contemptuously reported to his father:

"When the Cap of Freedom was presented to them, the poor mortals could not restrain their tears and the cry of *Viva el Librator* [*sic*] and *Viva la Republica* [*sic*] burst from the crowd at the end of the ceremony. The delighted freed-men . . . paraded the streets with the most grotesque demonstrations of joy. It was laughable to witness the ludicrous expression with a broad grin on their comical faces and the spring halt sort of step with which they skipped along receiving the congratulations of their friends"[112]

The 25 December ceremonies blew out of proportion the small achievements of the manumission junta. For example, in 1826 the junta's president publicly addressed the ten emancipated slaves with these words: "From this moment on, you are free, and you owe this precious gift to the Republic. Its laws, its wise institutions place you today in the group of citizens. . . . Manumitted! The Republic hopes that by breaking the bonds of slavery in which you moaned, it increases the number of its defenders, of its good citizens; and you will not evade this very fair expectation." The speech concluded with a recommendation to revere the "Father of Colombia," "President Liberator Simón Bolívar," who had initiated the process of emancipation.[113] Indeed, by performing a year's worth of manumissions on one day in Cartagena's main plaza, the junta appeared magnanimous and powerful. It taught the hundreds of cartageneros still in slavery that freedom rewarded loyalty and patience, and that protest and revolt had no place in that society. The manumission ceremonies also clearly underlined the boundaries between slaves and free persons of color—now raceless citizens united under the paternal protection of Bolívar—and emphasized the impossibility of their joint socioracial challenge.

Finally, in March 1828 Padilla was unable to find support outside of Cartagena, despite strong opposition to Montilla in several towns. In fact, Padilla's takeover had been so brief that Montilla could rapidly step up repression and prevent similar movements elsewhere. Although Mompox's santanderistas welcomed Padilla with enthusiasm when he stopped there on his way to Ocaña, when he returned, Montilla had given discretional powers to Colonel Federico Adlercreutz, a Swedish count with the Colombian army since 1820, to prevent any "sedition" or pardo movement in the city. Adlercreutz disarmed Mompox's militiamen and replaced them with more reliable forces from Cartagena; he also kept suspected sympathizers of Padilla in custody. Padilla was thus forced to leave immediately for Cartagena, where he was arrested on his arrival.[114]

Padilla's failure outside of Cartagena points to general characteristics in Caribbean New Granada's political culture that impeded the formation of an opposition movement headed in the capital of the Magdalena department. In reality, rather than providing the framework for building the future of the region, the creation of the department of Magdalena with its capital in Cartagena by the 1821 constitution only exacerbated tensions between that city and other towns and communities. Occupying now the position it had sought during the First Independence, Cartagena imposed levies in money and recruits everywhere but opposed the development of trade through Santa Marta and Sabanilla. The governorship of aristocrat Venezuelan general Montilla, who ruled the region from Cartagena with an iron hand during most of the 1820s, further set people against the capital.[115] In 1825, from Santa Marta, the newspaper *El Observador Samario* protested that all public jobs went to elite, well-connected "favored sons," when the "meritorious Republicans" who freed the country were "held back because they are not servile." It advocated the transformation of Santa Marta into a main international port to alleviate the misery of its merchants and laboring classes and to increase state revenues.[116]

Not surprisingly, in 1826 the leaders of several towns anticipated that if Bolívar was given dictatorial powers and if his authoritarian and centralist constitution was adopted, there would be no limit to Cartagena's despotism. Consequently, like most towns in Andean New Granada, they backed the constitution of 1821 and the government of Santander in Bogotá. On 20 July 1826 the municipal council of Mompox warned that "at the cost of the blood and sacrifices of its sons, this city is the one that fought the most under the banners of the hero Liberator to overthrow tyranny and conquer independence"; therefore, "this city is ready, in the literal sense, at the orders of the Government to support the sacred Constitution wherever it is necessary."[117] After the proclamation of Cartagena's pro-Bolívar act on 29 September 1826, Montilla ordered other towns in Magdalena to approve similar declarations. Soledad, Barranquilla, and Valledupar followed suit, but Mompox again refused and prominent leaders in Riohacha and Santa Marta declined to sign their city's manifestos. By 1827 these last two cities had declared their allegiance to the constitutional government in Bogotá.[118]

As these local stands indicate, during the 1820s people identified with their own cities, towns, and villages, rather than with New Granada or the Magdalena department. Towns and villages were still conceived as hierarchical, corporative entities whose heads were their respectable citizens, and bodies, the lower classes. Each town tended to respond to outside events as one united community or pueblo. Now about two generations after the Bourbon campaigns of forced resettlement, people had a strong sense of belonging to established entities. Yet, despite the growing reference to ciudadanos, there was no emerging notion of citizens as autonomous individuals. In fact, as before independence, the citizens with full rights continued to be the "respectable patresfamilias" with some education and property, to whom military leaders were now added. Simultaneously, the response of each city, town, and village was largely dictated by its relationship with neighboring communities. In this respect, independence did not reduce the competition between Caribbean New Granada's principal cities. Yet change in the demography, politics, and foreign relations of the new republic modified the comparative importance of these cities and their rapport with Andean Colombia.

First and foremost, the urban population of the Caribbean provinces in general had declined sharply.[119] The drop was sizable not only in Cartagena, but also in Mompox, whose population in 1835 was 8,067, compared with Alexander von Humboldt's estimate of 14,000 in 1801. The population in Valledupar and Riohacha had decreased as well. In fact, Santa Marta was the only city in which by 1835 the number of residents had increased to a still low 5,929, compared with 3,598 in the late 1770s. In all cities, persons of African and indigenous descent continued to represent the majority, and whites, the minority and the elite. In Mompox and Santa Marta, women over sixteen years of age outnumbered men (respectively, 121.5 and 128.0 women per 100.0 men).[120]

Mompox remained a trade and contraband center, the major stopover on the route between the coast and the interior, and the place where most champanes were built and most bogas contracted. It also comprised many skillful artisans, notably jewelers who worked the gold of Simití with great dexterity. But Mompox owed such a position to the absence of a challenger rather than its own advances. Like Cartagena, Mompox had lost its dynamic elite and its intermediate leaders of African descent in the war. The elevation of the city to capital of Mompox Province in 1826, with jurisdiction over a vast territory, including Simití and Ocaña, did little to reverse its demographic decline. By 1838 the bishop of Cartagena, Juan Hermenegildo de León, assessed that "the general backwardness and decadence that can be observed everywhere [in Mompox] are well-known. . . . The capitalists have disappeared. . . . Of the public wealth nothing is left but ruins in which everywhere one can see the consequences of the war of independence."[121] Santa Marta continued to be a city of secondary importance, despite being authorized to import and export after 1823. Its port still lacked docks, which made the loading and unloading of ships slow and perilous. The streets were unpaved, and most dwellings were modest one-story houses and mud-and-cane cabins. The fact that the city had been occupied and sacked by royalist Indians in 1823 affected its reputation in the commercial world. Trade, in reality, was limited to the import of luxury fabrics and goods from France and to the export of dyewood and hides. According to Swedish traveler Gosselman, in 1825 the city's few merchants usually met at sunset near the beach on a large log nicknamed "the Stock Market of Santa Marta" to talk about business. An 1826 report from a scornful British consul recommended closing Santa Marta's port, which in his view would only affect five or six individuals, and opening up exports from Sabanilla.[122] Valledupar languished as sugar production and cattle ranching had dropped due to the repeated crossing of troops during the war, and its trade and contraband remained limited. However, no town in the Caribbean region had been more destroyed by the war than Riohacha, burned to the ground by an Irish unit in 1820. It was left without a church, elementary school, or adequate buildings, and its inhabitants were so few and so poor that the national government had to allocate special funds for the construction of a church and a school. With a port lacking a wharf, no fertile lands in its surroundings, and hostile Wayúu in its proximity, Riohacha continued to live off smuggling.[123]

As Caribbean New Granada's principal cities struggled to recover their colonial standing and to collect revenues, some small towns were gaining importance, particularly Sabanilla and Barranquilla in the delta of the Magdalena River, and Ciénaga near Santa Marta. This was partly the result of a law in 1824 that not only divided the national territory into departments, provinces, and cantons, but also promoted the head of each canton to town (villa), with its own cabildo. The law also abolished the colonial distinctions between villages, pueblos de indios, and hamlets and elevated all of them to the category of parish. A more liberal approach to international trade and the development of local economies reinforced the demographic effects of administrative change. As early as 1826 the former colonial contraband site of Sabanilla, on the Caribbean Sea, interested the British enough for them to produce a report on "the conditions of Sabanilla being an open port."[124] Since the early 1800s, some foreign merchants had settled in Sabanilla's close neighbor, Barranquilla, from where they ran import and transportation businesses on the Magdalena River. According to Rensselaer, prominent among them was Canadian John Glen, who was "justly regarded as the patriarch of the village" and employed one hundred bogas, whom he reportedly transformed into neat and responsible heads of nuclear families. Glen had begun to import in Cartagena in 1809; although he had lost business during the war, he also made a fortune by managing to sell food to wealthy cartageneros during the siege of Morillo. His participation in the patriot army earned him the monopoly of legal foreign trade through Sabanilla in the early 1820s. His business grew steadily, and by 1829 he and his extended family "live[d] in grand style with three or four blacks to wait on the table and two or three in the kitchen."[125] By 1836 exports from Sabanilla already amounted to three times the value of those from Cartagena, and with 5,359 inhabitants, Barranquilla's population was almost on a par with that of Santa Marta.[126]

SANTANDERISTA CHALLENGE TO CARTAGENA

The fact that the hierarchical local community, or pueblo, continued to be the primary source of people's identification and sense of belonging, coupled with Caribbean New Granada cities' hatred for Cartagena and their rulers, explains, together with the region's difficult communications, General José Padilla's inability to rally other towns and villages behind his cause.[127] Moreover, these factors equally prevented the bolivaristas from dominating the Caribbean region beyond Cartagena, even after the annihilation of Padilla. At the national level, the bolivaristas realized in June 1828 that they could not get a majority of delegates at the Ocaña congress to vote for Bolívar's constitution. They walked away from the convention to prevent a quorum and resolved to achieve their goals through force and the dictatorship of the Liberator.[128] In Caribbean New Granada, with elitist merchant Juan de Francisco in charge of administrative matters, Montilla extended his extraordinary military powers. He ordered his subordinates in the Caribbean cities to use all means to neutralize santanderistas, notably recommending to Adlercreutz in Mompox: "Do not let any expression of discontent grow and less any action or violence, which need to be repressed with all might, even if it costs blood." The press was censured. Montilla also demanded that all cabildos, corporations, and patresfamilias endorse without delay acts requesting the "unlimited rule" of Bolívar "to save the republic," modeled on an act issued by bolivarista notables in Bogotá.[129]

After Bolívar officially assumed dictatorial powers in August 1828 and launched a series of conservative and pro-church reforms, Montilla stepped up repression and had opponents arrested, deported, imprisoned, or executed throughout the Caribbean provinces. The attempted murder of Bolívar in Bogotá in September by supporters of Santander and the subsequent shipment of Andean prisoners and exiles, including General Santander, on the Magdalena River and their incarceration in Cartagena intensified security measures in the region.[130] After Padilla's execution, rumors of conspiracies to avenge his death by killing Montilla and his subordinates multiplied, only to be refuted after military investigation.[131] For example, in Cartagena veteran officer Antonio Pérez was banned from the country for having said that Padilla "had made Colombia and should not be dead. That it seemed impossible . . . that they could kill such a brave general with so much service."[132] In 1829 resentment continued to mount as Montilla maneuvered to have all towns elect bolivarista candidates to a new national convention scheduled to take place in 1830.[133]

In the meantime, the Andean provinces of Cauca and Antioquia rebelled against Bolívar's dictatorship, and Venezuela, under General José Antonio Páez, had practically broken away from Gran Colombia. Although Bolívar managed to provisionally bring the two New Granadan provinces back into his fold, the rumor that his cabinet planned to crown him and institute a monarchy under a European prince after his death further eroded his popularity. From Venezuela, some supporters of Páez claimed that, as a monarch, Bolívar would reestablish all-white government and racial inequality and strengthen slavery.[134] Caribbean New Granada turned to open protest. Riohacha was the first city in the region to denounce the Liberator's dictatorship and the 1830 convention. In February 1830 a *riohachero* issued a call to the "honorable inhabitants of Valledupar and La Paz" to "throw off the yoke that oppresses [the people]." It protested the monarchist intentions of the "fraction of Bogotá," the "taxes that are excessive and above the citizen's capacities; and the work assignments and contributions imposed to enrich the agents of despotism with the meager substance of the communities [pueblos]." The riohachero concluded: "This is the freedom they offer us."[135]

Increasingly isolated, exhausted, and ill, Bolívar took a leave of absence from the presidency in March 1830, after having granted amnesty to Santander and some of his supporters. The convention elected two Andean aristocrat generals, Joaquín Mosquera, from Popayán, and Domingo Caicedo, from Bogotá, as president and vice president, respectively. During their brief tenure, Mosquera and Caicedo included some santanderistas in the government and attempted to reunify the nation, but in August 1830 the

The last days of General Simón Bolívar in Santa Marta (anonymous painter).
(*Bolívar de Cartagena a Santa Marta*, ed. Vicente Pérez Silva [Bogotá: Banco
Tequendamar–Litografía Arco, 1980])

bolivaristas deposed them in a military coup backed by acts and proclamations from several cities, notably Cartagena. The new president, Venezuelan General Rafael Urdaneta, assumed dictatorial powers, presumably until
Bolívar's resumption of the presidency. From Cartagena, Bolívar neither
condemned Urdaneta's coup nor left for Europe, as he had announced.
His health worsening, he traveled to Barranquilla and from there to Santa
Marta, where he died in December 1830.[136]

Before Bolívar's death, Venezuela and Ecuador had withdrawn from
Gran Colombia, and part of New Granada was up in arms against Urdaneta. In the Caribbean region, on 11 September 1830, the remote city of Riohacha was the first to rebel, unilaterally annexing its province to Venezuela
and requesting military protection. The small town of San Juan del César
joined in the rebellion. Venezuela did not send arms or troops but military
expertise in the person of Commander Pedro Carujo, who was directly implicated in the attempted murder of Bolívar in September 1828. Carujo had
no difficulty in finding volunteers for his militias among a population angry

with the governments in Cartagena and Bogotá. From Santa Marta, General Montilla sent by sea to Riohacha hundreds of soldiers who sacked and occupied the city but could not prevent the rebels from escaping to the vast province. The numerous reinforcements dispatched from Mompox to wipe out the insurgency by land met with disaster. As they left during the rainy season, floods, mud, and landslides hampered their march through Valledupar. Lacking food, many became sick and died, and the troops from Cartagena now safely in Riohacha failed to rescue them. Moreover, in the words of former minister of the interior José Manuel Restrepo, the inhabitants resorted to the traditional tactic of flight to the hinterland to avoid a military encounter:

> The defenders of the government of [Urdaneta in] Bogotá could not find a single human being. When they approached the villages, the haciendas, and even the huts in the wilderness, all men, women, and children [had] fled, taking whatever they could carry. The invaders could not find a guide, a peon, or a piece of news. In contrast, the countrymen gave to the armed riohacheros all the information they obtained. If asked about the cause for such a hatred and determination against the existing government, they answered: "that they had rebelled against the tyranny of General Bolívar and because the blood of Padilla called for revenge." They added, "that soon Páez would come to free the communities from the yoke of the 'tyrant.'"[137]

For the first time, opponents to the bolivarista faction not only contrasted tyranny with freedom, but also Bolívar with Padilla, whom they claimed to avenge. No doubt, this came partly from the fact that Padilla was a native of Riohacha. But, as people equated Bolívar's dictatorship with the restoration of whites' colonial privileges, the defense of Padilla was probably also an indirect way of emphasizing the rights of free people of color.

Concurrently, in October 1830 the area of Santa Marta became restless. According to Bolívar, then in Soledad, "the Bishop [santanderista José María Estévez], followed by his clergy and the vulgar rich from the region[,] are against [the government of Urdaneta] out of hatred for Cartagena and the cartageneros."[138] In November, under retired officer Carlos Hormechea, two hundred men from Ciénaga, joined by the customarily rebel Indians from nearby villages, attacked Santa Marta to remove it from the jurisdiction of Cartagena. They failed and fled to the province of Riohacha, but Montilla seized the opportunity to expel "some demagogues" from Santa Marta to Jamaica. He also transferred most of Santa Marta's arms and ammunition to Barranquilla so that angry inhabitants could not seize them.[139] By the time a dying Bolívar arrived in Santa Marta, in December 1830, a precarious calm had returned to Santa Marta and Riohacha Provinces. Montilla had entrusted the government of Riohacha to General José Sardá, a Spanish adventurer devoted to him who had accomplished a similar mission there in late 1820. Finding government troops and rebels exhausted by three months of hardship, Sardá built on his previous experience in the province. He obtained the surrender of many insurgents and forced others, including Carujo and Hormechea, to escape to the Guajira Peninsula and Maracaibo. For a short time, the department of Magdalena appeared to submit to the authorities of Cartagena.[140]

On 17 January 1831, by order of Juan de Francisco in Cartagena, every town and village in Magdalena solemnly mourned the death of Bolívar. Cartagena held grandiose obsequies in which most cartageneros participated, regardless of their political leanings. A monument was erected in the cathedral that comprised, among other artifacts, a gigantic obelisk, the statues of Liberty and Independence holding a portrait of the Liberator surmounted by the symbol of death, and the tearful statues of America and Religion. The vicar-general, Juan Marimón, one of the leaders of the First Independence, delivered the funeral homily.[141] Behind this display of unity, however, opposition to Montilla and Francisco was mounting and prompted Francisco to ship some of the numerous Andean political prisoners held in the city to Chagres and the island of San Andrés to prevent disorder.[142]

THE REVOLUTION OF THE LOWER MAGDALENA LIBERALS

It was not in Cartagena but in the towns and villages of the Lower Magdalena River that discontent turned into open rebellion. In a coordinated action during the night of 12 February 1831, a total of six hundred officers, soldiers, and men on foot and horseback, under militia captain Lorenzo Hernández, left Sabanalarga, Malambo, Santo Tomás, Baranoa, Sitionuevo, and several other villages on both sides of the river to meet in Soledad.[143] There, on the thirteenth, the officers issued a "solemn, patriotic and very free resolution" explaining the "rebellion" of the "communities of the cantons of Barranquilla, Soledad and some cantons of the Province of Santa Marta." They demanded the "restitution of the rights that they were able to conquer with immense sacrifices, which the satraps of the government suffocated despicably and atrociously." They denounced the repeated attacks against the constitution of 1821: the terror, deportations, forced conscription, and political appointments carried out by the enemies of the representative system. Finally, in the name of "God and Liberty," they demanded respect for the constitution, a federal system, the reinstatement of public employees removed during the dictatorship, and the departure of the "extremely hateful person" of Montilla.[144] Men from the villages on both banks of the river continued to arrive in Soledad, and on 14 February the rebels issued a new manifesto, this time entitled "Command of the 'Division Liberals of the Lower Magdalena.'" Signed by the chief commander, tax collector Antonio Pantoja, it lyrically contrasted the virtues of freedom and liberalism with tyranny, slavery, and despotism. Stating that the heroic struggle of Riohacha in 1830 had inspired the movement, the manifesto condemned "the intruding, illegal and despotic Government of Bogotá . . . [and] that of Cartagena, which is the only bulwark that shields the vicious administration of the former."[145] The insurgents entered Barranquilla "with the consent of the people" in order to seize the armaments that Montilla had pulled out of Santa Marta.[146]

As correctly seen by the rebels, Cartagena had become the last stronghold of the bolivaristas in New Granada, and any insurrection against Montilla in that city could precipitate the fall of Urdaneta's dictatorship in Bogotá.[147] Aware of this reality, Francisco assumed extraordinary powers to prevent the contamination of "the ignorant classes" by the "demagogic spirit" in Cartagena and the rest of the department and sent troops under General Ignacio Luque to Barranquilla. He accused Cartagena's Liberals of being the authors of the manifestos issued by the Lower Magdalena rebel officers. On 19 February he expelled to Jamaica fifteen men—all with strong ties to the city's popular sectors—including Manuel Marcelino Núñez, Calixto Noguera, Damián Berrío, and Juan José Nieto.[148]

Yet Cartagena's population remained faithful to the existing authorities, despite the discontent of many inhabitants. In fact, the decisive blow against Urdaneta came from General Luque. Unexpectedly, on 6 March, just as Luque was beginning to defeat the rebels in the Lower Magdalena, he switched sides and assumed leadership of the Liberals, now swollen by his own troops. Reportedly, Luque's move occurred during a banquet at the Barranquilla residence of bolivarista John Glen, where alcohol flowed freely, after the commanders of three battalions from Cartagena defamed Montilla.[149] The officers and Luque then publicly declared that the revolution in the Lower Magdalena was "legitimate," thus "just and legal," and that the "federal system" was the only viable one, because "the extension of the Republic and its various climates produce different necessities and different habits of the peoples." The troops that had gained independence had become "some blind instruments to defend and support the ambition of certain persons," when they should have been working for the good of the people and protecting their free institutions.[150] Two months later Luque justified his about-face by proclaiming himself "protector of the communities [pueblos] and their liberties." He had begun to question the mission entrusted to him by Montilla, he asserted, when he saw that the residents of the Lower Magdalena were not "rebels" but "property owners and honorable workers" for whom armed rebellion had become the only means to "shake off the weight of a dreadful slavery," and when he discovered that the prisoners in Barranquilla's jail were "respectable men" whose only crime had been to support freedom. Luque understood their complete rejection of the authorities in Cartagena and "decided to follow the footsteps of the people" into freedom, as he had done during the wars for independence.[151]

Two days after Luque's volte-face, on 8 March 1831, the town of Ciénaga, under General Francisco Carmona, rejected the authority of Montilla and Urdaneta in the name of "liberty and the iniquitously usurped rights of the pueblos."[152] The next day Santa Marta followed suit under General Trinidad Portocarrero. An assembly of the city's "patresfamilias and honorable vecinos" pronounced the province of Santa Marta "independent in its political and military Government from that of Cartagena."[153] Luque built further support in the region by eliminating some heavy taxes. The western area of Tolú also passed to the Liberals. On 24 March Luque began a one-month siege of Cartagena, demanding the resignations of Montilla and Francisco. Twelve hundred men, one schooner, and eighteen small boats besieged the capital, backed by the inhabitants of surrounding villages. Many hungry cartageneros abandoned their city, and individual soldiers deserted to join Luque's forces.[154] In early April, the authorities of Mompox, threatened by the advance of the troops led by Portocarrero, joined the Liberal movement and withdrew their province from the Magdalena department.[155]

On 26 April 1831, after news of these developments reached Riohacha, its inhabitants compelled their municipal council to issue a declaration whose rhetoric of liberty, civilization, and antityranny emulated that of 11 September 1830. Riohacha's new act declared "this Province independent so that it cannot be contaminated by the disorders prevailing in the rest of Colombia, but cooperating with the others in the surrender of the fortified city of Cartagena where the tyrants have taken refuge." However, the riohacheros still recognized Montilla's protégé, General Sardá, as their legitimate military commander and as "the people's protector and the guardian angel of its salvation." Every town and village in the province swore to abide by the declaration.[156]

Meanwhile, at dawn on 26 April, General Luque entered Cartagena with five hundred soldiers after a despairing Montilla agreed to surrender the city. Indeed, in central New Granada villages and towns had united against the dictatorship, the santanderista forces were winning everywhere, and Urdaneta's days in power were numbered. Contrary to their fears, Francisco and Montilla were not forced out by a pardo rebellion but by a declaration drafted by prominent citizens, "patresfamilias and other vecinos" led by Vicar-General Marimón, who demanded that they leave in order to end the civil war and the people's suffering.[157] The signatories, many of whom had been staunch supporters of Bolívar and Montilla, stated that, with few exceptions, most of the post-independence period had been characterized by "extraordinary powers," "banishments, persecutions and a sepulchral silence of the press; all this . . . has forced the communities [pueblos] to agree to proclaim their liberties, and it equally obliges us to agree with the opinion of all the Department." They urged Montilla and Francisco to accept Luque's propositions, because "the besiegers are our brothers, and in any circumstance they have to treat us as such."[158] Beyond their democratic claims, some of the signatories probably acted to secure their own futures.

The agreement signed by Luque and Montilla stipulated that the new departmental authorities would be the respectable Dr. Manuel Romay, for civil affairs, and Luque, for military affairs, but that in fact the provinces would be autonomous in most matters. All political prisoners would be released; all individuals who wished to leave would be allowed to do so; no one would be persecuted for his or her political ideas; and new elections of electors and representatives would be held shortly.[159] In reality, however, the provinces of Santa Marta, Mompox, and Riohacha refused to continue under the departmental system headed by Cartagena, even with substantial provincial autonomy and new, popular authorities.[160]

In May 1831 the Liberals had triumphed in almost all of New Granada. Joaquín Mosquera and Domingo Caicedo resumed the positions of president and vice president to which they had been elected in 1830, and Francisco de Paula Santander was recalled from his European exile. Elections were held, and in October a new constitutional convention opened in Bogotá. One of its first acts was to restore Santander's rank and titles and rehabilitate the memory of General José Padilla and others executed after the attempted assassination of Bolívar. The convention approved a new constitution—in many respects identical to that of 1821, except that it did away with the structure of the departments, leaving only the division into provinces, cantons, and parish districts. The political and military supremacy of Cartagena over the Caribbean region's other main cities had come to an end. Not surprisingly, the delegates elected Santander as New Granada's president and his close friend, lawyer José Ignacio Márquez, as vice president. In June 1832 Santander landed in Santa Marta. From there, he went to Barranquilla and Cartagena where, as a sign of the new times, Manuel Marcelino Núñez held a lavish reception in his honor at the Núñez residence. Santander then traveled up the Magdalena River and through several additional provinces to take the pulse of the country before arriving in Bogotá in October.[161]

THE LIBERAL TRIUMPH

Like the rest of New Granada, the Caribbean provinces witnessed rapid political change after the Liberal victory of May 1831. The pro-Santander prisoners recovered their freedom and the exiles returned, generally to take leading positions in the government. In July several Liberals headed by Juan Madiedo, a longtime opponent of Montilla, founded the Sociedad de Veteranos Defensores de la Libertad (Society of Veterans Defenders of Liberty) in Cartagena to protect the people and the new government. In addition to General Luque, the association comprised many men who had been persecuted by Montilla since the early 1820s, notably Calixto Noguera (secretary of the province), Mauricio José Romero (deputy to the national convention), Antonio del Real (professor of philosophy), and Damián Berrío (commander of the militia), as well as wealthy merchant Manuel Marcelino Núñez and Juan José Nieto. Among them, Noguera, Berrío, and Nieto were pardos, and in a letter to Caicedo recommending Nieto for a state position, Luque added: "If my word can warrant intentions in favor of men of this class."[162] The Sociedad's members also included leaders of the revolution of the Lower Magdalena, such as Antonio Pantoja (deputy to the national convention), many merchants, officers, and public employees, some teachers, one priest, one printer, and one British hacendado.[163]

The Liberal press flourished, celebrating freedom and the restored rights of the people, and recording the pioneer struggle of the riohacheros against Urdaneta's dictatorship. One notice entitled "To the Manes of Padilla," signed by "six thousand cartageneros," demanded revenge for his blood and, somewhat forgetful of his loneliness in 1828, asserted that the people "idolize him."[164] Moreover, in a symbolic reversal, Padilla received obsequies in Cartagena's cathedral in October 1831. According to a witness, the military trophies and the verses of a meaningful elegy prompted "at the same time sorrow and indignation." Similar to the funeral tribute to Bolívar, the attendance was enormous, and Vicar-General Marimón delivered the homily. The artifacts and the inscriptions on the catafalque pointed to Bolívar as responsible for the death of Padilla, "innocent victim of a tyrant." The members of the recently founded Society of the Veteran Defenders of Liberty attended in a single block, attired in mourning clothes but with red ribbons on their left breasts, in an imposing display of the new Liberal power.[165]

The departure of Montilla and Francisco was followed by a massive purge, repression, and banishment, especially after a conspiracy against the new government by military followers of Urdaneta was thwarted in Bogotá. The Liberal press of Cartagena played a major role in the repression. In early July 1831, for example, *Correo Semanal* demanded that all the "rebels" who still threatened public security in Santa Marta and Cartagena Provinces be expelled. It suggested raising funds to help the government pay for the transportation cost of their expulsion and warned that "the communities" were ready to take up arms to achieve justice. The newspaper later claimed that public jobs should be allocated only to reward "real merit," that is, "services and sufferings," which amounted to job distribution on a partisan basis.[166] *El Cartagenero Liberal* denounced the fact that, unlike other places, Mompox, inconsistent with its tradition of struggle for freedom, had not rid itself of the "satellites, spies, and servile dependents of Montilla and Francisco" and continued to be governed by the same clique. It then listed the names of "evildoers" who should be expelled.[167] Correspondents from villages and small towns wrote to Cartagena's newspapers to inform on authorities linked to the past dictatorship.[168] Even more aggressively, *El Latigazo*, as indicated by its name, lashed out against specific individuals still in the Caribbean region who had been "devoted to the would-be monarch [Bolívar]" or were "friend[s] of the wicked Montilla" and demanded their banishment. Similarly, *El Perro Registrón, con Rabia* (Searching Dog, with Rage) "bites the tyrants who stay," and, "arf! arf! arf! arf! ooowl!," barked and attacked, notably British consul Edward Watts and some assistants of Montilla.[169] A few targeted individuals attempted to redeem their reputations by printing broadsides defending their republican beliefs and past behavior.[170] But banishment became so common that by late August 1831 one Liberal paper protested that men were being indiscriminately deported, leaving their families behind in misery. Citing cases of arbitrary expulsion, it recommended that only the ringleaders be punished as they deserved, but that the "subaltern criminals" who followed them be treated "with more humanity."[171]

As vengeful as it was, the Liberal press made no mention of the race issue. Nevertheless, because many Veterans Defenders of Liberty were pardo, rumors that they intentionally exacerbated racial tensions in Cartagena spread in Bogotá in mid-1831. The rumors intensified after "the rabble of color" allegedly broke into the residence of a bolivarista patrician, arrested him, and forced him to leave for Jamaica, under the false accusation that he had asked Venezuela to intervene against the new government.[172] From Cartagena a correspondent warned Vice President Caicedo that "the pardo class is very insolent"; "the caste war is almost indicated and the spirit of separation very pronounced . . . we are [sitting] on a volcano." He repeatedly asked for a minimum of one thousand troops from the interior to contain them.[173] When he heard that Remigio Márquez might be appointed to the military command of Cartagena, Manuel Romay urged Caicedo not to send him to Cartagena, alleging that Márquez would take pleasure in dominating "the decent persons" and encourage "some aspirations that the people of color let seep through," creating serious trouble.[174] No doubt, Romay remembered that ten years earlier Márquez had been accused of pardocracia for his actions against the corrupt elite of Mompox. Rumors of pardos mobilizing against whites also circulated in Santa Marta and Mompox, raising fears that the whole department of Magdalena would secede from New Granada.[175]

By February 1832 news of the massive slave rebellion launched in Montego Bay, Jamaica, in December 1831, known as the Baptist War, had reached many parts of New Granada.[176] According to José Manuel Restrepo, "In Mompox, Cartagena and Santa Marta there were some movements of blacks, which are believed to be connected to those of Jamaica. Fortunately the plots were discovered, and the authors shot. With this and the subjugation of the black rebels of Jamaica, we hope that all will calm down."[177] No more is known of these incidents, which likely reflected more Restrepo's continuing fear of pardocracia and slave revolt than changing attitudes in Caribbean New Granada. Although the legal equality of the free had been firmly established with independence, the Liberals in power since 1831, regardless of color, made no attempt to end slavery. For example, the Liberal newspaper *Rejistro Oficial del Magdalena* dedicated an issue to the memory of Padilla and supported the Veterans Defenders of Liberty but did not discuss slavery. In November 1831 it listed in its "For Sale" section three female domestic slaves (one with her nine-month-old daughter), two male rural slaves, and one farm.[178] Few Liberals are recorded to have followed in the footsteps of the leader of Valledupar's 1813 independence movement, María de la Concepción Loperena, who stipulated in her will of 1835 that "the slaves and zambos who still live in my house" be set free at her death. In contrast, the Liberal bishop of Santa Marta, José María Estévez, included nothing in his will about freeing the two slaves he listed as property.[179]

In 1831–32 the most significant unrest took place in the cities' garrisons, not between whites and pardos or slaves. In Santa Marta, on 25 July 1831, two battalions of New Granadans and Venezuelans rebelled under the direction of their Venezuelan commanders against the Liberal government. Protesting overdue rations and ill treatment by the samarios, they attempted to rally General Carmona to their cause, on the basis of his Venezuelan roots, and arrested some of the province's new authorities. Much to their surprise, Carmona mobilized against them—assembling 600 troops in Ciénaga and the Indian villages near Santa Marta; in Santa Marta itself about 1,000 men "from all classes" rallied to protect "order . . . and . . . the honor of the nation. . . . Even the women took part, exhorting their sons to defend the city."[180] Outnumbered, the insurgents surrendered. Separated from their New Granadan mates, a total of 143 Venezuelan officers and soldiers were shipped back to their country of origin after receiving their rations, and 218 New Granadans were sent to Cartagena over land. Although the news of the failed revolt in Santa Marta increased anti-Venezuelan feelings in Andean New Granada, in the Caribbean provinces it did not affect the popularity of such Venezuelan generals as Carmona, Luque, and Portocarrero, who had replaced Montilla as the region's top commanders in Santa Marta, Cartagena, and Mompox, respectively.[181]

In remote Riohacha, however, the Spanish-born governor Sardá was unable to keep his post, despite his recognition of the new legal authorities in Bogotá in early May 1831, which prompted the departure for Maracaibo of the mostly Venezuelan battalion of Apure. In July New Granada's national government dismissed Sardá for his close connection to Montilla, a decision that divided Riohacha's population along class lines. Whereas a group of radical Liberals mobilized the lower classes against Sardá, recalling that "he came to conquer us," "a multitude of citizens," presumably patresfamilias, tried to convince the general to stay so that he would "restrain those who do not want to have a man to respect [in power], in order to keep the province restless and to live off the revolution." The sociopolitical conflict was complicated by Riohacha's traditional rivalry with Santa Marta Province: the advocates of Sardá argued that only he could stop the expansionism of the "sultan of Santa Marta," General Carmona.[182] In the end, the argument that Sardá was "not a son of the people [pueblo] although he declared himself in favor of liberty" prevailed, and the Liberal authorities in Bogotá upheld his removal. Nevertheless, Sardá, backed by santanderista bishop Estévez, was spared deportation and began to lobby in Bogotá for the reinstatement of his military rank.[183]

The Liberal revolt in 1831 shows that, in many respects, the notions of community and citizenship that had emerged around the institution of the cabildo after the abduction of King Ferdinand VII in 1808 had not disappeared after a decade of independence. The rebellion in Caribbean New Granada was one of whole communities (pueblos) led by their elite and military chiefs. In addition, the colonial hierarchy placing cities above small towns and villages continued as the heads of provinces or cantons ordered the communities in their jurisdiction to swear to adhere to proclamations identical to the ones they themselves had solemnly approved. The internal hierarchy of each community remained strong, as "respectable men" or "patresfamilias and honorable vecinos" headed the revolt and warranted its legitimacy.[184] Such social dynamics also prevailed in Cartagena, where in 1828 Padilla failed to rally "respectable men" and in 1831 the lower classes did not revolt autonomously, even during Luque's siege. Yet the whole city, led by its native elite, turned against Montilla once conditions became intolerable for everyone. Similar to the 1781 Comunero Revolt, people had a sense of what represented a just burden of recruitment, taxes, and political control and what required protest. Yet, with the exception of Riohacha, whose inhabitants showed their democratic spirit as early as September 1830, Caribbean New Granada's cities, towns, and villages tolerated governmental abuse much longer than those in Venezuela or Antioquia and Cauca, in the interior. They rebelled only after the death of Bolívar, as if with him alive, as under the king until his abduction in 1808, rebellion was not an option.

With Bolívar dead, Urdaneta's dictatorship and Montilla's repression became unacceptable, as expressed by Riohacha's manifesto of 26 April 1831: "For these reasons, the bonds that united us to the magistracy have been destroyed, the love and respect of the communities [pueblos] have been lost . . . and each city was left free to provide its preservation."[185] This proclamation and others issued during the rebellion of 1831 demonstrate time and again that the locus of sovereignty was the community, or pueblo, not individual citizens. But they also show that in many places in Caribbean New Granada some gains of independence were irreversible, notably a democratic government representing the good of all, which people identified with the constitution of 1821. The reestablishment of the monarchy and, concurrently, of white privileges became anathema. Instead of "God and the King," the popular cry had become "God and Liberty." Still, the manifestos did not demand equal liberty for all individuals but liberty of the rebel communities from the oppression of Cartagena and Bogotá. Within each pueblo, they requested the liberty of "property owners and honorable workers" rather than the liberty of day laborers, servants, and slaves.[186]

Despite General Luque's claim that the "different necessities and different habits" of Caribbean New Granadans made federalism the only legitimate system, the revolution of 1831 indicated how much the region was still divided and unable to develop a common plan for the future. The rebellion brought several cities and communities together against their common oppressor, Cartagena, embodied by Venezuelan aristocrat Montilla. However, for lack of a native elite with power and vision, the rebels replaced this ruler with other strong Venezuelan military men. Indeed, in the 1820s the Caribbean provinces did not witness the process of identity building that was taking place in Venezuela around Caracas and in Andean New Granada around Bogotá. Although Caribbean New Granada, like Venezuela, was subjected to Bolívar's excessive demand for recruits for his war in Peru, only in Venezuela did the draft produce broad-based resistance. Venezuelan opponents first challenged the authority of Bogotá's national government in matters of recruitment, rapidly reorientating their movement behind the caudillo Páez. The conflict of authority progressively evolved into a conflict between the civilian New Granadans and the military Venezuelans and between the center and the periphery. Identity building in Venezuela and Andean New Granada focused on distinguishing the alleged characteristics of one region from the other's. As the New Granadan elite promoted an image of the learned (culto), urban, and white Andean center against the rough, pardo, and llanero Venezuelan periphery, the elite in Caracas positioned the Venezuelans as glorious pioneers of Gran Colombia's independence struggle and portrayed New Granadans as exploitative pedants from which a second liberation was now necessary.[187] This growing dichotomy put Caribbean New Granada in an awkward position. Its culture and ethnic makeup were close to Venezuela's, and Mompox and Cartagena could easily share with Caracas the title of initiators of the independence struggle. In this context, understandably, Riohacha briefly annexed itself to Venezuela in 1830, when identification with the dictatorship of Urdaneta became impossible. Yet, historically, the administration of the Caribbean provinces depended on New Granada.

In reality, the political class of Caribbean New Granada lacked the two essential components that would make the separation of Venezuela possible: native "men in arms and men of quills and words, the military men and the lawyers," in the words of François-Xavier Guerra.[188] In 1828 the region's only native general, José Padilla, had shown that he did not have the qualities of a caudillo, and after his execution every military leader still in the region was Venezuelan. No native intellectual or politician distinguished himself by promoting a project that could represent Caribbean New Granada's general interests. Ignacio Muñoz's words failed to mobilize the cartageneros behind the pardo general. The costeño with the uppermost position, José María del Castillo y Rada, a minister in Urdaneta's dictatorship, did little for his region of origin but in 1829 initiated the government's highly unpopular project to establish a monarchy to solve the new nation's problems.[189] Moreover, throughout the period, unlike in 1810, Cartagena's small elite sided with the conservative forces at the national level. In 1826 they aligned themselves with the aristocrats of Bogotá and saw in the dictatorship of Bolívar an opportunity to restore the colonial powers and privileges of their city. In contrast with 1811, when Cartagena did not hesitate to autonomously proclaim the province's independence from the viceroyalty and from the king, in 1828 the city's elite remained loyal to Gran Colombia and to its Liberator, Bolívar; in 1830 it applauded Urdaneta's coup in Bogotá. Moreover, after independence, with equality and liberty of the free written into the constitution and the elimination of the status of limpieza de sangre, the lower classes of African descent acted more like followers than initiators. In 1828, if at first they accepted Padilla's seizure of power, they deserted him as soon as the balance of power tipped in favor of Montilla. In 1831, however, they massively participated in the Liberal revolution, initiating Caribbean New Granada's traditional alignment with the national politics of the Liberal Party for its support of equality and limited church intervention. Yet, despite the fact that in the early 1830s slaves still represented a substantial portion of the urban population, especially in Cartagena, the lower classes of color did not demand the abolition of slavery.

CONCLUSION:

AN ALL-AMERICAN

PERSPECTIVE

In 1835 Juan José Nieto bitterly complained to President Francisco de Paula Santander about Bogotá's neglect of the Caribbean region. He believed that in retaliation for the imprisonment of several Andean Liberal leaders (including Santander) by bolivaristas in Cartagena in 1828, authorities now "vomit[ed] their rancor" against the port city and "shockingly ridicule[d]" cartageneros for their alleged illiteracy, their "way of talking," and "their customs." Although he never mentioned the issue of race, Nieto denounced the insults heaped on Caribbean representatives in Bogotá and their "mortifying effects" as a result of the "pernicious rivalry [existing] between the inhabitants of the center and those of the coast." Federalism, he maintained, was the only solution to this conflict of interests.[1]

In the early 1830s, when the Liberals together with Santander gained power throughout New Granada, the four Caribbean provinces of Cartagena, Mompox, Santa Marta, and Riohacha went along with changes initiated in Bogotá. Although still loosely connected to the Andean interior, the Caribbean Coast did not form a separate nation when Venezuela and Ecuador broke away from Gran Colombia in 1830. Neither did the much dreaded pardocracia take control of the region to transform it into another Haiti. Nor did Caribbean New Granada join Venezuela, despite the facts that, during the first decade following independence in 1821, most of its leaders (those supporting Simón Bolívar as well as those behind Santander) were Venezuelan and culturally and racially Caribbean New Granada was closer to Venezuela than to its Andean counterpart. Nor did the region become a strong one within New Granada, united by its distinct economy, social organization, and culture, such as Antioquia, for example.[2]

Postcolonial fragmentation and dependency on Bogotá, this book shows, largely resulted from people's continuing identification, throughout the war for independence and after 1821, with individual cities, towns, and villages rather than with their province, their region, or New Granada. People still conceived of towns and villages as hierarchical, corporative entities whose heads were their "respectable citizens," and bodies, the lower classes. Only occasionally did autonomous and individual practices of citizenship emerge. In the region, the anticolonial war turned out to be a civil war in which proindependence Cartagena fought, first, against Mompox for declaring its independence not only from Spain but from Cartagena as well, and later, against Santa Marta for remaining royalist. Other cities and towns aligned themselves with one or the other side according to circumstance. Following the constitution of 1821, the formation of the department of Magdalena, with its capital in Cartagena, did not bring the main cities closer together but, on the contrary, revived and exacerbated tensions among them. Most towns in the region opposed renewed administrative centralization in Cartagena. In 1831 this conflict merged with the national conflict between pro-Santander Federalists and supporters of the late Bolívar's centralism. The hostilities escalated into another Caribbean New Granadan civil war, in which units from most towns and villages, under the banner of Liberals, besieged the bolivaristas in Cartagena. Yet, whereas in Andean New Granada the santanderistas built support for their cause and fostered patriotism by mobilizing the population against a common enemy—the Venezuelans, personified by Bolívar and his successor, the president-dictator General Rafael Urdaneta—in the Caribbean region the leaders of the Liberal revolution were Venezuelan, and no anti-Venezuelan sentiment grew out of the war.

In 1831 the surrender of Cartagena and the victory of Santander's supporters at the national level put an end to centralization in Cartagena, but it also reinforced the Caribbean region's alignment with Andean New Granada's bipartisan politics initiated by the opposing visions of Bolívar and Santander. Henceforth, it became essential for local communities to embrace national causes in order to gain favors from the government in Bogotá.[3] With a population and an economy already weakened by the war, the continuing rivalry between the major cities and subregions further debilitated the Caribbean region and prevented the elite from effectively representing its constituencies in Bogotá.

The alignment of the Caribbean New Granadan region with the former viceroyalty's center was not exceptional in Latin America. Following independence, most nations formed within the territorial limits of the colonial audiencias imposed by Spain and kept the same capitals. With the development of exports, some of these capitals, such as Lima and Buenos Aires, grew disproportionately vis-à-vis the rest of the country because they served simultaneously as the nation's administrative, economic, and political centers. In contrast, until the 1870s New Granada was marginal in the world economy, with limited exports from the interior and almost none from the Caribbean region itself. The proportion of Caribbean New Granadans in the total population of the country fell from 20.5 percent in 1778 to 14.2 percent in 1835 and continued to drop until 1905, when it began to slowly recover.[4] Cartagena did not regain its colonial importance. When eventually, in the late nineteenth century, coffee produced in the interior integrated New Granada into international markets, it was the port of Barranquilla, a village on the Magdalena River with little tradition of political leadership under Spain, that expanded into a city through rapidly increasing trade. The growth of Barranquilla, however, added a new player to the coastal cities' rivalry and failed to unite the Caribbean region.[5]

Caribbean New Granada's postcolonial fragmentation also resulted from its weak elite and lack of a strong regional caudillo. According to John Lynch, caudillos emerged throughout Spanish America after prolonged wars for independence. Caudillos often represented the economic and political interests of regional elites threatened by the new state's centralism. They also prevented, through patronage, lower-class insurgency. Almost all of the caudillos discussed by Lynch owned vast estates prior to the wars or acquired them shortly afterward, through which they built extensive clientage networks and from which they could levy troops.[6] In the process a few caudillos, notably Venezuelan José Antonio Páez, played a major role in early nation building. In Peru, in contrast, as Charles F. Walker explains, from Cuzco mestizo general Agustín Gamarra challenged the domination of the coastal capital of Lima by forming alliances between the highland's elite, Cuzco's mestizo urban population, and the rural Indian majority—alliances that, to bring in the Indians, included some Inca traditions. Although ultimately Gamarra failed and the centralism of Lima prevailed, resulting in the exclusion of the "dark-skinned lower classes" from Peruvian citizenship, his challenge was critical in strengthening, up to the present, the vision of an alternative Peru organized around the Cuzco region and its indigenous population.[7] Unlike in New Granada's interior, where a handful of caudillos rose to power, these patterns did not correspond to the Caribbean region, as shown in Chapter 6. The landless General José Padilla was unable to build a coalition uniting the lower classes of African descent and the white elite. Despite becoming a large landowner after the war, General Mariano Montilla could never gain popular support, more because of his aristocratic ways and contempt for the popular classes than because of his Venezuelan birth. The leaders of the 1831 Liberal rebellion against Montilla and Cartagena were all Venezuelan as well, which prevented them from playing an important political role in defending the distinctiveness of the coast in the fiercely anti-Venezuelan Bogotá of the time. This inability to forge a strong regional movement during the crucial years of nation building immediately following independence had a long-lasting, crippling effect on the relationship between the coast and the interior.[8]

ENCROACHMENT AND MESTIZAJE

Unlike Peru's dual-nation system, which maintained the colonial division between the "republic of Indians" and the "republic of Spaniards" by excluding the indigenous majority from full citizenship despite the growth of interstitial castes of mixed ancestry, New Granada opted for legal racial inclusion from the time of the First Independence.[9] The interstitial castes characterized late colonial and early independent New Granada. Far from being the majority, the "pure Indian" and the "pure black" existed mostly in a few Andean enclaves and at the underpopulated margins of the nation, the Guajira Peninsula, the vast tropical plains and forests, and the Pacific lowlands. In addition, broad participation of the local population, regardless of race, in the wars for independence precluded a racially exclusionary citizenship. Although everywhere in New Granada the white creole elite controlled most of the power, land, and wealth, visions of the new nation had to include the racially mixed majority. From the perspective of the Andean rulers, aside from white immigration that never materialized on a significant scale, the solution was to encourage Colombia's mestizaje, that is, to increase the Indo-European population to the detriment of the indigenous inhabitants.

During the First Independence, as after 1821, state policies regarding the pueblo Indians were based on gendered and racial concepts. They advocated the breaking up of Indian resguardos not only to privatize their lands but also to accelerate mestizaje between indigenous women and free peasants. The May 1811 edict by Cartagena's Supreme Junta opened up the pueblos to non-Indians and encouraged indigenous women to marry men "of other castes." It elevated Indians to equal citizens, which eliminated their protected colonial status and subjected them to the same taxes and military drafts as other residents. These policies resembled those adopted by patriots in Río de la Plata, Chile, and Venezuela as well as in Gran Colombia in 1821. In fact, only the ephemeral program of José María Morelos in Mexico in the early 1810s encompassed the protection of pueblos' communal lands.[10] After the division of Gran Colombia, New Granada's Liberals decreed by law in 1832 that up to thirty-two acres from each resguardo would be reserved for (presumably white or mestizo) settlers, leaving very little land for the Indians themselves. Worse, indigenous communities were ordered to rent a substantial portion of their remaining lands to pay for an elementary school. In addition, they were to pay all appraisal costs through the sale of resguardo lands to surveyors.[11] Not surprisingly, Indians immediately resisted a law so detrimental to their interests and managed to arouse some sympathy from the minister of the interior. In Cartagena Province, some pueblos de indígenas simply had no resguardos left; others lacked official documents indicating their boundaries. According to a petition from the province's chamber of deputies, the resguardos of many pueblos "comprise[d] such a diminished area that if it is divided, a minuscule portion would correspond to each indigene, which would result in no good for them." Most indigenous lands were so worthless that, if divided, all the proceeds from their sale would be used to pay the surveyors, appraisers, and judges according to the law of 1832.[12] In 1835 the interior minister suspended the division of resguardos in Cartagena Province, but in the region encroachment had already dramatically reduced indigenous lands and mestizaje was well advanced.[13]

On the other hand, the government showed no interest in promoting the decline of "full" blacks by encouraging the marriage of black women with men from other racial groups, as it did for indigenous women. At the same time, Caribbean New Granadans did not challenge the Andean-centered vision of mestizaje. Neither the white elite nor lower-class mulattoes and zambos claimed their region's "different mestizaje." In the race for nationhood and whitening, they tried to fit into the broad categories of mestizo and white. Consequently, the Afro-Caribbean population was pushed to the fringe of the mestizo nation, in a zone of allegedly inferior mestizaje and *zambaje*, whereas whites continued to be at the top of the racial pecking order, and blacks and Indians at the bottom. Nevertheless, for their participation in the economy and presumed support of the modern ideals of equality, blacks enjoyed a slightly higher status than Indians, who were stereotyped as clinging to colonial and indigenous traditions.

CONSTITUTIONAL EQUALITY WITH SLAVERY

The revolutionary character of the decision by Cartagena's white elite— reflected in the Supreme Junta's electoral law of December 1810 and the constitution of the State of Cartagena in 1812—to grant legal equality and suffrage to all adult men *regardless of race* who lived independently off their rents or labor, has seldom been recognized in the historiography. Neither has the fact that the constitution of Gran Colombia in 1821—similar to several other Latin American constitutions—embraced the same egalitarian principles. In addition, until 1827 all officers and soldiers in Gran Colombia's army, a majority of whom were not white, were allowed to vote, which further broadened the social base of the electorate.[14] This path-breaking racial inclusion erased the "stain of slavery," which for centuries had obsessed Spanish authorities and severely limited the options of individuals of African descent. Following shortly after the victory of the Haitian Revolution, it was a daring decision, even if it did not radically modify political and social institutions, which remained almost exclusively in white hands. Of course, formal equality did not mean universal male suffrage. Up to the mid-nineteenth century, constitutions in general stipulated that all men should defend their homeland but disenfranchised those without property or an independent income—namely, servants and wage laborers, the great majority of whom were of partial or full African or Indian descent. White men were thus overrepresented in the electorate. Yet the absence of restrictions on the rights of free men of African descent, even those recently emancipated, in the constitution of the State of Cartagena and the Gran Colombian constitution merits a brief comparison with the rights granted to them by the constitutions of other multiracial societies.

Distinct from the Gran Colombian constitution was that of the United States, where the issue of slavery threatened the fragile union between the free North and the proslavery South. The 1787 Constitutional Convention meeting in Philadelphia opted to ratify a constitution that began with "We, the People" without defining who among the "people" was included or excluded. It allowed each state to have its own constitution with its own notion of citizenship, and at that time, interestingly, most states granted suffrage to qualifying free African American men. Simultaneously, however, the southern states obtained from the North the concession that the number of their representatives be proportional to the number of their free citizens plus three-fifths of the number of their slaves, which inflated the pro-slavery representation and reflected the view that a slave equaled three-fifths of a human being.[15] As early as 1789, the first U.S. Congress tacitly endorsed blacks' exclusion from citizenship by approving the Bill of Rights without questioning slavery and some states' racial discrimination. As the number of states in the Union increased, so did the proportion of those excluding free African American men from citizenship: from 3 states out of 13 in 1790, they had swelled to 25 out of 32 in 1855, counting some northern states where blacks were an insignificant minority.[16] In contrast, among the territories still under British rule, in Jamaica, after many years of struggle, free Coloreds and blacks obtained equal rights with whites in 1830.[17]

France's American colonies, for their part, were swept along by the French Revolution. The Declaration of the Rights of Man prompted wealthy free men of color in the French Caribbean to demand equality with whites. Only in 1792, after a cruelly repressed insurrection of *gens de couleur* followed by a massive slave rebellion in northern Saint Domingue, did the French revolutionary legislature grant full equality to all free men of color as a means of gaining their support against the royalists. And only after a long and murderous war, Saint Domingue became the newly independent Haiti. Haiti's first constitution, in 1805, proclaimed all Haitians free, "black," and equal regardless of skin color. Signed by nine generals, it made military service compulsory without mentioning suffrage, and it entrusted all powers exclusively to an emperor for life, Jean-Jacques Dessalines. In 1816, after several civil wars and short-lived constitutions, Haiti adopted a republican constitution, but with a president for life who was to choose his successor (which inspired Bolívar's notion of a semimonarchical constitution). The 1816 Haitian constitution, in force until 1843, guaranteed suffrage to all adult men except debtors and domestic servants. Viewing Haiti as a sanctuary for nonwhites, it granted full citizenship to "all Africans, Indians, and those descended from their blood born in the colonies or in foreign countries" after one year of residency.[18]

The Spanish monarchy's first constitution, in 1812, can only be understood in the context of the American, French, and Haitian Revolutions and the Napoleonic invasion of Spain.[19] It granted full citizenship to male Spaniards, Indians, and mestizos, but not to free African men or those with full or partial African ancestry, except in rare cases. Such restrictions on free people of color continued a series of contradictory measures prompted by the turmoil in the Caribbean. After the launching of the Haitian Revolution, Spain allowed thousands of French refugees from Saint Domingue, regardless of color and often with their slaves, to settle in some of its island colonies, notably Cuba and Santo Domingo, but not on the mainland because they could bring in "the pernicious maxims" of the French National Assembly.[20] In 1795 the king extended the sale of gracias al sacar to pardos and quinterones seeking the status of whites, seemingly offering a way out of the "stain of slavery" to wealthy free individuals of African descent. However, protest by the creole elite in Cuba and Venezuela drastically limited the scope of the measure. Besides, according to Ann Twinam, the number of petitions for whiteness in all Spanish colonies totaled only twenty-six between 1795 and 1816.[21] This small number challenges well-accepted ideas among contemporaries and historians alike that people of African descent pursued the ideal of whitening. Even more paradoxically, after the beginning of the Haitian Revolution in 1791, Spain continued to entrust much of the defense of its colonies with a large population of castas and slaves to militiamen of African descent and to grant them the privileges of the military fuero. At the same time, to discourage free people of color in Spanish America from emulating the *affranchis* in Saint Domingue, the monarchy issued a series of cédulas that conceived of free castas as hereditarily corrupted—in terms of mores and political ideas—by their slave origins and defined castas' enthusiasm for the ideals of liberty, equality, and fraternity put forward by the French Revolution as innate vices. Building on this legacy, the 1812 constitution of the monarchy excluded people of African descent from the new rights it was extending to other racial categories, notably Indians and mestizos. In the Spanish colonies of Puerto Rico and Cuba, legal restrictions on people of African origin lasted until 1876.[22]

In contrast, some former Spanish colonies expunged the "stain of slavery" and eliminated all special provisions regarding free people of African descent as soon as they gained independence in the 1820s. The very exclusive constitution of the First Venezuelan Republic in 1811 did not refer to race in relation to the exercise of suffrage but used strict economic, social, and marital requirements to indirectly disenfranchise as many pardos as possible.[23] In Argentina, however, the Provisional Regulations of 1817, effective until 1826, stipulated that men with any degree of African ancestry could vote if born free, but could only be elected to public office if their ancestors had been free for four generations.[24] The former Portuguese colony of Brazil achieved independence with little fighting in 1822—during a period of rapid expansion of slavery—when the son of the king of Portugal crowned himself emperor. The imperial constitution, revised in 1824 and in force until 1846, granted citizenship to all free male Brazilians, regardless of race. As in Gran Colombia, all discriminatory laws, such as the interdiction of free men of color to bear arms, vanished. Nevertheless, unlike in Gran Colombia, the constitution excluded *libertos* (free men born in slavery) from voting in secondary elections. Because qualification as a second-degree elector was a prerequisite for almost all high posts, this stipulation de facto discriminated against libertos.[25]

Regarding liberty, or more precisely the abolition of slavery, the record of Caribbean New Granada and Gran Colombia is much less imposing than it is on the subject of the legal equality of free men of African descent. Like their peers elsewhere in Spanish America, neither the patriots promoting Cartagena's 1812 legislation nor those who designed Gran Colombia's 1821 laws perceived slavery as contradictory to democracy. In 1812 Cartagena's reformists, as patriots in other parts of New Granada, Venezuela, Chile, and Río de la Plata at that time, abolished the slave trade partly on British insistence. But the State of Cartagena, unlike Antioquia, Chile, and Río de la Plata, did not issue a free womb law. And of course, it did not replicate the full abolition of slavery issued by the patriot movements of Miguel Hidalgo and José María Morelos in Mexico.[26] In 1821 Gran Colombia's law of manumission, by only freeing the newborn, fell short of Bolívar's promise to President Alexandre Pétion, in 1816, to abolish slavery in the liberated territories in return for Haiti's support for independence. To his credit, in 1816 and 1818, after resuming the war, Bolívar issued four edicts that unconditionally abolished slavery in Venezuela and subjected former slaves to serve in the armed forces like all male inhabitants.[27] At the Congress of Angostura in 1819, Bolívar argued in vain that "the proscription of slavery" was necessary to maintain peace in independent Venezuela, but the Fundamental Law that congress adopted did not mention abolition and ignored his two edicts of 1818.[28] By the time of the debates on Gran Colombia's constitution in 1821, Bolívar had lowered his expectations. He implored the delegates at least to decree the "absolute freedom of all Colombians at the act of being born on the territory of the republic," in return for the blood shed by slaves for the country's freedom.[29] When slavery was finally abolished in New Granada thirty years later, it had already crumbled as a result of the end of the slave trade, natural death, the upheaval of the wars for independence, and slaves' self-purchase.

Like several other former Spanish colonies, New Granada freed its slaves more than three decades after independence—on 1 January 1852.[30] By then Haiti had abolished slavery forever, in 1805, following the short-lived emancipation by revolutionary France in 1793. Chile, Central America, and Mexico, where slaves were few, had ended slavery in the 1820s as a logical outcome of the principles of liberty and equality. After massive slave revolts, the British, in 1838, and the French, in 1848, emancipated all the slaves in their colonies. In 1852 solely the remaining Dutch and Spanish colonies as well as the U.S. South and Brazil upheld slavery, which fueled thriving tropical plantations. Abolition was decreed in the Dutch colonies only in 1863, in the United States in 1865, in Puerto Rico in 1873, in Cuba in 1886, and in Brazil in 1888 — and after bloody wars in the U.S. South and Cuba.[31] In the century-long process of slave emancipation in the Americas, thus, New Granada did not break new ground.

FROM MILITIAMEN OF ALL COLORS TO SOLDIERS

Let us briefly return to one of Spain's most contradictory policies — entrusting the armed defense of its colonies to those it held to be hereditarily unfit for most posts due to their slave origins. Although recent studies have shown the complexity of the colonial militia, this book is the first to chronicle militiamen of color's transition from "bearers of arms for the king" to freedom fighters and defenders of the republic. Ben Vinson's examination of the pardo and moreno militia in the overwhelmingly mestizo and Indian Mexico ends well before independence, when Spain began to disband these military units in the 1790s. Vinson concludes that, far from "whitening" its members, the militia's privileges, notably the military fuero and exemption from the tribute of the castas, fostered corporate *and* racial (pardo or moreno) identity among them. However, as militiamen's racial identity was rooted in their military incorporation and the benefits it brought to them, it progressively disappeared with the elimination of the militia of color. Focusing on the rapidly expanding slave society of Cuba from the 1790s to 1812, Matt Childs unveils a different dynamic. After militiamen of color played a decisive role in the defense of Havana against the British in 1762, the Spanish Crown increasingly relied on them to protect the island. As in Mexico and New Granada, in Cuba belonging to the militia was a source of privileges that placed pardo and moreno militiamen above the rest of the free population of African descent and, of course, the slaves. Moreover, Afro-Cuban militiamen routinely were required to hunt down runaway slaves and to suppress revolts; some officers of African descent were also slave-owners. Concurrently, however, several shared membership in the cabildos de nación with slaves. As a result, according to Childs, militiamen of color developed an ambiguous racial identity that both reinforced Cuba's corporate socioracial hierarchy and militated against the racial subordination required by a slave society, which explains why in 1812 some of them planned the Aponte Rebellion to end slavery and colonialism. Yet, curiously, after 1812 Spain did not downsize Cuba's pardo and moreno militias and only disbanded them after the failed conspiracy of La Escalera in 1844.[32]

The fact that Spain could only form militias along (blurry) racial lines in Cartagena meant that elsewhere in Caribbean New Granada the establishment of milicias de todos los colores limited the formation of racial or color identities. Moreover, because, unlike in Mexico, free people of African descent in New Granada did not pay the casta tribute, militiamen of color felt less privileged by the Crown than their Mexican peers.[33] Conversely, because, unlike in Cuba, there was no massive importation of slaves to Caribbean New Granada, militiamen did not witness the racial polarization of their society. In Cartagena, the pardo militia showed fidelity to the Crown in 1781, during the Comunero Revolt (even participating in its repression), and in 1799, when one of its officers denounced an alleged antiwhite slave conspiracy. However, when in 1810 royalist or reformist elites in Caribbean New Granadan cities formed juntas, the militiamen did not oppose them (see Chapter 4). Furthermore, in Mompox and Cartagena, the militia, reinforced by lower-class men (including slaves in the case of Mompox), participated in the junta's ousting of the Spanish authorities. Following on the heels of the Haitian Revolution, the crossclass and crossracial movement against Spain that took place in these two cities was unique among Latin American cities with large populations of African descent. For example, the aristocrats who in 1811–12 established the racially blind but socially exclusive First Venezuelan Republic in Caracas failed to obtain the backing of the militia and the lower classes. In fact, only the 1817 revolution in Recife, in the province of Pernambuco, Brazil, shared some common characteristics with Cartagena and Mompox. In all three cities, elite leaders and the popular classes united in a movement in which each group expressed specific aims in a common republican discourse: freedom from the restrictions imposed by colonial authorities for the elite and racial equality for the militia of color and the lower classes. Also in these cities, although not seeking to reverse the socioracial hierarchy, the multilayered movement was unable to remain in power for long.[34]

Although the militia in Mompox was neutralized with the occupation of the city by Cartagena's troops in January 1811, in Cartagena, the expanded pardo militia, renamed Pardo Patriots, rapidly exceeded the aristocrats' reformist agenda and became aggressively proindependence. In February 1811 Pardo Patriots attacked Spaniards and supporters of the monarchy, deepening the gap between Spanish and creole whites and causing the creole elite to split between autonomists and supporters of full independence. Soon afterward, the Pardo Patriots united with the most radical elite and, backed by a huge crowd, compelled the Supreme Junta to declare independence in November 1811. After this victory, however, mulatto and black militiamen did not transform their racially based military units into autonomous political organizations, largely because they immediately gained legal equality regardless of race. Furthermore, the remnants of their corporate identity as royal militiamen of color vanished with the increased racial and regional mixing during the war for independence. Continued fighting and devastation until 1823 achieved the destruction of racial divisions within the army.

Paradoxically, the status of men of African descent in New Granada's emerging republican army was far less prestigious than that of the king's militiamen of color, who often distinguished themselves as self-sufficient subjects and benefited from the military fuero. After independence most soldiers were forcibly recruited peasants and laborers with little or no chance for advancement in an army that tended to reproduce the socioracial hierarchy. Despite a different context, the fate of the Caribbean region's militia of color resembles that of the black and mulatto militia of Bahia, Brazil, uncovered by Hendrik Kraay. Afro-Bahian officers and militiamen too lost their prestige and privileges with the advent of liberalism and legal equality, especially after the replacement of the racially segregated royal militia battalions with a mixed National Guard in 1831. To prevent the rise of officers of color, the legislature required that they qualify as second-degree electors, a right denied to libertos by the 1824 constitution. Unlike their counterparts in Caribbean New Granada, Afro-Bahian officers attempted to defend their previous position by going to court and participating in the 1837 Sabinada Rebellion, in which they were crushed. In both regions, the army formed in these years was a two-tiered institution consisting of troops mostly of African descent dominated by white officers.[35] Yet on the Caribbean Coast, unlike in Bahia, discrimination was never legally justified by the "stain of slavery."

WAITING FOR THE HAITIAN REVOLUTION

As discussed in Chapters 1 and 3, the Haitian Revolution echoed in Caribbean New Granada, increasing fear among some elites and agitation among some slaves, notably after the discovery of the alleged antiwhite conspiracy of 1799 in Cartagena that the authorities linked to suspected conspiracies in Santa Marta, Riohacha, Maracaibo, and Santiago de Cuba. In 1803 rumors spread that two hundred black and mulatto deportees from Guadeloupe had landed on the Guajira Peninsula, presumably to launch a revolution along Haitian lines. In 1832, in the wake of the massive Baptist War by Jamaican slaves, new rumors of slave rebellion circulated in some Caribbean New Granadan cities, reportedly ending with a handful of executions. In reality, however, no slave revolt of any consequence troubled the region during the Age of Revolution.

This is not surprising. First and foremost, as argued by Michael Craton, slave revolt has to be understood from the standpoint of the *longue durée*: paralleling the continuing resistance and slow creolization of the slave population, it evolved from marronage in the seventeenth century to plots and full-range revolt, but the heroic figure of the maroon continued to inspire rebels and runaways until abolition.[36] During the heyday of the slave trade in Caribbean New Granada in the early seventeenth century, numerous Africans rejected enslavement by forming powerful palenques around Cartagena, in the lower Cauca River, and close to Valledupar and Riohacha. Although the army destroyed some of these settlements, others remained, and the maroons' descendants composed much of the local population, influencing its organization and culture.[37] After 1640 no massive importation of slaves occurred, which gradually lessened direct links with Africa. But small-scale marronage was still a preferred method of revolt in a region where slaves were a minority; large slave plantations were few, and vast frontiers and backlands remained out of the reach of the state and the church. As shown in Chapter 5, despite the renewed colonial assault on runaway communities in the eighteenth century, slaves continued to escape to the periphery during the wars for independence and until abolition in 1852. Had this escape valve not been always available, the likelihood of slave rebellion might have increased. In addition, the quasi absence of priests teaching the New Testament in the Caribbean New Granadan countryside precluded another cause of slave revolt identified by Craton: syncretic Christianity and the realization of the contradictions between slavery and the Catholic doctrine, which contributed to British Guayana's Demerara Revolt in 1823 and Jamaica's Baptist War in 1831–32.[38]

The absence of collective slave revolts does not mean that slavery was compassionate in Caribbean New Granada, as some scholars have argued, or that slaves were submissive.[39] The cases of severe master abuse and neglect mentioned in Chapters 2 and 3 attest to the contrary, as do slaves' actions to denounce their masters' cruelty, which the Crown attorney in Bogotá branded as "pride and arrogance."[40] The point is that even in Cartagena, several conditions conducive to revolt simply did not exist. Unlike in Cuba and Venezuela, after 1780 plantations did not expand, few slaves were imported, and slavery declined. As a result, masters were not powerful enough to challenge or ignore the Código Negro promulgated by the king in 1789. On the contrary, slaves were able to use this law, sometimes successfully, against owners' mistreatment. Furthermore, numerous slaves pursued freedom through self-purchase, which involved long-term planning, hard work, and sacrifice, but also avoidance of high risks, such as rebellion. Yet both coartación and the incrimination of masters called into question the essence of slavery and threatened its permanence.

As a minority scattered across a vast territory, slaves had no chance of revolting successfully without forming an alliance with another group, most likely the majority represented by free people of color. Both colonial and republican authorities were conscious of this fact, which explains why they feared the mobilization of free men of African descent, branding it pardocracia or a potential Haiti. Yet, in the few junctures in which free men of color held the balance of power, such as in Cartagena in 1811 and 1828, they demanded equality for themselves but not the abolition of slavery. Such a dissociation between slaves and free people of color was not unique to the region. In fact, everywhere in the Caribbean and South America, regardless of their proportion vis-à-vis slaves, free people of color seldom associated their struggle for equality with slaves' struggle for abolition—even if they had only recently been released from bondage.[41]

Even during the much dreaded Haitian Revolution, gens de couleur and slaves did not unite to fight for freedom, equality, and independence until 1802, when Napoleon sent thousands of troops to occupy Saint Domingue and enforce the restoration of slavery. Before 1789, the small minority of gens de couleur included wealthy and educated planters who owned about one-quarter of the colony's 500,000 slaves but suffered themselves from racial discrimination. After 1789, they fought against white colonists for their own equal rights but joined forces with whites against the slaves who rebelled. In early 1793, when whites fled and the French revolutionaries governed, the gens de couleur dominated Saint Domingue without questioning slavery. When in August 1793 French authorities declared the abolition of slavery in an attempt to gain mass support against foreign invasion, it triggered an intense struggle between former slaves and anciens libres.

Only after the 1802 Napoleonic invasion did racial consciousness (the recognition that despite color distinctions, all Haitians belonged to the black or African race, different but equal to other races) permit Haitian independence in 1804.[42]

In Jamaica, too, free Coloreds generally distanced themselves from slaves. By 1810 free people of color equaled whites in size, both groups being largely outnumbered by slaves. Although most free Coloreds were among the urban poor, some were rich slaveowners though excluded from politics and subjected to legal and social discrimination because of their race. A strong color hierarchy placed black freedmen at the bottom. Nevertheless, free Coloreds did not make common cause with slaves. On the contrary, many showed their willingness to defend the colonial order as militiamen actively repressing marronage and slave rebellions. Facing new racial restrictions in 1813, Jamaican free Coloreds began to make collective petitions for equal rights with whites without demanding an end to slavery, until they gained full civil rights in 1830. Even during the Baptist War, which speeded up the abolition of slavery in the British colonies, the involvement of free people of color was limited to a paternalistic support for progressive emancipation.[43]

In societies where they were less wealthy and proportionally less numerous than in Saint Domingue and Jamaica, free people of color were almost forced to act in alliance with other social groups. Their sphere of action was also limited by internal tensions related to phenotype and color. In Guadeloupe and Martinique, for example, the Declaration of the Rights of Man provided the framework within which free men of color demanded equal rights but ignored slave emancipation. But some made common cause with slaves and played a role in small slave rebellions. In Barbados the legal condition of the free Coloreds broadly followed the same development as in Jamaica; most attempted to distinguish themselves from slaves, struggling for their civil rights and supporting the slave system.[44]

Still, the 1795 antiwhite revolt in Coro, Venezuela, although understudied, seems to show that, under certain conditions—notably the expansion of slavery and increased racism—the two groups could unite. There, apparently, hundreds of slaves and free blacks, zambos, and pardos joined forces to attack whites and proclaim the abolition of slavery, social equality, and a republican government. But if during the wars for independence, Venezuela's free pardos and slaves joined first the royalist troops and later Bolívar's armies as the best route to their own equality and freedom, free pardos did not use their new power to destroy slavery, which slowly collapsed before its abolition in 1854.[45] In Cuba, in 1812 and 1844, some slaves and free persons of color coalesced to conspire and rebel to end colonialism and slavery, yet the magnitude of Spanish repression tended to blow out of proportion the relatively small number of individuals involved in these movements. The alliance of slaves and libres de color in the 1844 conspiracy can partly be explained by Cuba's late sugar boom, which boosted slavery when other islands around Cuba had already embraced the principles of legal equality and free wage labor.[46] In Bahia, Brazil, slave and freed men and women united in the Malê (Muslim) uprising of 1835. However, as shown by Joao José Reis, what brought them together was not race but a common religion and African (mostly Nagô) birth, which continued a trend of revolt by Africans, rather than the Brazilian-born, in the region. Slaves' and freedmen's emphasis on African origin points to the importance of ethnicity and, indirectly, color in Bahia, where some slave revolts targeted whites as well as mulattoes.[47] Such emphasis also existed elsewhere. From the evidence gathered by Matt Childs, it appears that almost all of the leaders of the 1812 Aponte conspiracy or rebellion in Cuba were black and envisioned black men in power.[48] Similarly, the 1799 conspiracy in Cartagena (see Chapter 3) involved only blacks, including a militia captain, who were denounced by a pardo officer. These cases indicate that when free people of African descent and slaves mobilized together, often ethnicity, gender, color, trade, or other shared characteristics strengthened their bond. In short, the conditions leading to the formation of an overarching racial consciousness in Saint Domingue after the Napoleonic invasion and in Coro in 1795 were unique—and short-lived.

In Caribbean New Granada, on the other hand, no external factors fundamentally altered the colonial socioracial hierarchy ascending from the poorer and darker to the wealthier and whiter. Nevertheless, after the outbreak of the Haitian Revolution, a portion of the aristocracy in power believed in the existence of a socioracial dichotomy—elite whites versus the popular classes of color. Moreover, the Spanish monarchy began to regard free people of African descent as essentially immoral, politically dangerous, and prone to launch a Haitian-like revolution as a result of racial inheritance (i.e., because of their slave origins). Following independence, elite creoles in power, such as Simón Bolívar and José Manuel Restrepo, referred to the same threat as pardocracia and in some cases repressed attempts by the lower classes of color to use their new equality to mobilize separately by accusing them of planning the elimination of whites. Thus after the Haitian Revolution colonial authorities began to promote "political racism," coined after Albert Sicroff's phrase "religious racism," to describe Spanish persecution of Jews who converted to Catholicism in the late fourteenth and fifteenth centuries.[49] Although after 1821 the republican establishment banned the mention of race in official documents, like the Crown, it equated castas with political trouble. Following the 1790s, several royalist and patriot leaders had assumed that free people of color and slaves shared common interests and represented a collective danger, despite the fact that throughout the period most of the armed resistance against elite rule in Caribbean New Granada came from Indians on the frontier and from some pueblos near Santa Marta. The socioracial dichotomy was also meaningful in the representations of the lower classes of color, as evidenced in their use of the collective "los blancos" to refer to the wealthy and the powerful. On occasion they resorted to mass demonstrations to instill white fear and demand concessions, especially to push the reformist elite from autonomy to independence from Spain in Cartagena in November 1811.[50]

A FUZZY YET ENDURING RACIAL HIERARCHY

If a black/white racial dichotomy appeared in moments of fear and crisis, most of the time a hierarchical "racial variety" predominated, one whose main categories in the colony were the black slave; the free black, zambo, and mulatto; the white and the Spaniard; and the Indian on the periphery. Still, the reality was far more complex, and Chapters 1, 2, and 3 examine the many inconsistencies, exceptions, and loopholes in colonial law. These chapters also expound on the colonial authorities' inability to classify individuals and peoples in these fixed categories when interracial unions of all kinds were plentiful, and status (free or slave, of legitimate or illegitimate birth), ethnicity, culture, location, occupation, economic standing, patronage connections, and marital status intertwined with skin color and other physical traits used in racial classification. Here are some reminders of this "racial disorder." First, some colonial agents classified poor light-skinned individuals who could not prove their limpieza de sangre as "blanco de la tierra." Second, Spanish law had created the category of "castas" for all free persons of full or mixed African descent; this gave them limited rights and subjected them to a casta tribute, justified by the alleged stain of slavery in their origins. Yet, despite the fact that (or because) the overwhelming majority of Caribbean New Granadans were castas, there is no record that they ever paid the tribute. At the same time, because they were the majority, men of African descent composed almost all militia units organized in the late eighteenth century to defend the Caribbean Coast. All of these men were armed and benefited from the military fuero, which gave them special rights, some of which nullified the restrictions imposed on castas. Although initially Spain tried to organize separate militias of whites, pardos, and negros in the region, as it did in Mexico and Cuba, it managed to do so (and imprecisely) only in the largest and whitest city, Cartagena, where colonial institutions were stronger. Everywhere else it failed and opted to relabel these units milicias de todos los colores. Another example of blurred racial categories is the large number of men and women whom the census of 1777 listed as pardo or cuarterón simultaneously with the honorific title of don or doña. Moreover, some men of African descent were army officers, and others served in the lower clergy and the colonial administration, despite regulations stipulating limpieza de sangre for these functions. Finally, there was little relationship between color and status: some mulattoes and blacks owned slaves, and slaves were themselves black, mulatto, zambo, or cuarterón.

Several factors account for this racial fuzziness, a major one being demography. In 1780 whites (including blancos de la tierra) made up only 10 percent of the region's total population, and only in the principal cities did they comprise up to one-third of the inhabitants. People of color represented the vast majority of the population, in some places almost its totality. But they were scattered over a vast territory characterized by difficult and slow communications, and there were important socioeconomic, status, color, racial, and cultural differences among them, which precluded the formation of common identities. At the same time, belonging to such a majority, few individuals of African descent experienced otherness more than occasionally, except those who gained positions of power and spent time in Bogotá and the Caribbean islands, such as José Padilla, Juan José Nieto, and Remigio Márquez. Of these three, only Padilla proudly asserted himself as an Other—a pardo—and unsuccessfully tried to mobilize his fellow pardo citizens against Cartagena's entrenched white aristocracy, which eventually led to his execution.[51]

Racial fuzziness, of course, was not unique to Caribbean New Granada. In fact, it characterized most colonial societies in which the encounter between colonizers and native people and, in the Americas, African slaves, resulted in mestizaje. Racial "purity" often did not survive the first generation after arrival, especially when the newcomers were single men rather than families. Thus, colonial authorities created new, interstitial racial categories to try to give definition to the fuzziness. According to Magnus Mörner, the eighteenth-century caste system of Mexico theoretically made distinctions among eighteen racial categories, that of Peru, sixteen; in practice, however, seven or less were in use. Even in the pre–Civil War United States, whiteness and blackness were not defined by the "one drop of black blood" rule, and the 1850 U.S. census included an ill-defined mulatto category for the "mixed-race" people.[52] In general, three processes explain the transformation of some Caribbean islands and portions of the continental Americas into two-tiered (black/white) or three-tiered (black/Colored/white) societies largely founded on racial criteria: first, the expansion of racial slavery and, with it, the need for slaveowners and administrators to dehumanize African slaves and rigidly separate them from free people; second, massive European immigration; and third, the rise of pseudo-scientific racism together with a discourse of liberal democracy and free labor.[53] In contrast, the Circum Caribbean, to which New Granada belongs, did not import many new slaves after 1776 (except for Venezuela) and failed to attract European immigrants after independence. Therefore, the leaders institutionalized racial fuzziness by acknowledging the mestizo (or pardo in the case of Venezuela) character of the nation while discreetly clinging to the colonial socioracial hierarchy.[54] After 1821 the coastal elite seldom claimed superiority on the basis of pure Spanish origin, but it hardly changed its behavior and beliefs grounded in colonialism and slavery. A small cluster of white elite families continued on top, a large majority of pardos, zambos, mestizos, and black artisans, workers, and servants below, and the still numerous slaves, often black, at the bottom of the social scale. Each individual had his or her own place in a multilayered socioracial hierarchy in which almost everyone could feel superior to someone else.

Fuzziness and fragmentation also characterized Caribbean New Granada's white minority, which influenced its control of the lower classes. To be fully effective, white domination requires a politically and economically strong elite that has no doubt about its superiority and is able to rally poor whites and close ranks in the face of challenge. This was true of the U.S. South and some Caribbean islands dominated by a planter elite, such as Cuba or Barbados, but not of Caribbean New Granada.[55] With an inefficient state and a weak Catholic Church, most social control depended on white hacendados, merchants, and entrepreneurs. These men and women were too divided among themselves (especially by birth, location, economic interests, and politics) to establish what could be called hegemony over the population. Even in moments of popular unrest, whites did not unite. In the process of creating local juntas in 1810, particularly, the upper class in

Cartagena and Mompox failed to form strong separate battalions of white militiamen uniting Spaniards and white creoles that could have prevented clashes between the two groups. Indeed, whiteness was multifaceted. On the one hand, it encompassed the blancos de la tierra, or the mulattoes and quadroons who passed for white. On the other hand, only Spaniards and white creoles who could prove limpieza de sangre, legitimate birth, Catholic marriage, property ownership, nonmanual occupation, education, and an honorable lifestyle were entitled to full rights and privileges. Thus only a small number of white elite families qualified for the full prerogatives of whiteness and monopolized the highest public and private positions in each city. Other whites had comparatively too few privileges for race to become a common bond between them and the elite. After independence, Caribbean New Granada's merchants, hacendados, and ranchers remained a small and moderately thriving group. Whiteness and nobility disappeared as criteria for holding higher office, and individuals from less prized social backgrounds, sometimes of partial African ancestry, managed to join these elite circles as long as they adopted elite norms and values. Yet the belief that birth determined capacities did not vanish. Political power and prestige remained largely a monopoly of elite white men. Like their predecessors, they divided along political, provincial, and local lines, and they avoided claiming racial superiority as a means of keeping the lower classes in check.

PATRONAGE AND FIESTAS

Under Spain as well as in the republic, the local elite exercised social control mostly through networks of patronage. The patron (or matron) guaranteed employment, access to land, protection against the draft, bailout fees, legal protection, and other resources necessary for survival in a society offering few economic opportunities. As the white elite was small and divided, the lower classes of color could play one patron against another, because whites needed their support and labor. Conversely, one patron could, for example, plot the military enlistment of his rivals' peones and tenant farmers. Lower-class individuals also competed against each other to become part of a network and to get the best deal possible from local bosses. Dependency on divided patrons effectively precluded collective lower-class action. Moreover, patronage weaved links across class, color, and gender lines that vertically integrated the local community and workforce, mediating antagonisms and strengthening the local sense of belonging. Local patrons themselves belonged to regional networks that loosely but durably connected the local to the national level. These alliances continued after 1808, allowing the First Independence to follow republican principles without destroying the socioracial hierarchy. In particular, Cartagena's white elite forged two competing crossclass and crossracial movements with the popular classes of color: the toledistas and the piñeristas. Not only did these alliances continue in the factions attached to Bolívar and Santander in the 1820s, but they also formed the local backbone of the two-party system Colombia adopted in the 1840s.[56] Similarly, the Conservative and Liberal Parties did not have fundamental ideological differences regarding economic and social policies. This precluded the conceptualization of two rival visions of society (even though the Conservatives promoted a much more interventionist Catholic Church than the Liberals). Moreover, as Conservative and Liberal leaders were able to channel lower-class men of African descent under their respective banners, they neutralized this group's autonomous socioracial challenge. As the two parties integrated local and regional constituencies into the Colombian nation, they eliminated the possibility of the Caribbean region's united challenge to the Andean center.

Although the endurance of Colombia's two-party system has few equivalents in the Western Hemisphere other than in the United States and Uruguay, patronage as a restraint to socioracial conflict can be found in several Latin American societies, from late-seventeenth-century Mexico to twentieth-century Brazil.[57] Nowhere did clientage erase hierarchies, but it complicated them. In the case of Caribbean New Granada, the relative fragmentation and the economic weakness of the small aristocracy made patronage all the more necessary since the armed forces comprised mostly men of color. Acquaintanceship or intimacy between white patrons and subordinates of color prevented overt class competition. At the same time, vertical patronage thwarted the envisioning of full equality.

As long as nonwhites "behaved" and did not challenge the socioracial hierarchy and existing power relations, they posed no problem to the elite. On the other hand, those individuals of color who, on the basis of the 1821 republican constitution, claimed full equality with the white aristocracy but lacked the racial, class, and cultural attributes for such a claim, threatened the social order and needed to be quickly eliminated—like General Padilla in 1828. For the same reason, the elite could not tolerate any attempts of the lower classes to mobilize collectively, which explains its brandishing of the specter of pardocracia each time the lower classes acted independently from white leadership. Such restrictions on the freedom of people of African descent, disguised in a discourse of legal equality, were far from unique to Caribbean New Granada. In fact, they exist today in many Latin American societies in which the official ideology considers nationalism and black (or mulatto) pride as fundamentally incompatible. Although black or pardo pride is repressed for allegedly dividing the nation and threatening the security of whites, in reality it is prohibited because it explicitly precludes the national pursuit of mestizaje and/or whitening. As a consequence, these societies also project themselves as free from racial discrimination, which in turn prevents oppressed minorities from demanding equality in the public and private spheres.[58]

If racial demands à la Padilla could not be tolerated by a society claiming legal equality for all, in Caribbean New Granada the continuing expression of lower-class alternative cultures encountered only sporadic elite repression, notably the failed campaigns against popular dancing by late colonial foreign bishops.[59] Some authors, such as Orlando Fals Borda and Edgar Rey Sinning, have exalted, not without some essentialism, the costeño subculture for its festive dimensions, sexual liberty, and insouciance, as well as its democracy and nonviolence.[60] Undoubtedly, costeño popular culture, with its triple—African, indigenous, and European—origins and its religious syncretisms, has helped Caribbean Colombians cope on a daily basis and has given meaning to their lives. Yet, as I show, this culture remained local and mostly festive. It seldom made claims against or directly challenged the power of the wealthy. Unlike some societies examined in the literature on popular resistance, in which a powerful elite repressed expressions of alternative cultures and forced these cultures to go underground, in Caribbean New Granada the leaders were conscious of their inability to exercise hegemony; thus they tolerated and often sponsored lower-class subcultures.[61] As Néstor García Canclini argues for Mexico, "The ambiguous strategy of the dominant classes toward subordinate cultures can be explained by this twofold movement: a desire to impose their economic and cultural models on subordinate cultures and, at the same time, to appropriate that which they cannot destroy or bring under their control."[62]

Indeed, if public festivals and carnivals could allow for irreverent, immoral, and unruly conduct, they also brought the whole community together and staged its power hierarchy. Most celebrations represented the political system and replicated the socioracial order, while at the same time offering spaces for enjoyment. Some elements remained unchanged. Throughout the period, white church dignitaries led public ceremonies, which generally included a *Te Deum* mass. In the transitional decade following independence in 1821, the figure of Bolívar replaced that of the king but similarly embodied the "common center" uniting all interests. Institutions such as municipal councils, always present at celebrations, became more racially inclusive. Also, the public manumission of slaves, though emancipating few men and women, marked a break with the colonial era. Nevertheless, ceremonies were not transformed into revolts. Perhaps the only celebrations that momentarily turned the socioracial hierarchy upside down were the all-night wakes preceding funerals, in which lower-class women, reputedly less threatening than men, could express their disrespect toward the wealthy. But balls and public rites served both as safety valves and as spaces where the old order gradually transformed into the new one. In fact, peoples' cultural autonomy was a price worth paying for an elite with limited means that wanted to maintain access to cheap labor and to ensure (and, after 1860, increase) its control of the region's best lands, economic opportunities, and political positions.[63] Funerals, fiestas, and official ceremonies validated the socioracial hierarchy and strengthened clientage bonds and the sense of local community. Already in the 1770s royal authorities had come to terms with this reality when they reversed a bishop's edict banning popular dances on the grounds that such a ban would be disregarded or spark violent protest.

Similarly, by the 1830s the understaffed church gave up trying to impose respect for Catholic norms in the sexual unions of the populace, after decades of campaigning for Catholic marriage. On the one hand, the continuing importance of free unions in the region attested to the resilience of the lower classes' alternative sexual and family views. It also reflected the fact that many men, such as ranchers and bogas, had migratory occupations. On the other hand, when the church gave up its goal of sanctifying unions, it tacitly admitted the well-established practice among employers and hacendados, among others, of exploiting their female slaves and dependents as sexual partners. In fact, much of the racial mixing that occurred in the Caribbean region originated in male domination and abuse of women, which had begun with the Spanish invaders' conquest of American women, followed by the Spanish and creole appropriation of African slave women. Although mestizaje could also be the result of mutually desired concubinage and intermarriage, racial and gender exploitation continued unabashed, especially during the eighteenth-century military campaigns of resettlement and the wars for independence. The demographic imbalance in the major cities, where women of African descent largely outnumbered men, also fostered exploitative unions and resulted in the high incidence of female-headed households.[64] Here again, my analysis distances itself from that of Fals, who, not unlike Gilberto Freyre for Brazil, locates the roots of the region's "triethnic race" in the sexual freedom characteristic of all costeños.[65] I take a more critical approach to Caribbean Colombian racial mestizaje and cultural syncretism in order to highlight the disparities resulting from complex hierarchies of power and wealth informed by gender, race, class, and ethnicity.

WOMEN'S INFLUENCE

Due to their demographic predominance in the cities and their overall socioeconomic importance, women, in their great majority nonwhite, profoundly influenced strategies of improvisation and resistance in the region. Even the rochelas and the nuclear settlements that were scattered across the hinterlands depended as much on the labor of women and children as that of men. With the exception of ranching and transportation, much of the agricultural production and small trade in the region involved women as well as men.[66] The brief cotton boom after 1800 fostered cottage industries in several areas based on women's weaving and sewing. In Caribbean New Granadan towns, as elsewhere in the Americas, free and slave women of African descent did most of the street and market selling; supplied food, charcoal, and entertainment; and provided all kinds of domestic service.[67]

As shown by Maria Odila Silva Dias for São Paulo, in Caribbean New Granada lower-class women seldom organized together to collectively defend themselves but usually resorted to adaptive improvisation to confront the challenges in their lives.[68] Women used three preferred avenues of resistance: counterculture, migration, and legal challenge. Although women and children were the primary targets of the eighteenth-century campaigns against arrochelados, once relocated in villages they did not become obedient followers of the norms imposed by the Catholic Church. As lamented by bishops, they often continued to barely cover their bodies and to worship in their own ways, and they were loud in church. Some took advantage of wakes and religious fiestas to be even more irreverent. Moreover, when they became pregnant out of wedlock, some chose abortion; others gave birth but entrusted the baptism of their children to acquaintances to avoid a church reprimand. In cities, some single mothers opted for blatant autonomy outside the Catholic canon and survived with their family by working relentlessly.

Women also migrated in search of better opportunities or to avoid hardship. Some moved from the countryside to cities in the hope of finding security, autonomy, and economic options in domestic service and the markets. (Similar movements also took place in the hinterland of Caracas, Lima, Mexico, São Paulo, New Orleans, and San Juan, for example.)[69] No doubt among these migrant women were single mothers and widows with children. For slave women, the city offered more chances for manumission than haciendas and villages. Conversely, during the wars for independence and the 1831 civil war, women abandoned some villages and small towns and took to the woods with their children and elderly relatives rather than suffer abuse by the enemy.

Some women exhibited resilience and the ability to use the justice system to their advantage. This was particularly true of the free and slave women who resorted to the law (notably the Código Negro) to redress injustices (see Chapter 3). Although not all of them won their suits, they contributed, at least in Cartagena and Mompox, to making authorities more sensitive to their human rights. Their strategies resembled those utilized by slave and freed women in Lima, uncovered by Christine Hünefeldt. Furthermore, this study, by linking women's higher rates of self-purchase than men with women's demographic preponderance among the urban slave population, seems to indicate that the principal factor explaining why more women than men achieved freedom was not women's preferential treatment but urban residence with its wider opportunities for wages.[70] Similarly, comparison with the largely mestizo Bogotá and the white and African-derived San Juan shows that it was not because lower-class women in Caribbean New Granada's cities were of African descent that a substantial proportion of them were single mothers, but because they were much more numerous than men in their socioracial category and in the urban population generally. Whether lower- and upper-class Caribbean New Granadan women challenged the continuing colonial patriarchal laws after independence by increasingly going to court to denounce spousal abuse, as they did in Caracas, is yet to be determined.[71]

In the Caribbean region as elsewhere, lower-class women of color employed nonconfrontational strategies to improve their lives and those of their loved ones. In addition to networks of solidarity within their own extended families and community, they established patronage and kinship relations with white elites that could prove helpful, especially when they were in trouble with the law. More exceptional in the American context was the low incidence of newborn and child abandonment registered in Cartagena's baptismal records, particularly among blacks and mulattoes. This suggests that indigent or unwilling mothers were able to have their offspring adopted or taken in as servants by relatives or higher-status households. In contrast, estimates for São Paulo in the early nineteenth century range between one-sixth and two-thirds of newborns abandoned.[72] As noted by several contemporary travelers, a strong tradition of charity and solidarity among Caribbean New Granada's lower-class women prevented extreme misery. No doubt, these traits reoriented overall urban mobilization toward compromise, without which the population of Cartagena could not have withstood three lengthy sieges—in 1815, 1820–21, and 1831—without revolt.

Lastly, women took part in the wars for independence in various ways. Although they remained nameless actors, some helped to shield villages and small towns from the destructive effects of repeated army occupation, whereas others accompanied the troops. Less anonymous, some elite women tied to powerful interests became leaders, organizers, suppliers, and fund-raisers for either the royalist or the proindependence cause, as well as the victims of banishment in cases of defeat. Yet women in general did not gain much with the establishment of the republic. Legal equality regardless of race had little impact on them, as it did not affect gender inequalities. True, racial barriers in legal marriages weakened, and reportedly a few leading creole men married pardo women. Starting in 1822, slave women gave birth to free children, even if the children were required to work without pay for their mother's master until age eighteen. But apparently Cartagena's women did not take part in the anti-Bolívar movement initiated by General Padilla in March 1828, perhaps because it was too brief and strictly focused on male demands. Three years later, however, women in Santa Marta actively supported General Francisco Carmona when he mobilized the population against the dictatorship of Urdaneta.

FRONTIERS AND SMUGGLING

In the end, the most abiding reason why the Caribbean region avoided large-scale social conflict and remained within New Granada was the continuing existence of vast uncontrolled hinterlands and frontiers as well as an unguarded littoral offering viable alternatives to rebellious and free-spirited individuals. As in some other parts of the Americas, the backlands and the sea represented a "safety valve" for releasing pressures built up in more settled areas to which defiant slaves and laborers, fugitives, and political opponents could escape with little risk of capture.[73] These fringe areas also corresponded to recent scholarship's broad definition of frontiers as "shifting membranes of contact between different peoples, where power was constantly being contested and negotiated."[74] Yet, unlike in the U.S. West and the Argentinian pampas, in Caribbean New Granada colonial and early republican authorities faced the quandary of "opening a frontier" that offered few legal opportunities for wealth and was inhabited by unsubdued Indians and runaways of color when there was no growing white population in the interior eager to colonize it. If some parallels can be drawn between Euclides da Cunha's nineteenth-century depiction of the inhabitants of northeastern Brazil's backlands (*os sertões*) as mixed-race savages and the descriptions of Caribbean New Granada's arrochelados by conquerors and travelers, neither the provincial elite nor New Granadan authorities had the means or incentive to conquer their backlands, as did their Brazilian counterparts.[75] Thus, the region's frontier continued to escape control. In addition, its location in the tropics, where survival was less arduous than in temperate climates, helps explain its endurance, like that of several other tropical frontiers in South and Central America.[76] In Caribbean New Granada, as in the Goiás examined by Mary Karash, for example, the colonial power tried and failed to impose Christianity and an Iberian way of life, because it could count on only a few white male settlers who would seek sexual partners among the local women, who as mothers transmitted the native culture. In both frontiers, the descendants of Indian nations and maroon communities have managed to survive up to the present through strategies ranging from warfare to flight and accommodation.[77]

Nonetheless, what was specific to Caribbean New Granada's frontier was its long littoral and access to the Atlantic trade that transformed its marginality into centrality for illegal activities. More precisely, the frontier provided a lucrative alternative to the lack of profitable export industries in the region: smuggling. Smuggling prospered and became fully irrepressible because it grew parallel to a culture in which many people in both the elites and the popular classes benefited from the lack of state and church control. While often racially stereotyped, smuggling was, to some extent, the social integrator uniting gold panners, cane distillers, and rustlers with carriers, muleteers, boatmen, and bogas; with hacendados, merchants, and officials; with female street sellers and peddlers. It linked the Andean center and the Pacific lowlands to the Caribbean Coast. Contraband also loosely connected cities to the countryside, the hinterlands, the indigenous nations on the frontier, and ultimately the Atlantic world. Because it also comprised the customs officials who failed to record, underrecorded, or misrecorded imports, it kept social and administrative hierarchies in place.[78] Smuggling even guaranteed the survival and autonomy of the Wayúu in the Guajira

Peninsula and the Kuna and Emberá in the Darién, without which the system of illegal trade could not have functioned. Not surprisingly, in 1822 republican authorities renounced their claim to jurisdiction over these territories and recognized them as indigenous "independent nations." But, in an attempt to channel some of the contraband profit into the national treasury, they requested that foreign ships purchase official Colombian licenses prior to trading with the frontier Indians.

In 1789 Archbishop-Viceroy Caballero y Góngora lamented that New Granada suffered from a fundamental problem of "disorder." Its richest lands were scarcely populated but its vast deserts and tropical forests sheltered unsubdued Indians and all the dregs of society. Accurately describing the Caribbean region more than two centuries ago, this statement still has validity today, as most of the region's lands are utilized for cattle ranching and most of its inhabitants congregate in cities. Moreover, since the 1990s the frontier and the hinterland have become a coveted terrain for illicit cultivation, laboratory work, and drug smuggling. Narcoproducers, guerrillas, and paramilitary units unrelentingly fight for control of land, resources, and people. In this spiralling violence, the indigenous communities and the descendants of the black, mulatto, and zambo arrochelados described in this book are vanishing. Either they are massacred by the battling factions or they escape, not farther beyond the frontier but to the cities, as destitute refugees.[79]

As stated in the introduction to this book, the 1991 constitution now guarantees indigenous and "black" communities their ethnic and cultural diversity, but the Colombian state is still too weak to protect their lives. Furthermore, to Caribbean Colombia's population of mixed and "full" African ancestry, neither the new constitution nor the 1993 Law of Negritudes has brought significant change. For most of them, equality as defined in 1821, with all its limitations, is still the rule. In the region, they continue, fragmented and divided, to face racial discrimination in their own communities without legal protection. They prefer negotiation and manipulation of elite divisions to overt confrontation. As in the past, they employ flight, legal action, patronage networks, and ritual kinship to individually improve their lot.

NOTES

ABBREVIATIONS

Colombia

AAC	Archivo del Arzobispado de Cartagena
AESM	Archivo Eclesiástico de Santa Marta
AHC	Archivo Histórico de Cartagena
FG	Fondo Gobernación
Justicia	Serie Justicia
AHNC	Archivo Histórico Nacional de Colombia, Bogotá
CO	Sección Colonia
AD	Fondo Aduana
CI	Fondo Caciques e Indios
CV	Fondo Censos Varios Departamentos
GN	Fondo Genealogías
MI	Fondo Miscelánea
NE	Fondo Negros y Esclavos
RE	Sección República
AC	Fondo Asuntos Criminales
AR	Archivo Restrepo
CB	Fondo Curas y Obispos
Censos	Fondo Censos
GM	Fondo Guerra y Marina
HI	Fondo Historia
NJ	Fondo Negocios Judiciales
APC	Archivo de la Parroquia de La Catedral, Cartagena
APST	Archivo de la Parroquia de la Santísima Trinidad, Getsemaní, Cartagena
BNC	Biblioteca Nacional de Colombia, Bogotá
SM	Sala Manuscritos
SP	Sala Pineda
SS	Sala Samper

France

MAE-Paris	Ministère des Affaires Etrangères, Paris
CCC	Correspondance Consulaire, Colombie, Carthagène
MD	Mission Diplomatique

Great Britain
PRO   Public Record Office, London
  FO   Foreign Office Papers

Spain
AGI   Archivo General de Indias, Seville
  Cuba   Papeles de Cuba
  Estado   Estado
  Santa Fe   Audiencia de Santa Fe
AGS   Archivo General de Simancas
  Guerra   Secretaría de Guerra

United States
NA   National Archives, Washington, D.C.
  DCC   Despatches from the U.S. Consuls in Cartagena, 1822–1906
                    (microcopy)

INTRODUCTION

1. *Constitución política de Colombia, 1991.* See also E. Sánchez, Roldán, and M. F. Sánchez, *Derechos e identidad.*

2. E. Sánchez, Roldán, and M. F. Sánchez, *Derechos e identidad*, 110; Arocha, "Afro-Colombia Denied," 30; Wade, *Blackness*, 352–55; Friedemann and Arocha, "Colombia," 68–69.

3. "Ley 70 sobre negritudes."

4. M. Zapata, *La rebelión de los genes*, 63–69; V. Moreno, *Negritudes.*

5. Gros, "Noirs, indiens et créoles," 60.

6. Cunin, "Le métissage dans la ville," 230–42.

7. Friedemann, "Negros en Colombia."

8. In 1970, 48 percent of Colombians were classified as mestizo; 24 percent, mulatto; 20 percent, white; 6 percent, black; and 2 percent, indigenous (Colombia, *Atlás básico*, 11). More recent atlases contain no data on race.

9. Wade, "Identités noires"; Aguledo, "Populations noires."

10. Revollo, *Costeñismos colombianos*, vi.

11. Nieto, "Geografía histórica" and "Bosquejo histórico"; [Corrales], *Documentos* and *Efemérides*; Urueta, *Documentos.*

12. Colombia, *Jeografia fisica.*

13. See Helg, "Los intelectuales frente a la cuestión racial" and "Esclavos y libres de color," 699–702; and Wade, *Blackness*, 12–19, and *Music*, 32–36, 42–47. For a rare nineteenth-century acknowledgment of the contribution of African slaves and their descendants to Colombia's economy and independence, see Camacho, *Notas de viaje*, 114–17.

14. Wade, *Music*, 187–212, 229.

15. Múnera, *El fracaso de la nación.*

16. Lemaître, *Contra viento y marea*; Park, *Rafael Núñez.*

17. Lemaître, *Historia general de Cartagena*, 4:171–239, and *Juan José Nieto*; Fals, *El Presidente Nieto*.

18. Pérez, *El negro Robles*. Although written in 1949, this biography, the first book-length study on Robles, was only published in 2000 as part of a special law passed by the Colombian Congress to honor the memory of the Liberal politician. Interestingly, its author, himself an Afro-costeño, imputes Robles's exceptional rise to the fact that "his idiosyncrasy differed a lot from that of the inhabitants of the Caribbean Coast" because he was reflective, controlled, and sober (p. 44).

19. Escalante, "Notas sobre el Palenque," 228–29; Cunin, "Le métissage dans la ville," 229, 257–58. According to Orlando Fals Borda (*Mompox y Loba*, 52A–56A), Bioho founded the palenque of Mantuna, not San Basilio.

20. Padilla's full name was José Prudencio Padilla, but he signed his letters "José Padilla." He is occasionally referred to as a zambo instead of a pardo. For brief mentions of Padilla in Bolívar's trajectory, see Liévano Aguirre, *Bolívar*, 501; Masur, *Simón Bolívar*, 447; Lynch, "Bolívar and the Caudillos," 30–31; and Bushnell, "The Last Dictatorship," 78. The most complete military biography of Padilla is Torres, *El Almirante*. See also E. Uribe, *Padilla*, and Otero, *Vida del Almirante*. For an illustration of Padilla's statue, see E. Uribe, *Padilla*, 380.

21. The territory considered in this book as Caribbean New Granada comprises the three colonial provinces of Riohacha, Santa Marta, and Cartagena, corresponding to today's departments of Guajira, César, Magdalena, Bolívar, Sucre, and Córdoba, and the coastal portion of northern Antioquia. For the geohistory of the region, see Avella, "Bases geohistóricas."

22. This book follows the racial categories mentioned in the sources. "Free people of color" is the equivalent of the Spanish "libres de color."

23. I have borrowed this expression from Matos, *Women and Urban Change*, 2.

24. McFarlane, *Colombia*; Bushnell, *Santander Regime*, 172, and *Making of Modern Colombia*.

25. König, *En el camino*; Garrido, *Reclamos y representaciones*; Safford, "Race, Integration, and Progress"; Jaramillo, *Ensayos sobre historia social*; Uribe-Urán, *Honorable Lives*; Earle, *Spain and the Independence of Colombia*.

26. One exception is geographer Theodore E. Nichols's 1951 Ph.D. dissertation, later published as *Tres puertos*.

27. Fals, "Influencia del vecindario pobre" and *Capitalismo*. See also Tovar, *Grandes empresas*, and Meisel, "Esclavitud, mestizaje y haciendas."

28. Fals, *Mompox y Loba*, *El Presidente Nieto*, *Resistencia en el San Jorge*, and *Retorno a la tierra*. For a sharp critique of Fals's work, see Bergquist, "In the Name of History," 164–65. For Fals's response, see Fals, "Comentarios a la mesa redonda."

29. Bell, *Cartagena de Indias* and "Conflictos regionales"; Sourdis, *Cartagena*; Múnera, *El fracaso de la nación*; Meisel and Aguilera, "Cartagena de Indias"; Romero, *Esclavitud*. Representative of the historiography focusing almost exclusively on the role of the elite are the studies by two members of Cartagena's Academia de Historia: Bossa, *Cartagena independiente*, and Lemaître, *Historia general de Cartagena*.

30. Posada-Carbó, *Colombian Caribbean*.

31. Escalante, "Notas sobre el Palenque"; Velásquez, "La canoa chocoana."

32. Friedemann and Arocha, *De sol a sol*; Taussig, *Devil*; Wade, *Blackness* and *Music*.

33. See, e.g., Sharp, *Slavery on the Spanish Frontier*; Chandler, *Health and Slavery*; McFarlane, "*Cimarrones* and *palenques*"; and Zuluaga, *Guerrilla y sociedad*.

34. V. Gutiérrez, *Familia y cultura*, 225–352.

35. Solaún and Kronus, *Discrimination*; Streicker, "Policing Boundaries"; Cunin, "Le métissage dans la ville."

36. See, e.g., Guardino, *Peasants, Politics*, and Walker, *Smoldering Ashes*. For an excellent discussion of the literature on nation making and citizenship in nineteenth-century Latin America, see Sabato, "On Political Citizenship."

37. The expression "mulatto escape hatch" comes from Degler, *Neither Black nor White*.

38. On frontiers, see, e.g., Guy and Sheridan, *Contested Ground*.

39. Genovese, *From Rebellion to Revolution*.

40. Geggus, "Slavery, War, and Revolution"; Craton, *Testing the Chains*, 241–53.

41. See, e.g., A. J. Díaz, "Gender Conflicts."

CHAPTER ONE

1. Caballero y Góngora, "Relación," 308–10. All translations in this book are mine unless otherwise noted.

2. Prebble, *Darien Disaster*; McFarlane, *Colombia*, 24–26; Kuethe, *Military Reform*, 23.

3. Representación de los comerciantes de Cartagena al Secretario de Estado Don Diego Gardoqui, 30 April 1795, in Spain, AGI, Santa Fe 1019. On contraband before 1770, see Grahn, *Political Economy of Smuggling*.

4. Pedro Mendinueta to Pedro Ceballos, 19 April 1803, in Spain, AGI, Estado, 52, no. 137, fol. 5.

5. Narváez, "Provincia de Santa Marta," 36. For additional estimates, see in Tovar, "*Convocatoria*": "Censo de los indios guajiros, [1760]" (pp. 531–32), "Indios en armas en la provincia de la Guajira, [1779]" (pp. 538–39), and "Censo de las misiones de los capuchinos en las provincias de Sta. Marta y Río Hacha, [1779]" (pp. 522–26).

6. Moreno y Escandón, "Estado del Virreinato," 185. On Moreno y Escandón, see McFarlane, *Colombia*, 205–7.

7. Xavier, "Reconocimiento," 483–84.

8. Moreno y Escandón, "Estado del Virreinato," 186–87.

9. Nichols, *Tres puertos*, 39–41; Fidalgo, "Expedición Fidalgo," 76 n; Consejo Regional, *Mapa cultural*, maps on 51, 85; McFarlane, *Colombia*, 39–40.

10. Múnera, *El fracaso de la nación*, 61. A local dictionary defines "rochela" as a group of bad or idle persons and the place where they gather (Revollo, *Costeñismos colombianos*, 236). On rochelas in the eastern plains of Venezuela, see Izard, *Orejanos, cimarrones y arrochelados*.

11. Torre, "Noticia individual," 43. See also Mollien, *Voyage*, 1:45.

12. Peredo, "Noticia historial," 143–44, 153; Silvestre, "Apuntes reservados," 104; Palacios, *Diario de viaje*, 39, 96.

13. Torre, "Noticia individual," 49.

14. Palacios, *Diario de viaje*, 72–73, 94.

15. Torre, "Noticia individual," 60. See also Palacios, *Diario de viaje*, 96.

16. Palacios, *Diario de viaje*, 72–73, 94. See also Peredo, "Noticia historial," 147.

17. Peredo, "Noticia historial," 147; Torre, "Noticia individual," 46. See also Caballero y Góngora, "Relación," 410, and Torre, "Noticia individual," 44, 54, 56, 60.

18. On women in rochelas in the Chocó and Cauca, see Sharp, *Slavery on the Spanish Frontier*, 153–57, and Zuluaga, *Guerrilla y sociedad*, 49–50, 57. On other frontier societies, see Socolow, "Women of the Buenos Aires Frontier," 78–81, and Thomas D. Hall, "Río de la Plata," 159–60.

19. Mollien, *Voyage*, 1:47, 49–50.

20. Torre, "Noticia individual," 55–56; Palacios, *Diario de viaje*, 47–48, 75–76, 95.

21. On palenques, see Borrego, *Palenques de negros*; McFarlane, "*Cimarrones and palenques*"; Fals, *Capitalismo*; and T. D. Gutiérrez, *Cultura vallenata*, 199–222.

22. Padrón del sitio de Santa Catalina, año 1780, in Colombia, AHNC, CO, CV, rollo 21, fols. 143–51v.

23. Torre, "Noticia individual," 47–51.

24. Escalante, "Notas sobre el Palenque," 228–29; McFarlane, "*Cimarrones* and *palenques*," 134–35.

25. Peredo, "Noticia historial," 140. On the evolution of the palenquero language, see Friedemann and Patiño, *Lengua y sociedad*, and Schwegler, "*Chi ma nkongo*."

26. Torre, "Noticia individual," 47–51.

27. Twinam, *Miners*, 16.

28. Palacios, *Diario de viaje*, 105; also 96. The palenque of Guamal, on the Cauca River, should not be confused with the new settlement of Guamal, founded by José Fernando Mier y Guerra on the Magdalena River south of Mompox.

29. These are only estimates. There is no census of New Granada's population before the one ordered by Archbishop-Viceroy Caballero y Góngora in the late 1770s, according to which the three Caribbean provinces had a total of 170,404 settled inhabitants (Tovar, "*Convocatoria*," 503, 519, 537).

30. On female honor, see Martinez-Alier, *Marriage, Class, and Colour*, 120–24, and Twinam, *Public Lives*, 32–33.

31. Eslava, "Defensa," 53–57; Solís, "Relación."

32. Silvestre, "Apuntes reservados," 103. See also Gil y Lemos, "Relación," 19–22; "Relación de los méritos y servicios de don José Fernando de Mier" (facsimile) (22 April 1778), in De-Mier, *Poblamientos*, 3:303–14; Fals, *Mompox y Loba*, 103AB–114AB; M. D. González, "La política de población"; and Mora, "Poblamiento y sociedad."

33. "Solicitud para que los ganados de don Nicolás Martínez no arruinen las tierras de los indios" (4 March 1785), in De-Mier, *Poblamientos*, 3:106–9; "Fray Bartolomé de Vinaroz, cura de Venero, expone algunas dificultades para el desempeño de su ministerio" (30 August 1788), ibid., 122–31.

34. "Censo de los indios guajiros, [1760]," in Tovar, *"Convocatoria,"* 531-32.

35. Messía, "Relación," 137-38, 144-47; Moreno y Escandón, "Estado del Virreinato," 188-89; Silvestre, "Apuntes reservados," 80-82, 102; Kuethe, "Pacification Campaign" and *Military Reform*, 137-38. On equally unsuccessful policies in the frontier areas of New Spain and Río de la Plata, see Slatta, "Spanish Colonial Military Strategy."

36. Fidalgo, "Expedición Fidalgo," 184-85 n.

37. Reichel, Introduction to Joseph Palacios de la Vega, *Diario*, 8.

38. "Pacificación general de los indios." For a detailed study of the process leading to the launching of the 1785 military campaign, see Luengo, "Génesis de las expediciones."

39. Antonio de Arévalo to Antonio Caballero y Góngora (16 July 1788), in Spain, AGI, Santa Fe 1068, no. 31.

40. Arguedas, "Diario," 385-89. See also Caballero y Góngora, "Relación," 459-67, and Silvestre, "Apuntes reservados," 104-5.

41. Ezpeleta, "Relación," 154-58; Fidalgo, "Expedición Fidalgo," 188 n.

42. Howe, *People Who Would Not Kneel*, 15; Mendinueta, "Relación," 165, 167.

43. Pombo, "Informe del real consulado," 243-48; Nieto, "Geografía histórica," 202. According to French resident Luis Striffler ("El Alto Sinú," pt. 1, 325-26), who visited the Alto Sinú in 1844, Montería, next to the indigenous pueblo of Cereté, was still then the "last civilized village" before entering Emberá territory.

44. Fidalgo, "Expedición Fidalgo," 48-49 n; also 38-41 n.

45. Anonymous letter quoted in Marchena, *La institución militar*, 172.

46. Fidalgo, "Expedición Fidalgo," 48-49 n.

47. Yet these indigenous communities could not be fully exterminated, and today's censuses still report about 16,000 Zenú and 400 Chimila (Consejo Regional, *El Caribe Colombiano*, 214-19).

48. By 1790, however, the numbers of the Kuna had been cut in half—to about 5,000—as a result of war and epidemics in the previous decades (Howe, *People Who Would Not Kneel*, 15).

49. For the mid-eighteenth-century campaigns against the Chimila, see documents in De-Mier, *Poblamientos*, 2:144-69, 198-99, 226-353, 363-65, 371-75, 379-420, and Fals, *Mompox y Loba*, 103AB-114AB.

50. Blanco, *Atlántico y Barranquilla*, 77-106.

51. Torre, "Noticia individual," 43. See also P. Moreno, *Antonio de la Torre*, 34-35, 39. For a more critical analysis, see Lucena, "Las nuevas poblaciones."

52. Torre, "Noticia individual," 72-73.

53. Ibid., 46-60; P. Moreno, *Antonio de la Torre*, chap. 4.

54. Torre, "Noticia individual," 46, 48, 51; P. Moreno, *Antonio de la Torre*, 66, 84.

55. Palacios, *Diario de viaje*, 105-6. On the Chocó Indians, see Faustino Lorenzo Gómez to Roque de Quiroga, 20 November 1782, in Colombia, AHNC, CO, CI, leg. 1, rollo 1, fols. 385v, 386v.

56. Palacios, *Diario de viaje*, 89; also 37-46, 86-87, 92, 96-100.

57. Ibid., 105-6.

58. Colmenares, "El tránsito a sociedades campesinas," 19; McFarlane, *Colom-*

bia, 45. Colmenares shows that during the same period, Cauca witnessed a process of land parceling that benefited the rural poor.

59. Tovar, *Hacienda colonial*, 119.

60. Palacios, *Diario de viaje*, 23; also 19–35. On the origins of the Indian pueblo of San Cipriano in an area of gold mining inhabited by blacks, see Faustino Lorenzo Gómez to Governor, "Los indios de San Cipriano de Ayapel," 20 November 1782, in [Corrales], *Efemérides*, 1:456–57.

61. "Solicitud para que los ganados de don Nicolás Martínez . . . ," in De-Mier, *Poblamientos*, 3:107; "Don Agustín de la Sierra solicita el envio de instrucciones relativas a tributos que deben pagar los hacendados" (April 1793), ibid., 143–45.

62. Fals, *Resistencia en el San Jorge*, 79A.

63. "Fray Bartolomé de Vinaroz," in De-Mier, *Poblamientos*, 3:122–31.

64. Peredo, "Noticia historial"; [Díaz de Lamadrid], "Visita pastoral." Although most pueblos consisted of the local native population previously entrusted to *encomiendas*, a few, such as San Nicolás, San Sebastián de Urabá, and Cereté, east of the Sinú River, had been forcibly populated with subjugated Indians of the Darién, whereas San Joseph de Puerto Martín, on the San Jorge River, was founded in 1762 in an unsuccessful attempt to resettle Indians from the Chocó who consequently fled to the adjacent mountains. The pueblo de indios of San Andrés, on the Sinú, was in 1772 the only one still belonging to an *encomienda*, that of the marquis of Villalta, a resident of Havana. With a total population of 2,393, it also included the Indians of Chimú and Pinchorroy (Peredo, "Noticia historial," 137–53).

65. Reichel, Introduction to Joseph Palacios de la Vega, *Diario*, 13.

66. Joseph de Andrade to capitán aguerra, 8 May 1791, in Colombia, AHNC, CO, CI, leg. 1, rollo 1, fol. 389.

67. Faustino Lorenzo Gómez to Governor, 8 July 1792, Colombia, AHNC, CO, CI, rollo 44, tomo 44, 1792, fol. 940v.

68. Declaración de don Bernardo de Agrazot y Villalobos, 4 July 1792, ibid., fols. 942–43.

69. [Díaz de Lamadrid], "Visita pastoral," 674–75.

70. Escalante, "Notas sobre el Palenque," 231.

71. Exp. de Manuel Josef de Escobar sobre que se lleve a efecto la demolición de un pueblo del sitio de San Basilio del Palenque, in Spain, AGI, Santa Fe 1068 (1789), no. 31. See also Permiso a Manuel José Escovar para introducir a Cartagena 300 Negros de otras colonias (1789–94), Spain, AGI, Sante Fe 1073, no. 13.

72. Exp. de Manuel Josef de Escobar, Spain, AGI, Santa Fe 1068, no. 31.

73. Procurador general Manuel de Otoya to H. M., 17 December 1795, Spain, AGI, Santa Fe 1011.

74. Basilio Pérez, interview with author, Palenque de San Basilio, 19 November 1995.

75. I have found no mention of Escobar's claim and of the destruction of Palenque de San Basilio in the secondary literature, which generally skips the years from 1790 to 1880 or assumes that palenqueros lived "totally isolated from our civilization" (Escalante, "Notas sobre el Palenque," 231; see also Friedemann and Cross, *MaNgombe palenque*). In the 1830s "San Basilio or the Palenque" is listed "with 1,073 inhabi-

tants and San Cayetano with 352" in Nieto, "Geografía histórica," 183, indicating that the resettlement of the palenqueros was a failure.

76. "Fray Bartolomé de Vinaroz," in De-Mier, *Poblamientos*, 3:126.

77. Moreno y Escandón, "Estado del Virreinato," 1:182–87; "Orden de remitir los padrones de familias dispersas y traslación de los pueblos de Tacaloa y Tacamocho" (21 April 1785), in De-Mier, *Poblamientos*, 3:109–21; Blanco, *Atlántico y Barranquilla*, 77–106; Peredo, "Noticia historial," 153; Fals, *Retorno a la tierra*, 119A.

78. Expediente sobre el abandono espiritual de familias en las montañas de Cartagena (1790), in Spain, AGI, Santa Fe 1069, no. 6.

79. Palacios, *Diario de viaje*, 49–61.

80. P. Moreno, *Antonio de la Torre*, 55.

81. On a fascinating case in the province of Cauca, see Zuluaga, *Guerrilla y sociedad*.

82. Mendinueta, "Relación," 55–56.

83. Ignacio Sánchez de Texada to Pedro Mendinueta, 28 February 1803, in Spain, AGI, Estado, 52, no. 137, fols. 15–16.

84. Mendinueta to Pedro Ceballos, 19 April 1803, ibid., fols. 1–10; see also Mendinueta to Sánchez de Texada, 9 April 1803, ibid., fols. 16–18.

85. On the opening and closing of frontiers, see Limerick, *Legacy of Conquest*, 23. For a comparative discussion of the colonial frontier, see Lockhart and Schwartz, *Early Latin America*, 253–304.

CHAPTER TWO

1. Silvestre, "Apuntes reservados," 101.

2. Pedro Mendinueta to Juan Manuel Alvarez, 19 May 1799, in Spain, AGI, Estado, 52, no. 76, fols. 147–48.

3. This figure includes the total population of the provinces of Cartagena (119,453), Santa Marta (46,985), and Riohacha (3,966) (Tovar, "Convocatoria," 503, 519, 537).

4. This percentage represents the 35,051 inhabitants living in the districts of Cartagena (13,396), Mompox (7,197), Santa Marta (3,598), Valledupar (3,677), Riohacha (1,515), and Ocaña (5,668) out of the official population of 170,404 in the three provinces in 1777–80 (censuses in Tovar, "Convocatoria," 487–519, 533–37). The interior city of Ocaña is not included in this study because it is closer to and shares more socioeconomic and cultural features with the northeastern colonial province of Pamplona (today the department of Norte de Santander, to which it belongs) than with the Caribbean region.

5. Another 21,483 free people of color lived in the main cities, bringing the total of the free population of color to 109,271 in the three provinces, according to the 1777–80 census (Tovar, "Convocatoria," 477–80, 512–14, 535). These figures do not include the thousands of Indians and free people of color living on the periphery (see Chapter 1).

6. Narváez, "Provincia de Santa Marta," 45.

7. Tovar, "*Convocatoria*," 477-80, 512-14, 535.

8. Among the *libres de color* in Riohacha Province, 67.3 percent were classified as mulatto (pardo); 26.6 percent, as zambo; 5.1 percent, as black; and less that 1.0 percent (27 persons), as mestizo (Tovar, "*Convocatoria*," 533).

9. Only the census returns of the city of Cartagena include the racial categories of individuals (see Chapter 3).

10. For example, Joseph [Fernández Díaz de Lamadrid], obispo de Cartagena, a arzobispo confesor Joaquin de Eletta, 6 February 1781, in Spain, AGI, Santa Fe 1171 (published in Bell, *Cartagena de Indias*, 152-61), and [Bache], *Notes on Colombia*, 256-57.

11. Mollien, *Voyage*, 1:26.

12. Colmenares, *Popayán*, 43; Peñas, *Los bogas*, 33-53. Eltis et al.'s *Trans-Atlantic Slave Trade: A Database on CD-ROM* has the records of 280 ships that disembarked 47,090 slaves in Cartagena between 1595 and 1793, chiefly in the peak years of 1595-1603 and 1618-40.

13. Gómez to Governor, "Los indios de San Cipriano," in [Corrales], *Efemérides*, 1:456-57; Gordon, *Human Geography*, 8-9; Twinam, *Miners*, 17, 40.

14. T. D. Gutiérrez, *Cultura vallenata*, 199-222.

15. Reclus, *Viaje*, 87; Fals, *Resistencia en el San Jorge*, 67A-73A, 67B-69B.

16. This figure does not include Indians in sovereign nations.

17. Tovar, "*Convocatoria*," 492-94, 510-12, 535.

18. Whereas in Cartagena Province only one-third of slaves resided in the principal cities of Cartagena and Mompox, a majority of slaves in Santa Marta and Riohacha Provinces lived in the cities of Ocaña, Valledupar, Santa Marta, and Riohacha. For a discussion of urban slavery, see Chapter 3.

19. The four villages were El Paso, San José Barrancas, Fonseca, and Becerril (Tovar, "*Convocatoria*," 514-16, 518-19).

20. Tovar, "*Convocatoria*," 497-99, 501-3.

21. Cited in Kuethe, *Military Reform*, 31. On limpieza de sangre, see Chapter 3.

22. A total of 7,727 whites lived in the main cities of Cartagena, Mompox, Santa Marta, Valledupar, Ocaña, and Riohacha (43.8 percent of all whites in the three coastal provinces) (censuses in Tovar, "*Convocatoria*," 489-92, 509-10, 534).

23. Pombo, "Informe de José Ignacio de Pombo," 132.

24. Fidalgo, "Expedición Fidalgo," 55 n. In addition to the trails from Cartagena and Santa Marta to the Magdalena Delta, one trail linked Mompox to Valledupar and Riohacha, and from there to the Lake of Maracaibo. Another trail connected San Benito Abad, on the San Jorge, to Sincelejo and Tolú, on the Caribbean Sea south of Cartagena. Sincelejo was also connected to Mahates, on the Canal del Dique. From Simití, on the Magdalena, one track went west to Ayapel, in the valley of the San Jorge, and another went east to Ocaña and Pamplona, in the eastern cordillera.

25. Nichols, *Tres puertos*, 39-41; Fidalgo, "Expedición Fidalgo," 76 n; Consejo Regional, *Mapa cultural*, maps on 51, 85; McFarlane, *Colombia*, 39-40.

26. Joseph a arzobispo confesor, in Spain, AGI, Santa Fe 1171.

27. For the difficulties of traveling in the interior, see [Díaz de Lamadrid], "Visita pastoral"; Mollien, *Voyage*; and Striffler, "El Alto Sinú," pt. 1, 317–46.

28. Colmenares, "El tránsito a sociedades campesinas," 19; McFarlane, *Colombia*, 45.

29. Pacheco, "La expulsión de los jesuítas."

30. Tovar, *Hacienda colonial*, 31–33, 36, 42.

31. "Solicitud para que los ganados de don Nicolás Martínez no arruinen las tierras de los indios" (4 March 1785), in De-Mier, *Poblamientos*, 3:106–9.

32. Tovar, *Hacienda colonial*, 39, 94–95. Other prominent landholding families were the Maestre, Araújo, Mozo de la Torre, Trespalacios, Díaz Granados, and Hoyos.

33. Peredo, "Noticia historial," 137–38, 140–43, 146–50, 153–54; [Díaz de Lamadrid], "Visita pastoral," 660–62, 673–74, 693–97. See also Tovar, *Hacienda colonial*, 28, 94, and T. D. Gutiérrez, *Valledupar*, 187.

34. Tovar, *Hacienda colonial*, 234–35. For the same trend in Caracas, see McKinley, *Pre-Revolutionary Caracas*, 59–61.

35. Tovar, *Hacienda colonial*, 48–54, 102; Romero, *Esclavitud*, 93, 95–96; Fals, *Mompox y Loba*, 119B; McFarlane, *Colombia*, 45–46.

36. Meisel, "Esclavitud, mestizaje y haciendas," 123–24; Fals, *Mompox y Loba*, 118B–123B; Colmenares, "El tránsito a sociedades campesinas," 19.

37. Romero, *Esclavitud*, 95–97.

38. P. Moreno, *Antonio de la Torre*, 48–62. For examples of hacendados's influence on justice, see Melchor de los Reyes esclavo de la testamentaria de Dn Martin de Zetuain clama por su libertad (tomo 4, 1806, fols. 1005–7) and Causa criminal contra don Pablo García, formada por el marqués de Torrehoyos (tomo 6, 1796–97, fol. 998), both in Colombia, AHNC, CO, NE.

39. Palacios, *Diario de viaje*, 49–52, 104.

40. Ibid., 71, 93, 95; Gil y Lemos, "Relación," 17–18.

41. Permiso a Manuel José Escovar para introducir a Cartagena 300 Negros de otras colonias (1789–94), in Spain, AGI, Santa Fe 1073, no. 13. On Escobar's petition to have Palenque de San Basilio destroyed and its inhabitants forcibly resettled, see Chapter 1.

42. "Litigio entre el alcalde de Tamalameque y el marqués de Torre Hoyos, por causa de jurisdicción y facultades concedidas a éste" (18 May 1794), in De-Mier, *Poblamientos*, 3:150.

43. "Fray Bartolomé de Vinaroz," ibid., 3:122–31. On the role of alcaldes ordinarios, see McFarlane, *Colombia*, 245–46.

44. "Orden de remitir los padrones de familias dispersas y traslación de los pueblos de Tacaloa y Tacamocho" (21 April 1785), in De-Mier, *Poblamientos*, 3:120–21. On the status of vecino, see Guerra, "El soberano y su reino," 41, and Herzog, *Defining Nations*, 43–63.

45. Causa criminal contra García por el marqués de Torrehoyos, in Colombia, AHNC, CO, NE, tomo 6, 1796–97, fols. 968–1021. On the marquis of Torre-Hoyos, see Tovar, *Hacienda colonial*, 117, and Fals, *Mompox y Loba*, 126A–B.

46. Moreno y Escandón, "Estado del Virreinato," 156–57; Palacios, *Diario de viaje*, 49–52, 71.

47. Humboldt, *En Colombia*, "Diario VII a y b," fol. 35.

48. "Solicitud para que los ganados de don Nicolás Martínez," in De-Mier, *Poblamientos*, 3:106–9; Romero, *Esclavitud*, 72.

49. "Fray Bartolomé de Vinaroz," in De-Mier, *Poblamientos*, 3:122–31.

50. "Litigio entre el alcalde de Tamalameque y el marqués de Torre Hoyos," ibid., 3:145–84; "Como consecuencia del litigio con el alcalde de Tamalameque, se reconocen y renuevan las facultades y jurisdicción en favor del marqués de Torre Hoyos" (11 December 1795), ibid., 3:184–248; "Vicente García, alcalde de Tamalameque, promueve nueva causa contra el marqués de Torre Hoyos" (20 October 1797), ibid., 3:259–70; "El marqués de Torre Hoyos renuncia a la jurisdicción sobre las nuevas poblaciones de la provincia de Santa Marta" (23 October 1797), ibid., 3:271–98.

51. Dominga Pérez, sobre su libertad, in Colombia, AHNC, CO, NE, tomo 9, 1799, fols. 564–633v. The *Ley de Siete Partidas*, compiled by King Alfonso the Wise of Castile in the thirteenth century, established the rights and obligations of slaves and regulated such aspects as slaves' manumission, marriage, punishment, and the status of their children (Sharp, *Slavery on the Spanish Frontier*, 127).

52. Barbier, "Commercial Reform," 96–102.

53. Narváez, "Provincia de Santa Marta," 19, 35–36, 53, 58–60.

54. Narváez, "Discurso," 71.

55. For an analysis of the dyewood monopoly, see McFarlane, *Colombia*, 144–50.

56. Ernesto Restrepo, *Historia de la provincia*, 469–70; Barbier, "Commercial Reform," 102–11; Acosta, *Vida de los esclavos*, 19–22, 58–64, 118.

57. Permiso a Manuel José Escovar para introducir a Cartagena 300 Negros de otras colonias, 1789–94, in Spain, AGI, Santa Fe 1073, no. 13.

58. Narváez, "Discurso," 93.

59. Ibid., 73; McFarlane, *Colombia*, 142–43.

60. Informe de los hacendados dueños de ingenios de trapiches al gobernador de la provincia de Cartagena, Joaquin de Cañaverales, 17 October 1789, in Spain, AGI, Santa Fe 1015; Tovar, *Hacienda colonial*, 48, 50, 249–54; Colmenares, "El tránsito a sociedades campesinas," 8–24; Jaramillo, *Ensayos sobre historia social*, 2:71–72.

61. McFarlane, *Colombia*, 297–307; Narváez, "Discurso," 98.

62. Pombo, "Informe de José Ignacio de Pombo," 121–34. On contraband, see Sindico a junta del consulado, 13 October 1795, in Spain, AGI, Santa Fe 1011.

63. On the Botanical Expedition, see Jara, *La expedición botánica*.

64. See, e.g., Informe del cura José Nicomedes de Fonseca y Mesa sobre la parroquia de Plato al obispo Cerrudo, 27 January 1809 (copy by Manuel José Ordoñez, priest in Plato, 12 November 1884), in Colombia, AESM, tomo 71a, 1884, fols. 76–77.

65. For an analysis of the Bourbon fiscal reforms, see McFarlane, *Colombia*, 208–27, and Phelan, *People and the King*, 29–34.

66. Kuethe, *Military Reform*, 7–13, 18–24, 196–97; Marchena, *La institución militar*, 431–61.

67. Kuethe, *Military Reform*, 22–23, 99–100; Marchena, *La institución militar*, 432, 450–53.

68. L. García, *Reseña histórica*, 250–51, 254.

69. [Díaz de Lamadrid], "Visita pastoral," 698.

70. Joseph a arzobispo confesor, in Spain, AGI, Santa Fe 1171.

71. [Díaz de Lamadrid], "Visita pastoral," 643–44, 650, 656, 677, 688; Joseph a arzobispo confesor, in Spain, AGI, Santa Fe 1171.

72. [Díaz de Lamadrid], "Visita pastoral."

73. Joseph a arzobispo confesor, in Spain, AGI, Santa Fe 1171. See also Peredo, "Noticia historial," 148–49.

74. [Díaz de Lamadrid], "Visita pastoral," 657, 671.

75. Ibid., 654; also 656–61, 675, 682–86.

76. Ibid., 656, 660, 698; Joseph a arzobispo confesor, in Spain, AGI, Santa Fe 1171; Peredo, "Noticia historial," 149–50; See also Bensusan, "Cartagena's Fandango Politics," 128.

77. [Díaz de Lamadrid], "Visita pastoral," 682.

78. Representación de Mompox, 21 January 1797, in Spain, AGI, Santa Fe 1073, doc. 10, no. 4.

79. Joseph a arzobispo confesor, ibid., Santa Fe 1171; [Díaz de Lamadrid], "Visita pastoral."

80. Joseph a arzobispo confesor, in Spain, AGI, Santa Fe 1171.

81. Bensusan, "Cartagena's Fandango Politics," 127–32.

82. [Díaz de Lamadrid], "Visita pastoral," 694; also 660–62, 673–74, 693–97. See also Joseph a arzobispo confesor, in Spain, AGI, Santa Fe 1171; Peredo, "Noticia historial"; and Tovar, *Hacienda colonial*, 94.

83. [Díaz de Lamadrid], "Visita pastoral," 693.

84. Pleito seguido por Melchor Sáenz Ortiz, Mompox, in Colombia, AHNC, CO, NE, tomo 4, 1796, fol. 534v.

85. [Díaz de Lamadrid], "Visita pastoral," 696; also 673–74, 693–97.

86. Martínez, *Cartas de los obispos*, 559–62.

87. Carta confidencial de A. Amar a C. Soler, [18 August 1805], in Spain, AGI, Santa Fe 579.

88. Pedro Mendinueta to Juan Manuel Alvarez, 19 May 1799, Spain, AGI, Estado, 52, no. 76, fols. 147–48.

89. On the Comunero Revolt, see Phelan, *People and the King*, and McFarlane, *Colombia*, 251–71.

90. Loy, "Forgotten Comuneros."

91. Phelan, *People and the King*, 110–11, 153, 193–94.

92. Orlando Fals Borda studied the late colonial period extensively looking for "mechanisms of popular counterpower" and "movements of armed resistance" by the Caribbean region's "working masses" emulating the Comunero Revolt, which he defines as a "revolution" and "the prologue to the war of national independence initiated in 1810." He found only two such occurrences, the "mutiny of the peasants of Ayapel" in 1785 and "the sedition of the 'Indians' of Jegua" in 1784. Although these cases show the ability of two rural communities—one mostly of African de-

scent, the other, indigenous—to resist abuse by the representatives of Spain, Fals presents no evidence that they had any links with the Comunero Revolt, that they questioned the authority of the king, or that they envisioned an independent egalitarian nation. In both cases the people renounced their revolt after the local priest intervened, a denouement not discussed by Fals. Moreover, Fals does not examine in depth why armed resistance was limited to these two cases (Fals, *Resistencia en el San Jorge*, 80B–95B).

93. Phelan, *People and the King*, 26.

94. "Consulta del Consejo de las Indias, sobre una representación de la Audiencia de Guatemala [. . .]," 31 October 1782, in Konetzke, *Colección de documentos*, 500. See also "Consulta del Consejo de las Indias sobre los motivos que ha tenido el gobernador e intendente de Nicaragua para no proceder a la exacción del tributo que se impone a los mulatos y negros libres," 10 September 1788, ibid., 628–31.

95. McFarlane, *Colombia*, 271, 252.

96. Tovar, *Hacienda colonial*, 119.

97. Julián, *La perla de la América*, 76–80; Fals, *Resistencia en el San Jorge*, 70A–79A, and *Mompox y Loba*, 95B, 111B; T. D. Gutiérrez, *Cultura vallenata*, 49, 254–55.

98. Phelan, *People and the King*, 161, 171.

99. In 1823 an anonymous British officer described the long-standing tensions between Andean and Caribbean New Granada as "a great want of cordiality" based on "the discordant modifications of habits and manners produced by diversity of climate and position" (*Present State of Colombia*, 262).

100. Jaramillo, *Ensayos sobre historia social*, 1:59, 67. This case is also analyzed in Tovar, *De una chispa*, 24–25, 31. For a similar case on a cattle-raising hacienda in Santa Marta Province in 1768, see McFarlane, "*Cimarrones* and *palenques*," 138–39. There, the slaves killed their overseer and were able to force their master into negotiations over labor conditions by threatening to destroy the hacienda and join the "wild Indians."

101. Tovar, *De una chispa*, 63.

102. Ibid., 18, 22–24, 53–58; Romero, *Esclavitud*, 119–39. For similar strategies in Peru, see Hünefeldt, *Paying the Price of Freedom*.

103. Geggus, "Slavery, War, and Revolution"; Brito, *Las insurrecciones de los esclavos*, 59–77. Slave rebellions are further discussed in Chapter 3 and the Conclusion.

104. Gómez to Governor, "Los indios de San Cipriano," in [Corrales], *Efemérides*, 1:456–57.

105. See, e.g., "Solicitud para que los ganados de don Nicolás Martínez," in De-Mier, *Poblamientos*, 3:107, and Fals, *Mompox y Loba*, 117A–118A.

106. Geggus, "Slavery, War, and Revolution," 21–22.

107. Kuethe, *Military Reform*, 134–36. On the militias' defense of the Sinú River against attacks from the Darién Indians, see Ezpeleta, "Relación," 293.

108. Informe sobre escasez de víveres en Cartagena, 17 November 1809, in Spain, AGI, Santa Fe 745.

109. Le Moyne, *Viaje*, 39.

110. Fidalgo, "Expedición Fidalgo," 81–83 n. For another denigrating comment, see J. M. Restrepo, *Historia de la revolución*, 1:41.

111. For more sympathetic comments, see Le Moyne, *Viaje*, 36–52, and Mollien, *Voyage*, 1:30–35.

112. For a detailed description of the bogas' technique, see Humboldt, *En Colombia*, "Diario VII a y b," fols. 11–15.

113. Mollien, *Voyage*, 1:35. See also Le Moyne, *Viaje*, 36–52, and Fidalgo, "Expedición Fidalgo," 81–83 n.

114. Humboldt, *En Colombia*, "Diario VII a y b," fol. 13. One real was worth one-eighth of a peso.

115. Le Moyne, *Viaje*, 39.

116. Fidalgo, "Expedición Fidalgo," 81–83 n; Mollien, *Voyage*, 1:45.

117. Narváez, "Discurso," 73. See also McFarlane, *Colombia*, 142–43.

118. Dominga Pérez, sobre su libertad, in Colombia, AHNC, CO, NE, tomo 9, 1799, fols. 572v–573v.

119. Informe sobre escasez de víveres, in Spain, AGI, Santa Fe 745.

120. Stern, "New Approaches," 11–18.

121. Taylor, *Drinking, Homicide, and Rebellion*, 145, 153. See also Guardino, *Peasants, Politics*, 24–27.

122. Pablo García sobre su noble ascendencia gallega, y la de Rafaela Montes, su consorte, 1799–1805, in Colombia, AHNC, CO, GN, rollo 3, fols. 34–34v.

123. "Litigio entre el alcalde de Tamalameque y el marqués de Torre Hoyos," in De-Mier, *Poblamientos*, 3:154–55; see also 3:213, 217. On Pedro Juan Tinoco, see Causa criminal contra García por el marqués de Torrehoyos, in Colombia, AHNC, CO, NE, tomo 6, 1796–97, fol. 969v.

124. "Los vecinos de El Banco reconocen la autoridad y jurisdicción del marqués de Torre Hoyos" (17 March 1796), in De-Mier, *Poblamientos*, 3:249–50, 252, 254, 257.

125. "Vicente García contra el marqués de Torre Hoyos," ibid., 3:268.

126. See Messía, "Relación," 139–41, and Guirior, "Instrucción," 295–303.

127. For general descriptions of the contraband trade, see Gil y Lemos, "Relación," 6–8; Manuel Trinidad Noriega, residente de Cartagena, representa el actual estado del comercio clandestino (20 April 1806), in Colombia, AHNC, CO, AD, fols. 285–94; Humboldt, *En Colombia*, "Diario VII a y b," fols. 39–40; Palacios, *Diario de viaje*, 49–52, 104; and Torre, "Noticia individual," 47.

128. Pombo, "Informe del real consulado," 145.

129. In 1777 the *quinto* collected on all bullion represented 3 percent of the value of gold dust (Sharp, *Slavery on the Spanish Frontier*, 62). On the importance of contraband in the Chocó, see ibid., 61–97.

130. Sindico to Junta del consulado, 13 October 1795, in Spain, AGI, Santa Fe 1011; Silvestre, "Apuntes reservados," 82.

131. Ezpeleta, "Relación," 237.

132. Manuel Trinidad Noriega, residente de Cartagena, representa el actual es-

tado del comercio clandestino, 20 April 1806, in Colombia, AHNC, CO, AD, leg. 4, fol. 289.

133. Mendinueta, "Relación," 102.

134. Narváez, "Discurso," 75.

135. Antonio Vacaro a presidente de la suprema junta de gobierno de España e Indias, 1 October 1808, in Spain, AGI, Santa Fe 745.

136. Pombo, "Informe del real consulado," 156, 203; Múnera, *El fracaso de la nación*, 48.

137. Caballero y Góngora, "Relación," 410.

138. Ezpeleta, "Relación," 207; Mendinueta, "Relación," 53; Narváez, "Discurso," 73.

139. Mendinueta, "Relación," 73-74.

140. Mollien, *Voyage*, 1:46.

141. On New Granada in general, see McFarlane, "*Cimarrones* and *palenques*," 138-43. For a mine recording fugitives, see Pleito seguido por Melchor Sanchez Ortiz, in Colombia, AHNC, CO, NE, tomo 4, 1796, fol. 552v.

142. Francisco Barcena Posada contra Melchor Saenz Ortiz, Mompox, in Colombia, AHNC, CO, NE, tomo 8, 1806, fols. 700-718.

143. Declaración de Rafaela Martínez, in Causa criminal contra García por el marqués de Torrehoyos, Colombia, AHNC, CO, NE, tomo 6, 1796-97, fol. 1013.

144. Melchor de los Reyes clama por su libertad, Colombia, AHNC, CO, NE, tomo 4, 1806, fols. 1005-7.

145. [Díaz de Lamadrid], "Visita pastoral," 654, 656, 660-61, 675; Palacios, *Diario de viaje*, 71, 75-76. On continuing burials in the 1840s in the woods in Plato, east of the Magdalena River, see Provincial Governor of Santa Marta to Bishop, 26 February 1845, in Colombia, AESM, tomo 57, 1845, fol. 134.

146. [Díaz de Lamadrid], "Visita pastoral."

147. Ibid., 684; also 646, 659-60.

148. Joseph a arzobispo confesor, in Spain, AGI, Santa Fe 1171.

149. [Díaz de Lamadrid], "Visita pastoral," 677. Sincelejo was then called San Francisco de Asís.

150. Sobre insurrección de los indígenas de la Villa de San Jerónimo de Ayapel, in Colombia, AHNC, CO, CI, rollo 19, tomo 18, 1794, fols. 249-70. See also Fals, *Resistencia en el San Jorge*, 83A-88A.

151. [Díaz de Lamadrid], "Visita pastoral," 669-70; also 689-90.

152. Ibid., 647, 663-64. On Barranquilla's population, see McFarlane, *Colombia*, 357.

153. [Díaz de Lamadrid], "Visita pastoral," 681, 675.

154. Ibid., 678-79, 681-82, 685-86, 688. On Indian pueblos in Santa Marta and Riohacha Provinces, see Saether, "Identities and Independence," 155-66.

155. [Díaz de Lamadrid], "Visita pastoral," 652-53. On the idolatry of Indians in Tetón, see also Peredo, "Noticia historial," 147.

156. See, e.g., Zoilo M. Arce, Informe de la parroquia de Remolino, 30 January 1884, in Colombia, AESM, tomo 122, fols. 80-82; *Carta pastoral*.

157. [Díaz de Lamadrid], "Visita pastoral," 681–82; also 679, 688.

158. Ibid., 684–85; Bensusan, "Cartagena's Fandango Politics," 128.

159. Ezpeleta, "Relación," 237.

160. Ibid., 207.

CHAPTER THREE

1. Pedro Mendinueta to Josef Antonio Caballero, 19 November 1800, in Spain, AGI, Estado 52, no. 102, fol. 2. In reality, a majority of slaves were natives of New Granada.

2. Mendinueta to Francisco de Saavedra, 19 July 1799, Spain, AGI, Estado 52, no. 81, fols. 1–2.

3. Mendinueta to Juan Manuel Alvarez, 19 May 1799, in Spain, AGS, Guerra 7247, exp. 26, fols. 147–48.

4. Guerra, *Modernidad e independencias*, 64–71; McFarlane, "Building Political Order," 14–15.

5. Censuses in Tovar, *"Convocatoria,"* 487–519, 533–37. Indians comprised no more than 0.5 percent of the inhabitants of Cartagena, 1.1 percent of those from Mompox and Riohacha, and 0.6 percent of those from Santa Marta; no Indians were registered in Valledupar.

6. Tovar, *"Convocatoria,"* 487–503. According to a detailed study of the 1777 census of Cartagena, 29.5 percent of its inhabitants were white; 49.3 percent, free people of color; 18.9 percent, slaves; 1.7 percent, ecclesiastics; and 0.6 percent, Indians (Meisel and Aguilera, "Cartagena de Indias," 31).

7. Fidalgo, "Expedición Fidalgo," 118 n; Bossa, *Cartagena independiente*, 29.

8. Padrón del barrio de Sto. Thoribio, año de 1777, in Colombia, AHNC, CO, MI, tomo 41, fols. 1004–79; Padrón que comprehende el barrio de Nra. Sa. de La Merced, y su vecindario, formado en el año de 1777, por su comisario Dn. Francisco Pedro Vidal, capitán de Milicias de Blancos, in Colombia, AHNC, CO, CV, tomo 8, fols. 134–64; Razón del barrio de San Sebastián, Año de 1777 (signed Pedro Thomás de Villanueva), in Colombia, AHNC, CO, MI, tomo 44, fols. 946–57; Padrón general ejecutado por Dn. Mariano José de Valverde, regidor interino de M.I.C.J. y Regimiento de esta ciudad de Cartagena de Indias y en ella comisario del barrio de la Sma. Trinidad de Gimaní en el presente año de 1777, in Colombia, AHNC, CO, CV, tomo 8, fols. 75–133. The census returns for the barrio of Santa Catalina are missing. Unfortunately, the parish and notarial records for this time period, with which the census data could have been complemented, have not been found. See also Urueta, *Cartagena*, and Sourdis, *Cartagena*, 15–16.

9. Marco, *Cartagena de Indias*, 297–301; Marchena, *La institución militar*, 314–19.

10. Mollien, *Voyage*, 1:45–50; McFarlane, *Colombia*, 41, 44–48.

11. Kuethe, *Military Reform*, 8–15; McFarlane, *Colombia*, 181–84.

12. Relación que comprende los artesanos que viven en el Barrio de Sn. Sebastián de esta ciudad con expresión de sus nombres, casas, edades y los que son milicianos, in Colombia, AHNC, CO, MI, rollo 31, fols. 1014–15; Relación que manifiesta los

artesanos que existen en el Barrio de Sto. Thoribio el presente año de 1780, ibid., fols. 148-54; Mendinueta to ministro de hacienda, Razón circunstanciada de la clase y cantidad de pesca que se hace en las costas de este virreinado, 3 June 1803, in Spain, AGI, Santa Fe 1016. See also Arévalo, "Informe"; Mollien, *Voyage*, 1:16-17; and McFarlane, *Colombia*, 43.

13. Informe de los hacendados dueños de ingenios de trapiches al gobernador de la provincia de Cartagena, Joaquin de Cañaverales, 17 October 1789, in Spain, AGI, Santa Fe 1015; Mendinueta, "Relación," 3:126. See also Barbier, "Commercial Reform," 106; Meisel, "Esclavitud, mestizaje y haciendas," 110-11; and McFarlane, *Colombia*, 142-52, 161-62.

14. "Apuntamientos para escribir una ojeada sobre la historia de la transformación política de la Provincia de Cartagena," n.d., in [Corrales], *Documentos*, 1:127; Bossa, *Cartagena independiente*, 124; Múnera, *El fracaso de la nación*, 103-10.

15. Mendinueta to Caballero, 19 November 1800, in Spain, AGI, Estado 52, no. 102, fol. 2.

16. Tovar, *"Convocatoria,"* 487-503.

17. Humboldt, "Diario VII a y b," fols. 16, 22.

18. Salzedo, *Apuntaciones*, 65, 69-70, 78-79, 81-82; "Exposición de los Representantes de la Provincia de Mompox al Congreso general de este Reino, para que se les admita en su seno," 1 January 1811, in [Corrales], *Documentos*, 1:232.

19. Tovar, *"Convocatoria,"* 507-19.

20. E. Restrepo, *Historia de la provincia*, 440; L. García, *Reseña histórica*, 253-54, 270, 282, 284-87, 290-91; Reclus, *Viaje*, 93-94.

21. Saether, "Identities and Independence," 68, 73-75, 85-88.

22. *Cartas escritas desde Colombia*, 124.

23. E. Restrepo, *Historia de la provincia*, 440; Silvestre, "Apuntes reservados," 86.

24. Romero, *Esclavitud*, 72. During the same years Cartagena legally imported 1,480 bozales (many of them for the Chocó), and Riohacha imported 57 (Barbier, "Commercial Reform," 106; E. Restrepo, *Historia de la provincia*, 479).

25. E. Restrepo, *Historia de la provincia*, 483-86.

26. Tovar, *"Convocatoria,"* 507-19.

27. T. D. Gutiérrez, *Valledupar*, 77-81, 183-88; Fidalgo, "Expedición Fidalgo," 71 n; Saether, "Identities and Independence," 102-4.

28. Tovar, *"Convocatoria,"* 533-37; Fidalgo, "Expedición Fidalgo," 48-49 n; Reclus, *Viaje*, 153-60; E. Restrepo, *Historia de la provincia*, 445; Robles, *Recuerdos del Riohacha*. On the pearl bonanza in Riohacha in the early 1750s, see Julián, *La perla de la América*, 10-24.

29. Ezpeleta, "Relación," 255-56; Fidalgo, "Expedición Fidalgo," 48-49 n; E. Restrepo, *Historia de la provincia*, 421, 464-65, 475, 479-86, 512; Pedraja, "La Guajira," 4; Romero, *Esclavitud*, 28-29.

30. Nichols, *Tres puertos*, 33.

31. Romero, *Esclavitud*, 28-29.

32. Germán, "Gobernantes de Mompox," 534. Mompox had already been elevated to a province from 1561 to 1680 (pp. 530-31).

33. "Exposición de los Representantes de la Provincia de Mompox," 1 January 1811, in [Corrales], *Documentos*, 1:233.

34. See, e.g., El cabildo de Cartagena previene sobre falsedad de un informe favorable a Joaquín Cañaveral, 1795, in Spain, AGS, Guerra 7085, exp. 8.

35. Saether, "Identities and Independence," 346-48; Múnera, *El fracaso de la nación*, 107, 156, 191; König, *En el camino*, 71-185.

36. On the role of sailors in the spread of revolutionary ideas, see Julius Scott, "Common Wind."

37. L. García, *Reseña histórica*, 245, 292.

38. Informe de los hacendados al gobernador, 17 October 1789, in Spain, AGI, Santa Fe 1015.

39. Pombo, "Informe de José Ignacio de Pombo," 121-34. On contraband, see Sindico a junta del consulado, 13 October 1795, in Spain, AGI, Santa Fe 1011. See also Múnera, *El fracaso de la nación*, 103-10, 128-36, 138-39; McFarlane, *Colombia*, 298-306; and König, *En el camino*, 71-125.

40. Salzedo, *Apuntaciones*, 73-89; Fals, *Mompox y Loba*, 127A-132A.

41. Joaquín de Cañaverales to conde de Lerena, 30 November 1791, in Spain, AGI, Santa Fe 1015.

42. Fals, *Mompox y Loba*, 132A; Garrido, *Reclamos y representaciones*, 156-59.

43. Domínguez, *Insurrection or Loyalty*, 36-40.

44. See, e.g., "Estatutos del colegio real y seminario de San Carlos en Cartagena de Indias," 29 December 1786, in Konetzke, *Colección de documentos*, 622-23.

45. See, e.g., ibid.; "R. C. que para el ejército de las artes y oficios no haya de servir de impedimento la ilegitimidad," 2 September 1784, ibid., 539-40; and "Real habilitación de un hijo natural para ejercer el oficio de escribano y notario real de las Indias," 23 May 1791, ibid., 691-92.

46. See, e.g., Información de cristianidad y limpieza de sangre acreditada a pedimiento de don Marcos Quezada, Cartagena, 1785, in Colombia, AHNC, CO, GN, rollo 5, fols. 692-710; Información que acredita la legitimidad, limpieza de sangre, vida y costumbres de don Manuel Francisco de Paula Pérez y sus ascendientes, Cartagena, 1787, ibid., fols. 511-49; Pablo García sobre su noble ascendencia gallega, 1799-1805, ibid., rollo 3, fols. 1-41v; and Certificación de don Marcos Carrasquilla, natural y vecino de Cartagena, 17 November 1797, in Spain, AGI, Santa Fe 1079.

47. "Consulta del Consejo de Indias sobre las reglas establecidas de la Audiencia de Méjico en cumplimiento de la real pragmática del año de 1778 referente a los matrimonios," 1 August 1781, in Konetzke, *Colección de documentos*, 477 (quotation); Martínez-Alier, *Marriage, Class, and Colour*, 11; Hanger, *Bounded Lives*, 92; Waldron, "Sinners and the Bishop," 162-63.

48. Martínez-Alier, *Marriage, Class, and Colour*, 12-13.

49. Twinam, "Is Race a 'Defect'?" Twinam notes that the dispensations of the condition (*calidad*) of pardo and quinterón are the last two in the list, that the fee for quinterones (1,100 reales) is higher than the fee for the darker pardos (700 reales), and that both fees are much lower than for most other dispensations (4,000 reales for illegitimate birth, for example). For the complete price list, see "R. C. insertando el

nuevo arancel de los servicios pecuniarios señalados a las gracias al sacar," 3 August 1801, in Konetzke, *Colección de documentos*, 778–83.

50. "Informe del ayuntamiento de Caracas," 28 November 1796, in Izard, *El miedo a la revolución*, 129–30, n. 16.

51. "Consulta del consejo sobre la habilitación de pardos para empleos y matrimonios," July 1806, in Konetzke, *Colección de documentos*, 822, 824, 827–28.

52. "Dictamen del fiscal en el Consejo de las Indias sobre declarar en América que las artes y oficios mecánicos son nobles," 24 January 1807, ibid., 832–34.

53. "Consulta del consejo sobre la habilitación de pardos," ibid., 826, 828.

54. In 1777, on average for the five cities, there were 136.5 free and slave women and girls of color per 100.0 males, and a very high 190.3 females per 100.0 males among Cartagena's free population of color (Tovar, *"Convocatoria,"* 487–519, 533–37).

55. Tovar, *"Convocatoria,"* 484, 489, 492, 494, 497; P. Rodríguez, *Sentimiento*, 83.

56. See, e.g., Colombia, APC, Libro de bautismos de pardos y morenos, 1803–11 (copiador); APC, Libro de bautismos de blancos, 1799–1820 (copiador); and APST, Libro de bautismos de pardos y morenos que empieza oy día nueve de noviembre deste año de 1795 por su actual cura rector Licenciado Andrés Navarro y Azevedo (termina 28 marzo 1803).

57. "Consulta del Consejo de las Indias sobre la declaración de que los espósitos debían considerarse exentos de la paga de tributo," 17 December 1802, in Konetzke, *Colección de documentos*, 786–91. In this document, the council recognizes the difficulty of classifying foundlings racially based on their physical appearance.

58. See McKinley, *Pre-Revolutionary Caracas*, 116–19.

59. Meisel and Aguilera, "Cartagena de Indias," 52. For a discussion of the title of "don," see Twinam, *Public Lives*, 4–5, and Jaramillo, *Ensayos sobre historia social*, 1:191–98.

60. On Santa Marta, see Romero, *Esclavitud*, 87.

61. Juan and Ulloa, *Relación histórica*, 41.

62. See, e.g., Causa criminal contra don Pablo García, formada por el marqués de Torrehoyos, in Colombia, AHNC, CO, NE, tomo 6, 1796–97, fol. 969v, and Francisco Barcena Posada contra Melchor Sáenz Ortiz, Mompox, ibid., tomo 8, 1806, fol. 785v.

63. Jaramillo, *Ensayos sobre historia social*, 1:189.

64. Padrón de La Merced, fol. 163; Razón de San Sebastián, ibid., fol. 949v.

65. Expediente de varias religiosas del Monasterio de Santa Clara de Cartagena quejándose de las violencias que dicen han sufrido en la admisión de una novicia inhábil, 25 November 1797, in Spain, AGI, Santa Fe 1077, 1798, Consejo, no. 10.

66. Expediente de varias religiosas, ibid.

67. Expediente sobre el abuso que hay en Cartagena de celebrarse matrimonios clandestinos, 18 May 1802, in Spain, AGI, Santa Fe 744, no. 7.

68. Expediente de varias religiosas. On the status of children of sacrilege, see Twinam, *Public Lives*, 128.

69. See, e.g., Causa criminal contra García por el marqués de Torrehoyos, in Colombia, AHNC, CO, NE, tomo 6, 1796–97, fol. 969v, and Barcena contra Sáenz, ibid., tomo 8, 1806, fol. 785v.

70. José Noble, vecino de Cartagena, solicitando se declare a Diego su hijo y demás hermanos por Españoles, libres del origen de pardos, y hábil para ser admitido en el colegio de San Carlos de Cartagena, in Spain, AGI, Santa Fe 1083A, 1801, no. 5. For octoroons, see Twinam, *Public Lives*, 44.

71. Jaramillo, *Ensayos sobre historia social*, 1:186–88; Jiménez, *Linajes cartageneros: Los Fernández de Sotomayor*, 14.

72. El obispo solicita se aprueba una casa cuna para niños expósitos, Cartagena, 19 May 1791, in Spain, AGI, Santa Fe 1070, no. 10; "R. C. que dispone la observancia en Indias del real decreto relativo a los niños expósitos," 19 February 1794, in Konetzke, *Colección de documentos*, 723–25. In 1791 Cartagena's orphanage sheltered only nineteen children. In 1802 the Council of the Indies ruled that although all foundlings should be declared legitimate and commoners, those whose "color, hair, and physiognomy were knowingly black, mulatto, Indian," or of other African-derived mixes, would have to pay the tribute of their class (Konetzke, *Colección de documentos*, 789).

73. The census returns, listing residents by place and household, distinguished between "married male," "single male," "married female," and "single female," often but not always giving their age. "Don" or "doña" preceded the names of men, women, and children with a higher status, and "slave" followed the names of those in bondage. For every city, the returns distinguished between whites, Indians, and others, whose race was not always indicated. Only for parts of Cartagena did they report whether men, women, and children were Spanish, white, quinterón, cuarterón, mulato, pardo, zambo, negro, moreno, mestizo, or indio. For all localities, gender and status affected information on gainful employment. The occupation of free male heads of household and free males over age twelve was generally listed, whereas it was seldom indicated for women (even when heads of household) and slaves (even when living independently from their master).

74. Padrón de Sto. Thoribio; Padrón de La Merced; Razón de San Sebastián. The census returns for Cartagena still reflect serious deficiencies in the collection of data. Notably, those for the barrio of Santa Catalina have disappeared, those for La Merced and San Sebastián do not give the racial classification for more than half of their inhabitants, and those for the suburb of Getsemaní do not provide racial information and rarely mention the occupation of free men. In fact, only those for Santo Toribio, the city's most densely populated and racially mixed barrio, present sufficient data for a close analysis. Yet Santo Toribio comprised mostly free persons of color and was home to 32.4 percent of Cartagena's slaves, about one-third of them living independently from their masters. The census returns of Santo Toribio thus provide unique insights into the intersection of color, class, and status among Cartagena's population of African descent.

75. Padrón de Gimaní, 1777.

76. Juan and Ulloa, *Relación histórica*, 41.

77. Saether, "Identities and Independence," 67–73, 85–94, 128–32.

78. Porto, *Plazas y calles*, 149–50. For a more detailed analysis, see Helg, "Limits of Equality," 10–13. On cabildos de nación in Cuba, see Childs, "Aponte Rebellion," 271–309.

79. J. Posada, *Memorias*, 2:195–99, 202–3.

80. Ibid., 2:204–9.

81. Fals, *Mompox y Loba*, 157B–158B.

82. E. Restrepo, *Historia de la provincia*, 494.

83. Gobernador Blas de Soria to virrey, 19 August 1808, in Spain, AGI, Santa Fé 745.

84. Mollien, *Voyage*, 1:18 (emphasis in original).

85. Kuethe, *Military Reform*, 26; J. Posada, *Memorias*, 2:207.

86. Padrón de Sto. Thoribio. See also Mendinueta to ministro de hacienda, 3 June 1803, in Spain, AGI, Santa Fe 1016.

87. Juan and Ulloa, *Relación histórica*, 55.

88. McAlister, *"Fuero Militar,"* 1–15; J. Sánchez, "African Freemen," 165–84; Archer, "Pardos, Indians, and the Army," 233; Montoya, "Milicias negras y mulatas," 102; Vinson, *Bearing Arms*; Childs, "Aponte Rebellion," 220–49.

89. Mendinueta to Alvarez, 19 May 1799, in Spain, AGS, Guerra 7247, no. 26, fols. 145–48; J. Sánchez, "African Freemen," 168.

90. Kuethe, *Military Reform*, 23–24.

91. Relación que comprende los artesanos que viven en el Barrio de Sn. Sebastián; Relación que manifiesta los artesanos que existen en el Barrio de Sto. Thoribio, 1780.

92. Mendinueta to Alvarez, 19 November 1799, in Spain, AGS, Guerra 7073, exp. 51; Kuethe, *Military Reform*, 31, 99, 217.

93. El baylio frey don Antonio Valdés, 1788–89, in Spain, AGS, Guerra 7073, exp. 30, 34; Don Juan Manuel Alvarez de Faría, 1798, ibid., exp. 38. For average salaries, see V. Gutiérrez and Pineda, *Miscegenación*, 395.

94. Filiación de Ignacio Xavier de Castro, 30 June 1798, in Spain, AGS, Guerra 7073, exp. 38. *Trigueño* also means olive-skinned or dark-complexioned.

95. Ibid.

96. Eduardo de Llamas, Libro de hojas de servicios de los ayudantes y sargentos garzones de la plana mayor de ejército agregada por S. M. al batallón de pardos libres de Cartagena, 31 December 1797, in Spain, AGS, Guerra 7281, exp. 6; ibid., 31 December 1800, Guerra 7282, exp. 4. For Mompox, see Cuerpo de cazadores urbanos del partido de Mompox, Marqués de Torre Hoyos, 15 June 1799, ibid., Guerra 7073, exp. 51. On racial discrimination among officers, see Kuethe, *Military Reform*, 38–39.

97. This conclusion is inferred from the absence of any mention of the tributo de castas in colonial records. The only non-Indians recorded as tribute payers were a few "españoles" (a category encompassing castas) residing in pueblos de indígenas where the tributo de indios was collected (Anthony McFarlane, e-mail message to author, 11 September 2002; Steinar Saether, e-mail message to author, 12 September 2002).

98. Mendinueta to Alvarez, 19 November 1799, in Spain, AGS, Guerra 7073,

exp. 51. See also J. Sánchez, "African Freemen," 167, and Montoya, "Milicias negras y mulatas."

99. Kuethe, *Military Reform*, 85–86.

100. See, e.g., Juan Vivanco, sobre la venta de una esclava llamada Petrona Pabla Bernal, in Colombia, AHNC, CO, NE, tomo 1, 1791, fols. 665–69v.

101. Nota reservada del secretario de guerra al virrey de Nueva Granada, 6 November 1797, in Spain, AGS, Guerra 7073, exp. 39. See also J. Sánchez, "African Freemen," and Kuethe, *Military Reform*, 177–78.

102. Zejudo to Mendinueta, 10 April 1799, in Spain, AGS, Guerra 7247, exp. 26, fols. 149–50.

103. Mendinueta to Alvarez, 19 May 1799, ibid., fols. 147–48. The viceroy alludes to the anti-Bourbon Comunero Revolt in 1781 (see Chapter 2).

104. Resolución del Consejo de Guerra, 2, 4, 8 October 1799, in Spain, AGS, Guerra 7247, exp. 26, fols. 18–20, 22–23, 157.

105. See, e.g., Mollien, *Voyage*, 1:16, 2:137, and Juan and Ulloa, *Relación histórica*, 42.

106. On gender imbalance and its causes in other Latin American cities during the same period, see Lombardi, *People and Places*, 82; Arrom, *Women of Mexico City*, 105–11; Kuznesof, *Household Economy*, 83; Hünefeldt, *Paying the Price of Freedom*, 93–94; and Hanger, *Bounded Lives*, 19–23. On Cartagena, see Meisel and Aguilera, "Cartagena de Indias," 33–39.

107. Gender ratios by racial category were as follows: pueblo Indians, 107.9 women per 100 men; libres de color, 106.9 women per 100 men; and slaves, 102.7 women per 100 men. With an average of 136.5 females for 100.0 males, the main cities fully absorbed the surplus of women and girls of African ancestry (my calculations, based on Tovar, *"Convocatoria,"* 487–519, 533–37).

108. See, e.g., Admiral José Padilla's beginnings as a sailor in Chapter 6. Padilla's own father spent four years in the early 1800s as a fugitive among the Wayúu following a dispute with the governor of Riohacha (Torres, *El Almirante*, 17–23; E. Uribe, *Padilla*, 5).

109. Padrón del barrio de Sto. Thoribio, año de 1777, fol. 1012.

110. El señor gobernador de la Plaza de Cartagena remite a esta superioridad testimonio íntegro de los autos obrados contra una negra bozal nombrada María Gervasia Guillén por haberle aprendido varios géneros de ilícita introducción, in Colombia, AHNC, CO, NE, tomo 5, 1796, fols. 317–29v.

111. Colombia, APC, Libro de bautismos de pardos y morenos, 1803–11; APC, Libro de bautismos de blancos, 1799–1820; APST, Libro de bautismos de pardos y morenos, 1795–1803. On *compadres*, see the classic essay by Mintz and Wolf, "Analysis of Ritual Co-Parenthood," and Gudeman and Schwartz, "Cleansing Original Sin."

112. In Cartagena, there were 2 foundlings out of 256 children of color baptized in the parish of Getsemaní in 1802, and 2 out of 95 children of color baptized in the parish of La Catedral in 1804. In contrast, in 1804 there were 2 foundlings out of 20 baptized whites in La Catedral (Colombia, APC, Libro de bautismos de pardos y

morenos, 1803-11; APC, Libro de bautismos de blancos, 1799-1820; APST, Libro de bautismos de pardos y morenos, 1795-1803).

113. Boswell, *Kindness of Strangers*, 15-20.

114. Ibid., 433. For a comparative analysis of child abandonment in eighteenth-century Spanish America, see Twinam, *Public Lives*, 133-39, 284-91, 298-306. On child abandonment in Bogotá and Tunja, see P. Rodríguez, *Sentimiento*, 104-11.

115. El obispo solicita se aprueba una casa cuna para niños expósitos, Cartagena, 19 May 1791, in Spain, AGI, Santa Fe 1070, no. 10.

116. Juan and Ulloa, *Relación histórica*, 49-50.

117. Pombo, "Informe de José Ignacio de Pombo," 131.

118. Don José Sorel médico y vecino de la ciudad de Cartagena sobre haberle encontrado a una esclava de su mujer una botella de licor veneno, in Colombia, AHNC, CO, NE, tomo 5, 1789, fol. 592. In this case a quarreling husband and wife accused each other of attempted murder through the intermediary of their slaves.

119. El contador general de aguardientes con las adjuntas copias representa lo conveniente sobre la compra de esclavos por cuenta de S. M. para el servicio de la fábrica de la renta de aguardiente de Cartagena, ibid., 1807, fols. 258-64v.

120. Marqués de Santa Cruz to Manuel de Guevara Vasconcelos, 21 May 1799, in Spain, AGI, Estado 71, no. 3, fols. 23-25, 29-31; Pedro Mendinueta to Francisco de Saavedra, 19 July 1799, ibid., Estado 52, no. 81, fols. 1-2; General Gouvion Saint Cyr to Pedro Cevallos, 29 Prairial [May] de l'an 10 de la République française, ibid., Estado 71, no. 5, fols. 9-11.

121. Anastasio Zejudo to viceroy, 9 April 1799, ibid., Estado 53, no. 77, fol. 10.

122. Josef Munive y Mozo to Zejudo, 24 April 1799, in Spain, AGS, Guerra 7247, exp. 26, fols. 122-23.

123. Zejudo to Viceroy, 9 April 1799, in Spain, AGI, Estado 53, no. 77, fols. 9-11. See also Mendinueta to Saavedra, 19 May 1799, ibid., Estado 52, no. 76, fols. 5-7.

124. Zejudo to Saavedra, 30 April 1799, ibid., Estado 53, no. 77, fols. 1-4.

125. Zejudo to Mendinueta, 9 April 1799, ibid., fol. 12; Joaquin Francisco Fidalgo to Zejudo, 20 April 1799, in Spain, AGS, Guerra 7247, exp. 26, fols. 109-10; Mendinueta to Zejudo, 29 April 1799, in Spain, AGI, Estado 52, no. 76, fols. 25-27, and Mendinueta to Alvarez, 19 May 1799, fols. 29-35.

126. Marquis of Santa Cruz to Manuel de Guevara Vasconcelos, 21 May 1799, in Spain, AGI, Estado 71, no. 3, fols. 23-25, 29-31. On the alleged conspiracy of Maracaibo, see Helg, "Fragmented Majority," 157-60.

127. Consejo pleno extraordinario de guerra, 9 October 1799, in Spain, AGS, Guerra 7247, exp. 26, fols. 34-45.

128. Salzedo, *Apuntaciones*, 75; Fals, *Mompox y Loba*, 132A.

129. See, e.g., Padrón del barrio de Sto. Thoribio; Padrón . . . [d]el barrio de Nra. Sa. de la Merced; Razón del barrio de San Sebastián.

130. Tovar, *De una chispa*, 18, 22-24, 53-58. For a similar trend in Peru, see Hünefeldt, *Paying the Price of Freedom*, 65.

131. Juan and Ulloa, *Relación histórica*, 110-11.

132. Romero, *Esclavitud*, 126, 129, anexos 6–7; Klein, *African Slavery*, 226–30. For the manumission of some newborns, see Colombia, APC, Libro de bautismos de pardos y morenos, 1803–11.

133. "Consulta del Consejo de las Indias sobre la coartación de los esclavos en beneficio de su libertad," 5 December 1788, in Konetzke, *Colección de documentos*, 631–35.

134. Pombo, "Informe del real consulado," 143.

135. On the lawyers of slaves in Lima, see Hünefeldt, *Paying the Price of Freedom*, 65.

136. Doña Juana Masa con Gertrudis Subisa sobre sevicia, Cartagena, in Colombia, AHNC, CO, NE, tomo 7, 1782, fols. 1012, 1020.

137. Masa con Subisa, ibid., fols. 1012v, 1020. For an example of a slave granted freedom for heroism, see "Consulta del Consejo de Indias sobre la instancia hecha por el negro Manuel Huevo, esclavo de V. M., solicitando su libertad," 26 September 1785, in Konetzke, *Colección de documentos*, 583–85.

138. See Drescher, *Capitalism and Antislavery*.

139. "R. instrucción sobre la educación, trato y ocupación de los esclavos," 31 May 1789, in Konetzke, *Colección de documentos*, 3:643–52.

140. See, e.g., Criminales contra Pedro Joseph Catalán, negro esclavo de Dn Ignacio de Narváez por ladrón sacrilego, in Colombia, AHNC, CO, NE, tomo 2, 1790, fols. 920–68, and Criminales contra Anselmo Miranda, mulato esclavo de Dn Simón González, por robar dos polleras que vendió en 4 pesos a un mozo de una canoa en Tolú, ibid., tomo 3, 1797, fols. 1052–1100.

141. "Consulta del Consejo de las Indias sobre el reglamento expedido en 31 de mayo de 1789 para la mejor educación, buen trato y ocupación de los negros esclavos de América," 17 March 1794, in Konetzke, *Colección de documentos*, 726–32; Geggus, "Slavery, War, and Revolution," 11; Childs, "Aponte Rebellion," 73–76.

142. Tovar, *De una chispa*, 18.

143. Vivanco sobre la venta de Bernal, in Colombia, AHNC, CO, NE, tomo 1, 1791, fol. 651.

144. For example, in the late 1790s the marquis of Torre-Hoyos wrongly accused hacendado García (d. 1799) of having whipped a slave to death, but, as the grudge between the two men was well known, García was absolved after several witnesses declared that the elderly, insane slave had died of natural causes (Causa criminal contra García por el marqués de Torrehoyos, in Colombia, AHNC, CO, NE, tomo 6, 1796–97, fols. 968–1021). A few years later Mompox's alcalde ordinario, Sáenz, falsely accused hacendado and brick producer Barcena of keeping in bondage a slave supposedly freed by her deceased mistress. Sáenz also claimed that Barcena had whipped a rural slave to death. Although from several accounts Barcena punished his slaves excessively, the slave he allegedly had killed had run away and was captured in Nechí (Don Melchor Sáenz Ortiz contra don Francisco de la Barcena Posada, sobre la libertad de una esclava, María Magdalena Soto, Mompox, ibid., tomo 9, 1805, fols. 207–88; Barcena contra Sáenz, ibid., tomo 8, 1806, fols. 700–924; Desistencia de don Francisco de la Barcena y don Melchor Sáenz Ortiz en la causa seguida sobre sevicia de esclavos, ibid., tomo 4, 1807, fols. 1001–4).

145. Masa con Subisa, in Colombia, AHNC, CO, NE, tomo 7, 1782, fol. 1012v.

146. Ibid., fols. 1027-27v.

147. Vivanco sobre la venta de Bernal, ibid., tomo 1, 1791, fols. 703v-705.

148. Pedro Mendinueta to Josef Antonio Caballero, 19 November 1800, in Spain, AGI, Estado 52, no. 102, fols. 1-3.

149. Masa con Subisa, in Colombia, AHNC, CO, NE, tomo 7, 1782, fols. 1017v-1022; Vivanco sobre la venta de Bernal, ibid., tomo 1, 1791, fols. 701v, 702v.

150. Masa con Subisa, ibid., tomo 7, 1782, fols. 1017v-1019v, 1021v.

151. Juan Chacón contra María de los Angeles Barraza, ibid., tomo 4, 1808, fol. 1060v. For an excellent discussion of honor in colonial Spanish America, see Twinam, *Public Lives*, 32-33.

152. Chacón contra Barraza, in Colombia, AHNC, CO, NE, tomo 4, 1808, fol. 1077.

153. When Chacón ignored Valverde's legal marriage to his slave, Ana Escobar, and sold him separately to María de los Angeles Barraza, Valverde obtained permission from the ecclesiastical tribunal to spend two nights a week with his wife, so that they could "consummate the marriage." Since Chacón resisted the ecclesiastical decision, Valverde denounced him to the protector of slaves, in front of whom the exchange of insults took place. After spending four days in prison for impertinence, Valverde repeatedly sneaked into Chacón's house to ridicule him.

154. Sáenz contra Barcena, in Colombia, AHNC, CO, NE, tomo 9, 1805, fols. 265v-266.

155. Pleito seguido por Melchor Sáenz Ortiz, Mompox, ibid., tomo 4, 1796, fols. 435-555v.

156. Barcena contra Sáenz, ibid., tomo 8, 1806, fols. 756v-757.

157. Jaramillo, *Ensayos sobre historia social*, 1:232-33.

158. Causa criminal contra García por el marqués de Torrehoyos, in Colombia, AHNC, CO, NE, tomo 6, 1796-97, fol. 969v. Throughout the first independence, Tinoco was alcalde of Guamal, a village that remained faithful to Spain ("Ocupación de la ciudad de Ocaña por las fuerzas al mando de don Ignacio de la Rus, January 1815," in [Corrales], *Documentos*, 2:9-10).

159. Barcena contra Sáenz, in Colombia, AHNC, CO, NE, tomo 8, 1806, fols. 755, 785v-786, 823.

160. Mendinueta to Alvarez, 19 May 1799, in Spain, AGI, Estado 52, no. 76, fol. 145; Munive to Zejudo, 24 April 1799, in Spain, AGS, Guerra 7247, exp. 26, fols. 122-23.

161. Mendinueta to Alvarez, 19 May 1799, in Spain, AGI, Estado 52, no. 76, fol. 145.

162. Zejudo to virrey, 9 April 1799, ibid., Estado 53, no. 77, fol. 11; Mendinueta to Saavedra, 19 May 1799, Estado 52, no. 76, fol. 6.

163. Uribe-Urán, "Birth of a Public Sphere," 433.

164. Assunção, "L'adhésion populaire," 308-9.

165. See also Bennett, "Research Note," 208.

CHAPTER FOUR

1. "Alegato del Dr. García de Toledo," in Arrázola, *Los mártires responden*, 15, 17, 21. For a biography of García de Toledo, see Jiménez, *Linajes cartageneros*, 3–60.

2. For comparative analyses of Spanish American independence movements, see Lynch, *Spanish American Revolution*; J. E. Rodríguez, *Independence of Spanish America*; and Hamnett, "Process and Pattern."

3. On New Granada as a whole, see Earle, *Spain and the Independence of Colombia*; McFarlane, "Building Political Order"; Tovar, "Guerras de opinión"; and Hamnett, "Popular Insurrection."

4. Los diputados del Ayuntamiento de Cartagena hacen presente las continuas escaseces de víveres, 1 December 1809, in Spain, AGI, Santa Fe 745. See also Múnera, *El fracaso de la nación*, 127–28.

5. "Oficios cambiados entre los señores Gobernador de Cartagena y Alcaldes ordinarios, sobre los temores de una subversión del orden," 15 May 1810, in [Corrales], *Documentos*, 1:65–66; Confesión de J. M. Toledo, in Colombia, BNC, SM, Proceso de los mártires de Cartagena, 1816, fols. 88–89; Resolución de establecimiento de una Junta Superior de gobierno en Cartagena, 23 May 1810, in Spain, AGI, Santa Fe 747.

6. "Apuntamientos para escribir una ojeada," in [Corrales], *Documentos*, 1:127; "Memorial de S. Verástegui al general Luque sobre el coronel B. Rodríguez," 24 April 1834, ibid., 1:413.

7. "El comandante del apostadero a la corte," 30 May 1810, in Arrázola, *Documentos*, 57; Arrázola, *Secretos*, 69; Meisel and Aguilera, "Cartagena de Indias," 47.

8. "Apuntamientos," in [Corrales], *Documentos*, 1:127; Bossa, *Cartagena independiente*, 124.

9. "Acta de la sesión del Cabildo de Cartagena tenida el 14 de Junio de 1810," in [Corrales], *Documentos*, 1:81–90; Antonio de Narváez to virrey de Santa Fe, 19 June 1810, in Spain, AGI, Santa Fe 1011; and "Defensa hecha por el señor J. M. de Toledo, de su conducta pública y privada," 30 November 1811 (1:385–89), and "Apuntamientos" (1:127–28), both in [Corrales], *Documentos*.

10. "Edicto por el cual el Cabildo de Cartagena excita a los habitantes de la ciudad a procurar la unión," 19 June 1810, in [Corrales], *Documentos*, 1:94–95.

11. "Informe que el Comandante de ingenieros don Vicente Talledo dirige al Virrey Amar, sobre las ideas que abrazan algunos vecinos de Mompox de subvertir el orden," 13 November 1809, ibid., 1:20–21.

12. Informe del Comandante de Ingenieros don Vicente Talledo, al Virey [*sic*] Amar, sobre conatos de revolución en Cartagena y Mompox, 3 May 1810, ibid., 1:53.

13. Salzedo, *Apuntaciones*, 93, also 119. See also "Informe de . . . Talledo," 3 May 1810, in [Corrales], *Documentos*, 1:53; "Informe del Comandante don Vicente Talledo dirige al Virey [*sic*] Amar, sobre los rumores que se hacen valer en Mompox," 23 March 1810 (1:49–51), and "Exposición de la Junta de Cartagena de Indias, sobre los sucesos de Mompox," 4 December 1810 (1:209–10), ibid.

14. "Párrafos de la exposición del Comandante don Vicente Talledo . . . relativos

a los primeros sucesos de Mompox en al año de 1810," n.d., in [Corrales], *Documentos*, 1:119-21. See also "Los señores Villavicencio y Narváez dan aviso al Virey [*sic*] Amar de haber llegado a Mompox," 3, 4 July 1810, ibid., 1:149-50. After 1810 Muñoz and Galván continued to fight for New Granada's independence. Muñoz was promoted to colonel and later served as military commander of the Panama Isthmus; Galván became a captain and was executed by Spain in 1816 (Salzedo, *Apuntaciones*, 94).

15. On the process in Bogotá, see McFarlane, "Building Political Order," 17-20.

16. "El mes de Agosto de 1810 en la Villa de Mompox," n.d., in [Corrales], *Documentos*, 1:197.

17. "Exposición de la Junta de Cartagena," ibid., 1:205.

18. Salzedo, *Apuntaciones*, 86-87, 98.

19. "El mes de Agosto," in [Corrales], *Documentos*, 1:187-88; Salzedo, *Apuntaciones*, 97-100.

20. Salzedo, *Apuntaciones*, 117-18.

21. "Exposición de la Junta de Cartagena" (1:206-7) and "El mes de Agosto" (1:192-94, 198), both in [Corrales], *Documentos*.

22. J. M. de Toledo and J. M. Benito Revollo, A todos los estantes y habitantes de esta Plaza y Provincia, 9 November 1810, in Spain, AGI, Santa Fe 747.

23. Jiménez, *Los mártires de Cartagena*, 1:147-48, 238-39; "Reorganización de la Junta Suprema de Cartagena de Indias" (*Semanario Ministerial*, 7 March 1811), in [Corrales], *Documentos*, 1:182.

24. "El representante de Mompox contesta al Manifiesto de la Junta Suprema de Cartagena, que antecede," 28 January 1811, in [Corrales], *Documentos*, 1:226.

25. Junta de la Provincia de Cartagena de Indias a las demás de este nuevo Reyno de Granada, 19 September 1810, in Spain, AGI, Santa Fe 747; J. M. Restrepo, *Historia de la revolución*, 1:147-48, 160-68; Salzedo, *Apuntaciones*, 110-11.

26. "El representante de Mompox contesta," in [Corrales], *Documentos*, 1:219. See also Salzedo, *Apuntaciones*, 112. The text of the constitution has since disappeared.

27. "Reorganización de la Junta Suprema" (1:183) and "Exposición de la Junta de Cartagena" (1:213), both in [Corrales], *Documentos*. These documents mention the secession of Simití but do not provide any details.

28. Pombo, "Informe del real consulado," 197; "Decreto de la Junta de Gobierno," 10 December 1810, in Arrázola, *Documentos*, 92-96.

29. "Defensa hecha por . . . Toledo," in [Corrales], *Documentos*, 1:390; Jiménez, *Los mártires de Cartagena*, 1:149-53.

30. "Acuerdo que reorganiza el gobierno provincial," 11 December 1810, in [Corrales], *Efemérides*, 2:48. See also "Decretos de la Junta," 12, 29 November 1810, *El Argos Americano*, 24 December 1810, supp.

31. "Exposición de la Junta de Cartagena," in [Corrales], *Documentos*, 1:205; Salzedo, *Apuntaciones*, 117-18.

32. Salzedo, *Apuntaciones*, 115; "El representante de Mompox contesta," in [Corrales], *Documentos*, 1:218.

33. Salzedo, *Apuntaciones*, 113, 117; "Alegato del Dr. D. Antonio José de Ayos," in Arrázola, *Los mártires responden*, 180; "Defensa hecha por . . . Toledo," in [Corrales], *Documentos*, 1:370, 372.

34. *El Argos Americano*, 4 February 1811, supp.; "Carta primera de P.," 9 March 1811, *El Argos Americano*, 18 March 1811; M. Gutiérrez to capitán general de la isla de Cuba, 3 March 1811, in Spain, AGI, Santa Fe 747.

35. "Carta en que se refieren muchos hechos relacionados y consiguientes a la sublevación del Regimiento Fijo de Cartagena," 10 February 1811, in [Corrales], *Efemérides*, 2:67-68. See also "Defensa hecha por . . . Toledo," in [Corrales], *Documentos*, 1:391-92, and Alegato del gobierno de Cartagena, 8 February 1811, in Spain, AGI, Santa Fe 747.

36. "Carta en que se refieren muchos hechos," in [Corrales], *Efemérides*, 2:64-70; "Extracto de las causas seguidas a don Tomás Torres y a don Juan de Francisco," n.d., in [Corrales], *Documentos*, 1:399. For a watered-down narrative, see "Suceso del día 4 de Febrero," *El Argos Americano*, 4 February 1811, supp.

37. Del virrey don Benito Pérez a la Corte, 26 April 1811, in Spain, AGI, Santa Fe 630.

38. Del obispo de Cartagena al rey, ibid., Santa Fe 580; "Representación para que se expida la Constitución," 19 June 1811, in [Corrales], *Efemérides*, 2:72-73; "Defensa hecha por . . . Toledo," in [Corrales], *Documentos*, 1:368.

39. Although the Cortes agreed that all free natives residing in any Spanish territory were Spaniards, in late 1810, in order to win Spanish support for parity in representation of Spaniards and Americans based on the count of the free population, the American representatives (also motivated by their own racial prejudices) agreed to limit apportionment and the rights of citizenship to "Spaniards who on both sides draw their origin in the Spanish dominions of both hemispheres," purposely excluding Africans and their full or mixed descendants. Over strong objections from some American deputies, this exclusion became part of the 1812 constitution of the Spanish monarchy ("Constitución política de la monarquía española" [1812], 5-6. See also Anna, "Spain and the Breakdown of the Imperial Ethos," 257-59, and Demélas and Guerra, "Hispanic Revolutions").

40. "Carta primera," 25 March 1811, in *El Argos Americano*, 15 April 1811; "Carta segunda," 26 March 1811, ibid., 29 April 1811.

41. "Representación para que se expida la Constitución," in [Corrales], *Efemérides*, 2:72-73; "Defensa hecha por . . . Toledo," in [Corrales], *Documentos*, 1:368. The petition was presented by Germán Gutiérrez Piñeres, Miguel Díaz Granados, Manuel Rodríguez Torices, and José Fernández de la Madrid, among others.

42. [Núñez], *Exposición*, 5.

43. Proposiciones presentadas por los diputados del pueblo y aprobadas y sancionadas el 11 de Noviembre de 1811, in Carta del comandante general de Panamá a ministro de justicia, 30 November 1811, in Spain, AGI, Santa Fe 745.

44. On these events, see "Acta de independencia de la Provincia de Cartagena en la Nueva Granada," 11 November 1811 (1:351-56), and "Defensa hecha por . . . Toledo" (1:365, 371, 394-95), both in [Corrales], *Documentos*; Urueta, *Cartagena*,

567-68; F. de P. Ribón, "Estadística de Mompox," in [Corrales], *Efemérides*, 4:339; and Salzedo, *Apuntaciones*, 113.

45. Copia de la correspondencia entre la Suprema Junta de Cartagena de Indias y el obispo Fraile Custodio, 1 June 1812, in Spain, AGI, Santa Fe 747; Jiménez, *Los mártires de Cartagena*, 1:238-81.

46. "Alegato de . . . Ayos," in Arrázola, *Los mártires responden*, 183-84, 196; Jiménez, *Los mártires de Cartagena*, 1:281, 285-86.

47. J. M. Restrepo, *Historia de la revolución*, 1:187-89; McFarlane, "Building Political Order," 19-26.

48. "Constitución política del Estado de Cartagena de Indias, expedida el 14 de Junio de 1812," in [Corrales], *Documentos*, 1:532. For the whole constitution, see ibid., 1:485-546.

49. Vicencio Ruiz de Gómez a virrey, 22 May 1810, in P. Castro, *Culturas aborígenes*, 59-60.

50. P. Castro, *Culturas aborígenes*, 57-61; T. D. Gutiérrez, *Valledupar*, 207-15.

51. Alarcón, *Compendio de historia*, 70.

52. "Instalación de la Junta Superior de la plaza de Santa Marta y su provincia," 10 August 1810, in [Corrales], *Documentos*, 1:136-40; Saether, "Identities and Independence," 206-8, 225.

53. Romero, *Esclavitud*, 86-88.

54. "Elección e instalación de la nueva Junta Superior provincial de Santa Marta," n.d., in [Corrales], *Documentos*, 1:184-85. See also E. Restrepo, *Historia de la provincia*, 499-507.

55. "Nota oficial por la cual el Gobierno de la Provincia de Santa Marta da cuenta al Virey [*sic*] electo de este Reino del estado de relaciones entre dicha Provincia y las demás del mismo Reino," 23 July 1811, in [Corrales], *Documentos*, 1:342.

56. "Correspondencia cruzada entre el gobierno de la provincia de Cartagena de Indias y las autoridades residentes en la ciudad de Santa Marta, sobre comercio entre ambas provincias," January-March 1811, in [Corrales], *Documentos*, 1:240-42; "Nota de la Junta de Cartagena, dirigida a la de Santa Marta, relativa al envío del diputado que represente a la segunda en el congreso de este reino," March 1811, ibid., 1:242-44.

57. "Copia de la representación [de algunos pueblos de la Provincia de Santa Marta]," 30 June 1811, in [Corrales], *Documentos*, 1:259-73.

58. "Oficio del Gobierno de Cartagena, en que excita al de la Provincia de Santa Marta," 8 July 1811, in [Corrales], *Documentos*, 1:258.

59. "Contestación del Gobierno de la Provincia de Santa Marta a la nota precedente del de la de [*sic*] Cartagena," 2 August 1811 (1:273-76), and "Oficio del Gobernador de la Provincia de Santa Marta al Virey [*sic*] don Benito Pérez, en que le avisa haber movilizado fuerzas sobre el pueblo del Guáimaro," 11 August 1811 (1:276-94), both in [Corrales], *Documentos*; La Junta Suprema de Cartagena a los habitantes de su provincia, 31 August 1811, in Spain, AGI, Santa Fe 747.

60. E. Restrepo, *Historia de la provincia*, 512-14, 526-28; Torres, *El Almirante*, 22.

61. E. Restrepo, *Historia de la provincia*, 530; "Parte que el Comandante del batallón 'Albuera,' Juan Jiménez, da al Virey [*sic*] de la pérdida de la plaza de Santa Marta," 13 January 1813, in [Corrales], *Documentos*, 1:575–77.

62. On family and professional links between the members of the revolutionary juntas throughout New Granada, see Uribe-Urán, *Honorable Lives*, 60–65.

63. "Discurso del Excelentísimo señor Presidente del estado independiente de Cartagena, en la apertura de las sesiones de la Cámara de Representantes del mismo estado," 8 January 1813, in [Corrales], *Documentos*, 1:557.

64. "Informe de . . . Talledo . . . sobre conatos de revolución en Cartagena y Mompox" (1:53) and "Exposición de la Junta de Cartagena" (1:209-10), both in [Corrales], *Documentos*; Salzedo, *Apuntaciones*, 119; Fals, *Mompox y Loba*, 136A.

65. Barcena contra Sáenz, Mompox, in Colombia, AHNC, CO, NE, tomo 8, 1806, fols. 700–924; Desistencia de Barcena y Sáenz, Mompox, ibid., tomo 4, 1807, fols. 1001–4.

66. See, e.g., García de Toledo's opposition to the Congress of Bogotá in 1810 and Manuel del Castillo's refusal to participate in the forces of the Federation of the United Provinces in 1815, in contrast to the piñeristas' inclusion of the representative of Bogotá, bogotano priest Nicolás Mauricio de Omaña, in the events of November 1811 in Cartagena, the participation of Manuel Rodríguez Torices in the government of the Federation, and the intervention of priest Juan Marimón endorsing Cartagena's support of Bolívar in 1815.

67. "El mes de Agosto," in [Corrales], *Documentos*, 1:192–94.

68. Ibid., 1:198.

69. "Carta de un Criollo," *El Argos Americano*, 28 January 1811.

70. [Corrales], *Efemérides*, 2:48–56, and *Documentos*, 1:497, 502, 508, 532.

71. "Constitución . . . de Cartagena," in [Corrales], *Documentos*, 1:538–39.

72. "Alegato de . . . Ayos," in Arrázola, *Los mártires responden*, 153, 161, 196, 204–5, 213.

73. "Apuntamientos," in [Corrales], *Documentos*, 1:128–29.

74. "Defensa hecha por . . . Toledo," ibid., 1:379.

75. "Alegato del Dr. García de Toledo," in Arrázola, *Los mártires responden*, 17, 21–22.

76. "Representación para que se expida la Constitución," in [Corrales], *Efemérides*, 2:72–73.

77. "Carta primera," in *El Argos Americano*, 15 April 1811. Signed by J. M., the letter was probably written by Juan Marimón, a priest and member of the junta. See also "Carta segunda," in *El Argos Americano*, 29 April 1811. This second letter is signed by J. F. de M., probably José Fernández de la Madrid.

78. "Artículos tomados del número 1.o del periódico de Santafé titulado 'El Efímero,' sobre temores de perturbación del orden público," 1812, in [Corrales], *Documentos*, 1:422–23. The substance of the Lancers' demands is unknown.

79. "Constitución . . . de Cartagena," in [Corrales], *Documentos*, 1:539. On gender in the French Revolution, see Melzer and Rabine, *Rebel Daughters*.

80. For a similar pattern in revolutionary France, see Geggus, "Racial Equality, Slavery, and Colonial Secession."

81. Pombo, "Informe del real consulado," 143.

82. Bushnell, *Making of Modern Colombia*, 42.

83. "Constitución . . . de Cartagena," in [Corrales], *Documentos*, 1:540–41.

84. M. González, "El proceso de manumisión," 161.

85. Pombo, "Informe del real consulado," 139–40.

86. Edicto, 6 May 1811, *El Argos Americano*, 13 May 1811, in Arrázola, *Documentos*, 173–77. Racially inclusive military units were established after the adoption of the 1812 constitution.

87. J. M. Restrepo, *Historia de la revolución*, 1:242. There are no estimates of the number of royalist, proindependence, or neutral priests in Caribbean New Granada in the period 1810–15. Uribe-Urán's (*Honorable Lives*, 47) study of New Granada's political elite, which focuses mainly on lawyers in the Andean regions, only gives data on priests for Bogotá's 1810 Supreme Junta, where they accounted for about 20 percent of the members.

88. "Acuerdo que reorganiza el gobierno provincial," 11 December 1810, in [Corrales], *Efemérides*, 2:48.

89. "Constitución . . . de Cartagena," in [Corrales], *Documentos*, 1:486, 495; J. M. Restrepo, *Historia de la revolución*, 1:204. The first Masonic lodge in New Granada was the lodge of the Three Theological Virtues, founded in Cartagena in 1808. Its members included toledistas and piñeristas: José María García de Toledo, Manuel Rodríguez Torices, Juan Fernández de Sotomayor, and José Fernández de la Madrid, among others (Carnicelli, *La masonería*, 1:78–83).

90. "El Obispo felicita al Rey por su liberación y narra brevemente los hechos revolucionarios de Cartagena," 12 July 1814, in Martínez, *Cartas de los obispos*, 587.

91. "El gobernador de Santa Marta envia al Virey [*sic*] el Acta de adhesión de Tolú a la causa realista," 18 November 1812, in [Corrales], *Documentos*, 1:445–47; J. M. Restrepo, *Historia de la revolución*, 1:242–43.

92. Gutiérrez de Piñeres to Pantaleón Germán Ribón, 16 October 1812, in Colombia, AHNC, RE, AR, fondo I, caja 1, rollo 1, fols. 116–17 (microfilm).

93. Juan Salvador Anselmo Daza to José Medina Galindo, 20 January 1813, in P. Castro, *Culturas aborígenes*, 79.

94. "Piezas relativas al abandono de la ciudad de Santa Marta por las autoridades y fuerzas realistas," 30 January 1813, in [Corrales], *Documentos*, 1:561–74; T. D. Gutiérrez, *Valledupar*, 92.

95. "Medidas adoptadas por el Congreso de las Provincias Unidas de la Nueva Granada respecto de la de Santa Marta," 25 April 1813 (1:597–601), and "Alocución del vice-gobernador de Cartagena, con motivo de la derrota que sufrieron las fuerzas republicanas en 'Papares,'" 14 May 1813 (1:595–96), both in [Corrales], *Documentos*; Ortiz, *Franceses en la independencia*, 103–8.

96. E. Restrepo, *Historia de la provincia*, 540–41.

97. P. Castro, *Culturas aborígenes*, 65; José María de Quiróz to Medina, 1813, ibid., 75.

98. Acta de independencia, 4 February 1813, in P. Castro, *Culturas aborígenes*, 86, 206; T. D. Gutiérrez, *Valledupar*, 229–38.

99. "Edicto por el cual se excita a la formación de un ejército que se encargue de

someter la plaza de Santa Marta," 16 May 1813, in [Corrales], *Documentos*, 1:596–97.

100. "El poder ejecutivo de la unión se dirige al gobierno de Cartagena," 14 June 1813, ibid., 1:603–6.

101. E. Restrepo, *Historia de la provincia*, 534–35, 537; Earle, *Spain and the Independence of Colombia*, 45–46.

102. See, e.g., "Correspondencia interceptada, embarcaciones apresadas y declaraciones recibidas por el capitán del corsario particular titulado 'Nuestra Señora de la Luz,'" 16 February 1813, in [Corrales], *Documentos*, 1:585–93.

103. McKinley, *Pre-Revolutionary Caracas*, 170–74.

104. Montalvo, "Instrucción," 229; Sourdis, *Cartagena*, 77–86.

105. José María García de Toledo to Manuel del Castillo, 10 January 1815, in Colombia, AHNC, RE, AR, fondo I, caja 1, rollo 1, fols. 262–66; Varios diputados to pueblos de la Sabana del Cauca y Sinú, 12 January 1815, ibid., fols. 266–69.

106. Ribón to Bolívar, 23 December 1814, ibid., rollo 1, fol. 292; Vicente Celedonio Gutiérrez de Piñeres to Gabriel Gutiérrez de Piñeres, 7 January 1815, ibid., fol. 260; Montalvo, "Instrucción," 230.

107. Sourdis, *Cartagena*, 71–72.

108. Petición a Pedro Gual, 28 January 1815, in Colombia, AHNC, RE, AR, fondo I, caja 1, rollo 1, fols. 303–6; Montalvo, "Instrucción," 235. See also Sourdis, *Cartagena*, 83–92.

109. "El mes de Agosto," in [Corrales], *Documentos*, 1:187–89; Salzedo, *Apuntaciones*, 117–18.

110. Barcena contra Sáenz, Mompox, in Colombia, AHNC, CO, NE, tomo 8, 1806, fol. 755.

111. "Alegato de . . . Ayos," in Arrázola, *Los mártires responden*, 153.

112. J. Posada, *Memorias*, 2:195–209; "Carta [sobre] la sublevación del Regimiento Fijo de Cartagena," in [Corrales], *Efemérides*, 2:64–70.

113. Montalvo, "Instrucción," 230.

114. Nuevos dirigentes, 24 January 1815, in Colombia, AHNC, RE, AR, fondo I, caja 1, rollo 1, fols. 342–43.

115. Proposiciones presentadas por los diputados del pueblo, 30 November 1811, in Spain, AGI, Santa Fe 745.

116. "Copia de la representación [de algunos pueblos de la Provincia de Santa Marta]," in [Corrales], *Documentos*, 1:270.

117. Cited in Alarcón, *Compendio de historia*, 70.

118. See Colombia, APC, Libro de bautismos de pardos y morenos, 1811–19, and APST, Libro donde se sientan las partidas de los bautismos de pardos y morenos que comienza en dos de Agosto del año 1812. Both also list white women owning slaves as *ciudadanas*.

119. Jorge Tadeo Lozano to María Loperena de Fernández de Castro, 28 March 1813, in P. Castro, *Culturas aborígenes*, 88.

120. Daza to Medina, 20 January 1813, in P. Castro, *Culturas aborígenes*, 79.

121. Ibid., 206.

122. "Testamento de la Señora María de la Concepción Loperena," 1 February

1835, in T. D. Gutiérrez, *Valledupar*, 252–53; P. Castro, *Culturas aborígenes*, 66–75, 203–6.

123. Salzedo, *Apuntaciones*, 161, 164, 166; Fals, *Mompox y Loba*, 133A–41A; Monsalve, *Mujeres de la independencia*, 106–9, 130–31.

124. Salzedo, *Apuntaciones*, 115; Cherpak, "Participation of Women"; Salzedo, *Apuntaciones*, 159–60; Monsalve, *Mujeres de la independencia*, 109, 121–24.

125. F. Gómez, "Los censos en Colombia," 20, table 3; McFarlane, *Colombia*, 353.

126. The son of Luis de Rieux abandoned his haciendas to his slaves after being drafted (Luis de Rieux to secretario del despacho universal de Indias, 26 July 1815, in Spain, AGI, Santa Fe 747). See also Alexander, *Life of Alexander*, 216–18, and Francisco de Paz al gobernador político y militar, 20 September 1816, in Spain, AGI, Cuba 715.

127. Bell, *Cartagena de Indias*, 80–95.

128. "Piezas relativas al abandono de la ciudad de Santa Marta por las autoridades y fuerzas realistas," 9–31 January 1813, in [Corrales], *Documentos*, 1:571–72.

129. "Thomas de Acosta, gobernador de Santa Marta, al Virey [sic] sobre envio a La Habana de varios negros esclavos hechos prisioneros," 6 March 1812, ibid., 1:424–25.

130. Romero, *Esclavitud*, 76–79, 91, anexo 4; E. Posada, *La esclavitud*, 47.

131. Bossa, *Cartagena independiente*, 24–26.

132. "Thomas de Acosta . . . al Virey," in [Corrales], *Documentos*, 1:424–25.

133. If manumission had taken place on a large scale, it is likely that defendants would have mentioned it in their 1816 court-martial.

134. Del virrey don Benito Pérez a la Corte, 26 April 1811, in Spain, AGI, Santa Fe 630; "Parte que el Comandante del batallón 'Albuera,'" in [Corrales], *Documentos*, 1:575–77; P. Castro, *Culturas aborígenes*, 86, 206.

135. Tercera proclama de Castillo a todos los habitantes del Estado de Cartagena, in Colombia, BNC, SM, Proceso de los mártires de Cartagena, 1816, fols. 173–76.

136. T. D. Gutiérrez, *Valledupar*, 225.

137. "Constitución política de la monarquía española" [1812], 5–6; Bentivenga, *Cedulario indígena venezolano*, 314–15.

138. "Parte que el Comandante del batallón 'Albuera,'" in [Corrales], *Documentos*, 1:575–77.

139. T. D. Gutiérrez, *Valledupar*, 225.

140. "Copia de la representación," in [Corrales], *Documentos*, 1:259–73; "Oficio del Gobernador de la Provincia de Santa Marta al Virey [sic] don Benito Pérez," 11 August 1811, ibid., 1:276–77.

141. "Correspondencia interceptada, embarcaciones apresadas," 16 February 1813, ibid., 1:592.

142. Fernández de Sotomayor, *Catecismo*.

143. "Ocupación de la ciudad de Ocaña por las fuerzas al mando de don Ignacio de la Rus," January 1815, in [Corrales], *Documentos*, 2:9–10.

144. Conde, *Espacio, sociedad y conflictos*, 115.

145. At his 1816 court-martial, Castillo vainly attempted to save his life by claiming that his opposition to Bolívar, his mismanagement of the army of the Magdalena

Line, his attack against Cartagena and the piñeristas in early 1815, and his defense strategy during Morillo's siege were all maneuvers to restore the king's sovereignty ("Alegato de Manuel Castillo," in Arrázola, *Los mártires responden*, 96, 101, 118, 128).

146. "Reminiscencias del sitio de Cartagena, hechas por el esclarecido ciudadano Lino de Pombo," 8 April 1862, in [Corrales], *Documentos*, 2:172–74.

147. Ibid., 2:167–74; García del Rio, "Sitio de Cartagena de 1815."

148. Montalvo, "Instrucción," 247.

149. "Reminiscencias del sitio," in [Corrales], *Documentos*, 2:167–74; García del Rio, "Sitio de Cartagena." The demographic effects of the siege clearly appear in the baptism registers of the city. In the parish of La Catedral, 141 black and mulatto babies were baptized in 1814, 93 in 1815, 76 in 1816, 145 in 1817, and 136 in 1818 (Colombia, APC, Libro de bautismos de pardos y morenos, 1811–19). In the same parish, 47 white babies were baptized in 1814, 53 in 1815, 33 in 1816, 56 in 1817, and 57 in 1818 (APC, Libro de bautismos de blancos, Parroquia La Catedral, 1799–1820). In Getsemaní, 204 black and mulatto babies were baptized in 1814, 180 in 1815, 124 in 1816, 265 in 1817, and 249 in 1818 (Colombia, APST, Libro donde se sientan las partidas de los bautismos de pardos y morenos que comienza en dos de Agosto del ano 1812). In the three registers, the number of foundlings did not increase significantly in 1815–16.

150. "Reminiscencias del sitio," in [Corrales], *Documentos*, 2:167–74; "Sitio de Cartagena por el General don Pablo Morillo," 1823, ibid., 2:287–89; [Núñez], *Exposición*, 10–12.

151. On the impact of reconquest in New Granada as a whole, see Earle, "Popular Participation."

152. "Memorial que el Brigadier don Gabriel Torres y Velazco . . . elevó al Rey de España," 15 July 1819, in Lemaître, *Antecedentes y consecuencias*, 147–48.

153. Gabriel de Torres to Secretario de Estado, 23 July 1818, in Spain, AGI, Santa Fe 1017.

154. Montalvo, "Instrucción," 274–75, 279.

155. Ibid., 251, 254. On the Comunero Revolt and the role of Cartagena's pardo militia in its repression, see Chapters 2 and 3.

156. "La Real Audiencia relaciona al Consejo las iniquidades cometidas en el Reino por la autoridad militar," 9 September 1817, in [Corrales], *Documentos*, 2:374–75.

157. Tisnes, *La independencia*, 343–46; Bossa, *Cartagena independiente*, 124–26; Jiménez, *Los mártires de Cartagena*, 2:365.

158. "Documentos que revelan las iniquidades de las autoridades militares españolas, cometidas en las poblaciones de la Nueva Granada en los años de 1815 a 1819," in [Corrales], *Documentos*, 2:377–81.

159. "Pastoral del obispo, Fray Gregorio José Rodríguez, O.S.B., en la cual fustiga la usura de los clerigos y anuncia castigos," 12 January 1818, in Martínez, *Cartas de los obispos*, 589–90.

160. Cited in Bell, *Cartagena de Indias*, 97. See also Gregorio José, obispo de

Cartagena, sobre el estado de esta Santa Iglesia, 17 March 1818, in Spain, AGI, Santa Fe 1171.

161. "Pastoral del obispo, Fray Gregorio José Rodríguez, O.S.B., en que ataca a Bolívar y los patriotas, 3 September 1819, in Martínez, *Cartas de los obispos*, 608.

162. José María del Castillo a Santander, 10 September 1820, in E. Rodríguez, *La vida de Castillo y Rada*, 340–43.

163. Correspondencia del gobernador militar de Mompox, September 1819, in Spain, AGI, Cuba 746; J. M. Restrepo, *Historia de la revolución*, 4:110–15, 138–39; Earle, *Spain and the Independence of Colombia*, 145–63.

164. "Constitución política de la monarquía española" (1812), 5–6.

165. Pasto Province in the south remained royalist until the end of 1822.

CHAPTER FIVE

1. J. M. Restrepo, *Diario político*, 1:222. See also Bushnell, *Santander Regime*, 172.

2. "Consejo extraordinario de gobierno del sábado 25 de enero de 1823," in *Acuerdos del consejo . . . , 1821–1824*, 107; "Consejo ordinario de gobierno del lunes 29 de septiembre de 1823," ibid., 152; Hamilton, *Travels*, 1:20–21, 35–36; Cochrane, *Journal*, 58–59; Alarcón, *Compendio de historia*, 104–15.

3. *Constituciones de Colombia*, 712–13; "Ley," 29 August 1827, in República de Colombia, Sala de Negocios Generales, *Codificación*, 3:307; Bushnell, *Santander Regime*, 13–14.

4. "Ley," 21 July 1821, in República de Colombia, Sala de Negocios Generales, *Codificación*, 1:14–17. The law was more restrictive than Bolívar's proposal, which included the "absolute freedom of all the Colombians upon the act of being born in the territory of the republic" (Simón Bolívar to President of the Sovereign Congress of Colombia, 14 July 1821, in Bolívar, *Obras completas*, 2:1176).

5. "Ley," 11 October 1821, in República de Colombia, Sala de Negocios Generales, *Codificación*, 1:116–18.

6. República de Colombia, *Memoria que el secretario de estado . . . de 1823*, 15.

7. For British praise of the measure, see Francis Hall, *Colombia*, 14. For an example of notices of fugitives, see Relación de reos, Juzgado orden 1º de 1er cantón de Cartagena, 1 July 1824, in Colombia, AHNC, RE, NJ, rollo 2, fol. 287.

8. "Ley," 6 August 1821, in República de Colombia, Sala de Negocios Generales, *Codificación*, 1:23–30.

9. "Consejo ordinario del lunes 28 de marzo de 1825," in *Acuerdos del consejo . . . , 1825–1827*, 30–31; "Ley," 18 April 1825, in República de Colombia, Sala de Negocios Generales, *Codificación*, 2:94–95; Uribe-Urán, *Honorable Lives*, 77.

10. "Ley," 7 April 1826, in República de Colombia, Sala de Negocios Generales, *Codificación*, 2:272–75.

11. "Ley," 4 March 1826, ibid., 2:201–2.

12. J. M. Restrepo, *Historia de la revolución*, 1:19. See also McFarlane, *Colombia*, 36.

13. J. M. Restrepo, *Historia de la revolución*, 1:15–18, 40–44. For a broader discussion of Restrepo's *Historia*, see Colmenares, "La Historia de la revolución."

14. Bolívar to Francisco de Paula Santander, 7 April 1825, in Bolívar, *Obras completas*, 1:1076.

15. See, e.g., Simón Bolívar to [Jefe de las Fuerzas de Tierra de S. M. B.], 17 June 1814, ibid., 1:97–9.

16. J. E. Rodríguez, *Independence of Spanish America*, 187–88. For an uncritical view of Bolívar's elimination of Piar, see Liévano, *Bolívar*, 223–30. For a narrative sympathetic to Piar, see Zapata, *Piar, Petión y Padilla*, 31–106.

17. Bolívar to Santander, 13 June 1826, in Bolívar, *Obras completas*, 1:1371.

18. Santander to Bolívar, 6 March 1825, in Santander, *Cartas Santander-Bolívar*, 4:322. See also Bushnell, *Santander Regime*, 300–301.

19. Groot, *Historia eclesiástica y civil*, 14–30; Bushnell, *Santander Regime*, 282–86; Maingot, "Social Structure, Social Status," 317. For testimony supporting the execution, see Hamilton, *Travels*, 2:242–46.

20. Edward Watts to Under-Secretary of State, 23 April 1824, in Great Britain, PRO, FO 18–6, 33.

21. "Consejo extraordinario de gobierno del jueves 8 de julio de 1824," in *Acuerdos del consejo . . . , 1821–1824*, 235–36.

22. Bushnell, *Making of Modern Colombia*, 58.

23. The government also wasted a considerable portion of a 30 million peso loan from British investors on impracticable projects. See Bushnell, *Santander Regime*, 76–126.

24. McFarlane, *Colombia*, 353; F. Gómez, "Los censos en Colombia," 20, table 3. Although the first postcolonial census of 1825 similarly indicates that the inhabitants of Caribbean Colombia had dropped to 14.5 percent of the total population of New Granada, historians prefer to use the census of 1835. By listing 177,983 inhabitants in the Caribbean provinces and 1,229,259 in the entire country, the 1825 census seriously undercounted the population, as a result of New Granadans' strong resistance to a census they perceived as a scheme for taxation and military recruitment (F. Gómez, "Los censos en Colombia," 13–14, 18).

25. Colombia, AHNC, RE, Censos, Censo de 1835. See also Chapter 3.

26. For an interesting discussion of the population of the canton of Cali, Cauca, in 1830, whose census returns exceptionally included racial categories, see Escorcia, "La formación de las clases sociales."

27. See, e.g., "Decreto sobre expulsión de desafectos," 7 January 1823, in [Corrales], *Efemérides*, 2:321–23.

28. Bossa, *Cartagena independiente*, 25–26.

29. *Present State of Colombia*, 291–92.

30. Mollien, *Voyage*, 1:26.

31. J. M. Restrepo, *Diario político*, 2:71; Bossa, *Cartagena independiente*, 175–77.

32. [Bache], *Notes on Colombia*, 257. For a colonial example, see the case of zambo captain of justice Pedro Juan Tinoco in Guamal, discussed in Chapters 3 and 4.

33. Hamilton, *Travels*, 1:47-48; Rensselaer Van Rensselaer to his father, 12 July 1829, in Bonney, *Legacy*, 1:496; Gosselman, *Viaje por Colombia*, 107-8.

34. See, e.g., Lista de causas criminales pendientes, Sabanalarga, 1 July 1839, AHC, FG, Justicia, Leg. 23.

35. See, e.g., Colombia, APC, Libro de bautismos de pardos y morenos, desde 16 de Octubre de 1828 hasta 28 de Febrero de 1830; APC, Libro de bautismos de blancos, 1820-1832 (copiador); and APST, Libro de bautismos de pardos, 18 de Febrero de 1818 a 17 de Mayo de 1824.

36. República de Colombia, *Memoria que el secretario de estado . . . de 1823*, 25-26, and *Esposición que el secretario de estado . . . de 1824*, 9; J. A. Castro, "De Neiva a Cartagena," 424-25; F. Díaz, *Letras e historia del Bajo Sinú*, 46.

37. Nieto, "Geografía histórica," 175-76; Támara, *Historia de Sincelejo*, 206.

38. Romero, "La esclavitud en Barranquilla," 18.

39. "Ley," 21 October 1821, in República de Colombia, Sala de Negocios Generales, *Codificación*, 1:14-17. Priests registered the baptism of the children of slaves in the pardo registers as "hijo/a de esclava/os" and concluded the record with "libre por ley de manumisión del 19 de diciembre de 1821" (free by Law of Manumission of 19 December 1821).

40. República de Colombia, *Esposición del secretario de estado . . . de 1834*, 46.

41. "Ley," 21 October 1821, in República de Colombia, Sala de Negocios Generales, *Codificación*, 1:14-17.

42. Romero, *Esclavitud*, 146; Bierck, "Struggle for Abolition," 371-77.

43. Salzedo, *Apuntaciones*, 201-2. Salzedo mistakenly gives 1834 as the year of the first manumission ceremony.

44. "Fiestas nacionales en diciembre de 1826," *Gaceta de Cartagena de Colombia*, 31 December 1826, in [Corrales], *Efemérides*, 2:343-44; Rensselaer to his father, 1 January 1829, in Bonney, *Legacy*, 1:446.

45. A new law in February 1825, approved in the context of British recognition of Gran Colombia's independence, considered foreign slave trade an act of piracy and imposed the death penalty on importers of slaves from Africa ("Ley," 18 February 1821, in República de Colombia, Sala de Negocios Generales, *Codificación*, 2:9-11).

46. *El Mundo Observador*, 3, 12 July 1826. For ads of slaves for sale, see, e.g., the Cartagena newspapers *Las Reformas*, *Gaceta de Cartagena*, *Correo Semanal*, *El Hércules*, and *Rejistro oficial del Magdalena*. The price for male slaves was about 300 pesos and for female slaves, 150 pesos.

47. Romero, *Esclavitud*, 138, 150, 156, anexo 7.

48. Congreso de Cúcuta, 1821, *Libro de Actas*, 423.

49. "Ley 1a de 21 julio de 1821," in República de Colombia, Sala de Negocios Generales, *Codificación*, 1:16.

50. Congreso de Cúcuta, *Libro de Actas*, 254-55.

51. Ibid., 195; also 184-86, 190, 210, 227.

52. Carlos Soublette, Orden para que los pueblos del departamento del Magdalena gocen de su vida social, 4 October 1824, in Colombia, AHNC, RE, GM, tomo 373, fol. 361. For an example of detailed news of runaway slaves, see *El Constitucional del Magdalena*, 20 January 1833.

53. F. Gómez, "Los censos en Colombia," table 3; McFarlane, *Colombia*, 353; Tovar, *"Convocatoria,"* 93–96. In 1835, 2.3 percent of the population of New Granada was registered as slave; the provinces with the highest percentage of slaves were Chocó (17.5 percent), Buenaventura (15.4 percent), Popayán (12.2 percent), and Cauca (10.1 percent), followed by Pasto (4.2 percent), Riohacha (3.6 percent), Santa Marta (3.1 percent), Cartagena (2.9 percent), Antioquia (2.2 percent), and Mompox (2.1 percent). The remaining provinces, including Panama, had less than 2 percent of their population in slavery (F. Gómez, "Los censos en Colombia," table 3).

54. Hamilton, *Travels*, 1:68–69; Gosselman, *Viaje*, 99.

55. M. T. Uribe and Alvarez, *Poderes y regiones*, 232.

56. Colombia, AHNC, RE, Censos, Censo de 1835.

57. Meisel, "Esclavitud, mestizaje y haciendas," 116–17.

58. Romero, *Esclavitud*, 160.

59. Colombia, AHNC, RE, Censos, Censo de 1835.

60. República de Colombia, *Memoria que el secretario de estado . . . de 1823*, 14–15.

61. "Resolución," 15 October 1828, in *Decretos del Libertador*, 3:171–78.

62. Safford, "Race, Integration, and Progress," 12–13.

63. República de Colombia, *Esposición que el secretario de estado . . . de 1824*, 14.

64. "Consejo ordinario de gobierno del martes 5 de marzo de 1822," in *Acuerdos del consejo . . . , 1821–1824*, 29–30; "Consejo ordinario de gobierno del lunes 29 de marzo de 1824," ibid., 193–94; Merchants from Kingston to Admiral Halsted, 21 June 1824, in Great Britain, PRO, FO 18–6, 261.

65. República de Colombia, *Esposición que el secretario de estado . . . de 1824*, 14–15.

66. "Consejo ordinario de gobierno del lunes 15 de noviembre de 1824," in *Acuerdos del consejo . . . , 1821–1824*, 276; Bushnell, *Santander Regime*, 149, n. 76.

67. "Decreto," 1 May 1826, in República de Colombia, Sala de Negocios Generales, *Codificación*, 2:333–34. For a subsequent project involving colonization by deported criminals, see also República de Colombia, *Esposición del secretario de estado . . . de 1834*, 43–45.

68. Legrand, *Frontier Expansion*, 6–7.

69. Esteban Díaz Granados to Domingo Caycedo, 17 May 1831, in *Archivo epistolar*, 2:247; *Present State of Colombia*, 281; Fals, *Mompox y Loba*, 140A–43A.

70. Hamilton, *Travels*, 1:62; Cochrane, *Journal*, 91; Gosselman, *Viaje*, 104.

71. Posada-Carbó, *Colombian Caribbean*, 31.

72. Fals, *Capitalismo*, 32–35, 40–41; F. Díaz, *Letras*, 44; Fals, *Retorno a la tierra*, 78–79.

73. Bushnell, *Santander Regime*, 143–46.

74. Edward Watts to John Bidwell, 19 August 1827, in Great Britain, PRO, FO 18–45, 356; Gosselman, *Viaje*, 72; Lemaître, *Historia general de Cartagena*, 4:56; Nichols, *Tres puertos*, 46, 48. On Francisco's involvement in the Conspiracy of the Fijo, see Chapter 4 and [Corrales], *Efemérides*, 2:66–69.

75. Fals, *Mompox y Loba*, 142A-43A.

76. Bushnell, *Santander Regime*, 278-79; Maingot, "Social Structure, Social Status," 313-14.

77. Hamilton, *Travels*, 1:15; Fidel Rivas to Santander, 1 March 1828, in *Archivo Santander*, 17:255-58. Although an 1826 law created a national militia, it never fully materialized ("Ley," 1 April 1826, in República de Colombia, Sala de Negocios Generales, *Codificación*, 2:251-68; Bushnell, *Santander Regime*, 260-61).

78. Bolívar to Santander, 21 December 1823, in Bolívar, *Obras completas*, 1:851.

79. J. M. Macpherson to Henry Clay, 6 May 1826, in United States, NA, DCC, roll 1.

80. Le Moyne, *Viaje*, 79-81, 202.

81. *Present State of Colombia*, 278, 282. According to Charles S. Cochrane (*Journal*, 119), the total cost of his one-month trip from Mompox to Honda amounted to U.S. $1,200, including the food for passengers and bogas.

82. "Ley," 11 April 1825, in República de Colombia, Sala de Negocios Generales, *Codificación*, 2:72-85.

83. Nichols, *Tres puertos*, 45-49.

84. "Ley," 3 May 1826, in República de Colombia, Sala de Negocios Generales, *Codificación*, 2:356-63.

85. "Ley," 1 May 1826, ibid., 2:330-33.

86. Le Moyne, *Viaje*, 33-88. The bogas both sickened and captured the imagination of foreign travelers. In addition to the works cited in Chapter 2, see Cochrane, *Journal*, 74-75, 89-173; Hamilton, *Travels*, 1:79-82; and Gosselman, *Viaje*, 117, 124, 127-28. Interestingly, none of these accounts describes a conversation with bogas.

87. Burgos, *El general Burgos*, 46, 62. For a similar case in Ciénaga, see Cochrane, *Journal*, 67.

88. Bushnell, *Santander Regime*, 229-36. Colombia was the first independent Spanish American nation to have diplomatic relations with the Vatican—in 1836 (Bushnell, *Making of Modern Colombia*, 89).

89. Mecham, *Church and State*.

90. "Decreto," 18 March 1826, in República de Colombia, Sala de Negocios Generales, *Codificación*, 2:243-44.

91. República de Colombia, *Memoria que el secretario de estado . . . de 1823*, 36-39.

92. For example, in 1825 out of the 34 members of the electoral college of Cartagena Province, 9 were clergymen (among them José María Berástegui) and only 2 were generals (among them José Padilla) ("Acta de instalación," 2 October 1825, in [Corrales], *Efemérides*, 2:330).

93. L. García, *Reseña histórica*, 333-52.

94. Visita pastoral del Sr. obispo de Cartagena, Juan Hermenegildo de León, y disposiciones de su diócesis, in Colombia, AHNC, RE, CB, tomo 17, 1838, fols. 36-68, 76. On Díaz de Lamadrid's diocesan tour, see Chapter 2. For an informative comment by New Granada's minister of the interior on Juan Fernández de Soto-

mayor's visit to the region in 1834, when he was the apostolic vicar of Cartagena, see Lino de Pombo to Obispo de Leuca, vicario apostólico de Cartagena, 1834, in [Corrales], *Efemérides*, 3:237–39.

95. Visita pastoral . . . de León, fol. 38v.

96. Bushnell, *Santander Regime*, 200.

97. Visita pastoral . . . de León, fols. 54, 51, 54v.

98. "Se ordena," 15 October 1827, in *Decretos del Libertador*, 2:373–76.

99. Visita pastoral . . . de León, fol. 62.

100. José María [Estévez], obispo de Santa Marta, to secretario del interior, 20 June 1833, in Colombia, AHNC, RE, CB, tomo 15, fol. 286.

101. José María [Estévez] to ministro de estado, 24 August 1828, ibid., tomo 28, fol. 700.

102. Nicolás P. Prieto to secretario del interior, 9 April 1833, ibid., tomo 15, fols. 283–85.

103. Prieto to secretario del interior, ibid., fol. 285; José María to secretario del interior, 20 June 1833, ibid., fols. 284–85.

104. José Francisco Escudero to intendente del Magdalena, 11 September 1823, 29 October 1823, in Colombia, AHNC, RE, GM, tomo 373, fols. 306, 312. See also Valentin Arcía moviliza contra los blancos en Majagual, ibid., AC, 1822, leg. 61, fols. 1166v.

105. Arcía moviliza contra los blancos en Majagual, in Colombia, AHNC, RE, AC, 1822, leg. 61, fols. 1166, 1167, and leg. 96, fols. 317v–318.

106. Disturbios en Mompox, 1823, ibid., leg. 66, fol. 808.

107. Bernabé Noguera to Manuel Pardo, 4 June 1823, in Colombia, AHNC, RE, HI, leg. 1, no. 027, fols. 168–69.

108. Disturbios en Mompox, 1823, ibid., AC, leg. 66, fol. 808v.

109. Ibid., fols. 804–6; Santander to President of the Senate, 6 August 1823, in Santander, *Cartas y mensajes*, 241; "Consejo ordinario de gobierno del lunes 11 de agosto de 1823," in *Acuerdos del consejo . . . , 1821–1824*, 145.

110. Defensa presentada por el señor Remigio Márquez a la comisión nombrada por el Senado para instruir el proceso de la acusación que contra él puso la Cámara de Representantes, 17 February 1824 (Bogotá: Imprenta de Jayme Cowie, 1824), in Colombia, AHNC, RE, AR, fondo II, caja 32, vol. 54, fols. 5–17. Marixa Lasso, in a study to demonstrate the popularity of the Haitian Revolution among Caribbean New Granada's pardo population, did not refer to the documents indicating that the authors of the broadside were Márquez's enemies (Lasso, "Haiti as an Image," 181–84).

111. "Consejo ordinario de gobierno del lunes 5 de enero de 1824," in *Acuerdos del consejo . . . , 1821–1824*, 175; "Consejo ordinario de gobierno del lunes 19 de enero de 1824," ibid., 177–78; Márquez al supremo poder ejecutivo, 23 March 1824, in Colombia, AHNC, RE, NJ, rollo 1, fols. 483–89; Santander to President of the Senate, 28 April 1824, in Santander, *Cartas y mensajes*, 4:387. See also Bushnell, *Santander Regime*, 65–66.

112. Arcía moviliza, in Colombia, AHNC, RE, AC, 1822, leg. 61, fols. 1147–1147v.

113. Ibid., fol. 1163.

114. Ibid., leg. 96, fol. 25, and leg. 61, fol. 1166; also leg. 96, fol. 314.

115. Ibid., leg. 61, fol. 1167.

116. Ibid., leg. 96, fols. 310–22v.

117. *Present State of Colombia*, 208.

118. Watts to Col. P. Campbell, 19 April 1825, in Great Britain, PRO, FO 135-3.

119. Rafael Tono to comandante general del departamento del Magdalena, 10 July 1822, in Colombia, AHNC, RE, GM, tomo 360, 1824, fol. 47; "Consejo ordinario de gobierno del martes 18 de noviembre de 1823," in *Acuerdos del consejo . . . , 1821-1824*, 164–65; *Present State of Colombia*, 208.

120. Gosselman, *Viaje*, 57, 114; Striffler, "El Alto Sinú," pt. 1, 324–25.

121. Nieto, "Geografía histórica," 167–84; Macpherson to Secretary of State, 18 January 1834, in United States, NA, DCC, roll 2; Ramón León Sánchez to Secretary of State, 14 May 1840, NA, DCC, roll 3.

122. Nieto, "Geografía histórica," 168, 183, 204–5.

123. Macpherson to Secretary of State, 20, 25 August 1835, in United States, NA, DCC, roll 2.

124. J. Posada, *Memorias*, 4:284; Cochrane, *Journal*, 96.

125. Nieto, "Geografía histórica."

126. Hamilton, *Travels*, 1:60–61, 92 (quotation).

127. Watts to Earl of Aberdeen, 25 March 1829, in Great Britain, PRO, FO 135-13.

128. Nieto, "Geografía histórica," 192; also 171, 173, 176, 195.

129. Ibid., 163–206.

130. Colombia, AHNC, RE, Censos, Censo de 1835. See also Chapter 6.

131. Nieto, "Geografía histórica," 170, 192–97; Hamilton, *Travels*, 1:45–46; Macpherson to Secretary of State, 18 January 1834, in United States, NA, DCC, roll 2.

132. Striffler, "El Alto Sinú," pt. 1, 326–27; Nieto, "Geografía histórica," 182; Mollien, *Voyage*, 1:26.

133. Striffler, "El Alto Sinú," pt. 2, 377–83.

134. Prieto to secretario del interior, fols. 283–85; Visita pastoral . . . de León, fols. 52v–54v.

135. Mollien, *Voyage*, 1:24; [Bache], *Notes on Colombia*, 261.

136. Colmenares, "El tránsito a sociedades campesinas," 20–21. Whereas the total population of New Granada increased by 212.7 percent between 1778 and 1835, that of the Caribbean provinces grew only by 147.4 percent (F. Gómez, "Los censos en Colombia," tables 1, 3).

137. Fals, *Mompox y Loba*, 140A–46A, 145B–146B; Posada-Carbó, *Colombian Caribbean*, 31.

138. On the massive distribution of public lands to private entrepreneurs after 1870 and the rapid expansion of the cattle industry partly under antioqueño control, see Legrand, *Frontier Expansion*, 41–45, and Posada-Carbó, *Colombian Caribbean*, 76–81, which stresses the positive role of cattle ranching as formative of an integrated market and well adapted to the region's scant resources.

139. Arcía moviliza, in Colombia, AHNC, RE, AC, 1822, leg. 96, fol. 310.

140. See Bolívar to Santander, 21 December 1823, in Bolívar, *Obras completas*, 1:851.

141. Macpherson to Clay, 6 May 1826, in United States, NA, DCC, roll 1.

142. Whereas Sargeant Eustaquio Ponzales was sentenced to death and executed for stealing some cartridges and greatcoats for other soldiers in Ciénaga, Lieutenant Guillermo Thompson got his death sentence, for abandoning the guard and beating up a sargeant, commuted to four years of prison ("Consejo ordinario del miércoles 25 de mayo de 1825" and "Consejo ordinario del miércoles 12 de abril de 1826," in *Acuerdos del consejo . . . , 1825-1827*, 53, 146).

143. Macpherson to Clay, 30 March 1827, in United States, NA, DCC, roll 1.

144. Maingot, "Social Structure, Social Status," 313. For a general discussion of the nineteenth-century Colombian army, see Tirado, *Aspectos sociales*. Only veterans who had joined the patriot army before February 1819 and had at least two years of service could claim a bonus in national property, a program that chiefly benefited the high-ranking officers and for which most Caribbean New Granadan veterans did not qualify (Bushnell, *Santander Regime*, 275-77).

145. Pombo to Obispo de Leuca, in [Corrales], *Efemérides*, 3:238.

146. Rensselaer to his father, 17 March 1829, in Bonney, *Legacy*, 1:465, 467, 469.

147. Hamilton, *Travels*, 1:20, 85-86.

148. Cochrane, *Journal*, 149-50.

149. Rensselaer to his father, 17 March 1829, in Bonney, *Legacy*, 1:469; Cochrane, *Journal*, 78-85.

150. Visita pastoral . . . de León, fol. 41.

151. Gosselman, *Viaje*, 116. See also Hamilton, *Travels*, 1:78.

152. Hamilton, *Travels*, 1:93. Hamilton gives this translation of the Spanish verses: "Perish the miserable Spanish Tyrants / Long live the American Republicans!"

153. Rensselaer to his father, 1 January 1829, in Bonney, *Legacy*, 1:447-48; J. J. Aversenc to Minister, 30 December 1837, in France, MAE-Paris, CCC, no. 1, fol. 283.

154. See, e.g., Hamilton, *Travels*, 1:88; Mollien, *Voyage*, 1:24; [Bache], *Notes on Colombia*, 256, 261; Camille de Saint-Germain, Notice sur la République de Colombie, année 1824, in France, MAE-Paris, MD, Amérique, no. 39; Gosselman, *Viaje*, 59, 91; Macpherson to Clay, 6 May 1826, in United States, NA, DCC, roll 1; Rensselaer to his father, 6 February 1829, in Bonney, *Legacy*, 1:462; and Le Moyne, *Viaje*, 43. For recent interpretations along comparable lines, see Fals, *Mompox y Loba*, 154B-161B, and Rey, *El hombre y su río*, 107-12. See also the Conclusion below.

155. Rensselaer to his father, 17 March 1829, in Bonney, *Legacy*, 1:467.

156. Mollien, *Voyage*, 1:17; also 1:26.

157. *Present State of Colombia*, 282.

158. Hamilton, *Travels*, 1:64.

CHAPTER SIX

1. General José Padilla, *Al respetable público de Cartagena*, 15 November 1824, in Colombia, AHNC, RE, AR, fondo XI, caja 88, vol. 170, fols. 125-26 (emphasis in the original).

2. Bolívar to Santander, 7 April 1825, in Bolívar, *Obras completas*, 1:1076.

3. Santander to Bolívar, 21 July 1825, in Santander, *Cartas Santander-Bolívar*, 5:16.

4. Bolívar to Santander, 20 May 1825, in Bolívar, *Obras completas*, 1:1097. The Colombian-Mexican project to liberate Cuba was definitively abandoned because the United States and Britain feared that it would provoke a slave uprising and produce a reduction in U.S.-Cuban trade (Santander to Bolívar, 6 March 1826, in Santander, *Cartas Santander-Bolívar*, 5:154; J. M. Restrepo, *Historia de la revolución*, 5:237-45).

5. Padilla, *Al respetable público de Cartagena*.

6. E. Uribe, *Padilla*, 65-133, 194-278, 306. On Montilla's and other generals' attempts to disprove the leading role of Padilla in Maracaibo, see Torres, *El Almirante*, 319-24. For the private aspects of this rivalry, see J. Zapata, *Piar, Petión y Padilla*, 189-265.

7. Montilla to Santander, 10, 30 April 1822, in Montilla, *General*, 2:922-23, 927. See also Conde, "Provincias, ciudadanía y 'clase,'" 100.

8. Montilla to Santander, 20 August 1822, in Montilla, *General*, 2:943.

9. Montilla to Santander, 10 August 1822, ibid., 2:941.

10. Montilla to Santander, 20 February 1823, ibid., 2:969.

11. Padilla to Santander, 30 August 1824, in E. Uribe, *Padilla*, 301-3.

12. Torres, *El Almirante*, 155; Bushnell, *Santander Regime*, 319-21.

13. Santander to Bolívar, 6 October, 6 November 1825, in Santander, *Cartas Santander-Bolívar*, 5:60, 101-2.

14. Bolívar to Santander, 27 October 1825, in Bolívar, *Obras completas*, 1:1222.

15. For example, in Getsemaní in 1822, out of 233 baptized black or mulatto infants, only 80 were born to legally married parents; in 1829, out of 130 baptized infants of African descent, only 23 had legally married parents (Colombia, APST, Libro bautismos de pardos, Febrero 18 1818 a 17 de Mayo 1824 and Libro de bautismos de pardos y morenos, desde 16 de Octubre de 1828 hasta 28 de Febrero de 1830). In contrast, among the white parishioners of La Catedral, out of 60 infants baptized in 1829, 38 were born to legally married parents and only 10 to unwed parents, but as many as 12 were foundlings—more than three times the rate of child abandonment in Getsemaní for the same year (Colombia, APC, Libro de Blancos, 1820-32 [copiador]).

16. Edward Watts to Joseph Planta, 30 November 1824, in Great Britain, PRO, FO 18-7, 231v.

17. "Apelación a la razón" (Bogotá, 1828), in Torres, *El Almirante*, 351.

18. "10 de Octubre de 1825 en la ciudad de Cartagena," *Correo del Magdalena*, 13 October 1825, in [Corrales], *Efemérides*, 2:333; Torres, *El Almirante*, 147-48.

19. E. Uribe, *Padilla*, 306.

20. Gosselman, *Viaje*, 98-100.

21. Bolívar to Antonio José Sucre, 12 May 1826, in Bolívar, *Obras completas*, 1:1323.

22. Bolívar to Santander, 7 May 1826, ibid., 1:1322. See also Bolívar to Santander, 7 June 1826, ibid., 1:1365.

23. Bolívar to Santander, 27 December 1825, 13 June 1826, ibid., 1:1252-54, 1371; Bolívar to Sucre, 12 May 1826, ibid., 1:1323-24; Liévano, *Bolívar*, 462; Nicholls, *From Dessalines to Duvalier*, 59.

24. Bolívar to Rafael Urdaneta, Cristóbal Mendoza, Francisco Javier Yanes, José Padilla, Mariano Montilla, Tomás Cipriano de Mosquera, Juan Paz del Castillo, and Pedro Briceño Méndez, 6-8 August 1826, in Bolívar, *Obras completas*, 1:1408-15. See also Bolívar to Páez, 4 August 1826, ibid., 1:1406-8. On Antonio Leocadio Guzmán and his appreciation of Bolívar's constitutional project, see Duarte, *Poder y política*, 468-72, 480-85.

25. See Montilla's correspondence with Bolívar, in Montilla, *General*, 1:217-49, 565-77; Padilla to Santander, 20 August 1826, and Padilla to Páez, 29 July 1826, in *Archivo Santander*, 15:125-29.

26. Padilla to Bolívar, 6 October 1826, in O'Leary, *Memorias del General O'Leary*, 7:423-25.

27. Manuel Marcelino Núñez to Santander, 25 September 1826, in *Archivo Santander*, 15:216-17.

28. "Acta de la municipalidad de Cartagena," 29 September 1826, in [Corrales], *Efemérides*, 2:336-38.

29. Antonio L. Guzmán to Bolívar, 1 October 1826, in O'Leary, *Memorias del General O'Leary*, 2:354-55.

30. Calixto Noguera to Santander, 2 October 1826, in *Archivo Santander*, 15:238.

31. Padilla to Santander, 2 October 1826, ibid., 15:229-32.

32. Cited in Torres, *El Almirante*, 189.

33. Juan de Dios Amador to Santander, Núñez to Santander, and Noguera to Santander, 2 October 1826, in *Archivo Santander*, 15:233, 235, 238-39.

34. Guzmán to José Gabriel Pérez, 1 October 1826, in O'Leary, *Memorias del General O'Leary*, 2:357-59.

35. "Acta de la municipalidad de Cartagena," 337-38. See also "Fiestas nacionales en diciembre de 1826," *Gaceta de Cartagena de Colombia*, 31 December 1826, in [Corrales], *Efemérides*, 2:343-44; *La Lanza Llanera* (Cartagena), 1826 (n.d.), in Colombia, AHNC, RE, AR, fondo XI, caja 88, vol. 170, fols. 141-42.

36. J. M. Macpherson to Henry Clay, 24 March 1827, in United States, NA, DCC, roll 1; "Decreto," 23 November 1826, "Reglamentación," 8 March 1827, in *Decretos del Libertador*, 2:30-31, 98-155; Bushnell, *Santander Regime*, 338-43.

37. Watts to George Canning, 27 March 1827, and Watts to John Bidwell, 29 March 1827, in Great Britain, PRO, FO 18-45.

38. Macpherson to Clay, 30 March 1827, in United States, NA, DCC, roll 1.

39. Bolívar to Páez, 11 July 1827, in Bolívar, *Obras completas*, 2:141.

40. For a description of the banquet at Padilla's home, see *Aurora de Colombia*,

2 August 1827. On Bolívar's policy toward the navy in 1826–27, see Torres, *El Almirante*, 161–63, 180–82, 188.

41. Salzedo, *Apuntaciones*, 188–89; "Entrada del Libertador en Cartagena," *Gaceta de Cartagena de Colombia*, in [Corrales], *Efemérides*, 2:347–48.

42. For examples of anti-Santander publications in Cartagena, see Se ve frecuentemente la verdad sufrir algun eclipse, Cartagena, 1827, in Colombia, AHNC, RE, AR, fondo XI, caja 88, vol. 170, fols. 144–47; Los facciosos se destruyen por su propia malignidad, Cartagena, 1827, ibid., fols. 148–55; and Juan Bautista Calcaño a sus conciudadanos, Cartagena, 8 July 1827, ibid., fols. 158–59.

43. "Ley," 29 August 1827, in República de Colombia, Sala de Negocios Generales, *Codificación*, 3:307; P. Moreno, *Santander*, 393–408; Bushnell, *Santander Regime*, 269–70; Uribe-Urán, *Honorable Lives*, 90.

44. Bolívar to Montilla, 6 November 1827, in Bolívar, *Obras completas*, 2:194.

45. Padilla to Santander, 9 February 1828, in *Archivo Santander*, 17:245–46.

46. Exposición dirigida a la Gran Convención por la división del Magdalena, 25 February 1828, in Colombia, AHNC, RE, AR, fondo XI, caja 88, vol. 170, fols. 161–67.

47. Montilla to secretario de estado del despacho del interior, 7 March 1828, in [Corrales], *Efemérides*, 2:359–61; Padilla to director de la comisión de la Gran Convención, 12 March 1828, in *Gaceta de Colombia* (Bogotá), no. 342, 1 May 1828.

48. "Se fijan," 20 February 1828, and "Autorización," 23 February 1828, in *Decretos del Libertador*, 3:27–32.

49. "Proceso por los tumultos de Cartagena levantado por el general Mariano Montilla . . . contra el general Padilla y los oficiales que se negaron a firmar la representación militar contra la convención de Ocaña," 12 March 1828, in Torres, *El Almirante*, 331.

50. Ibid., 334.

51. Montilla to secretario de estado, in [Corrales], *Efemérides*, 2:361.

52. Ibid., 2:361–62; Padilla to director de la comisión, 12 March 1828; "Apelación a la razón," in Torres, *El Almirante*, 348; José Montes to Montilla, n.d., in Montilla, *General*, 1:388–90. For a version of the events that hypothesizes the direct participation of Montes in Montilla's scheme, see Otero, *Vida del Almirante*, 92–95.

53. *La Cotorra*, 23 April 1828; "Apelación a la razón," in Torres, *El Almirante*, 345–51; Manifestación que Manuel Pérez de Recuero hace a sus conciudadanos, Cartagena, 20 July 1831, in Colombia, BNC, SP, no. 573; Otero, *Vida del Almirante*, 91–98; Torres, *El Almirante*, 209.

54. Padilla to director de la comisión, 12 March 1828.

55. "Apelación a la razón," in Torres, *El Almirante*, 350. See also Watts to Earl of Dudley, 7 March 1828, in Great Britain, PRO, FO 18–57, 113–18; *El Calamar*, 13 March 1828, in Colombia, AHNC, RE, AR, fondo XI, caja 77, vol. 5.

56. "Proceso por los tumultos," in Torres, *El Almirante*, 329, 333–34.

57. *El Amanuense*, 16 March 1828.

58. "Proceso por los tumultos," in Torres, *El Almirante*, 329, 333–34, 337–38.

59. Ibid., 327–30.

60. Torres, *El Almirante*, 145–48.

61. Vicente Ucrós to secretario de estado del despacho del interior, 9 March 1828, in [Corrales], *Efemérides*, 2:355-57; *El Amanuense*, 16 March 1828, in United States, NA, DCC, roll 1.

62. "Proceso por los tumultos," in Torres, *El Almirante*, 331, 333.

63. Padilla to director de la comisión, 12 March 1828; Vicente Ucrós, Al público, Cartagena, 19 May 1832, in Colombia, BNC, SS, Sala 1, no. 12881, pieza 32.

64. Padilla to consul de los Estados Unidos de la América del Norte, 9 March 1828, in United States, NA, DCC, roll 1.

65. Otero, *Vida del Almirante*, 97-98.

66. Padilla to Bolívar, 12 March 1828, partly cited in Torres, *El Almirante*, 214-15. See also J. Posada, *Memorias*, 1:128.

67. Padilla to director de la comisión, 12 March 1828.

68. Padilla to Montilla, 13 March 1828, in Montilla, *General*, 1:394-95.

69. *Documentos sobre el proceso de la conspiración*, 13-15, 249. See also Cordovez, *Reminiscencias*, 732-33, 741.

70. Bolívar to Briceño, 16 November 1828, and Bolívar to Páez, 16 November 1828, in Bolívar, *Obras completas*, 2:505-8.

71. "Proceso por los tumultos," in Torres, *El Almirante*, 337; Bossa, *La vida novelesca*, 9.

72. Padilla to Santander, 10 May 1825, in *Archivo Santander*, 11:355-56; Montilla to Santander, 20 September 1825, in Montilla, *General*, 2:991-92; Torres, *El Almirante*, 149-50.

73. Padilla to Santander, 25 February 1827, in *Archivo Santander*, 16:245-46.

74. *La Cotorra*, 23 April 1828. For a later confirmation of this accusation, see Ucrós, Al público, in Colombia, BNC, SS, Sala 1, no. 12881, pieza 32.

75. Urdaneta to Montilla, 28 July 1828, in *Archivo Santander*, 17:374; "Declaración del señor doctor Ignacio Muñoz," 7 June 1828, in O'Leary, *Memorias del General O'Leary*, 26:292-93. On 1 October 1828 Muñoz, on his way to be prosecuted in Bogotá, escaped near Nare. He took temporary refuge in Riohacha, from where he wrote an obsequious letter to Bolívar. First confined to Riohacha, Muñoz went into exile in Venezuela, where he remained until 1855. He died in Cartagena at age seventy-four. Until the end, he continued to practice law and to be involved in disputes, but he never again achieved political recognition (Adlercreutz to jefe superior del distrito, 5 October 1828, in Colombia, AHNC, RE, GM, tomo 432, fol. 470; Muñoz to Bolívar, 10 December 1828, in O'Leary, *Memorias del General O'Leary*, 9:569-70; Bossa, *La vida novelesca*, 17-24).

76. Watts to Earl of Dudley, 8 March 1828, in Great Britain, PRO, FO 18-57, 118-19.

77. *El Amanuense*, 16 March 1828.

78. Daniel O'Leary to Bolívar, 5 April 1828, in Cordovez, *Reminiscencias*, 693.

79. J. Posada, *Memorias*, 1:127.

80. F. Gómez, "Los censos en Colombia," 20, table 3.

81. [Bache], *Notes on Colombia*, 277.

82. M. Rodríguez and J. Restrepo, "Los empresarios extranjeros," 142-43; Bell, "Conflictos regionales," 40-43.

83. See, e.g., Macpherson to John Quincy Adams, 12 October 1823, and Macpherson to Clay, 16 October 1823, in United States, NA, DCC, roll 1; B. Chassériau, Compte-rendu d'une mission remplie à [sic] Colombie, 20 October 1824, in France, MAE-Paris, MD, Fonds Divers, Amérique, no. 39, fol. 148.

84. Gosselman, *Viaje*, 33.

85. Colmenares, "El tránsito a sociedades campesinas," 23.

86. Joaquin Mosquera to Santander, 18 February 1833, in *Archivo Santander*, 20:103.

87. Colombia, AHNC, RE, Censos, Censo de 1835. See also Chapter 3.

88. Colombia, AHNC, RE, Censos, Censo de 1835. As another indicator of the continuing importance of slavery, in Getsemaní 20 percent of the 130 pardo and black infants baptized in 1829 were born to slave mothers (Colombia, APST, Libro de bautismos de pardos y morenos, desde 16 de Octubre de 1828 hasta 28 de Febrero de 1830).

89. Macpherson to Clay, 24 March 1827, in United States, NA, DCC, roll 1; Mollien, *Voyage*, 1:16.

90. Macpherson to Clay, 30 March 1827, in United States, NA, DCC, roll 1.

91. Watts to Bidwell, 3 February 1827, in Great Britain, PRO, FO 18-45, 69. On the 1823 mutiny, see Watts to Colonel P. Campbell, 19 April 1825, ibid., FO 135-3.

92. Watts to Canning, 27 March 1827, ibid., FO 18-45.

93. "Consejo ordinario del sábado 7 de julio de 1827," in *Acuerdos del consejo . . . , 1825-1827*, 260-61; Manifestos públicos de los oficiales de los cuerpos militares de Cartagena en favor de Bolívar, 16-18 June 1827, in Great Britain, PRO, FO 18-45.

94. Exposición dirigida a la Gran Convención, 25 February 1828.

95. Macpherson to Clay, 6 May 1826, in United States, NA, DCC, roll 1.

96. Escudero to intendente del Magdalena, 11 September 1823, and Padilla to intendente, 20 March 1825, in Colombia, AHNC, RE, GM, tomo 373, fols. 306-9, 347.

97. Bolívar to Santander, 27 October 1825, in Bolívar, *Obras completas*, 1:1222.

98. For a comparison with Juan José Nieto, see the Introduction.

99. On Páez's leadership, see A. Gómez, *Páez*, 182-298, and Hébrard, "Pueblos y actores municipales."

100. Padilla to Santander, 18 March, 2 April, 18 August 1827, in *Archivo Santander*, 16:299, 322-23, 17:154.

101. Bonifacio Rodríguez to Santander, 31 March, 16 April 1827, ibid., 16:319, 333.

102. Contiene quince cartas dirigidas por mi hermana a sujetos respetables y su contestación, in Colombia, AHNC, RE, HI, tomo 1, fols. 375-411.

103. Magdalena Padilla, A la impostura y la intriga. La justicia y la verdad, in Colombia, AHNC, RE, AR, Documentos varios de Cartagena, rollo 5, fondo 1, vol. 9, fol. 339.

104. "Defensa hecha por . . . Toledo," in [Corrales], *Documentos*, 1:379.

105. Aversenc, Etat commercial, industriel, politique et moral de la province de Carthagène, 27 September 1837, in France, MAE-Paris, CCC, no. 1, fol. 236.

106. Notably José María del Real, Vicente Ucrós, and Ignacio Muñoz had pardo wives (Montilla to Santander, 20 February 1823, in Montilla, *General*, 2:969).

107. Macpherson to Clay, 4 October 1829, in United States, NA, DCC, roll 1.

108. Macpherson to Clay, 6 May 1826, ibid.; Adolphe Barrot to ministre, 4 May 1832, in France, MAE-Paris, CCC, no. 1, fols. 15-16.

109. Aversenc, Etat commercial, 27 September 1837, in France, MAE-Paris, CCC, no. 1, fols. 234-35. See also Juan and Ulloa, *Relación histórica*, 50-55.

110. J. Posada, *Memorias*, 2:195-99, 202-3.

111. Rensselaer to his father, 1 January 1829, in Bonney, *Legacy*, 1:447-48. See also Aversenc to ministre, 30 December 1837, in France, MAE-Paris, CCC, no. 1, fol. 283.

112. Rensselaer to his father, 1 January 1829, in Bonney, *Legacy*, 1:446. See also "Fiestas nacionales en diciembre de 1826," in [Corrales], *Efemérides*, 2:343-44.

113. "Fiestas nacionales en diciembre de 1826," 2:343-44.

114. Pedro Rodríguez to Adlercreutz, Cartagena, 21 March 1828, in Parra-Pérez, *La Cartera del coronel*, 40-43; Salzedo, *Apuntaciones*, 191; F. Díaz, *Letras*, 36.

115. Bell, "Conflictos regionales," 44.

116. *El Observador Samario*, 2 November 1825.

117. Salzedo, *Apuntaciones*, 188.

118. Montilla to Bolívar, 7 October, 13 December 1826, in Montilla, *General*, 1:576-77, 579; Miguel Arismendi to Bolívar, 13 December 1826, in O'Leary, *Memorias del General O'Leary*, 2:475-77; Se ve frecuentemente la verdad sufrir algun eclipse, in Colombia, AHNC, RE, AR, fondo XI, caja 88, vol. 170, fols. 144-47.

119. Nichols, *Tres puertos*, 134, 151; Salzedo, *Apuntaciones*, 190; Hamilton, *Travels*, 1:15.

120. Colombia, AHNC, RE, Censos, Censo de 1835.

121. Visita pastoral del Sr. obispo de Cartagena, Juan Hermenegildo de León, y disposiciones de su diócesis, ibid., CB, tomo 17, 1838, fol. 41v.

122. Gosselman, *Viaje*, 58-59; Consul Fauche to James Henderson, 10 January 1826, in Great Britain, PRO, FO 135-8; Le Moyne, *Viaje*, 20; Bermúdez, *Materiales para la historia*, 313.

123. "Consejo ordinario de gobierno del martes 3 de agosto de 1824, in *Acuerdos del consejo . . . , 1821-1824*, 256; Decree of 18 March 1826, in República de Colombia, Sala de Negocios Generales, *Codificación*, 2:243-44.

124. Fauche to Henderson, 10 January 1826, in Great Britain, PRO, FO 135-8. See also Nichols, *Tres puertos*, 171-72, 175.

125. Rensselaer to his father, 1 January, 13 May 1829, in Bonney, *Legacy*, 1:453, 477-78.

126. Colombia, AHNC, RE, Censos, Censo de 1835; Nieto, "Geografía histórica," 168-69; Posada-Carbó, *Una invitación a la historia de Barranquilla*, 17. Barranquilla fully developed only in the 1870s.

127. For this hatred, see, e.g., Bolívar to Urdaneta, 25 October 1830, in Bolívar, *Obras completas*, 2:939-40.

128. Liévano, *Bolívar*, 502-13.

129. Montilla to Adlercreutz, 20, 25 June 1828, 2, 18 July 1828, in Parra-Pérez,

La Cartera del coronel, 54–59, 63–66. See also Bushnell, *Making of Modern Colombia*, 67. For examples of bolivarista propaganda in the press, see *Las Reformas*, August–October 1828, and *La Luna*, October–November 1828.

130. Salzedo, *Apuntaciones*, 193; L. García, *Reseña histórica*, 341.

131. Montilla to secretario del estado, 10 October 1828, in Colombia, AHNC, RE, GM, tomo 432, fol. 449.

132. Se denuncia al subteniente retirado Antonio Pérez, 21 October 1828, ibid., fols. 569–74.

133. Montilla to Adlercreutz, January–July 1829, in Parra-Pérez, *La Cartera del coronel*, 71–72, 77, 80, 89–98; Montilla to Urdaneta, 9 July 1829, in *El Hércules*, 13 June 1831; Rensselaer to his father, 17 November 1829, in Bonney, *Legacy*, 2:7.

134. Liévano, *Bolívar*, 535–36. See also Bushnell, *Making of Modern Colombia*, 67–73.

135. Honrados Vallenatos y Paceños, 9 February 1830, in Colombia, AHNC, RE, AR, Documentos varios de Cartagena, rollo 5, fondo 1, vol. 9, fol. 346.

136. For a sympathetic account of Bolívar's last years, see G. García Márquez, *El general en su laberinto*.

137. J. M. Restrepo, *Historia de la revolución*, 6:417.

138. Bolívar to Urdaneta, 25 October 1830, in Bolívar, *Obras completas*, 2:939–40.

139. J. M. Restrepo, *Historia de la revolución*, 6:419, and *Diario político*, 2:160.

140. Salzedo, *Apuntaciones*, 196; J. M. Restrepo, *Historia de la revolución*, 6:407–9, 415–20. On Sardá, see P. Moreno, *Santander*, 585–87.

141. "Exequias fúnebres," 17 January 1831, in [Corrales], *Efemérides*, 2:461–64.

142. Juan de Francisco Martín to ministro de estado, 2 February 1831, ibid., 3:5.

143. "Movimientos contra el régimen dictatorial," ibid., 3:10–13.

144. Pronunciamiento de los cantones de Barlovento, 13 February 1813, in Colombia, AHNC, RE, AR, fondo XI, caja 88, vol. 170, fols. 171–73.

145. Antonio Pantoja, "A la autoridades civiles y militares," 14 February 1831, in [Corrales], *Efemérides*, 3:17–18.

146. M. J. del Castillo to general comandante de armas de la provincia, 15 February 1831, ibid., 3:14–15.

147. J. M. Restrepo, *Diario político*, 2:160.

148. Francisco to ministro de estado, 16 and 25 February 1831, in [Corrales], *Efemérides*, 3:10, 19–21; *Gaceta de Colombia*, no. 508, 20 March 1831, 3.

149. J. M. Restrepo, *Historia de la revolución*, 6:476–79.

150. "Acta de los cuerpos que componen la división que, al mando del señor general José Ignacio Luque, existen en los cantones de Barranquilla y Soledad," 6 March 1831, in [Corrales], *Efemérides*, 3:41–43.

151. Ignacio Luque to ministro de estado, 27 April 1831, ibid., 3:86–87.

152. Francisco Carmona to ministro secretario de estado, 2 May 1831, in *Gaceta de Colombia*, no. 528, 7 August 1831.

153. Carmona to Montilla, 13 March 1831, in *Rejistro oficial del Magdalena*, 23 August 1831; "Acta de la parroquia de San Juan de la Ciénaga," 8 March 1831, and

"Acta de la capital de la provincia de Santa Marta," 9 March 1831, both in [Corrales], *Efemérides*, 3:43–45.

154. Macpherson to Secretary of State, 31 March 1831, in United States, NA, DCC, roll 2; J. M. Restrepo, *Historia de la revolución*, 6:479–88; Lemaître, *Historia general de Cartagena*, 4:67–75.

155. "Pronunciamientos habidos en Mompox," 8 April 1831, in [Corrales], *Efemérides*, 3:79–85; Salzedo, *Apuntaciones*, 198–99.

156. José María Cataño to Caicedo, 10 May 1831, in *Gaceta de Colombia*, no. 521, 19 June 1831; "Acta de la ciudad de Riohacha," 26 April 1831, ibid., no. 522, 26 June 1831.

157. Mauricio José Romero to Domingo Caycedo [Caicedo], 9 May 1831, in *Archivo epistolar*, 2:234–36; "Enérgica representación de los padres de familia y otros vecinos de la plaza de Cartagena," 21 April 1831, in [Corrales], *Efemérides*, 3:72–74.

158. "Enérgica representación," 3:73.

159. "Capitulación de la plaza de Cartagena," 23 April 1831, in *Gaceta de Colombia*, no. 517, 22 May 1831.

160. *Gaceta de Colombia*, no. 519, 5 June 1831.

161. P. Moreno, *Santander*, 547–49, 567–70.

162. Luque to Caycedo [Caicedo], 18 June 1831, in *Archivo epistolar*, 3:72–74.

163. *Correo Semanal*, 8 July 1831; "Sociedad de 'Veteranos Defensores de la Libertad,'" in [Corrales], *Efemérides*, 3:104–5.

164. *Correo Semanal*, 24 June 1831. See also other issues of *Correo Semanal*; *El Cartagenero Liberal*, June–August 1831; and *El Hércules*.

165. *Rejistro oficial del Magdalena*, 13 October 1831.

166. *Correo Semanal*, 8 July, 2 September 1831.

167. *El Cartagenero Liberal*, 17 August 1831. For similar accusations, see also Los liberales, El cañón está cargado, Cartagena, 1831, and Los liberales, Al público, Cartagena, 1831, in Colombia, BNC, SP, no. 573.

168. *Correo Semanal*, 19 August 1831.

169. *El Latigazo*, no. 2, 1831 (n.d.); *El Perro Registrón*, nos. 3–5, 1831 (n.d.).

170. Manifestación que Manuel Pérez de Recuero hace a sus conciudadanos, Cartagena, 20 July 1831, in Colombia, BNC, SP, no. 573; Ucrós, Al público, BNC, SS, Sala 1, no. 12881, pieza 32.

171. *El Hércules*, 24 August 1831.

172. J. M. Restrepo, *Diario político*, 2:204.

173. J. Manuel Montoya to Caycedo [Caicedo], 29 July 1831, 25 August 1831, in *Archivo epistolar* 3:126–27, 150–51. See also J. M. Restrepo, *Diario político*, 2:204, 213.

174. Manuel Romay to Caycedo [Caicedo], 2 September 1831, in *Archivo epistolar*, 3:159–62.

175. Montoya to Caycedo [Caicedo], 9 September 1831, ibid., 3:170–71.

176. On the Baptist War, see Craton, *Testing the Chains*, 291–321.

177. J. M. Restrepo, *Diario político*, 2:230.

178. *Rejistro oficial del Magdalena*, 17 November 1831. For another example, see *El Hércules*, 24 August 1831.

179. "Testamento de Loperena," in T. D. Gutiérrez, *Valledupar*, 251; "Codicilo del Ilmo. Obispo Dr. José María Estévez," 13 October 1834, in L. García, *Reseña histórica*, 360. Many Liberals implicated in the attempted assassination of Bolívar in 1828 went to jail with their personal slaves or servants (*Los Riohacheros defensores*, 30 May 1833).

180. *Gaceta [de Colombia] extraordinaria*, 24 August 1831.

181. *El Hércules*, 3 August 1831; *Correo Semanal*, 19 August 1831; J. M. Restrepo, *Historia de la revolución*, 6:574–75, 581.

182. Riohacha to editor del *Rejistro oficial del Magdalena*, 30 August 1831, supp. to *Rejistro oficial del Magdalena*, 1831 (n.d.) ("he came to conquer us"); Al general José Sardá, por una multitud de ciudadanos, Fonseca, 20 July 1831, supp. to *Rejistro oficial del Magdalena*, 1831 ("a multitude of citizens" and "restrain those . . . of the revolution"). See also J. M. Restrepo, *Diario político*, 2:187.

183. Los Samarios, Censura política, 5 July 1832, in Colombia, AHNC, RE, AR, fondo XI, caja 88, vol. 170, fols. 177–83. Sardá ended up being one of the leaders of the conspiracy of 23 July 1833 against Santander's government; his accomplices were other dismissed officers as well as clergymen and bolivaristas from the elite of Bogotá. Sentenced to death, Sardá escaped from prison and was shot when discovered (P. Moreno, *Santander*, 588–608).

184. See, e.g., Carmona to Montilla, 13 March 1831, in *Rejistro oficial del Magdalena*, 23 August 1831, and *Gaceta de Colombia*, no. 520, 12 June 1831.

185. "Acta de la ciudad de Riohacha," 26 April 1831, *Gaceta de Colombia*, no. 522, 26 June 1831.

186. Luque to ministro de estado, 27 April 1831; *Constituciones de Colombia*, 712–13.

187. J. M. Restrepo, *Historia de la revolución*, 1:19; Hébrard, "Pueblos y actores municipales." Such stereotypical representations still inspire some scholarship. Notably, Claudio Véliz (*Centralist Tradition*, 160–61) attributes the failure of Gran Colombia to Bolívar's attempt to federate three already centralized and culturally different societies, adding: "The most symbolically appropriate man in Venezuela was probably the llanero, the cow-hand, in Colombia, the scholar, in Ecuador, the monk."

188. Guerra, "Le peuple souverain," 35.

189. P. Moreno, *Santander*, 534.

CONCLUSION

1. Nieto to Santander, 7 August 1835, in Bell, "Una temprana argumentación." Federalism briefly became a reality in November 1840, when various Caribbean cities as well as the towns and communities in their jurisdiction, like other areas in New Granada, rejected the authority of Bogotá in the civil war of the "Supremes" (1839–42). The rebellion on the coast started in Santa Marta and Ciénaga, under the same Venezuelan general—Francisco Carmona—as in 1831. Nieto participated and was promoted to general. Yet the movement rapidly lost momentum as a result of the continuing antagonism between Caribbean cities and the usual attempt by Car-

tagena to disassociate itself from the others. Once again, the region's fragmentation benefited the Andean center (Bell, "Conflictos regionales," 47-48).

2. There is extensive scholarship on Antioquia. See, e.g., Parsons, *Antioqueño Colonization*; Christie, *Oligarcas, campesinos*; and Santa, *La colonización antioqueña*.

3. For example, in 1833 Valledupar and Riohacha competed for jurisdiction over the area of San Juan del César, each claiming loyalty to Santander (*Los Riohacheros defensores*, 30 April 1833).

4. Bell, *Política, políticos*, 8.

5. On the growth of Barranquilla, see Nichols, *Tres puertos*, 171-84, 261-68, and Posada-Carbó, *Colombian Caribbean*, 113-46.

6. Lynch, *Caudillos*, 132-82, 402-9.

7. Walker, *Smoldering Ashes*, 4.

8. As shown by a critical review of Fals's *El Presidente Nieto*, the profoundly republican and urban Juan José Nieto, who presided over the sovereign state of Bolívar in the early 1860s, cannot be characterized as a caudillo (Archila, "Creamos").

9. On Peru, see Thurner, *From Two Republics*, 5-19.

10. Edicto, 6 May 1811, *El Argos Americano*, 13 May 1811, in Arrázola, *Documentos*, 173-77; Lynch, *Spanish American Revolution*, 84, 154, 197, 311, 315-16. Morelos and his followers, however, did not promote land distribution or peasant recovery of hacienda lands (Van Young, *The Other Rebellion*, 434-35, 502-3; Guardino, *Peasants, Politics*, 64).

11. República de Colombia, *Exposición que el secretario del interior . . . de 1833*, 36, 64-68; Safford, "Race, Integration, and Progress," 12-13.

12. "Peticiones de la Cámara de provincia al poder ejecutivo," *El Constitucional de Cartagena* 13, 10 January 1836.

13. "Comunicaciones," *El Constitucional de Cartagena* 14, 20 January 1836.

14. Bushnell, "Aspectos de historia electoral," 29-30; Bushnell, *Santander Regime*, 268-70.

15. Nieman, *Promises to Keep*, 10-14.

16. Keyssar, *Right to Vote*, 2-25, 56.

17. Heuman, *Between Black and White*, 44-53.

18. Janvier, *Les constitutions d'Haiti*, 117. For Haiti's 1805 and 1816 constitutions, see ibid., 30-41, 112-42. See also Fick, "French Revolution," 51-75.

19. "Constitución política de la monarquía española" (1812).

20. E. Restrepo, *Historia de la provincia*, 469-70.

21. Twinam, "Is Race a 'Defect'?"

22. "Constitución política de la monarquía española" (1876), 67-83.

23. Bushnell, "La evolución del derecho de sufragio," 190-94.

24. Bushnell, "El sufragio en la Argentina," 11-14.

25. Graham, "Ciudadanía y jerarquía," 358-62; Flory, "Race and Social Control," 204.

26. Lynch, *Spanish American Revolution*, 84-85, 156, 197, 311, 315-16.

27. Bolívar, Habitantes de la Costa Firme, 23 May 1816, A los habitantes de Río Caribe, Carúpano y Cariaco, 2 June 1816, Bando de Villa de Cura, 11 March 1818,

and Bando de La Victoria, 13 March 1818, in Bolívar, *Obras completas*, 2:1092–93, 1120–21.

28. "Ley fundamental de la república de Colombia" (17 December 1819).

29. Bolívar al presidente del soberano congreso de Colombia, 14 July 1821, in Bolívar, *Obras completas*, 1:576.

30. The other former Spanish colonies that freed their slaves were Ecuador (1852), Argentina and Uruguay (1853), Venezuela and Peru (1854), and Bolivia (1861).

31. For a comparative study of abolition in the Americas, see Blackburn, *Overthrow of Colonial Slavery*; Klein, *African Slavery*, 243–71; Drescher, *Capitalism and Antislavery*; and Davis, *Slavery and Human Progress*, 231–315.

32. Vinson, *Bearing Arms*, 5, 226–27; Childs, "Aponte Rebellion," 211–61; Paquette, *Sugar Is Made with Blood*, 228.

33. Apparently, the collection of the casta tribute was exceptional to Mexico. According to David Cahill, Spain failed to introduce it in Peru in 1779–80 (e-mail message to author, 14 November 2002). In 1788 it gave up trying to levy it in Nicaragua due to the resistance of "this province's exorbitant number of mulattoes" ("Consulta del Consejo de las Indias," 10 September 1788, in Konetzke, *Colección de documentos*, 628–31). Matt Childs found no mention that it was levied in Cuba (e-mail message to author, 10 December 2002).

34. On the Pernambuco rebellion, see Viotti, *Brazilian Empire*, 11–12. On Venezuela, see McKinley, *Pre-Revolutionary Caracas*, 173, and Hamnett, "Process and Pattern," 317–19. Although the 1797–99 abortive Gual-España conspiracy in La Guaira and Caracas, Venezuela, included Spaniards, free men of color, and white creoles and sought independence, tax reforms, and racial equality, as well as the abolition of slavery and the Indian tribute, it had the characteristics of a military coup and received no support from the creole elite (McKinley, *Pre-Revolutionary Caracas*, 135–38; Domínguez, *Insurrection or Loyalty*, 151).

35. Kraay, "Politics of Race."

36. Craton, *Testing the Chains*, 11–17.

37. Borrego, *Palenques de negros*; T. D. Gutiérrez, *Cultura vallenata*, 199–222.

38. Craton, *Testing the Chains*, 241–53.

39. See, e.g., Cunin, "Le métissage dans la ville," 66–68.

40. Vivanco sobre la venta de Bernal, in Colombia, AHNC, CO, NE, tomo 1, 1791, fols. 703v–705.

41. Sharp, *Slavery on the Spanish Frontier*, 148–54; Geggus, "Slavery, War, and Revolution."

42. Nicholls, *From Dessalines to Duvalier*, 1–43.

43. Heuman, *Between Black and White*, 3–96; Craton, *Testing the Chains*, 291–321.

44. Pérotin-Dumon, "Free Colored and Slaves"; Geggus, "Slaves and Free Coloreds"; Handler, *Unappropriated People*, 190–218; Beckles, "On the Backs of Blacks."

45. Brito, *Las insurrecciones de los esclavos*, 59–77; Lombardi, *Decline and Abolition*; Wright, *Café con leche*, 25–35.

46. Childs, "Aponte Rebellion," 324–408; Paquette, *Sugar Is Made with Blood*.

47. Reis, *Slave Rebellion in Brazil*.

48. Childs, "Aponte Rebellion," 409–26.

49. Cited by Burns, "Unfixing 'Race,'" September 2002.

50. See, e.g., Lucena, "Las nuevas poblaciones," 777.

51. About his youth in Martinique, Frantz Fanon (1925–61) wrote: "In the Antilles, there was also that little hiatus that exists between the hordes of creole whites, mulattoes, and niggers [*la békaille, la mulâtraille et la négraille*]. But I was satisfied with an intellectual understanding of these differences." It was in France, when "the white man's eyes" transformed him into the Other, a "nigger," that Fanon (himself a *mulâtre*) understood that the only way to overcome alienation was "to assert myself as a BLACK MAN" above the differences in color, class, and education. (Fanon, *Peau noire masques blancs*, 109, 113).

52. Mörner, *Race Mixture*, 56–60; Williamson, *New People*.

53. See, e.g., Holt, *Problem of Freedom*.

54. Wright, *Café con leche*; Hoetink, "'Race.'"

55. Childs, "Aponte Rebellion," 68–77; Watson, "Salmagundis *vs.* Pumpkins."

56. Fals, *El Presidente Nieto*, 65B, 70B–72B.

57. See esp. Cope, *Limits of Racial Domination*; Graham, *Patronage and Politics*; and Butler, *Freedoms Given*, 21–24. On the endurance of Colombia's two-party system, see Bergquist, *Labor in Latin America*, 274–375.

58. Wright, *Café con leche*; Viotti, *Brazilian Empire*, 234–46; Helg, *Our Rightful Share*; Hanchard, *Orpheus and Power*.

59. For a comparative examination of political versus cultural strategies by Afro-Brazilians, see Butler, *Freedoms Given*.

60. Fals, *Mompox y Loba*, 154B–161B; Rey, *El hombre y su río*.

61. See, e.g., James C. Scott, *Domination and the Arts of Resistance*. For a more balanced discussion, see Kertzer, *Ritual, Politics*.

62. N. García, *Transforming Modernity*, 171.

63. For this practice in the early 1960s, see Havens, Montero, and Romieux, *Cereté*, 106–8.

64. Recent scholarship has shown a high incidence of female-headed households and single motherhood *regardless of race* in several Latin American cities in the late eighteenth and early nineteenth centuries. See Dueñas, *Los hijos del pecado*, 245–65; Hünefeldt, *Paying the Price of Freedom*, 138; Kuznesof, *Household Economy*, 162–63, 181; and Kinsbruner, *Not of Pure Blood*, 109–12. For an example in a small town linked to the expansion of the latifundio at the expense of small farms, see Metcalf, *Family and Frontier*, 144–48. For free unions, polygamy, and machismo in mid-twentieth-century Caribbean Colombia, see V. Gutiérrez, *Familia y cultura*, 281–312; Dussán, "La estructura de la familia"; and Havens, Montero, and Romieux, *Cereté*, 11, 57–58, 96–98, 103–6, 248–52.

65. Fals, *Mompox y Loba*, 150B–152B, and *El Presidente Nieto*, 150B–154B; Freyre, *Masters and the Slaves*. For an analysis of the exploitative effects of latifundio and caudillismo in the early 1960s, see Havens, Montero, and Romieux, *Cereté*.

66. For the similar importance of family labor to the survival of small farms in a Brazilian rural community, see Metcalf, *Family and Frontier*, 132–35.

67. On women's economic role in San Juan, Puerto Rico, see Matos, *Women and Urban Change*, 84–100.

68. Silva Dias, *Power and Everyday Life*.

69. Lombardi, *People and Places*, 82; Hünefeldt, *Paying the Price of Freedom*, 93–94; Arrom, *Women of Mexico City*, 105–11; Kuznesof, *Household Economy*, 83; Hanger, *Bounded Lives*, 19–23; Kinsbruner, *Not of Pure Blood*, 82–84.

70. See Nishida, "Manumission and Ethnicity," 375–76, n. 47.

71. Hünefeldt, *Paying the Price of Freedom*, 167–72; A. J. Díaz, "Gender Conflicts." The disappearance of pre-1850 notary and judicial records of several Caribbean Colombian archives has made thorough research impossible.

72. Kuznesof, *Household Economy*, 73. Few studies of child abandonment exist for late-colonial and early-republican Latin America, but interestingly Bogotá, with its mostly mestizo population, also exhibits a low rate of *expósitos* (below 5 percent) similar to that of Cartagena (Dueñas, *Los hijos del pecado*, 230–31). On adoption and employment of unwanted children in the 1960s, see Havens, Montero, and Romieux, *Cereté*, 104–5.

73. Weber and Rausch, Introduction to *Where Cultures Meet*, xxix.

74. Guy and Sheridan, "On Frontiers," 15.

75. Cunha, *Rebellion in the Backlands*; Langfur, "Forbidden Lands," 322–23.

76. Degler, *Neither Black nor White*, 51–52.

77. Karash, "Interethnic Conflict and Resistance."

78. See Grahn, *Political Economy of Smuggling*, 1–8, and Zuluaga, *Guerrilla y sociedad*.

79. Rosero, "Los afrodescendientes y el conflicto."

BIBLIOGRAPHY

MANUSCRIPTS AND ARCHIVAL SOURCES

Colombia
Archivo del Arzobispado de Cartagena
Archivo Eclesiástico de Santa Marta
Archivo Histórico de Cartagena
    Fondo Gobernación
      Serie Justicia
Archivo Histórico Nacional de Colombia, Bogotá
    Sección Colonia
      Fondo Aduana
      Fondo Caciques e Indios
      Fondo Censos Varios Departamentos
      Fondo Genealogías
      Fondo Miscelánea
      Fondo Negros y Esclavos
    Sección República
      Archivo Restrepo
      Fondo Asuntos Criminales
      Fondo Censos
      Fondo Curas y Obispos
      Fondo Guerra y Marina
      Fondo Historia
      Fondo Negocios Judiciales
Archivo de la Parroquia de La Catedral, Cartagena
Archivo de la Parroquia de la Santísima Trinidad, Getsemaní, Cartagena
Biblioteca Nacional de Colombia, Bogotá
    Sala Manuscritos
    Sala Pineda
    Sala Samper

France
Ministère des Affaires Etrangères, Paris
    Correspondance Consulaire, Colombie, Carthagène
    Mission Diplomatique

Great Britain
Public Record Office, London
  Foreign Office Papers

Spain
Archivo General de Indias, Seville
  Audiencia de Santa Fe
  Estado
  Papeles de Cuba
Archivo General de Simancas
  Secretaría de Guerra

United States
National Archives, Washington, D.C.
  Dispatches from the U.S. Consuls in Cartagena, Colombia, 1822–1906
    (Microcopy)

NEWSPAPERS AND PERIODICALS

Amanuense o Rejistro político y militar, El (Cartagena), 16 March 1828
Argos Americano, El (Cartagena), 1810–11
Aurora de Colombia (Cartagena), August 1827
Calamar, El (Cartagena), 1828
Cartagenero Liberal, El, June–August 1831
Constitucional de Cartagena, El, 1836
Constitucional del Magdalena, El (Cartagena), 1833
Correo Semanal (Cartagena), 1831
Cotorra, La (Cartagena), April 1828
Gaceta de Cartagena, 1830
Gaceta de Cartagena de Colombia, 1822
Gaceta de Colombia, 1831
Gaceta de Colombia (Bogotá), 1821–31. Facsimile ed. 5 vols. Bogotá: Banco de la
  República, 1973.
Gaceta [de Colombia] extraordinaria, August 1831
Hércules, El (Cartagena) 1831
Latigazo, El (Cartagena), 1831
Luna, La (Cartagena), October–November 1828
Mundo Observador, El (Cartagena), 1826
Observador Samario, El (Santa Marta), November 1825
Perro Registrón, con Rabia, El (Cartagena), 1831
Reformas, Las (Cartagena), 1828
Rejistro oficial del Magdalena (Cartagena), 1831
*Riohacheros defensores de la constitución y leyes del Estado de la Nueva Granada,
  Los* (Riohacha?), 30 May 1833

Acuerdos del consejo de gobierno de la república de Colombia, 1821-1824. 1892.
Reprint, Bogotá: Fundación para la Conmemoración del Bicentenario del
Natalicio y el Sesquicentenario de la Muerte del General Francisco de Paula
Santander, 1988.

Acuerdos del consejo de gobierno de la república de Colombia, 1825-1827. 1892.
Reprint, Bogotá: Fundación para la Conmemoración del Bicentenario del
Natalicio y el Sesquicentenario de la Muerte del General Francisco de Paula
Santander, 1988.

Alexander, Alexander. *The Life of Alexander Alexander Written by Himself.*
Edited by John Howell. Vol. 2. Edinburgh: William Blackwood, 1830.

Archivo epistolar del general Domingo Caycedo [Caicedo]. 3 vols. Bogotá: Editorial
A.B.C., 1943, 1946-47.

Archivo Santander. 24 vols. Edited by Ernesto Restrepo Tirado (1913-20); Diego
Mendoza Pérez, J. M. Henao, and Gerardo Arrubla (1923-32). Bogotá:
Aguila Negra Editorial, 1913-32.

Arévalo, Antonio de. "Informe rendido al virrey, Cartagena de Indias a 9 de
diciembre de 1766." In *Tercer Congreso Hispanoamericano de Historia-Segundo
de Cartagena de Indias,* 327-52. Cartagena: Talleres Gráficos Mogollón, 1962.

Arguedas, Luis. "Diario de una expedición reservada a cargo del capitán de
fragata Luis Arguedas (Reconocimiento de la costa de Tiburón) (Fundación de
Carolina)," 1786-87. In *Colección de documentos inéditos sobre la geografía y la
historia de Colombia,* edited by Antonio B. Cuervo, 1:371-429. Bogotá:
Imprenta de Vapor de Zalamea Hermanos, 1891.

Arrázola, Roberto. *Los mártires responden. . . .* Cartagena: Ediciones Hernández,
1973.

———, ed. *Documentos para la historia de Cartagena.* Vol. 1. Cartagena: Edición
Oficial, 1963.

[Bache, Richard]. *Notes on Colombia, Taken in the Years 1822-23.* Philadelphia:
H. C. Carey and I. Lea, 1827.

Bentivenga de Napolitano, Carmela, ed. *Cedulario indígena venezolano, 1501-
1812.* Caracas: Universidad Católica Andrés Bello, 1977.

Bolívar, Simón. *Obras completas.* Edited by Vicente Lecuna. 2 vols. La Habana:
Editorial Lex, 1947.

Bonney, Catharina V.[issher Van] R.[ensselaer], ed. *Legacy of Historical
Gleanings.* 2 vols. Albany, N.Y.: J. Munsell, 1875.

Caballero y Góngora, Antonio. "Relación del estado del Nuevo Reino de
Granada," 1789. In *Relaciones e informes de los gobernantes de la Nueva
Granada,* edited by Germán Colmenares, 1:361-492. Bogotá: Banco Popular,
1989.

Camacho Roldán, Salvador. *Notas de viaje (Colombia y Estados Unidos de
América).* Vol. 1. 1890. Reprint, Bogotá: Banco de la República, 1973.

*Cartas escritas desde Colombia: Durante un viaje de Caracas a Bogotá y desde allí
a Santa Marta en 1823.* 1824. Reprint, Bogotá: Banco de la República, 1975.

Carta pastoral del Ilustrísimo señor don Pedro A. Brioschi al clero y pueblo de la diócesis de Cartagena con motivo de la santa visita. Cartagena: Tipografía de "San Pedro Claver," 1898.

Cochrane, Charles Stuart. *Journal of a Residence and Travels in Colombia during the Years 1823 and 1824.* Vol. 1. 1825. Reprint, New York: AMS Press, 1971.

Colombia, Comisión Corográfica. *Jeografia física i politica de las provincias de la Nueva Granada.* Por la Comisión Corográfica bajo la dirección de Agustín Codazzi. Compiled by Eduardo Acevedo Latorre. 4 vols. 1856. Reprint, Bogotá: Banco de la República, 1957-59.

Congreso de Cúcuta, 1821. *Libro de Actas.* 1921. Reprint, Bogotá: Publicaciones del Banco de la República, 1971.

Constitución política de Colombia, 1991. Mexico, D.F.: Universidad Nacional Autónoma de México-Fondo de Cultura Económica, 1994.

"Constitución política de la monarquía española" (1812). In *Textos de las constituciones de Cuba, 1812-1940,* edited by Antonio Barreras, 3-59. Havana: Editorial Minerva, 1940.

"Constitución política de la monarquía española" (1876). In *Textos de las constituciones de Cuba, 1812-1940,* edited by Antonio Barreras, 67-83. Havana: Editorial Minerva, 1940.

Constituciones de Colombia, Las. Vol. 2. Edited by Diego Uribe Vargas. Madrid: Ediciones Cultura Hispánica, 1977.

[Corrales, Manuel Ezequiel, ed.]. *Documentos para la historia de la provincia de Cartagena de Indias, hoy estado soberano de Bolívar en la Unión colombiana.* 2 vols. Bogotá: Imprenta de Medardo Rivas, 1883.

[————, ed.]. *Efemérides y anales del estado de Bolívar.* 4 vols. Bogotá: Casa Editorial de J. J. Pérez, 1889.

Cuervo, Antonio B., ed. *Colección de documentos inéditos sobre la geografía y la historia de Colombia.* Vol. 1. Bogotá: Imprenta de Vapor de Zalamea Hermanos, 1891.

Decretos del Libertador. 3 vols. Caracas: Imprenta Nacional, 1961.

De-Mier, José María, ed. *Poblamientos en la provincia de Santa Marta: Siglo XVIII.* 3 vols. Bogotá: Colegio Máximo de las Academias de Colombia-Libreros Colombianos, 1987.

Dessalines d' Orbigny, Alcide. *Voyage pittoresque dans les deux Amériques: Résumé général de tous les voyages de Colomb, Las-Casas, Oviedo [. . .].* Paris: L. Tenré, 1836.

[Díaz de Lamadrid, José Fernández]. "Visita pastoral de la ciudad y diócesis de Cartagena de Indias, 1778-1781, practicada por el Ilmo. Fray José Fernández Díaz de Lamadrid." In *Cartas de los obispos de Cartagena de Indias durante el período hispánico, 1534-1820,* edited by Gabriel Martínez Reyes, 639-98. Medellín: Editorial Zuluaga, 1986.

Documentos sobre el proceso de la conspiración del 25 de Septiembre de 1828. Originales del Fondo Pineda y del Archivo Histórico que reposan en la Biblioteca Nacional, edited by Enrique Ortega Ricaurte. Bogotá: Prensa de la Biblioteca Nacional, 1942.

Eslava, Sebastián de. "Defensa del Gobierno del virrey Eslava, hecha por el oidor Eslava" (October 1751). In *Relaciones e informes de los gobernantes de la Nueva Granada*, edited by Germán Colmenares, 1:41-101. Bogotá: Banco Popular, 1989.

Ezpeleta, Josef de. "Relación del gobierno del Excmo Sor. Dn. Josef de Ezpeleta, etc., en este Nuevo Reino de Granada con expresión de su actual estado en los diversos ramos que abraza [. . .]" (1796). In *Relaciones e informes de los gobernantes de la Nueva Granada*, edited by Germán Colmenares, 2:153-311. Bogotá: Banco Popular, 1989.

Fernández de Sotomayor, Juan. *Catecismo o instrucción popular*. Cartagena: Imprenta del Gobierno, 1814.

Fidalgo, Joaquín Francisco. "Expedición Fidalgo" (1790s). In *Colección de documentos inéditos sobre la geografía y la historia de Colombia*, edited by Antonio B. Cuervo, 1:1-305. Bogotá: Imprenta de Vapor de Zalamea Hermanos, 1891.

García del Rio, Juan. "Sitio de Cartagena de 1815." In *Antecedentes y consecuencias del once de noviembre de 1811 (Testimonios y documentos relacionados con la gloriosa gesta de la independencia absoluta de Cartagena de Indias)*, edited by Eduardo Lemaître, 76-104. Cartagena: Impresora Marina, 1961.

Gil y Lemos, Francisco. "Relación de D. Francisco Gil y Lemos" (1789). In *Relaciones e informes de los gobernantes de la Nueva Granada*, edited by Germán Colmenares, 2:5-33. Bogotá: Banco Popular, 1989.

Gosselman, Carl August. *Viaje por Colombia, 1825 y 1826*. Translated by Ann Christien Pereira. Bogotá: Banco de la República, 1987.

Guirior, Manuel. "Instrucción que deja a su sucesor en el mando el virrey Manuel Guirior." (1776). In *Relaciones e informes de los gobernantes de la Nueva Granada*, edited by Germán Colmenares, 1:271-359. Bogotá: Banco Popular, 1989.

Hall, Francis. *Colombia: Its Present State, in Respect of Climate, Soil, Productions, Population, Government, Commerce, Revenue, Manufactures, Arts, Literature, Manners, Education and Inducements to Emigration*. London: Baldwin, Cradock and Joy, 1825.

Hamilton, J[ohn] P[otter]. *Travels through the Interior Provinces of Columbia* [*sic*]. 2 vols. London: John Murray, 1827.

Humboldt, Alexander von. "Diario VII a y b." In Alexander von Humboldt, *En Colombia: Extractos de sus Diarios preparados y presentados por la Academia colombiana de ciencias exactas, físicas y naturales y la Academia de Ciencias de la República democrática alemana*, 11,a-136,a. Bogotá: Flota Mercante Grancolombiana, 1982.

Juan, Jorge, and Antonio de Ulloa. *Relación histórica del viage hecho de orden de S. Mag. a la América meridional [. . .]*. Madrid: Antonio Marín, 1748.

Julián, Antonio. *La perla de la América, provincia de Santa Marta (Edición facsimilar)*. 1787. Reprint, Bogotá: Academia Colombiana de Historia, 1980.

Konetzke, Richard, ed. *Colección de documentos para la historia de la formación* social de Hispanoamérica, 1493-1810. Vol. 3. Madrid: Consejo Superior de Investigaciones Científicas, 1962.

Le Moyne, Augusto. *Viaje y estancia en la Nueva Granada.* Bogotá: Editorial Incunables, 1985.

"Ley fundamental de la república de Colombia" (17 December 1819). In *Las Constituciones de Colombia*, edited by Diego Uribe Vargas, 2:699-702. Madrid: Ediciones Cultura Hispánica, 1977.

"Ley 70 sobre negritudes aprobada por el congreso en 1993." In Carlos Calderón Mosquera, *Investigaciones históricas y temas económicos*, 119-211. Cali: Editorial Claridad Ltda., 1993.

Martínez Reyes, Gabriel, ed. *Cartas de los obispos de Cartagena de Indias durante el período hispánico, 1534-1820.* Medellín: Editorial Zuluaga, 1986.

Mendinueta, Pedro. "Relación del estado del Nuevo Reino de Granada: Año 1803." In *Relaciones e informes de los gobernantes de la Nueva Granada*, edited by Germán Colmenares, 3:5-191. Bogotá: Banco Popular, 1989.

Messía de la Zerda, Pedro. "Relación del estado del Virreinato de Santafé, que hace el Excmo. Sr. D. Pedro Messía de la Zerda a su sucesor el Excmo. Sr. D. Manuel Guirior. Año 1772." In *Relaciones e informes de los gobernantes de la Nueva Granada*, edited by Germán Colmenares, 1:123-52. Bogotá: Banco Popular, 1989.

Mollien, Gaspard. *Voyage dans la république de Colombia, en 1823.* 2 vols. Paris: Arthus Bertrand, 1824.

Montalvo, Francisco de. "Instrucción sobre el estado en que deja el Nuevo Reino de Granada en 1818." In *Relaciones e informes de los gobernantes de la Nueva Granada*, edited by Germán Colmenares, 3:193-336. Bogotá: Banco Popular, 1989.

Montilla, Mariano. *General de División, Homenaje en el bicentenario de su nacimiento, 1782-1982.* 2 vols. Caracas: Ediciones de la Presidencia de la República, 1982.

Moreno y Escandón, Francisco Antonio. "Estado del Virreinato de Santafé, Nuevo Reino de Granada, y relación de su gobierno y mando del excelentísimo señor Bailio Frey Pedro Messía de la Cerda [. . .]," 1772. In *Relaciones e informes de los gobernantes de la Nueva Granada*, edited by Germán Colmenares, 1:153-270. Bogotá: Banco Popular, 1989.

Narváez y la Torre, Antonio de. "Discurso del mariscal de campo de los reales ejércitos D. Antonio de Narváez y la Torre sobre la utilidad de permitir el comercio libre de neutrales en este reyno" (5 June 1805). In *Ensayos de dos economistas coloniales: Don Antonio de Narváez y la Torre y don José Ignacio de Pombo*, edited by Sergio Elías Ortiz, 67-120. Bogotá: Banco de la República, 1965.

———. "Provincia de Santa Marta y Río Hacha del Virreynato de Santafé. Informe del gobernador" (19 May 1778). In *Ensayos de dos economistas coloniales: Don Antonio de Narváez y la Torre y don José Ignacio de Pombo*, edited by Sergio Elías Ortiz, 17-65. Bogotá: Banco de la República, 1965.

Nieto, Juan José. "Bosquejo histórico de la revolución que regeneró al Estado de

Bolívar." In Juan José Nieto, *Selección de textos políticos, geográfico e históricos*, edited by Gustavo Bell Lemus, 51-115. Barranquilla: Ediciones Gobernación del Atlántico, 1993.

———. "Geografía histórica, estadística y local de la provincia de Cartagena, República de la Nueva Granada descrita por cantones." In Nieto, *Selección de textos políticos, geográfico e históricos*, 119-208.

[Núñez, Manuel Marcelino]. *Exposición de los acontecimientos memorables relacionados con mi vida política, que tuvieron lugar en este país desde 1810 en adelante*. Cartagena: Imp. de Hernández e Hijos, 1864.

O'Leary, Daniel Florencio. *Memorias del General O'Leary publicadas por su hijo, Simón B. O'Leary, por orden del gobierno de Venezuela y bajo los auspicios de su presidente, general Guzmán Blanco*. 32 vols. Caracas: Imprenta de la "Gaceta Oficial," 1874-1914.

"Pacificación general de los indios del Darién," 21 July 1787. *Boletín de Historia y Antigüedades* 148 (June 1920): 197-202.

Palacios de la Vega, Joseph. *Diario de viaje del P. Joseph Palacios de la Vega entre los indios y negros de la provincia de Cartagena en el nuevo reino de Granada, 1787-1788*. Edited by Gerardo Reichel Dolmatoff. Bogotá: Editorial ABC, 1955.

Parra-Pérez, Caracciolo, ed. *La cartera del coronel conde de Adlercreutz: Documentos inéditos relativos a la historia de Venezuela y de la Gran Colombia*. Paris: Editions Excelsior, 1928.

Peredo, Diego de. "Noticia historial de la provincia de Cartagena de Indias, año 1772." *Anuario Colombiano de Historia Social y de la Cultura* 6-7 (1971-72): 125-54.

Pombo, José Ignacio de. "Informe de José Ignacio de Pombo del consulado de Cartagena sobre asuntos económicos y fiscales" (18 April 1807). In *Ensayos de dos economistas coloniales: Don Antonio de Narváez y la Torre y don José Ignacio de Pombo*, edited by Sergio Elías Ortiz, 121-34. Bogotá: Banco de la República, 1965.

———. "Informe del real consulado de Cartagena de Indias a la junta provincial de la misma. Por el prior de ese cuerpo, D. José Ignacio de Pombo" (12 November 1810). In *Ensayos de dos economistas coloniales*, 135-271.

Posada Gutiérrez, Joaquín. *Memorias histórico-políticas*. 4 vols. Bogotá: Imprenta Nacional, 1929.

Present State of Colombia; Containing an Account of the Principal Events of Its Revolutionary War; The Expeditions Fitted Out in England to Assist in Its Emancipation; Its Constitution; Financial and Commercial Laws; Revenue, Expenditure and Public Debt; Agriculture; Mines; Mining and Other Associations, The, by an Officer, Late in the Colombian Service. London: John Murray, 1827.

Reclus, Elisée. *Viaje a la Sierra Nevada de Santa Marta*. 1914; reprint, Bogotá: Instituto Colombiano de Cultura-Colcultura, 1992.

República de Colombia. *Exposición del secretario de estado, en del despacho del interior i relaciones esteriores del gobierno de la Nueva Granada, al congreso constitucional del año de 1834, sobre los negocios de su departamento.* Bogotá: Imp. de B. Espinosa, 1844.

———. *Esposición que el secretario de estado del despacho del interior de la república de Colombia hizo al congreso de 1824, sobre los negocios de su departamento.* Bogotá: Imprenta de la República, 1824.

———. *Exposición que el secretario del interior i relaciones esteriores del gobierno de la Nueva Granada hace al congreso constitucional del año de 1833, sobre los negocios de su departamento.* Bogotá: Imp. de B. Espinosa, 1833.

———. *Memoria que el secretario de estado y del despacho del interior presentó al congreso de Colombia, sobre los negocios de su departamento, año de 1823.* Bogotá: Espinosa, 1823.

———. Sala de Negocios Generales del Consejo de Estado. *Codificación nacional de todas las leyes de Colombia desde el año de 1821, hecha conforme a la ley 13 de 1912.* 24 vols. Bogotá: Imprenta Nacional, 1924-33.

Restrepo, José Manuel. *Diario político y militar: Memorias sobre los sucesos importantes de la época para servir a la historia de la revolución de Colombia y de la Nueva Granada desde 1819 para adelante.* Vols. 1, 2. Bogotá: Imprenta Nacional, 1954.

———. *Historia de la revolución de la república de Colombia.* 6 vols. 1827. Reprint, Medellín: Editorial Bedout, 1969-70.

Santander, Francisco de Paula. *Cartas y mensajes del General Francisco de Paula Santander.* Vol. 4, *1822-1824,* edited by Roberto Cortazar. Bogotá: Talleres Editoriales de Librería Voluntad, 1954.

———. *Cartas Santander-Bolívar.* 5 vols. Bogotá: Fundación para la Conmemoración del Bicentenario del Natalicio y el Sesquicentenario de la Muerte del General Francisco de Paula Santander, 1988-90. Biblioteca de la Presidencia de la República.

Silvestre, Francisco. "Apuntes reservados particulares y generales del estado actual del Virreinato de Santafé de Bogotá [. . .]" (1789). In *Relaciones e informes de los gobernantes de la Nueva Granada,* edited by Germán Colmenares, 2:35-152. Bogotá: Banco Popular, 1989.

Solís, José de. "Relación del estado del Virreinato de Santafé, hecha por el Excmo. Sr. D. José de Solís al Excmo. Sr. Zerda. Año 1760." In *Relaciones e informes de los gobernantes de la Nueva Granada,* edited by Germán Colmenares, 1:103-21. Bogotá: Banco Popular, 1989.

Striffler, Luis. "El Alto Sinú: Historia del primer establecimiento para extracción de oro en 1844." Pt. 1. *Boletín Historial,* nos. 43-44 (November-December 1918): 317-46.

———. "El Alto Sinú." Pt. 2. *Boletín Historial,* nos. 45-46 (January-February 1919): 377-98.

———. "El Alto Sinú." Pt. 3. *Boletín Historial,* nos. 47-48 (March-April 1919): 513-36.

Torre y Miranda, Antonio de la. "Noticia individual de las poblaciones nuevamente fundadas en la Provincia de Cartagena" (1774-78). In *Documentos para la historia de Cartagena*, compiled by José P. Urueta, 4:33-78. Cartagena: Tipografía de Antonio Araújo L., 1890.

Urueta, José P., comp. *Documentos para la historia de Cartagena*. 6 vols. Cartagena: Tipografía de Antonio Araújo L., 1887-91.

Xavier Monty, Francisco. "Reconocimiento y exploración de la costa de Carolina y golfo del Darién por el teniente de navío D. Francisco Xavier Monty y otros ingenieros, 1761." In *Colección de documentos inéditos sobre la geografía y la historia de Colombia*, edited by Antonio B. Cuervo, 1:481-504. Bogotá: Imprenta de Vapor de Zalamea Hermanos, 1891.

SECONDARY SOURCES

Acosta Saignes, Miguel. *Vida de los esclavos negros en Venezuela*. Prologue by Roger Bastide. Caracas: Hesperides Distribución-Ediciones, 1967.

Aguledo Alvarado, Carlos Efrén. "Populations noires et politique dans le Pacifique colombien: Paradoxes d'une inclusion ambigüe." Ph.D. diss., Université de Paris III, 2002.

Alarcón, José C. *Compendio de historia del departamento del Magdalena (Desde 1.525 hasta 1.895)*. 1900. Reprint, Bogotá: Editorial El Voto Nacional, 1963.

Anna, Timothy E. "Spain and the Breakdown of the Imperial Ethos: The Problem of Equality." *Hispanic American Historical Review* 62 (1982): 242-72.

Archer, Christon I. "Pardos, Indians, and the Army of New Spain: Inter-Relationships and Conflicts, 1780-1819." *Journal of Latin American Studies* 6 (1974): 231-55.

Archila Neira, Mauricio. "Creamos: Cachacos violentos, costeños pachangosos. . . ." *Boletín Cultural y Bibliográfico* 21, no. 2 (1984): 112-13.

Arocha Rodríguez, Jaime. "Afro-Colombia Denied." In *Report on the Americas* 25 (February 1992): 28-31.

Arrázola, Roberto. *Secretos de la historia de Cartagena*. Cartagena: Tipografía Hernández, 1967.

Arrom, Silvia M. *The Women of Mexico City, 1790-1857*. Stanford, Calif.: Stanford University Press, 1985.

Assunção, Matthias Röhrig. "L'adhésion populaire aux projects révolutionnaires dans les sociétés esclavagistes: Le cas du Vénézuela et du Brésil, 1780-1840." *Caravelle* (Toulouse) 54 (1990): 291-313.

Avella Esquivel, Francisco. "Bases geohistóricas del Caribe colombiano." In Observatorio del Caribe colombiano. *Respirando el Caribe: Memorias de la cátedra del Caribe colombiano*, comp. Ariel Castillo Mier, 1:3-28. Bogotá: Editorial Gente Nueva Ltda., 2001.

Barbier, Jacques A. "Commercial Reform and *Comercio Neutral* in Cartagena de Indias, 1788-1808." In *Reform and Insurrection in Bourbon New Granada and Peru*, edited by John R. Fisher, Allan J. Kuethe, and Anthony McFarlane, 96-120. Baton Rouge: Louisiana State University Press, 1990.

Beckles, Hilary. "On the Backs of Blacks: The Barbados Free-Coloureds' Pursuit of Civil Rights and the 1816 Slave Rebellion." *Immigrants and Minorities* 3 (July 1984): 167–88.

Bell Lemus, Gustavo. *Cartagena de Indias: De la colonia a la república*. Bogotá: Fundación Simón y Lola Guberek, 1991.

———. "Conflictos regionales y centralismo: Una hipótesis sobre las relaciones políticas de la Costa Caribe con el gobierno central en los primeros años de la República, 1821–1840." In *El Caribe colombiano: Selección de textos históricos*, edited by Gustavo Bell Lemus, 39–48. Barranquilla: Editorial Uninorte, 1988.

———. *Política, políticos y desarrollo socio-económico de la costa atlántica: Una visión histórica*. Series Documentos, no. 5. Barranquilla: Universidad del Norte, 1989.

———. "Una temprana argumentación en favor del federalismo en la Costa caribe de la Nueva Granada." *Huellas* 19 (April 1987): 20–22.

———, ed. *El Caribe colombiano: Selección de textos históricos*. Barranquilla: Editorial Uninorte, 1988.

Bennett, Herman L. "A Research Note: Race, Slavery, and the Ambiguity of Corporate Consciousness." *Colonial Latin American Historical Review* 3 (Spring 1994): 207–13.

Bensusan, Guy. "Cartagena's Fandango Politics." *Studies in Latin American Popular Culture* 3 (1984): 127–34.

Bergquist, Charles. "In the Name of History: A Disciplinary Critique of Orlando Fals Borda's *Historia doble de la Costa*." *Latin American Research Review* 25 (Summer 1990): 156–76.

———. *Labor in Latin America: Comparative Essays on Chile, Argentina, Venezuela, and Colombia*. Stanford, Calif.: Stanford University Press, 1986.

Bermúdez y Bermúdez, Arturo. *Materiales para la historia de Santa Marta (Recopilación histórica)*. Bogotá: Editorial Kimpres Ltda, 1997.

Bierck, Harold A., Jr. "The Struggle for Abolition in Gran Colombia." *Hispanic American Historical Review* 33 (August 1953): 365–86.

Blackburn, Robin. *The Overthrow of Colonial Slavery, 1776–1848*. London: Verso, 1988.

Blanco Barros, José Agustín. *Atlántico y Barranquilla en la época colonial*. Barranquilla: Ediciones Gobernación del Atlántico, 1994.

Borrego Pla, María del Carmen. *Palenques de negros en Cartagena de Indias a fines del siglo diecisiete*. Sevilla: Escuela de Estudios Hispanoamericanos, 1973.

Bossa Herazo, Donaldo. *Cartagena independiente: Tradición y desarrollo*. Bogotá: Ediciones Tercer Mundo, 1967.

———. *La vida novelesca e infortunada del doctor Ignacio Múñoz, paladín de la libertad*. Cartagena: Impresora Marina, 1961.

Boswell, John. *The Kindness of Strangers: The Abandonment of Children in Western Europe from Late Antiquity to the Renaissance*. New York: Pantheon Books, 1988.

Brito Figueroa, Federico. *Las insurrecciones de los esclavos negros en la sociedad colonial venezolana*. Caracas: Editorial Cantaclaro, 1961.

Burgos Puche, Rubio Remberto. *El general Burgos*. Bogotá: Editorial ABC, 1965.

Burns, Kathryn. "Unfixing 'Race.'" September 2002. In author's possession.

Bushnell, David. "Aspectos de historia electoral colombiana del siglo XIX." In *Política y sociedad en el siglo XIX*, 28–38. Tunja, Colombia: Ediciones "Pato Marino," 1975.

———. "La evolución del derecho de sufragio en Venezuela." *Boletín Histórico* (Caracas) 29 (1972): 189–206.

———. "The Last Dictatorship: Betrayal or Consummation?" *Hispanic American Historical Review* 63 (February 1983): 65–105.

———. *The Making of Modern Colombia: A Nation in Spite of Itself.* Berkeley: University of California Press, 1993.

———. *The Santander Regime in Gran Colombia.* Newark: University of Delaware Press, 1954.

———. "El sufragio en la Argentina y en Colombia hasta 1853." *Revista del Instituto de Historia del Derecho Ricardo Levene* 19 (1968): 11–29.

Butler, Kim D. *Freedoms Given, Freedoms Won: Afro-Brazilians in Post-Abolition São Paulo and Salvador.* New Brunswick, N.J.: Rutgers University Press, 1998.

Carnicelli, Américo. *La masonería en la historia de la independencia de América, 1810–1830.* 2 vols. Bogotá: Cooperativa Nacional de Artes Gráficas, 1970.

Castro, Juan A. "De Neiva a Cartagena." In *Crónica grande del río de la Magdalena: Recompilación, notas, advertencias,* edited by Aníbal Noguera Mendoza, 1:421–28. Bogotá: Ediciones Sol y Luna, 1980.

Castro Trespalacios, Pedro. *Culturas aborígenes cesarenses e independencia de Valle de Upar.* Bogotá: Biblioteca de Autores Cesarenses, 1979.

Chandler, David L. *Health and Slavery in Colonial Colombia.* New York: Arno Press, 1981.

Cherpak, Evelyn. "The Participation of Women in the Independence Movement of Gran Colombia, 1780–1830." In *Latin American Women: Historical Perspectives,* edited by Asunción Lavrin, 219–34. Westport, Conn.: Greenwood Press, 1978.

Childs, Matt D. "The Aponte Rebellion of 1812 and the Transformation of Cuban Society: Race, Slavery, and Freedom in the Atlantic World." Ph.D. diss., University of Texas at Austin, 2001.

Christie, Keith H. *Oligarcas, campesinos y política en Colombia: Aspectos de la historia socio-política de la frontera antioqueña.* Translated from the English by Fernan González. Bogotá: Universidad Nacional de Colombia, 1986.

Colmenares, Germán. "La Historia de la revolución por José Manuel Restrepo: Une prisión histórica." In Germán Colmenares et al., *La independencia: Ensayos de historia social,* 7–23. Bogotá: Instituto Colombiano de Cultura, 1986.

———. *Popayán: Una sociedad esclavista, 1680–1800.* Vol. 2 of *Historia económica y social de Colombia.* Bogotá: La Carreta, 1979.

———. "El tránsito a sociedades campesinas de dos sociedades esclavistas en la Nueva Granada, Cartagena y Popayán, 1780–1850." *Huellas* (Barranquilla) 29 (1990): 8–24.

————, ed. *Relaciones e informes de los gobernantes de la Nueva Granada.* 3 vols.
Bogotá: Banco Popular, 1989.

Colombia, Instituto Geográfico Agustín Codazzi. *Atlás básico de Colombia.*
Bogotá: Banco de la República, 1970.

Conde Calderón, Jorge Enrique. *Espacio, sociedad y conflictos en la provincia de
Cartagena, 1740–1815.* Barranquilla: Fondo de Publicaciones de la Universidad
del Atlántico, 1999.

————. "Provincias, ciudadanía y 'clase' en el Caribe colombiano, 1821–1855."
Tesis de Diploma de Estudios Avanzados, Universidad Pablo de Olavide,
Programa de Doctorado "Las máscaras del poder en el imaginario
latinoamericano," Seville, Spain, 2001.

Consejo Regional de Planificación de la Costa Atlántica. *El Caribe Colombiano:
Realidad ambiental y desarrollo.* Santa Marta: Consejo Regional de
Planificación de la Costa Atlántica, 1992.

————. *Mapa cultural del Caribe colombiano.* Santa Marta: Consejo Regional de
Planificación de la Costa Atlántica, 1993.

Cope, R. Douglas. *The Limits of Racial Domination: Plebeian Society in Colonial
Mexico, 1660–1720.* Madison: University of Wisconsin Press, 1994.

Cordovez Moure, José María. *Reminiscencias de Santafé de Bogotá.* Edited by
Elisa Mújica. Madrid: Aguilar, 1957.

Craton, Michael. *Testing the Chains: Resistance to Slavery in the British West
Indies.* Ithaca: Cornell University Press, 1982.

Cunha, Euclides da. *Rebellion in the Backlands.* Translated from the Portuguese
by Samuel Putnam. Chicago: University of Chicago Press, 1944.

Cunin, Elisabeth. "Le métissage dans la ville: Apparences raciales, ancrage
territorial et construction de catégories à Cartagena (Colombie)." Ph.D. diss.,
Université de Toulouse le Mirail, 2000.

Davis, David Brion. *Slavery and Human Progress.* Oxford: Oxford University
Press, 1984.

Degler, Carl N. *Neither Black nor White: Slavery and Race Relations in Brazil and
the United States.* 1971. Reprint, Madison: University of Wisconsin Press,
1986.

Demélas-Bohy, M. D., and F.-X. Guerra, "The Hispanic Revolutions: The
Adoption of Modern Forms of Representation in Spain and America, 1808–
1810." In *Elections before Democracy: The History of Elections in Europe and
Latin America,* edited by Eduardo Posada-Carbó, 33–60. London: Institute of
Latin American Studies, 1996.

Díaz, Arlene J. "Gender Conflicts in the Courts of the Early Venezuelan
Republic: Caracas, 1811–1840." Special issue of *Crime, Histoire & Sociétés* 2,
no. 2 (1998): 35–53.

Díaz Díaz, Fernando. *Letras e historia del Bajo Sinú.* Montería: Universidad de
Córdoba-Fondo Editorial, Librería Domus, 1998.

Domínguez, Jorge I. *Insurrection or Loyalty: The Breakdown of the Spanish
American Revolution.* Cambridge: Harvard University Press, 1980.

Drescher, Seymour. *Capitalism and Antislavery*. Cambridge: Cambridge University Press, 1987.

Duarte French, Jaime. *Poder y política: Colombia, 1810-1827*. Bogotá: Carlos Valencia Editores, 1980.

Dueñas Vargas, Guiomar. *Los hijos del pecado: Ilegitimidad y vida familiar en la Santafé de Bogotá colonial*. Bogotá: Universidad Nacional de Colombia, 1997.

Dussán de Reichel, Alicia. "La estructura de la familia en la costa caribe de Colombia." In *Actas del XXXIII congreso internacional de americanistas. San José, 20-27 julio 1958*, 2:692-703. San José, Costa Rica: Lehmann, 1959.

Earle, Rebecca. "Popular Participation in the Wars of Independence in New Granada." In *Independence and Revolution in Spanish America: Perspectives and Problems*, edited by Anthony McFarlane and Eduardo Posada-Carbó, 87-101. London: Institute of Latin American Studies, University of London, 1999.

———. *Spain and the Independence of Colombia, 1810-1825*. Exeter: University of Exeter Press, 2000.

Eltis, David, Stephen D. Behrendt, David Richardson, and Herbert S. Klein, eds. *The Trans-Atlantic Slave Trade: A Database on CD-ROM*. Cambridge: Cambridge University Press, 1999.

Escalante, Aquiles. "Notas sobre el Palenque de San Basilio, una comunidad negra de Colombia." *Divulgaciones Etnológicas* 3, no. 5 (1954): 207-358.

Escorcia, José. "La formación de las clases sociales en el período de la Independencia." In Germán Colmenares et al., *La independencia: Ensayos de historia social*, 71-110. Bogotá: Instituto Colombiano de Cultura, 1986.

Fals Borda, Orlando. *Capitalismo, hacienda y poblamiento en la costa atlántica*. Bogotá: Punta de Lanza, 1976.

———. "Comentarios a la mesa redonda sobre la *Historia doble de la Costa*." *Anuario Colombiano de Historia Social y de la Cultura* 16-17 (1988-89): 231-40.

———. "Influencia del vecindario pobre colonial en las relaciones de producción de la Costa atlántica." In Francisco Leal Buitrago et al., *El agro en el desarrollo histórico colombiano: Ensayos de economía política*, 129-60. Bogotá: Punta de Lanza, 1977.

———. *Mompox y Loba*. Vol. 1 of *Historia doble de la Costa*. Bogotá: Carlos Valencia Editores, 1979.

———. *El Presidente Nieto*. Vol. 2 of *Historia doble de la Costa*. Bogotá: Carlos Valencia Editores, 1981.

———. *Resistencia en el San Jorge*. Vol. 3 of *Historia doble de la Costa*. Bogotá: Carlos Valencia Editores, 1984.

———. *Retorno a la tierra*. Vol. 4 of *Historia doble de la Costa*. Bogotá: Carlos Valencia Editores, 1986.

Fanon, Frantz. *Peau noire masques blancs*. Paris: Editions du Seuil, 1952.

Fick, Carolyn E. "The French Revolution in Saint Domingue: A Triumph or a Failure?" In *A Turbulent Time: The French Revolution and the Greater*

Caribbean, edited by David Barry Gaspar and David Patrick Geggus, 51-75. Bloomington: Indiana University Press, 1997.

Flory, Thomas. "Race and Social Control in Independent Brazil." *Journal of Latin American Studies* 9 (November 1977): 199-224.

Freyre, Gilberto. *The Masters and the Slaves: A Study of the Development of Brazilian Civilization*. Translated from the Portuguese by Samuel Putnam. New York: Knopf, 1946.

Friedemann, Nina S. de. *Carnaval en Barranquilla*. Bogotá: Editorial La Rosa, 1985.

———. "Negros en Colombia: Identidad e invisibilidad." *América Negra* 3 (1992): 25-35.

Friedemann, Nina S. de, and Jaime Arocha. "Colombia." In Minority Rights Group, *No Longer Invisible: Afro-Latin Americans Today*, 47-76. London: Minority Rights Group, 1995.

Friedemann, Nina S. de, and Jaime Arocha. *De sol a sol: Génesis, transformación y presencia de los negros en Colombia*. Bogotá: Planeta Colombiana Editorial, 1986.

Friedemann, Nina S. de, and Richard Cross. *MaNgombe palenque: Ganaderos negros*. Bogotá: Carlos Valencia Editores, 1980.

Friedemann, Nina S. de, and Carlos Patiño Roselli. *Lengua y sociedad en el Palenque de San Basilio*. Bogotá: Instituto Caro y Cuervo, 1983.

García Benítez, Luis. *Reseña histórica de los obispos que han regentado la diócesis de Santa Marta: Primera parte, 1534-1891*. Bogotá: Editorial Pax, 1953.

García Canclini, Néstor. *Transforming Modernity: Popular Culture in Mexico*. Translated from the Spanish by Lidia Lozano. Austin: University of Texas Press, 1993.

García Márquez, Gabriel. *Cien años de soledad*. Buenos Aires: Editorial Sudamericana, 1967.

———. *El general en su laberinto*. Madrid: Mondadori, 1989.

Garrido, Margarita. *Reclamos y representaciones: Variaciones sobre la política en el Nuevo Reino de Granada, 1770-1815*. Bogotá: Banco de la República, 1993.

Geggus, David P. "Racial Equality, Slavery, and Colonial Secession during the Constituent Assembly." *American Historical Review* 94 (December 1989): 1290-1308.

———. "Slavery, War, and Revolution in the Greater Caribbean, 1789-1815." In *A Turbulent Time: The French Revolution and the Greater Caribbean*, edited by David Barry Gaspar and David Patrick Geggus, 1-50. Bloomington: Indiana University Press, 1997.

———. "The Slaves and Free Coloreds of Martinique during the Age of the French and Haitian Revolutions." In *The Lesser Antilles in the Age of European Expansion*, edited by Robert L. Paquette and Stanley L. Engerman, 280-301. Gainesville: University Press of Florida, 1996.

———, ed. *The Impact of the Haitian Revolution in the Atlantic World*. Columbia: University of South Carolina Press, 2001.

Genovese, Eugene D. *From Rebellion to Revolution: Afro-American Slave Revolts in the Making of the Modern World*. Baton Rouge: Louisiana State University Press, 1980.

Germán de Ribón, Segundo. "Gobernantes de Mompox." *Boletín historial: Organo del Centro de Historia de Santa Cruz de Mompox* 14 (March 1950): 526-54.

Gómez, Fernando. "Los censos en Colombia antes de 1905." In *Compendio de estadísticas históricas de Colombia*, edited by Miguel Urrutia and Mario Arrubla, 9-30. Bogotá: Universidad Nacional de Colombia, 1970.

Gómez Picón, Alirio. *Páez: Fundador del estado venezuelano*. Bogotá: Ediciones Tercer Mundo, 1978.

González Luna, María Dolores. "La política de población y pacificación indígena en las poblaciones de Santa Marta y Cartagena (Nuevo Reino de Granada), 1750-1800." *Boletín Americanista* 28 (1978): 87-118.

González, Margarita. "El proceso de manumisión en Colombia." *Cuadernos Colombianos* 2 (1974): 145-240.

Gordon, B. Le Roy. *Human Geography and Ecology in the Sinú Country*. Berkeley: University of California Press, 1957.

Graham, Richard. "Ciudadanía y jerarquía en el Brazil esclavista." In *Ciudadanía política y formación de las naciones: Perspectivas históricas de América Latina*, edited by Hilda Sabato, 345-70. Mexico: Colegio de México-Fideicomiso Historia de las Américas-Fondo de Cultura Económica, 1999.

———. *Patronage and Politics in Nineteenth-Century Brazil*. Stanford: Stanford University Press, 1990.

Grahn, Lance. *The Political Economy of Smuggling: Regional Informal Economies in Early Bourbon New Granada*. Boulder, Colo.: Westview Press, 1997.

Groot, José Manuel. *Historia eclesiástica y civil de Nueva Grenada*. Vol. 5. 1869. Reprint, Bogotá: Ministerio de Educación Nacional, Ediciones de la Revista, 1953.

Gros, Christian. "Noirs, indiens et créoles en Amérique latine et aux Antilles: Identité sociale et action collective." *Cahiers des Amériques Latines* 17 (1994): 53-63.

Guardino, Peter F. *Peasants, Politics, and the Formation of Mexico's National State: Guerrero, 1800-1857*. Stanford, Calif.: Stanford University Press, 1996.

Gudeman, Stephen, and Stuart B. Schwartz. "Cleansing Original Sin: Godparenthood and the Baptism of Slaves in Eighteenth-Century Bahia." In *Kinship Ideology and Practice in Latin America*, edited by Raymond T. Smith, 35-58. Chapel Hill: University of North Carolina Press, 1984.

Guerra, François-Xavier. *Modernidad e independencias: Ensayos sobre las revoluciones hispánicas*. Madrid: Editorial MAPFRE, 1992.

———. "Le peuple souverain: Fondements et logiques d'une fiction (le XIXe siècle)." In Centre National de la Recherche Scientifique, *Quel avenir pour la démocratie en Amérique latine?*, 19-54. Paris: Editions du Centre National de la Recherche Scientifique, 1989.

———. "El soberano y su reino: Reflexiones sobre la génesis del ciudadano en América Latina." In *Ciudadanía política y formación de las naciones:*

Perspectivas históricas de América Latina, edited by Hilda Sabato, 33–61. Mexico City: Colegio de México-Fideicomiso Historia de las Américas-Fondo de Cultura Económica, 1999.

Gutiérrez de Pineda, Virginia. *Familia y cultura en Colombia.* Bogotá: Instituto Colombiano de Cultura, 1975.

Gutiérrez de Pineda, Virginia, and Roberto Pineda Giraldo. *Miscegenación y cultura en la Colombia colonial, 1750–1810.* Vol. 1. Bogotá: Uniandes-Colciencias, 1999.

Gutiérrez Hinojosa, Tomás Dario. *Cultura vallenata: Origen, teoría y pruebas.* Bogotá: Plaza & Janes, 1992.

———. *Valledupar: Música de una historia.* Bogotá: Editorial Grijalbo, 2000.

Guy, Donna J., and Thomas E. Sheridan. "On Frontiers." In *Contested Ground: Comparative Frontiers on the Northern and Southern Edges of the Spanish Empire.* Edited by Donna J. Guy and Thomas E. Sheridan, 3–15. Tucson: University of Arizona Press, 1998.

Guy, Donna J., and Thomas E. Sheridan, eds. *Contested Ground: Comparative Frontiers on the Northern and Southern Edges of the Spanish Empire.* Tucson: University of Arizona Press, 1998.

Hall, Thomas D. "The Río de la Plata and the Greater Southwest: A View from World-System Theory." In *Contested Ground: Comparative Frontiers on the Northern and Southern Edges of the Spanish Empire,* edited by Donna J. Guy and Thomas E. Sheridan, 150–66. Tucson: University of Arizona Press, 1998.

Hamnett, Brian B. "Popular Insurrection and Royalist Reaction: Colombian Regions, 1810–1823." In *Reform and Insurrection in Bourbon New Granada and Peru,* edited by John R. Fisher, Allan J. Kuethe, and Anthony McFarlane, 292–326. Baton Rouge: Louisiana State University Press, 1990.

———. "Process and Pattern: A Re-Examination of the Ibero-American Independence Movements, 1808–1826." *Journal of Latin American Studies* 29 (May 1997): 279–328.

Hanchard, Michael George. *Orpheus and Power: The Movimento negro of Rio de Janeiro and São Paulo, Brazil, 1945–1988.* Princeton, N.J.: Princeton University Press, 1994.

Handler, Jerome S. *The Unappropriated People: Freedmen in the Slave Society of Barbados.* Baltimore: Johns Hopkins University Press, 1974.

Hanger, Kimberly S. *Bounded Lives, Bounded Places: Free Black Society in Colonial New Orleans, 1769–1803.* Durham: Duke University Press, 1997.

Havens, A. Eugene, L. Eduardo Montero, and Michel Romieux. *Cereté, un area de latifundio (Estudio económico y social).* Bogotá: Universidad Nacional de Colombia, Facultad de Sociología, 1965.

Hébrard, Véronique. "Pueblos y actores municipales en la estructuración de la región venezolana, 1821–1830." *Anuario de Historia Regional y de las Fronteras* (Bucaramanga) 5 (2000): 99–149.

Helg, Aline. "Esclavos y libres de color, negros y mulatos en la investigación y la historia de Colombia." *Revista Iberoamericana* 65, nos. 188–89 (July–December 1999): 697–712.

————. "A Fragmented Majority: Free 'of All Colors,' Indians, and Slaves in Caribbean Colombia during the Haitian Revolution." In *The Impact of the Haitian Revolution in the Atlantic World*, edited by David Geggus, 157–75. Columbia: University of South Carolina Press, 2001.

————. "Los intelectuales frente a la cuestión racial en el decenio de 1920: Colombia entre México y Argentina." *Estudios Sociales* (Medellín) 4 (March 1989): 37–53.

————. "The Limits of Equality: Free People of Color and Slaves during the First Independence of Cartagena, Colombia, 1810–1815." *Slavery and Abolition* 20 (August 1999): 1–30.

————. *Our Rightful Share: The Afro-Cuban Struggle for Equality, 1886–1912.* Chapel Hill: University of North Carolina Press, 1995.

Herzog, Tamar. *Defining Nations: Immigrants and Citizens in Early Modern Spain and Spanish America.* New Haven: Yale University Press, 2003.

Heuman, Gad J. *Between Black and White: Race, Politics, and the Free Coloreds in Jamaica, 1838–1865.* Westport, Conn.: Greenwood Press, 1981.

Hoetink, H[arry]. "'Race' and Color in the Caribbean." In *Caribbean Contours*, ed. Sidney W. Mintz and Sally Price, 55–84. Baltimore: Johns Hopkins University Press, 1985.

Holt, Thomas C. *The Problem of Freedom: Race, Labor, and Politics in Jamaica and Britain, 1832–1938.* Baltimore: Johns Hopkins University Press, 1992.

Howe, James. *A People Who Would Not Kneel: Panama, the United States, and the San Blas Kuna.* Washington, D.C.: Smithsonian Institution Press, 1998.

Hünefeldt, Christine. *Paying the Price of Freedom: Family and Labor among Lima's Slaves, 1800–1854.* Berkeley: University of California Press, 1994.

Izard, Miguel. *El miedo a la revolución: La lucha por la libertad en Venezuela, 1777–1830.* Madrid: Editorial Tecnos, 1979.

————. *Orejanos, cimarrones y arrochelados: Los llaneros del Apure.* Barcelona: Sendai Ediciones, 1988.

Janvier, Louis Joseph. *Les constitutions d'Haiti, 1801–1885.* Vol. 1. 1886. Reprint, n.p.: Editions Fardin, 1977.

Jara, Victor Emilio. *La expedición botánica de Mutis y la cultura hispánica.* Bogotá: Editorial Kelly, 1981.

Jaramillo Uribe, Jaime. *Ensayos sobre historia social colombiana.* 2 vols. Bogotá: Tercer Mundo Editores, 1989.

Jiménez Molinares, Gabriel. *Linajes cartageneros.* Vol. 2. Cartagena: Imprenta Departamental, 1958.

————. *Linajes cartageneros: Los Fernández de Sotomayor.* Vol. 1. Cartagena: Imprenta Departamental, 1950.

————. *Los mártires de Cartagena de 1816 ante el consejo de guerra y ante la historia.* 2 vols. Cartagena: Imprenta Departamental, 1947.

Karash, Mary. "Interethnic Conflict and Resistance on the Brazilian Frontier of Goaiás, 1750–1890." In *Contested Ground: Comparative Frontiers on the Northern and Southern Edges of the Spanish Empire*, edited by Donna J. Guy and Thomas E. Sheridan, 115–34. Tucson: University of Arizona Press, 1998.

Kertzer, David I. *Ritual, Politics, and Power*. New Haven: Yale University Press, 1988.

Keyssar, Alexander. *The Right to Vote: The Contested History of Democracy in the United States*. New York: Basic Books, 2000.

Kinsbruner, Jay. *Not of Pure Blood: The Free People of Color and Racial Prejudice in Nineteenth-Century Puerto Rico*. Durham: Duke University Press, 1996.

Klein, Herbert S. *African Slavery in Latin America and the Caribbean*. New York: Oxford University Press, 1986.

König, Hans-Joaquim. *En el camino hacia la nación: Nacionalismo en el proceso de formación del estado y la nación de la Nueva Granada, 1750 a 1856*. Translated from the German by Dagmar Kusche and Juan José de Narváez. Bogotá: Banco de la República, 1994.

Kraay, Hendrik. "The Politics of Race in Independence-Era Bahia: The Black Militia Officers of Salvador, 1790–1840." In *Afro-Brazilian Culture and Politics: Bahia, 1790s to 1990s*, edited by Hendrik Kraay, 158–75. Armonk, N.Y.: M. E. Sharpe, 1998.

Kuethe, Allan J. *Military Reform and Society in New Granada, 1773–1808*. Gainesville: University Presses of Florida, 1978.

——. "The Pacification Campaign on the Riohacha Frontier, 1772–1779." *Hispanic American Historical Review* 50 (1970): 467–81.

Kuznesof, Elizabeth Anne. *Household Economy and Urban Development: São Paulo, 1765–1836*. Boulder, Colo.: Westview Press, 1986.

Langfur, Harold Lawrence. "The Forbidden Lands: Frontier Settlers, Slaves, and Indians in Minas Gerais, Brazil, 1760–1830." Ph.D. diss., University of Texas at Austin, 1999.

Lasso, Marixa. "Haiti as an Image of Popular Republicanism in Caribbean Colombia, Cartagena Province, 1811–1828." In *The Impact of the Haitian Revolution in the Atlantic World*, edited by David Geggus, 176–90. Columbia: University of South Carolina Press, 2001.

Legrand, Catherine. *Frontier Expansion and Peasant Protest in Colombia, 1850–1936*. Albuquerque: University of New Mexico Press, 1986.

Lemaître, Eduardo. *Contra viento y marea: La lucha de Rafael Núñez por el poder*. Bogotá: Instituto Caro y Cuervo, 1990.

——. *Historia general de Cartagena*. 4 vols. Bogotá: Banco de la República, 1983.

——. *Juan José Nieto y su época*. Bogotá: C. Valencia Editores, 1983.

——, ed. *Antecedentes y consecuencias del once de noviembre de 1811 (Testimonios y documentos relacionados con la gloriosa gesta de la independencia absoluta de Cartagena de Indias)*. Cartagena: Impresora Marina, 1961.

Liévano Aguirre, Indalecio. *Bolívar*. 1950. Reprint, Caracas: Ediciones de la Presidencia de la República-Academia Nacional de la Historia, 1988.

Limerick, Patricia N. *The Legacy of Conquest: The Unbroken Past of the American West*. New York: W. W. Norton, 1988.

Lockhart, James, and Stuart B. Schwartz. *Early Latin America: A History of*

Colonial Spanish America and Brazil. New York: Cambridge University Press, 1983.

Lombardi, John V. *The Decline and Abolition of Negro Slavery in Venezuela, 1820–1854.* Westport, Conn.: Greenwood Press, 1971.

———. *People and Places in Colonial Venezuela.* Bloomington: Indiana University Press, 1976.

Loy, Jane M. "Forgotten Comuneros: The 1781 Revolt in the Llanos of Casanare." *Hispanic American Historical Review* 61 (1981): 235–57.

Lucena Giraldo, Manuel. "Las nuevas poblaciones de Cartagena de Indias, 1774–1794." *Revista de Indias* 53, no. 199 (1993): 761–81.

Luengo Muñoz, Manuel. "Génesis de las expediciones militares al Darién en 1785–6." *Anuario de Estudios Americanos* 18 (1961): 333–416.

Lynch, John. "Bolívar and the Caudillos." *Hispanic American Historical Review* 63 (February 1983): 3–35.

———. *Caudillos in Spanish America, 1800–1850.* New York: Oxford University Press, 1992.

———. *The Spanish American Revolution, 1808–1826.* 2d ed. New York: W. W. Norton, 1986.

Maingot, Anthony P. "Social Structure, Social Status, and Civil-Military Conflict in Urban Colombia, 1818–1858." In *Nineteenth-Century Cities: Essays in the New Urban History*, edited by Stephan Thernstrom and Richard Sennet, 297–355. New Haven: Yale University Press, 1969.

Marchena Fernández, Juan. *La institución militar en Cartagena de Indias en el siglo XVIII.* Seville: Escuela de Estudios Hispanoamericanos, 1982.

Marco Dorta, Enrique. *Cartagena de Indias: Puerto y plaza fuerte.* Madrid: Alfonso Amadó, 1960.

Martinez-Alier, Verena. *Marriage, Class, and Colour in Nineteenth-Century Cuba: A Study of Racial Attitudes and Sexual Values in a Slave Society.* 1974. Reprint, Ann Arbor: University of Michigan Press, 1989.

Masur, Gerhard. *Simón Bolívar.* 1948. Reprint, Albuquerque: University of New Mexico Press, 1968.

Matos Rodríguez, Félix V. *Women and Urban Change in San Juan, Puerto Rico, 1820–1868.* Tallahassee: University Press of Florida, 1999.

McAlister, Lyle N. *The "Fuero Militar" in New Spain, 1764–1800.* Gainesville: University Presses of Florida, 1957.

McFarlane, Anthony. "Building Political Order: The 'First Republic' in New Granada, 1810–1815." In *In Search of New Order: Essays on the Politics and Society of Nineteenth-Century Latin America*, edited by Eduardo Posada-Carbó, 8–33. London: Institute of Latin American Studies, 1998.

———. "*Cimarrones* and *palenques*: Runaways and Resistance in Colonial Colombia." *Slavery and Abolition* 6 (1985): 131–51.

———. *Colombia before Independence: Economy, Society, and Politics under Bourbon Rule.* Cambridge: Cambridge University Press, 1993.

McKinley, P. Michael. *Pre-Revolutionary Caracas: Politics, Economy, and Society, 1777–1811.* Cambridge: Cambridge University Press, 1985.

Mecham, J. Lloyd. *Church and State in Latin America: A History of Politico-Ecclesiastical Relations.* Rev. ed. Chapel Hill: University of North Carolina Press, 1966.

Meisel Roca, Adolfo. "Esclavitud, mestizaje y haciendas en la provincia de Cartagena, 1533–1851" (1980). In *El Caribe colombiano: Selección de textos históricos,* edited by Gustavo Bell Lemus, 69–139. Barranquilla: Editorial Uninorte, 1988.

Meisel Roca, Adolfo, and María Aguilera Díaz. "Cartagena de Indias en 1777: Un análisis demográfico." *Boletín Cultural y Bibliográfico* 34, no. 45 (1997): 21–57.

Melzer, Sara E., and Leslie W. Rabine, eds. *Rebel Daughters: Women and the French Revolution.* New York: Oxford University Press, 1992.

Metcalf, Alida. *Family and Frontier in Colonial Brazil: Santana de Parnaíba, 1520–1822.* Berkeley: University of California Press, 1992.

Mintz, Sidney W., and Eric R. Wolf. "An Analysis of Ritual Co-Parenthood (Compadrazgo)." *Southwestern Journal of Anthropology* 6, no. 4 (Winter 1950): 341–67.

Monsalve, José D. *Mujeres de la independencia.* Biblioteca de Historia Nacional, vol. 38. Bogotá: Imprenta Nacional, 1926.

Montoya, Salvador. "Milicias negras y mulatas en el reino de Guatemala, siglo XVIII." *Caravelle* (Toulouse) 49 (1987): 93–104.

Mora de Tovar, Gilma. "Poblamiento y sociedad en el Bajo Magdalena durante la segunda mitad del siglo XVIII." *Anuario Colombiano de Historia Social y de la Cultura* 21 (1993): 40–57.

Moreno de Angel, Pilar. *Antonio de la Torre y Miranda, viajero y poblador.* Bogotá: Planeta Colombiana Editorial S.A., 1993.

———. *Santander: Biografía.* Bogotá: Planeta Colombiana Editorial S.A., 1989.

Moreno Salazar, Valentín. *Negritudes.* Cali: Editores XYZ, 1995.

Mörner, Magnus. *Race Mixture in the History of Latin America.* Boston: Little, Brown, 1967.

Múnera, Alfonso. *El fracaso de la nación: Región, clase y raza en el Caribe colombiano (1717–1810).* Bogotá: Banco de la República-El Ancora Editores, 1998.

Nicholls, David. *From Dessalines to Duvalier: Race, Colour, and National Independence in Haiti.* 1979. Reprint, New Brunswick, N.J.: Rutgers University Press, 1996.

Nichols, Theodore E. *Tres puertos de Colombia: Estudio sobre el desarrollo de Cartagena, Santa Marta y Barranquilla.* Bogotá: Banco Popular, 1973.

Nieman, Donald G. *Promises to Keep: African-Americans and the Constitutional Order, 1776 to the Present.* New York: Oxford University Press, 1991.

Nishida, Mieko. "Manumission and Ethnicity in Urban Slavery: Salvador, Brazil, 1808–1888." *Hispanic American Historical Review* 73 (August 1993): 361–91.

Otero D'Costa, Enrique. *Vida del Almirante José Padilla, 1778–1828.* 1921. Reprint, Bogotá: Imprenta y Litografía de las Fuerzas Militares, 1973.

Ortiz, Sergio Elías. *Franceses en la independencia de la Gran Colombia.* Bogotá: Editorial ABC, 1971.

————, ed. *Ensayos de dos economistas coloniales: Don Antonio de Narváez y la Torre y don José Ignacio de Pombo*. Bogotá: Banco de la República, 1965.

Pacheco, Juan Manuel. "La expulsión de los jesuítas del Nuevo Reino de Granada." In Aurelio Carvajalino Cabrales et al., *Antología histórica*. Vol. 16 of *Biblioteca de autores ocañeros*, 408-54. Ocaña: Publicaciones de la Escuela de Bellas Artes, 1979.

Paquette, Robert L. *Sugar Is Made with Blood: The Conspiracy of La Escalera and the Conflict between Empires over Slavery in Cuba*. Middletown, Conn.: Wesleyan University Press, 1988.

Park, James William. *Rafael Núñez and the Politics of Colombia Regionalism, 1863-1886*. Baton Rouge: Louisiana State University Press, 1985.

Parsons, James J. *Antioqueño Colonization in Western Colombia*. Berkeley: University of California Press, 1949.

Pedraja, René de la. "La Guajira en el siglo XIX: Indígenas, contrabando y carbón." In *El Caribe colombiano: Selección de textos históricos*, edited by Gustavo Bell Lemus, 1-38. Barranquilla: Editorial Uninorte, 1988.

Peñas Galindo, David Ernesto. *Los bogas de Mompox: Historia del zambaje*. Bogotá: Tercer Mundo Editores, 1988.

Pérez Escobar, Jacobo. *El negro Robles y su época*. Bogotá: Centro para la Investigación de la Cultura Negra, 2000.

Pérotin-Dumon, Anne. "Free Colored and Slaves in Revolutionary Guadaloupe: Politics and Political Consciousness." In *The Lesser Antilles in the Age of European Expansion*, edited by Robert L. Paquette and Stanley L. Engerman, 259-79. Gainesville: University Press of Florida, 1996.

Phelan, John Leddy. *The People and the King: The Comunero Revolution in Colombia, 1781*. Madison: University of Wisconsin Press, 1978.

Porto del Portillo, Raúl. *Plazas y calles de Cartagena*. Cartagena: Tipografía Mogollón, 1950.

Posada, Eduardo. *La esclavitud en Colombia*. Bogotá: Imprenta Nacional, 1933.

Posada-Carbó, Eduardo. *The Colombian Caribbean: A Regional History, 1870-1950*. New York: Oxford University Press, 1996.

————. *Una invitación a la historia de Barranquilla*. Bogotá: Fondo Editorial CEREC, 1987.

Prebble, John. *The Darien Disaster*. London: Secker and Warburg, 1968.

Reichel Dolmatoff, Gerardo. Introduction to Joseph Palacios de la Vega, *Diario de viaje del P. Joseph Palacios de la Vega entre los indios y negros de la provincia de Cartagena en el nuevo reino de Granada, 1787-1788*, edited by Gerardo Reichel Dolmatoff, 5-16. Bogotá: Editorial ABC, 1955.

Reis, Joao José. *Slave Rebellion in Brazil: The Muslim Uprising of 1835 in Bahia*. Translated from the Portuguese by Arthur Brakel. Baltimore: Johns Hopkins University Press, 1993.

Restrepo Tirado, Ernesto. *Historia de la provincia de Santa Marta*. 1921. Reprint, Bogotá: Instituto Colombiano de Cultura, 1975.

Revollo, Pedro María. *Costeñismos colombianos o apuntamientos sobre lenguaje costeño de Colombia*. Barranquilla: Talleres Tipográficos de la Ed. Mejoras, 1942.

Rey Sinning, Edgar. *El hombre y su río*. Santa Marta: Gráficas Gutenberg, 1995.

Robles Cataño, Osvaldo. *Recuerdos del Riohacha que se fue (La casa de la calle de los Almendros)*. Bogotá: Gobernación de la Guajira, Junta Regional de Cultura de la Guajira, 1986.

Rodríguez, Pablo. *Sentimiento y vida familiar en el Nuevo Reino de Granada.* Bogotá: Ariel, 1997.

Rodríguez Becerra, Manuel, and Jorge Restrepo Restrepo, "Los empresarios extranjeros de Barranquilla, 1820-1900." In *El Caribe colombiano: Selección de textos históricos*, edited by Gustavo Bell Lemus, 139-97. Barranquilla: Editorial Uninorte, 1988.

Rodríguez O., Jaime E. *The Independence of Spanish America.* Cambridge: Cambridge University Press, 1998.

Rodríguez Piñeres, Eduardo, ed. *La vida de Castillo y Rada*. Biblioteca de Historia Nacional, vol. 79. Bogotá: Academia de Historia, 1949.

Romero Jaramillo, Dolcey. "La esclavitud en Barranquilla, 1814-1851." *Huellas* 35 (August 1992): 13-21.

———. *Esclavitud en la provincia de Santa Marta, 1791-1851*. Santa Marta: Fondo de Publicaciones de Autores Magdalenenses-Instituto de Cultura y Turismo del Magdalena, 1997.

Rosero, Carlos. "Los afrodescendientes y el conflicto armado en Colombia: La insistencia en lo propio como alternativa." In *Afrodescendientes en las Américas: Trayectorias sociales e identitarias: 150 años de la abolición de la esclavitud en Colombia*, edited by Claudia Mosquera, Mauricio Pardo, and Odile Hoffman, 547-59. Bogotá: Universidad Nacional de Colombia, 2002.

Sabato, Hilda. "On Political Citizenship in Nineteenth-Century Latin America." *American Historical Review* 106 (October 2001): 1290-1315.

Saether, Steinar A. "Identities and Independence in the Provinces of Santa Marta and Riohacha (Colombia), ca. 1750-ca. 1850." Ph.D. diss., University of Warwick, October 2001.

Safford, Frank. "Race, Integration, and Progress: Elite Attitudes and the Indian in Colombia, 1750-1870." *Hispanic American Historical Review* 71 (February 1991): 1-33.

Salzedo del Villar, Pedro. *Apuntaciones historiales de Mompox: Edición conmemorativa de los 450 años de Mompox*. 1939. Reprint, Cartagena: Gobernación del Departamento de Bolívar, 1987.

Sánchez, Joseph. "African Freemen and the Fuero Militar: A Historical Overview of Pardo and Moreno Militiamen in the Late Spanish Empire." *Colonial Latin American Historical Review* 3 (Spring 1994): 165-84.

Sánchez S., Enrique, Roque Roldán, and María Fernanda Sánchez. *Derechos e identidad: Los pueblos indígenas y negros en la Constitución política de Colombia de 1991*. Bogotá: Disloque Editores, 1993.

Santa, Eduardo. *La colonización antioqueña: Una empresa de caminos*. Bogotá: Tercer Mundo Editores, 1993.

Schwegler, Armin. *"Chi ma nkongo": Lengua y rito ancestrales en El Palenque de San Basilio (Colombia).* 2 vols. Frankfurt: Vervuert, 1996.

Scott, James C. *Domination and the Arts of Resistance: Hidden Transcripts.* New Haven: Yale University Press, 1990.

Scott, Julius. "The Common Wind: Currents of Afro-American Communication in the Era of the Haitian Revolution." Ph.D. diss., Duke University, 1986.

Sharp, William F. *Slavery on the Spanish Frontier: The Colombian Chocó, 1680–1810.* Norman: University of Oklahoma Press, 1976.

Silva Dias, Maria Odila. *Power and Everyday Life: The Lives of Working Women in Nineteenth-Century Brazil.* Translated from the Portuguese by Ann Frost. Cambridge: Polity Press, 1995.

Slatta, Richard W. "Spanish Colonial Military Strategy and Ideology." In *Contested Ground: Comparative Frontiers on the Northern and Southern Edges of the Spanish Empire*, edited by Donna J. Guy and Thomas E. Sheridan, 83–96. Tucson: University of Arizona Press, 1998.

Socolow, Susan M. "Women of the Buenos Aires Frontier (or the Gaucho Turned Upside Down)." In *Contested Ground: Comparative Frontiers on the Northern and Southern Edges of the Spanish Empire*, edited by Donna J. Guy and Thomas E. Sheridan, 67–82. Tucson: University of Arizona Press, 1998.

Solaún, Mauricio, and Sidney Kronus. *Discrimination without Violence: Miscegenation and Racial Conflict in Latin America.* New York: Wiley, 1973.

Sourdis de De la Vega, Adelaida. *Cartagena de Indias durante la primera república, 1810-1815.* Bogotá: Banco de la República, 1988.

Stern, Steve J. "New Approaches to the Study of Peasant Rebellion and Consciousness: Implications of the Andean Experience." In *Resistance, Rebellion, and Consciousness in the Andean Peasant World, 18th to 20th Centuries*, edited by Steve J. Stern, 3–25. Madison: University of Wisconsin Press, 1987.

Streicker, Joel. "Policing Boundaries: Race, Class, and Gender in Cartagena, Colombia." *American Ethnologist* 22 (1995): 54–74.

Támara Gómez, Edgardo. *Historia de Sincelejo: De los Zenúes al Packing House.* Bogotá: Impreandes Presencia, 1997.

Taussig, Michael. *The Devil and Commodity Fetishism in South America.* Chapel Hill: University of North Carolina Press, 1980.

Taylor, William B. *Drinking, Homicide, and Rebellion in Colonial Mexican Villages.* Stanford, Calif.: Stanford University Press, 1979.

Thurner, Mark. *From Two Republics to One Divided: Contradictions of Postcolonial Nationmaking in Andean Peru.* Durham: Duke University Press, 1997.

Tirado Mejía, Alvaro. *Aspectos sociales de las guerras civiles en Colombia.* Bogotá: Instituto Colombiano de Cultura, 1976.

Tisnes Jiménez, Roberto M. *La independencia en la costa atlántica.* Biblioteca de Historia Nacional, vol. 134. Bogotá: Editorial Kelly, 1976.

Torres Almeyda, Jesús C. *El Almirante José Padilla (epopeya y martirio).* 1983. Reprint, Bogotá: Imprenta y Publicaciones de las Fuerzas Militares, 1990.

Tovar Pinzón, Hermes. *"Convocatoria al poder del número": Censos y estadísticas de la Nueva Granada*. Bogotá: Archivo General de la Nación, 1994.

———. *De una chispa se forma una hoguera: Esclavitud, insubordinación y liberación*. Tunja: Universidad Pedagógica y Tecnológica de Colombia, 1992.

———. *Grandes empresas agrícolas y ganaderas: Su desarrollo en el siglo XVIII*. Bogotá: Ediciones CIEC, 1980.

———. "Guerras de opinión y represión en Colombia durante la independencia (1810–1820)." *Anuario Colombiano de Historia Social y de la Cultura* 11 (1983): 187–232.

———. *Hacienda colonial y formación social*. Barcelona: Ediciones Sendai, 1988.

Twinam, Ann. "Is Race a 'Defect'? Official and Popular Debates over Whitening in Late Colonial Spanish America." Paper presented at the 117th Annual Meeting of the American Historical Association, Chicago, 3 January 2003.

———. *Miners, Merchants, and Farmers in Colonial Colombia*. Austin: University of Texas Press, 1982.

———. *Public Lives, Private Secrets: Gender, Honor, Sexuality, and Illegitimacy in Colonial Spanish America*. Stanford, Calif.: Stanford University Press, 1999.

Uribe de Hincapié, María Teresa, and Jesús María Alvarez. *Poderes y regiones: Problemas en la constitución de la nación colombiana, 1810–1850*. Medellín: Departamento de Publicaciones, Universidad de Antioquia, 1987.

Uribe-Urán, Victor M. "The Birth of a Public Sphere in Latin America during the Age of Revolution." *Comparative Studies in Society and History* 42 (2000): 425–58.

———. *Honorable Lives: Lawyers, Family, and Politics in Colombia, 1780–1850*. Pittsburgh: University of Pittsburgh Press, 2000.

Uribe White, Enrique. *Padilla: Homenaje de la armada colombiana al héroe de la batalla del lago de Maracaibo*. Bogotá: Imprenta y Litografía de las Fuerzas Militares, 1973.

Urueta, José P. *Cartagena y sus cercanías*. 1886. Reprint, Cartagena: Tip. de Vapor "Mogollón," 1912.

Van Young, Eric. *The Other Rebellion. Popular Violence, Ideology, and the Mexican Struggle for Independence, 1810–1821*. Stanford, Calif.: Stanford University Press, 2001.

Velásquez Murillo, Rogerio. "La canoa chocoana en el folclor." *Revista Colombiana de Folclor* 3 (1959): 107–26.

Véliz, Claudio. *The Centralist Tradition in Latin America*. Princeton, N.J.: Princeton University Press, 1980.

Vinson, Ben, III. *Bearing Arms of His Majesty: The Free-Colored Militia in Colonial Mexico*. Stanford, Calif.: Stanford University Press, 2001.

Viotti da Costa, Emilia. *The Brazilian Empire: Myths and Histories*. Chicago: University of Chicago Press, 1985.

Wade, Peter. *Blackness and Race Mixture: The Dynamics of Racial Identity in Colombia*. Baltimore: Johns Hopkins University Press, 1993.

———. "Identités noires, identités indiennes en Colombie." *Cahiers des Amériques Latines* 17 (1994): 125–39.

————. *Music, Race, and Nation: Música Tropical in Colombia*. Chicago: University of Chicago Press, 2000.

Waldron, Kathy. "The Sinners and the Bishop in Colonial Venezuela: The *Visita* of Bishop Mariano Martí, 1771-1784." In *Sexuality and Marriage in Colonial Latin America*, edited by Asunción Lavrin, 156-77. Lincoln: University of Nebraska Press, 1989.

Walker, Charles F. *Smoldering Ashes: Cuzco and the Creation of Republican Peru, 1780-1840*. Durham: Duke University Press, 1999.

Watson, Karl. "Salmagundis *vs.* Pumpkins: White Politics and Creole Consciousness in Barbadian Slave Society, 1800-1834." In *The White Minority in the Caribbean*, edited by Howard Johnson and Karl Watson, 17-31. Princeton, N.J.: Markus Wiener, 1997.

Weber, David J., and Jane M. Rausch. Introduction to *Where Cultures Meet: Frontiers in Latin American History*, edited by David J. Weber and Jane M. Rausch, xxiii-xli. Wilmington, Del.: Scholarly Resources, 1994.

Williamson, Joel. *New People: Miscegenation and Mulattoes in America*. New York: Free Press, 1980.

Wright, Winthrop R. *Café con leche: Race, Class, and National Image in Venezuela*. Austin: University of Texas Press, 1990.

Zapata Olivella, Juan. *Piar, Petión y Padilla: Tres mulatos de la revolución*. Barranquilla: Ediciones Universidad Simón Bolívar, 1986.

Zapata Olivella, Manuel. *La rebelión de los genes: El mestizaje americano en la sociedad futura*. Bogotá: Altamir Ediciones, 1997.

Zuluaga R., Francisco U. *Guerrilla y sociedad en el Patía: Una relación entre clientelismo político y la insurgencia social*. Cali: Universidad del Valle, Facultad de Humanidades, 1993.

215, 223, 238, 257; and Palenque de San Basilio, 38; and wars for independence, 143, 144–47, 149, 161; and Spanish reconquest, 156, 159; and Peru, 163; Indians serving under, 172; and republican policies, 176; and loss of soldiers, 189; and Padilla, 195–96, 197, 201, 203, 205, 206–9, 231; and manumission, 218; dictatorial powers of, 222–23; death of, 224, 226, 234; and slavery, 245

Bolivia, 202

Boswell, John, 108

Boves, José Tomás, 165, 166

Brazil, 2, 14, 244–45, 246, 247, 248, 252, 257, 260, 262, 263

Britain: and pressure for abolition of slavery, 8, 112, 245; and contraband trade, 20, 28, 29, 41, 50, 72, 88, 173; war with, 55, 56, 58, 64, 73, 101–2; and slave trade, 140

Bundes (popular dances), 62, 76–77, 78, 79, 191

Bushnell, David, 11

Bussa's Rebellion, 15

Caballero y Góngora, Antonio, 18, 29, 33, 37, 51, 52, 55, 57, 74, 85, 264

Caicedo, Domingo, 223–24, 229, 232

Canal del Dique, 33, 48, 88, 212

Cañaverales, Joaquín de, 37–38, 90, 114, 115

Caribbean Colombia, 2, 3–4, 7, 11, 47, 264

Caribbean New Granada: population of, 7, 11, 47, 54, 167, 187, 239, 300 (n. 24), 305 (n. 136); fragmentation of territory, 9, 17, 21, 40–41, 238–40; and republican reforms, 16; and regionalism, 17; economy of, 53, 168, 184–89, 237; postwar society of, 167–69; and Venezuela, 237
—frontier: uncontrolled nature of, 9, 14, 15, 18, 41; Indians of, 11, 14, 15,

18–20, 21; role of, 17; and smuggling, 18, 262–64; geography of, 19, 20–21; population of, 20; and rochelas, 21–23; and palenques, 23–25; challenges of, 25–26; and Spanish forced resettlement, 26, 27–36, 40, 41; and survival, 187

Carmona, Francisco, 233, 234, 262, 315 (n. 1)

Carnivals and fiestas, 98–100, 119, 190–93, 217, 258–60

Carracedo, Pedro, 96

Cartagena: and racial equality, 7–8; slave population of, 7, 44, 83–84, 212, 236, 273 (n. 12), 311 (n. 88); competition with Santa Marta, 9; race relations in, 13; and socioracial hierarchy, 15, 94, 96, 97, 101, 212, 217, 284 (n. 74); and independence, 16, 120, 121–23, 124, 125, 126–29, 131, 134–35, 138, 178, 212, 235, 238; French fleet's seizure of, 18; Bogotá compared to, 42; as administrative center, 43, 238; and trade, 54, 56, 81, 82, 88, 89–90, 122, 132, 211–12, 219; and contraband trade, 73, 74; and political power, 80, 83, 119, 211–18; and slave resistance, 80, 83, 112, 115–16; economy of, 81, 82–83, 89–90, 161; population of, 81, 157, 211, 220, 298 (n. 149); and white elites, 81, 83, 89, 212, 214, 215, 236, 242, 257; and Haitian Revolution, 83, 84, 109; and women of color, 83; and Mompox, 88; and single motherhood, 93; and education, 95–96; and carnivals and fiestas, 98; and militia system, 101, 102, 247, 256; alleged slave conspiracy in, 104, 109–10, 115, 118, 249; and wars for independence, 143–47, 148, 149–50, 152, 153, 211, 238; and racial categories, 147; and Spanish reconquest, 156–58, 160, 298

(n. 149); and Bolívar, 204-5, 236; and Padilla, 210-18; lack of confrontation in, 216-17; and civil war of 1831, 227, 228, 229, 238; and constitution of 1831, 229-230

Cartagena Province: and Nieto, 4; and hacienda development, 12; and frontier, 18; and Spanish forced resettlement, 29, 33; population of, 43; and hacendados' land acquisition, 50; and agriculture, 56; and Catholic Church, 60; and revenues to support Cartagena, 81; and independence, 128, 129, 145; and Liberalism, 237; and resguardos, 241

Carujo, Pedro, 224-25, 226

Castillo, Manuel del, 138, 145-47, 149, 150, 152, 153, 156, 158, 197, 294 (n. 66), 297-98 (n. 145)

Castillo y Rada, José María, 201, 236

Catalonia, 56, 83

Catholic Church: and education, 1; and white elites' position, 7; official control of, 9, 15, 21, 25, 48, 63, 79; and rochelas, 22, 23; and frontier, 25-26, 40, 41; and Spanish forced resettlement, 36; and rural areas, 42, 60-63, 76-79, 193; and hacendados, 52; relationship with state, 61-62; and slaves, 62-63; and Cartagena, 82; and socioracial hierarchy, 94, 142, 169; and independence, 130, 141, 142; and wars for independence, 155; and Spanish reconquest, 158; land of, 174; and republican policies, 177-80, 190-92; norms of, 260. *See also* Missionaries; Priests

Cattle ranching: and white elites, 9; and Spanish forced resettlement, 32; and slaves, 46, 65, 171; and hacendados, 50; and trade, 56; and free people of color, 65-66; and Car-

tagena, 82; and Santa Marta, 85; and Valledupar, 86, 87; and Spanish reconquest, 158; and constitution of 1821, 174; and republican policies, 186

Caudillos, 239-40

Central America, 246

Centralism, 1, 124, 129, 136, 194, 238

Children: and rochelas, 23, 26; and palenques, 25, 26; and Spanish forced resettlement, 36, 39; and Catholic Church, 61, 76, 78, 190; and child abandonment, 107-8, 286 (n. 112); godparents of, 107; of slaves, 111, 113, 153, 169-70

Childs, Matt, 246-47, 252

Chile, 241, 245, 246

Chimila Indians, 20, 27-28, 31, 35, 38, 40, 77, 86, 145, 154

Chocó, 12, 13, 32, 34, 35, 72

Cities: socioracial hierarchy of, 10, 15, 91-97; women's population in, 10; state control of, 42; population of, 47, 80, 220; and military recruitment, 57; and militiamen, 68, 80, 100-105; migration to, 79, 105, 186, 261; profiles of, 80-88; and slaves, 80, 81, 83, 108-18, 171-72; and white elites, 88-91; and women of color, 93, 105-8; carnivals and fiestas in, 98-100; decline of, 219-21. *See also* Intercity rivalries

Citizenship, 126; and Indians, 141; and free men of color, 147-49; and education, 169; and Padilla, 196, 199-200, 216; and militia system, 213-14; and manumitted slaves, 218; and civil war of 1831, 219-20, 234, 238; in other nations in the Americas, 239, 240, 242-45. *See also* Suffrage

Civil war of 1831: and Caribbean New Granada, 7; and intercity rivalries, 9, 16; and constitution of 1821, 16,

226-27; and Liberalism, 16, 226-30, 238; and Montilla, 227, 228, 229, 234

Civil war of the "Supremes" (1839-42), 4, 315 (n. 1)

Class issues. See Socioracial hierarchy

Cocoa cultivation, 46, 50, 56

Codazzi, Agustín, 4

Código Negro, 112-15, 117, 119, 171, 250, 261, 288 (n. 144)

College and Seminary of San Carlos, 95-96

Colmenares, Germán, 187

Colombia: Andean-centered histories of, 3, 4; as mestizo nation, 3, 7, 9

Colonization law of 1823, 175, 187

Comisión Corográfica, 4

Communication: in Caribbean New Granada, 9, 21, 48-49, 65; and Spanish forced resettlement, 48, 49; and slave resistance, 67; and Mompox, 84, 89; and Santa Marta, 85; and Cartagena, 89; and transportation, 203

Comunero Revolt, 55, 63-66, 67, 104, 234, 247, 276-77 (n. 92)

Congress of Cúcuta, 161, 162, 163, 171, 172

Conservatism, 4, 136

Conspiracy of the Fijo, 175

Constitution of 1812, 129-31, 138, 139-40, 142, 144, 149, 154, 160, 163, 242, 245

Constitution of 1821: supporters of, 9; and civil war of 1831, 16, 226-27; impact of, 16; adoption of, 162, 238; and racial equality, 163-64, 180, 242; and suffrage, 163; and education, 164, 169; and Bolívar, 202, 203, 204, 205; and Montilla, 207; and intercity rivalries, 219, 238; and slavery, 245

Constitution of 1831, 229-30

Constitution of 1886, 1, 4

Constitution of 1991, 1, 2, 7, 264

Constitutions: in other nations in the Americas, 242-45

Contraband trade: and white elites, 9; and frontier, 14, 20, 30, 41, 263; and rochelas, 23; and Mompox, 43, 84; and beef, 50; stimulation of, 56; and rural areas, 72-74; and cattle ranching, 73; and Santa Marta, 85-86; and Riohacha, 87-88; and Cartagena, 89; and women, 107; and Spanish reconquest, 158; and republican policies, 185. See also Smuggling; Trade

Cortes of Cadiz, 128, 129, 135, 138, 154, 292 (n. 39)

Costeños, 3-4

Cotton production, 56, 57, 70, 90, 185, 260

Council of the Indies, 39, 61-64, 91, 92-94, 95, 284 (n. 72)

Council of the Regency, 121-22, 124, 126, 131, 133-34, 137

Counterculture, 75-79, 189-94. See also Bundes; Carnivals and fiestas; Marriage

Craton, Michael, 15, 249

Crespo, Narciso Vicente, 132, 144, 148

Cuba: and trade, 53, 56; and slave trade, 55, 85; and taxation, 57; and militia, 58, 246-47; importation of liquor from, 83; and white elites, 91; and Código Negro, 114; slaves exported to, 153; liberation of, 196, 307 (n. 4); and French refugees, 244; and slavery, 246, 250, 252; and socioracial hierarchy, 255

Cundinamarca, 129, 146, 150

Cunha, Euclides da, 263

Cunin, Elizabeth, 13

Curaçao, 20, 73, 87

Darién, 18, 19, 28-29, 30, 33, 34, 35, 55, 67, 173

Darién Indians, 29
Declaration of the Rights of Man and
    Citizen, 89, 243, 251
Demerara Revolt, 15
Deserters, 67, 145, 159, 162, 189
Dessalines, Jean-Jacques, 243
Díaz de Lamadrid, José Fernández, 37,
    49, 60-63, 76-78, 94, 179
Díaz Granados family, 132
Dutch, 20, 28

Earle, Rebecca, 11
Ecuador, 165, 224, 237
Education: and Catholic Church, 1;
    and white elites, 89; in Mompox,
    90; and class issues, 91, 95-96, 122;
    and constitution of 1812, 140; of
    Indians, 141, 172, 173; and Spanish
    reconquest, 158; and suffrage, 163;
    and constitution of 1821, 164, 169
Elbers, Juan Bernardo, 175, 177
Electoral Law of 1811, 141
Emberá Indians, 19, 30, 31, 44, 153,
    154, 264
Encinoso, Mauricio, 173
Encomiendas, 32, 271 (n. 64)
Enlightenment, 83, 134
Epalza, Mateo de, 136, 151
Equality. See Racial equality
Escalante, Aquiles, 12
Escobar, Manual Josef de, 37, 51
Escudero, José Francisco, 180-81, 214
Estévez, José María, 178, 180, 225,
    233, 234
Ezpeleta, Josef de, 30, 55-56, 73, 79

Fals Borda, Orlando, 12, 110-11, 175,
    260, 276-77 (n. 92)
Faris, Laureano, 94
Federalism, 124, 129, 136, 194, 204,
    227, 235, 237, 238, 315-16 (n. 1)
Federation of the United Provinces of
    New Granada, 129, 145, 146, 147
Ferdinand VII (king of Spain), 121,

123, 124, 131, 133, 143, 145, 147, 161,
    234
Fernández de Sotomayor, Juan, 90, 96,
    123, 124, 127, 141, 155, 157, 190
Fidalgo, Joaquín Francisco, 30-31, 49,
    68
Fijo, 81, 122, 123, 126, 127, 128, 149,
    175
Flight. See Runaway Indians; Runaway
    slaves
Flores, Manuel Antonio, 58
France, 122, 126
Francisco, Juan de, 175, 197, 208, 214,
    222, 226, 227, 229, 231
Free people of color: and mixed Afri-
    can ancestry, 1-3, 13, 14, 34, 43, 44,
    91, 92, 95, 128, 138, 149, 160, 242,
    292 (n. 39); and full African ances-
    try, 2, 3, 10, 43, 44, 128, 138, 149,
    160, 241, 242, 292 (n. 39); of Carib-
    bean Colombia, 7; legal equality of,
    7, 16, 17; and men's suffrage, 7-8,
    16, 126, 130, 137, 138, 242; relation-
    ship with Indians, 7, 10, 35, 42, 65,
    79; relationship with slaves, 7, 8,
    10, 14, 65, 79, 149; internal divi-
    sions among, 14; relationship with
    white elites, 15, 42, 66, 147, 148,
    162, 181-84, 193, 208, 215-16; and
    palenques, 24; and Spanish forced
    resettlement, 39, 40; population of,
    43, 48, 167, 272 (n. 5); of Riohacha
    Province, 43; and slave ownership,
    46; and patronage networks, 67;
    as squatters, 67; and cities, 80, 93;
    and Cartagena, 81, 83, 148, 212;
    and Mompox, 84, 148; and Santa
    Marta, 85, 86; and Valledupar, 86,
    87; and Riohacha, 87; as blancos
    de la tierra, 94; and class issues,
    95; and marriage, 97; and carnivals
    and fiestas, 98; and independence,
    126, 127, 134, 135, 137, 147-50; and
    wars for independence, 145, 167-

68; and Haitian Revolution, 165; administrative positions of, 168; and conscription, 175, 213, 214; and racial equality, 200. *See also* Lower-class people of color; Militiamen of African descent

Free womb laws, 8, 140, 163, 169–70, 245

French Revolution, 14, 83, 89, 93, 115, 118, 119, 139, 243

Freyre, Gilberto, 260

Friedemann, Nina S. de, 2, 12

Galán, José Antonio, 64

Gálvez, José de, 29

Gamarra, Agustín, 239

García, Pablo, 90, 118

García, Vicente, 53, 71, 90, 136

García Canclini, Néstor, 258

García de Toledo, José María, 121, 122, 125, 127–29, 135, 138–40, 146, 149, 158, 214, 294 (n. 66)

García Márquez, Gabriel, 11

Garrido, Margarita, 11

Geggus, David, 15, 67

Gender ratio: and Indians, 46; and slaves, 46, 111; in cities, 47, 105, 119, 220, 286 (n. 107); in rural areas, 47, 48; and total population, 47; of Cartagena, 81, 212

Genovese, Eugene, 14

Germán Ribón, Pantaleón, 90, 124, 127, 129, 136, 147

Getsemaní, 81, 82, 122, 207, 211, 212

Gil y Lemos, Francisco, 30

Glen, John, 222, 227

Gold exports, 54

Gold mines: and slaves, 44, 64, 67, 140, 171

Gold panning, 46, 72

Gonzaga Galván, Luis, 123, 127, 148, 158

Gosselman, Carl August, 191, 201, 221

Gracias al sacar, 92–94, 119

Gran Colombia: republican reforms of,

16; and constitution of 1821, 163–67; and slaves, 169–71; and Indians, 172–73, 176; and rural areas, 173–77; and Catholic Church, 177–78; and Bolívar's fears of pardocracia, 202; and Venezuela, 223, 224, 235, 237; division of, 241; and discriminatory laws, 245

Guadeloupe, 39, 251

Guajira Peninsula, 19, 20, 28, 29, 39, 45, 173, 240, 249

Gual, Pedro, 146

Guatemala, 64, 92

Guerra, François-Xavier, 236

Gutiérrez, Virginia, 13

Gutiérrez de Caviedes, José María, 124, 137

Gutiérrez de Piñeres, Gabriel, 128–29, 135, 138–39, 143, 145–46, 149, 157, 175, 214

Gutiérrez de Piñeres, Germán, 128, 129, 135, 139, 146, 149, 157, 175, 214

Gutiérrez de Piñeres, Juan Francisco, 57–58, 64

Gutiérrez de Piñeres, Vicente Celedonio, 90, 124–25, 127–29, 135–36, 139–40, 146–47, 149, 153, 157, 175, 214

Guzmán, Antonio Leocadio, 202–4

Hacendado class: and socioracial conflict, 16; and Spanish forced resettlement, 34, 35, 36, 37, 40, 49, 84; and mestizaje, 36; and state control, 42; expansion of land properties, 49–50, 188; and patronage networks, 50–53, 65, 79; and titles of nobility, 51; and military recruitment, 59; and revolt, 63; profits of, 74; and Mompox, 84, 90; and independence, 136; and republican policies, 174, 187–88

Haciendas: development of, 12, 15; and palenques, 24, 25; Indian raids on, 28, 30; and Spanish forced resettle-

ment, 34–35; and slaves, 42, 50,
62–63, 66, 67, 75, 152, 153, 171, 277
(n. 100)
Haiti, 166–67, 197, 198, 202, 243, 245
Haitian Revolution: and slave resistance, 14–15, 66, 115, 118, 119–20;
white elites' fears concerning, 14, 16,
39, 42, 248–53; and Caribbean New
Granada, 19, 66; Mendinueta on,
42; and Cartagena, 83, 84, 109, 121;
and militiamen of African descent,
104; and free people of color, 165;
and pardocracia, 200; and Spanish
colonies, 243–44
Hamilton, John P., 190, 191, 192–93
Hatos y Banda, Oleto Marcelino, 53
Herskovits, Melville J., 12
Historiography, 11–13
Hormechea, Carlos, 225, 226
Hoyos, Gonzalo Josef de, 51–53, 71,
90
Humboldt, Alexander von, 52, 68, 69,
84, 220
Hünefeldt, Christine, 261

Ibarra, José Ignacio, 208
Illegitimacy, 93, 95, 96, 164, 169
Indians: and constitution of 1991, 1, 2,
7; and Caribbean Colombia, 7; relationship with free people of color,
7, 10, 35, 42, 65, 79; fragmentation
of population, 10–11; of frontier, 11,
14, 15, 18–20, 21, 25; and Spanish
forced resettlement, 11, 26, 27–31,
32, 33–34, 35, 36, 38, 39–40, 48,
271 (n. 64); defiance of Spain, 20,
26, 27–31; pueblos de indios, 22,
29, 32, 38, 42, 45, 46, 48, 50, 52, 65,
77, 140–41, 154, 172; and rochelas,
22; communal lands of, 32, 34, 35,
65, 164, 174, 240–41; runaway, 35,
263; and rural areas, 45–46; and
haciendas, 50, 67; and resistance to
Catholic Church, 77; and carnivals
and fiestas, 98; and independence,

125, 133–34, 140–41, 153–54, 162,
240; and suffrage, 126, 128, 138,
242; and Spanish conquest, 159;
and Law of 11 October 1821, 163–
64; and republican policies, 172–
73, 176; and socioracial hierarchy,
242; and cities, 280 (n. 5). See also
specific Indian nations
Infante, Leonardo, 166
Inquisition, 127, 129, 142
Intendents, 58
Inter-American Congress, 167
Intercity rivalries: and civil war of
1831, 9, 16, 229–30; and regionalism, 12; and socioracial hierarchy,
15; and trade, 88, 194, 211–12; and
white elite competition, 90; and
political power, 119; and independence, 125, 126–27, 129, 132–33,
144, 161, 220, 238; and constitution
of 1821, 219, 238
Intraregional rivalries, 9, 16

Jamaica, 20, 73, 87, 151, 156, 173, 243,
251
Jamaican Baptist War (1831–32), 15,
232, 249, 251
Jaramillo, Jaime, 66
Jesuits, 50
Juan, Jorge, 94, 96, 100, 108, 216
Juntas, 121–22, 124, 125
Justiciano, 116

Karash, Mary, 263
Kogi Indians, 19, 31, 40
König, Hans-Joaquim, 11
Kraay, Hendrik, 248
Kronus, Sidney, 13
Kuna Indians, 19, 20, 21, 29–31, 33,
39, 40, 153, 154, 173, 264

Labatut, Pedro, 143–44, 145, 154
Lancaster, Joseph, 169
Land: resguardos, 32, 34, 35, 65, 164,
174, 240–41; and Spanish forced re-

settlement, 34-35, 38, 40, 79; state control of, 42; and rural areas, 45; hacendados' acquisition of, 49-50, 52, 65; and squatters, 67, 74-75, 174, 188; and republican policies, 174-75, 187

Lanz, Micaela de, 50

Law 70 of Negritudes (1993), 1, 3, 6, 7, 264

Le Moyne, Auguste, 69, 176, 177

Lemus, Gustavo Bell, 169

Lenoit, Anita, 151

León, Juan Hermenegildo, 178-79, 190, 220

Ley de Siete Partidas, 53

Liberalism: and political leaders, 4-5; and civil war of 1831, 16, 226-30, 238; and Cartagena, 83; and independence, 134, 136; triumph of, 230-34; and slavery, 232-33; and Caribbean New Granada, 237

Limpieza de sangre, 48, 91, 93, 164, 236

Liquor monopolies, 58, 74

Localism, 9, 17, 65, 219, 222, 238

Loperena de Fernández de Castro, María Concepción, 144-45, 150-51, 153, 233

López, Antonio, 39

López, José Hilario, 4

López, Marcos, 188

Lower-class people of color: historical portrayals of, 4; relationship with white elites, 6, 7, 16, 124; and patronage networks, 8, 119; resistance strategies of, 15; and Spanish forced resettlement, 39; and bundes, 62; and Santa Marta, 85, 150; and socioracial hierarchy, 98; and independence, 125, 126, 127, 128, 131, 132, 134, 135, 136-39, 144, 161; women as, 151, 161, 261; and cultural patterns, 189-94; and racial equality, 204, 216; and Cartagena, 215

Luque, Ignacio, 227, 228, 229, 230, 233, 234, 235

Lynch, John, 239

Madiedo, Juan, 230

Madriaga, Andrés de, 50

Madriaga family, 50

Magdalena River, 2, 11, 20, 21, 23, 31-33, 35, 38, 43, 48-49, 72-73, 171, 177

Manumission, 66, 105, 111, 140, 169-70, 217-18, 245, 261

Manumission Law of 21 July 1821, 163, 169-70, 217, 245

María Juliana, 94-95

Marimón, Juan, 141, 226, 229, 231, 294 (n. 66)

Mariño, Santiago, 166

Márquez, José Ignacio, 230

Márquez, Remigio, 162, 181-82, 183, 184, 200, 232, 254

Marriage: and rochelas, 22; and palenques, 25, 37; and rural areas, 61, 78; and Royal Pragmatic of 1778, 92, 95; and free unions, 93, 190, 201, 215, 307 (n. 15); and Cartagena, 96-97; and Santa Marta, 97; and women in cities, 106, 108; and slaves, 113; and constitution of 1821, 164

Martínez de Aparicio, José María, 132

Martínez de Pinillos, Pedro, 90, 123

Martinique, 251

McFarlane, Anthony, 11, 65

Medellín, 124

Medino Galindo, José, 88, 133, 135, 144

Meisel Roca, Adolfo, 12, 94

Méndez, Pedro Briceño, 209

Mendinueta, Pedro: and Kuna Indians, 30, 39; and frontier, 39-40; and mulattoes, 42, 48; and possible revolution of nonwhites, 43, 63, 80; and trade, 56; and contraband trade, 73; and wages, 74; and

Santa Marta, 85–86; and militiamen of African descent, 102, 103, 104, 105, 120; and Cartagena's slave conspiracy, 110

Mestizaje, 1, 3, 13, 36, 164, 172, 240, 241, 259

Mestizos, 2, 3, 43, 45, 126, 128, 241

Mexico, 58, 71, 246, 247, 255, 257, 258, 317 (n. 33)

Mier family, 50

Mier y Guerra, José Fernando, 28, 31, 38, 51, 71

Military fuero, 101, 103, 110, 147, 180, 213

Militiamen of African descent: and racial equality, 7, 100–101, 104, 148–49; military positions of, 8, 100–105, 213; resistance of, 67; and cities, 80, 100–105; and gracias al sacar, 92, 93; and socioracial hierarchy, 94, 100–105; and Cartagena's slave conspiracy, 109–10; and independence, 120, 130, 133, 135, 147–50; compared before and after independence, 180–81, 213, 215; and Padilla, 206; and suffrage, 213

Militia system: and racial equality, 7, 15; and recruitment, 57, 58–59; and racial categories, 59, 79, 101, 123, 124–25, 147, 150, 216, 246–48, 254; and training, 59; and avenues of advancement, 68; and military reform, 81–82; and conscription, 175, 213, 214, 227; and republican policies, 175–76, 184, 188–89

Mina, Diego, 109

Mining, 44, 50, 56, 63, 64, 67, 75, 140, 171

Missionaries, 27–28, 34, 35, 36, 173, 177, 180

Mollien, Gaspard, 23, 43, 68–69, 75, 78, 99, 105, 168, 192

Mompox: socioracial hierarchy of, 15; and independence, 16, 120, 123–24, 125, 126–27, 128, 129, 131, 132, 134–38, 140, 142, 151, 220–21, 235, 238; and intercity rivalries, 16; and contraband trade, 43, 84; and trade, 43, 84, 220; and hacendados, 51–52; and slave resistance, 66, 110–11, 114, 115–18; and bundes, 76–77; and political power, 80, 84, 119; economy of, 84; population of, 84, 220; and slaves, 84; and white elites, 84, 89; and women of color, 84; and carnivals and fiestas, 99; and militia system, 101, 102, 103, 247–48, 256; and racial categories, 147; and Spanish reconquest, 156; and manumission, 170; and mulattoes, 181; and Padilla, 208, 209, 218

Mompox Province, 88, 125, 129, 171, 220, 229, 237

Montalvo, Francisco de, 145, 156

Montes, Francisco, 122, 123, 126, 135

Montes, José, 206, 207

Montilla, Mariano: and desertion of troops, 162; as governor, 168, 219, 222–23, 225–26; and land, 175, 187; and Márquez, 182; and mutiny of troops, 184; and Padilla, 197–201, 203, 206, 208, 216, 218; and mulattoes, 199, 200; and Ocaña convention, 213–14; and civil war of 1831, 227, 228, 229, 234; departure of, 231; replacements for, 233; and Cartagena, 234; lack of popular support, 240

Morelos, José María, 241, 316 (n. 10)

Mores: and Spanish forced resettlement, 36, 37; and rural areas, 60–61, 78, 79; and Peredo, 62; and independence, 141; and republican policies, 190; and Padilla, 201

Morillo, Pablo, 151, 156, 157, 158, 160, 211

Mörner, Magnus, 254–55

Mosquera, Joaquín, 223–24, 229

Motilón Indians, 19–20, 27–28, 31, 40

Mountain of María, 33

160–61; and militiamen of African descent, 104; and women, 107, 108; and slaves, 118; and Cartagena, 212; and white elites, 256–57

Peasants, 11, 50, 64, 70, 71, 174

Peredo, Diego de, 23, 24, 62, 78

Pérez, Basilio, 38

Pérez, Dominga, 53, 70

Pérez Dávila, José, 59

Pérez de Vargas, Francisco, 31–32

Pérez Prieto, Pedro, 133

Peru, 58, 163, 166, 172, 176, 195, 202, 204, 235, 239, 240, 255

Pétion, Alexandre, 245

Phelan, John, 64

Piar, Manuel, 166, 197, 209

Pimienta, Juan, 112

Piñeres, Juan Antonio, 207, 208

Pita, Juan Josef, 198

Pointis, Jean Bernard Louis Desjean, 18

Political organization: of Indians, 1; of free people of color, 7, 10, 67, 148; and diversity of multiracial society, 14; and Spanish forced resettlement, 65

Pombo, José Ignacio de, 48, 56–57, 72, 90, 112, 126, 136, 140

Portocarrero, General, 233

Posada-Carbó, Eduardo, 12, 174

Posada Gutiérrez, Joaquín, 98, 211

Priests: as hacendados, 51; payment of, 51; and hacendados, 52, 53; in rural areas, 60–61, 76, 77, 79; negligence of, 61, 178, 180; and contraband trade, 73; resistance to, 76, 77; and Código Negro, 113; and independence, 141–42, 294 (n. 87); and Spanish reconquest, 158–59; and republican policies, 177–80

Puerto Rico, 55, 244, 246

Quakers, 112

Quinterones, 92

Racial categories: class issues not overlapping with, 9–10; fuzziness of, 10, 22, 91, 108, 253–56; in rural areas, 10, 43; and militia system, 59, 79, 101, 123, 124–25, 147, 150, 216, 246–48, 254; and independence, 147, 149; and suffrage, 148; and constitution of 1821, 164; republican avoidance of, 168

Racial equality: steps toward, 7–8; strategies for achieving, 80; and independence, 138, 147, 148, 149, 163; and constitution of 1821, 163–64; and republican policies, 181–84; and Bolívar, 196, 223; and Montilla, 198; and Padilla, 199–200, 202; in other constitutions in the Americas, 242–45

Racial identity, 3, 6–7, 14, 149, 246–47

Racial issues: and Law 70 of Negritudes, 2, 13; and Caribbean Colombia, 4; Nieto's avoidance of, 5; and race as organizational category, 6, 8, 14; suppression of reference to race in laws and constitution, 8; and regionalism, 13; and Spanish forced resettlement, 35; and cities, 91–97

Racism, 4, 8, 13, 197, 211

Real, Antonio del, 199, 230

Rebustillo, Antonio, 155

Regionalism, 1, 2, 3–4, 13, 71, 142–43, 154

Rensselaer, Rensselaer Van, 192, 217, 221–22

Resguardos, 32, 34, 35, 65, 164, 174, 240–41

Resistance: and Afro-Caribbean Colombians, 8; and survival, 10, 15, 16, 39, 187; slave resistance, 14–15, 55, 66, 80, 111–19; of Indians, 31; and relationship of free people of color and Indians, 35; and Spanish forced resettlement, 36–40; and rural areas, 67–71; individual strategies of, 70, 75; to Catholic Church, 76–79, 91; and militia system, 188

Restrepo, José Manuel, 162, 164, 165, 225, 232, 252

Revollo, Manuel Benito, 90, 141, 142, 157

Revollo, Pedro María, 3

Ribón, Juan Pantaleón, 147, 158, 175

Río de la Plata, 241, 245

Riohacha: and intercity rivalries, 16; and Wayúu Indians, 30, 87, 88, 133, 144, 160; as administrative center, 43; and zambos, 44; and transportation, 49; and trade, 54; and political power, 80, 119; population of, 87, 220; and white elites, 87, 89; and education, 89; and militia system, 101; as royalist stronghold, 120, 133, 134, 135, 144, 162; and wars for independence, 144, 221; and constitution of 1821, 219; rebellion of, 223, 224–25, 227, 235–36; and civil war of 1831, 228–29, 234; and Sardá, 233–34

Riohacha Province: and frontier, 18; and Wayúu Indians, 19; population of, 43; and trade, 55; and Catholic Church, 60; separation from Santa Marta Province, 87, 88; and civil war of 1831, 229; and Liberalism, 237

Roblendo, Carlos, 181

Robles, Luis A., 5–6, 267 (n. 18)

Rochelas: descriptions of, 21–23; population of, 22, 25; disorder of, 26; and Spanish forced resettlement, 26, 31–36, 39, 40, 41, 48; and hacendados, 50, 51; and squatters, 74; and independence, 152

Rodríguez, Gregorio José, 158, 159

Rodríguez Torices, Manuel, 135–36, 139, 146, 294 (n. 66)

Rojas, Francisco, 70

Romay, Manuel, 229, 232

Romero, Anita, 196, 197, 199, 201

Romero, Dolcey, 12, 111, 171

Romero, Mauricio José, 198, 230

Romero, Pedro, 6, 122, 128, 129, 148, 149, 157, 196, 214

Ruiz de Noriega, Bernardo, 28

Runaway Indians, 35, 263

Runaway slaves: and rochelas, 22; and palenques, 23–25; and rural areas, 45; and resistance, 66, 75, 111; sanctuaries for, 67, 79; and independence, 152; and Spanish conquest, 159; repression of, 171, 263

Rural areas: and Law 70 of Negritudes, 1; and fluid color distinctions, 10; fragmentation of, 15, 66; autonomy of, 42, 75; and Catholic Church, 42, 60–63; and state, 42, 57–59; villages of, 42, 43, 44; and agriculture, 53–57; and military recruitment, 57, 58–59; lack of revolts in, 63–67; and resistance, 67–71; and squatters, 67, 74–75; and smuggling, 72–74; counterculture in, 75–79; and republican policies, 173–77

Sáenz de Maza, Juana María, 112

Sáenz Ortiz, Melchor, 117, 136

Saether, Steinar, 85

Safford, Frank, 11

Saint Domingue, 54–56, 80, 83, 110, 243–44, 250, 252

Salazar, José María, 124, 137–38

Salcedo, Víctor de, 131, 135

San Andrés, 46

San Cipriano, 34, 35, 36

San Jorge River, 20–21, 22, 33, 35, 38, 44

San Jorge Valley, 32–33

San Juan de la Ciénaga, 46

Santa Coa, marquis of, 50, 51, 67, 84

Santa Marta: competition with Cartagena de Indias, 9; and Indians fighting for Spain, 11; socioracial hierarchy of, 15; and intercity rivalries, 16; Spanish allegiance of, 16; Bogotá compared to, 42; as administrative center, 43; and transportation, 49; and trade, 54, 85, 88, 219, 221; and political power, 80, 119; isolation of, 84-85; economy of, 85; and lower-class people of color, 85, 150; population of, 85, 220; and white elites, 85, 86, 89; and education, 89; and marriage, 97; and carnivals and fiestas, 99; and militia system, 101; and independence, 120, 125, 126, 145; as royalist stronghold, 120, 125, 126, 127, 129, 131-34, 144, 146, 148, 162, 221, 238; and wars for independence, 143-44, 145, 146; and Spanish reconquest, 156, 160; and manumission, 170; and constitution of 1821, 219; and Bolívar, 225-26; rebellion in, 233

Santa Marta Province: and frontier, 18; and Indians, 27-28; population of, 43; slaves in, 46; and hacendados' land acquisition, 50; and Catholic Church, 60; separation from Riohacha Province, 87, 88; as royalist stronghold, 133, 135, 162; and republican policies, 176; and civil war of 1831, 229; and Liberalism, 237

Santander, Francisco de Paula: and Bolívar, 16, 159, 176, 202, 203, 205, 213, 215, 223, 238, 257; and Boves's race war, 166; and Estévez, 178; and Padilla, 193, 195, 196, 198, 201, 203, 206, 209, 210, 215; exile of, 209; and Mompox, 219; and civil war of 1831, 229, 230; and Nieto, 237

Santo Domingo, 55, 121, 244

Sardá, José, 226, 228-29, 233-34, 315 (n. 183)

Sharp, William, 72

Sicroff, Albert, 253

Sierra, Agustín de la, 52

Sierra Nevada, 19, 20

Silva Dias, Maria Odila, 260

Silvestre, Francisco, 28, 42

Single heads of households, 10, 93, 106-7, 150, 213, 318 (n. 64)

Sinning, Edgar Rey, 258

Sinú River, 21, 32, 35, 38, 44

Slave resistance, 14-15, 55, 66, 80, 111-19

Slavery: in Caribbean Colombia, 7, 13; abolition of, 8, 236, 245; and Spanish forced resettlement, 32; and gold mines, 44; and *Ley de Siete Partidas*, 53; slave trade, 55–56, 57, 73, 81, 83, 85, 110, 140, 163, 170, 245, 301 (n. 45); and socioracial hierarachy, 92-93, 103; and independence, 136, 140; and Law of 21 July 1821, 163, 169-70, 217; and Liberalism, 232-33; and United States, 242-43. *See also* Código Negro

Slaves: and Cartagena, 7, 44, 81, 83-84, 212, 236, 273 (n. 12), 311 (n. 88); relationship with free people of color, 7, 8, 10, 14, 79, 149; and self-purchase, 8, 14, 66, 75, 111–12, 119, 152, 171, 250; women as, 10, 81, 152; relationship with white elites, 15, 66; and haciendas, 42, 50, 51, 62-63, 67; population of, 44, 46, 80, 152, 171, 273 (n. 12), 302 (n. 53); and rural areas, 46; and agriculture, 54-56, 57; and Catholic Church, 62-63; and Comunero Revolt, 64, 66; and cities, 80, 81, 83, 108-18, 171-72; and Mompox, 84, 114, 288 (n. 144); and Santa Marta, 85, 111; and Valledupar, 86; and Riohacha, 87; and socioracial hierarchy, 97; and carnivals and fiestas, 98-99; freeing of, 124, 166, 233; and independence, 130-31, 136, 140, 152-53, 161; and wars for independence, 153; and republican policies, 169-72. *See also* Runaway slaves

Smuggling: role of, 17; and frontier,

18, 262–64; and Spanish forced resettlement, 33; and beef, 50; and hacendados, 50; and gold, 72, 73, 74; and rural areas, 72–74, 79; and Mompox, 84, 90; and Santa Marta, 85, 86, 88; and Riohacha, 87, 88, 221; and white elites, 89; and Indians, 173. *See also* Contraband trade

Social mobility: and Afro-Caribbean Colombians, 8–9

Sociedad Económica de Amigos del País, 90

Society of the Veteran Defenders of Liberty, 230, 231, 232

Socioracial hierarchy, 9; of cities, 10, 15, 91–97, 119; and Padilla, 16, 195, 196–205; and frontier, 26, 40; and Council of the Indies, 91, 92–94, 95, 284 (n. 72); and Catholic Church, 94, 142, 169; and militiamen of African descent, 94, 100–105; and occupations, 97, 168; and carnivals and fiestas, 98–100, 119, 258–60; and racial mixing, 99–100; and women, 105–8; and independence, 134, 160; loosening of restrictions of, 168; inconsistencies of, 253

Socorro, 64, 65, 66, 70

Solaún, Mauricio, 13

Soria, Blas de, 127

Soublette, Carlos, 168

Soudis de De la Vega, Adelaida, 12

Spain: Indians' defiance of, 20, 26, 27–31; and trade, 88; and regional juntas, 121

Spanish Capuchins, 28, 35

Spanish Empire: and Caribbean New Granada's economy, 53, 57; and military defense, 81

Spanish forced resettlement: and Caribbean New Granada, 7; and Indians, 11, 26, 27–31, 32, 33–34, 35, 36, 39–40, 48, 271 (n. 64); and rochelas and palenques, 26, 31–39, 40, 41,

48; and resistance, 36–40; and integration of population into colony, 42; and Indian labor, 50; and political organization, 65; and squatters, 74; and Valledupar, 86; and white elites, 90

Spanish reconquest: failure of, 12; and white elites, 16; and independence, 135; and Montalvo, 145; and Ferdinand VII, 147; and Cartagena, 156–58, 160, 298 (n. 149); and repression, 158; and Catholic Church, 159

Squatters, 67, 74–75, 174, 188

State: and white elites' position, 7; official control of, 9, 15, 21, 25, 42, 48, 63, 79; and Indians, 11, 26; and frontier, 25–26, 40, 41; and cities, 42; and rural areas, 42, 57–59; and hacendados, 52; relationship with Catholic Church, 61–62

Steamboats, 69

Stern, Steve J., 70

Streicker, Joel, 13

Striffler, Luis, 187

Subisa, Gertrudis, 112, 115, 116

Suffrage, male, 7–8; and First Independence, 129–30, 132, 137–38, 148, 150; in Spanish constitution of 1812, 138, 160, 243–44; and constitution of 1821, 163, 169; and conflict between Bolívar and Santander, 202, 204–6, 213–14; in other constitutions in the Americas, 242–45

Sugar cultivation and production, 46, 50, 56, 64, 82, 85–87, 89, 171, 174, 185

Supreme Junta of Bogotá, 124

Supreme Junta of Cartagena, 125, 126, 128, 132–33, 140, 149

Talledo y Rivera, Vicente, 123–24, 125, 135, 153

Tamalameque, 71

Taussig, Michael, 12–13

Taxation: and trade, 56, 57, 89–90;
and rural areas, 57, 58; and Comunero Revolt, 64; collection of taxes,
71; and gold panning, 72; and
contraband trade, 73, 89; and Span-
ish reconquest, 158; and Gran Co-
lombia, 167; and transportation,
177; and Bolívar, 204, 213, 223
Taylor, William B., 71
Thomistic University, 96
Tinoco, Pedro Juan, 71, 118, 156
Tobacco monopolies, 58
Tobacco production, 57, 64, 70
Torre-Hoyos, María Josefa Isabel de,
151
Torre-Hoyos, marquis of, 52–53, 71,
84, 90, 111, 118, 136, 151
Torres y Velazco, Gabriel, 157, 159
Torre y Miranda, Antonio de la, 21, 22,
23, 25, 32–33, 36, 37, 48, 187
Tovar, Hermes, 50, 66
Trade: cities' competition for, 9; and
Mompox and Valledupar, 43; and
hacendados, 50; and agriculture,
53–57; and Cartagena, 54, 56, 81,
82, 88, 89–90, 122, 132, 211–12,
219; and Santa Marta, 54, 85, 88;
slave trade, 55–56, 57, 73, 81, 83, 85,
110, 140, 163, 170, 245, 301 (n. 45);
and importation of foreign liquor,
56, 83, 89; and intercity rivalries,
88; and white elites, 89; and independence, 126, 136; and bogas, 177;
and republican policies, 184–85. See
also Contraband trade; Smuggling
Transitory Article 55, 1
Transportation: in rural areas, 21, 48–
49, 58, 60, 61, 273 (n. 24); and
tax collection, 58; and priests, 60,
61; and bogas, 68–70; and smuggling, 73; and slaves, 108–9; and
republican policies, 176–77; and
trade, 184; and agriculture, 192;
and communication, 203
Twinam, Ann, 92, 244, 282 (n. 49)

Ucros, José, 181–82
Ucrós, Vicente, 207, 208
Ulloa, Antonio de, 94, 96, 100, 108,
216
United States: black population of,
2; and frontier, 14, 263; and trade,
55, 122; banishment to, 146; and
racial equality and slavery, 242–43,
246; and racial categories, 255; and
patronage, 257
Urdaneta, Rafael, 224, 225, 227, 229,
230, 231, 234, 236, 238, 262
Uribe, Jaime Jaramillo, 11
Uribe-Urán, Victor, 11, 118
Uruguay, 257

Valde-Hoyos, marquis of, 51, 131, 154
Valest y Valencia, Nicolás, 124, 127
Valledupar: and trade, 43; and zambos, 44; and Santa Marta/Riohacha
route, 49; and political power, 80,
119; population of, 86, 220; and
Spanish forced resettlement, 86;
and white elites, 86–87, 89; and
Santa Marta, 88; and education,
89; and militia system, 101, 102,
103; and independence, 120, 131,
134, 144–45, 154, 162; and wars for
independence, 144–45; economy of,
221
Vatican, 61, 178
Velásquez, Rogerio, 12
Venezuela: and Padilla, 6, 197; independence in, 14, 132, 197; and
trade, 53, 57; and slavery, 55, 244,
245, 250, 251–52; and contraband
trade, 73; and white elites, 91;
and militiamen of African descent,
104; and slave conspiracy, 110; and
Código Negro, 114; and juntas,
121; proindependence armies of,
143; and wars for independence,
145; and Spanish reconquest, 156;
destabilization of, 162; and mulattoes, 165; and pardocracia, 165, 166;

white elites of, 168; and republican
policies, 175; and Páez, 202, 215,
223; and Bolívar, 206; and Gran
Colombia, 223, 224, 235, 237; and
Indians, 241; and militia system,
247, 317 (n. 34)

Viana, Antonio, 132

Villages: and Spanish forced resettlement, 40, 41, 65, 77; state control of,
42; population of, 43, 44, 48; and
transportation, 49; and hacendado
class, 51; and military recruitment,
58–59; and Catholic Church, 60;
and political organization, 70–71;
and wars for independence, 145,
154–56, 162; and free people of
color, 150, 168; and Spanish reconquest, 158, 160; and education, 169;
and slaves, 171; ascending power of,
221–22; and trade, 221–22; and civil
war of 1831, 238

Vinaroz, Bartolomé de, 52

Vinson, Ben, 246

Virgin of Candelaria, 98, 191, 217

Wade, Peter, 4, 13

Walker, Charles F., 239

Wars for independence: and Caribbean
New Granada, 7; and slavery, 8;
and Indians, 11; and Palenque of
San Basilio, 38; and Bolívar, 143,
144–47, 149, 161; and Cartagena,
143–47, 148, 149–50, 152, 153, 211,
238; and free people of color, 145,
167–68; and villages, 145, 154–56,
162

Watts, Edward, 231

Wayúu Indians: and Guajira Peninsula, 19, 28, 30; and contraband
trade, 20, 173; and Riohacha, 30,
87, 88, 133, 144, 160; resistance
of, 31, 39–40; and independence,
153; and regional instability, 162;
and Catholic Church, 180; and
smuggling, 263–64

White elites: and Transitory Article
55, 1; and Caribbean Colombia's
history, 4; relationship with lower-
class people of color, 6, 7, 8, 16;
and franchise for free black men,
7–8; population of, 7, 167; divisions
of, 8, 9, 16, 88–91, 135, 161, 203;
weaknesses of, 8, 9, 16, 91, 239;
and fears of Haitian Revolution,
14, 16, 39, 42, 248–53; relationship
with free people of color, 15, 42, 147,
148, 162, 181–84, 193, 208, 215–
16; and rochelas, 26; and Spanish
forced resettlement, 31, 34; gender
ratio of, 48; in rural areas, 48; and
military recruitment, 59, 100, 101,
124–25, 189; and contraband trade,
74; and Mompox, 84, 90; and Santa
Marta, 85, 86, 89; and Valledupar,
86–87, 89; and Riohacha, 87, 89;
and cities, 88–91; and marriage, 95,
96–97; and carnivals and fiestas,
98; women as, 99, 105, 150–51; and
socioracial hierarchy, 119, 241; and
suffrage, 126; and independence,
127, 128, 131–32, 134–36, 138; as
political leaders, 168, 212, 240; domestic slaves of, 171; and Padilla,
196–97, 215; and pardocracia, 200

White Patriots, 128

Women: as reproducers and producers,
10; socioeconomic importance of,
10, 15, 23, 105, 260–62; and rochelas, 22, 26; and palenques,
26; and Spanish forced resettlement, 33, 36, 39; and mestizaje,
36; and morality, 61; and resistance
to Catholic Church, 78, 106, 108,
260; women of color in cities, 81,
83, 84, 93, 105–8, 119, 283 (n. 54);
and socioracial hierarchy, 105–8,
212–13; as slaveowners, 108, 112,
114, 116–17; as urban slaves, 108,
111, 112, 114–15; and independence,
139–40, 150–52, 161; exclusion from

suffrage, 150; and wars for independence, 151–52; education of, 164; and trade, 185. *See also* Gender ratio

Yturen, Manuel, 104–5, 109, 118

Zambo artisans, 83
Zambos: and Law 70 of Negritudes, 1; of Caribbean Colombia, 7; and class issues, 9–10; and rochelas, 22; and palenques, 25, 45; of Riohacha Province, 43; of villages, 44–45; and Valledupar, 87; and cities, 93; and carnivals and fiestas, 98; and suffrage, 126; and independence, 127, 134; population of, 167; and Padilla, 198

Zejudo, Anastasio, 104, 105, 109
Zenú Indians, 28, 31, 32